SCARECROW CONCORDANCES

Scarecrow Concordances, No. 4

A CONCORDANCE TO THE POEMS OF HART CRANE

by
Hilton & Elaine Landry
with the assistance of
Maurice Kramer

Revised by
Robert DeMott

The Scarecrow Press, Inc.
Metuchen, N.J.   1973

Library of Congress Cataloging in Publication Data

Landry, Hilton.
   A concordance to the poems of Hart Crane.

   "Based on The complete poems and selected letters
and prose of Hart Crane, edited by Brom Weber."
   1. Crane, Hart, 1899-1932--Concordances.
I. Landry, Elaine, joint author. II. DeMott,
Robert. III. Crane, Hart, 1899-1932. The complete
poems and selected letters and prose of Hart Crane.
IV. Title.
PS3505.R272Z49 1973   811'.5'2   72-10663
ISBN 0-8108-0564-2

Preface

This concordance is based on THE COMPLETE POEMS AND SELECTED LETTERS AND PROSE OF HART CRANE, edited by Brom Weber, and published by Liveright Publishing Corporation of New York in 1966. The paper-bound Anchor Books edition, with identical pagination and lineation, was published by Doubleday & Company, Inc. in the same year.

The concordance ignores or merely samples words usually omitted in such works, like a, about, an, be, can, of, said, very, who, but certain others which normally fall into this class--I, me, my, O, thee, thy--are included because of the nature of Hart Crane's work. Since he is primarily a lyric poet, it was the opinion of some members of the American Philosophical Society, as well as of certain Crane scholars, that the occurrence of first person pronouns, especially I and me, should be recorded. Other personal pronouns have been liberally sampled. But Crane is not only a lyric poet, he is one of unusual rhetorical formality, with a tendency toward the use of apostrophe and prayer that is rare in modern American poetry. Thus it was necessary to include all archaic words and forms, such as doth, thee, and thy, in addition to O, a word which occurs most frequently in The Bridge. In the case of as and like, both of which are also customarily omitted, it was decided to increase the usefulness of the concordance by listing all instances which signify a comparison or simile, including those where there might be some doubt.

An early unpublished version of the concordance, supported by a grant from the American Philosophical Society (1962), was based on THE COMPLETE POEMS OF HART CRANE, edited by Waldo Frank and published in 1958. Unfortunately, our work was nearly finished when Maurice Kramer and I learned that the Frank edition was to be replaced by another within three or four years. We were left with a manuscript which would require revision to fit the new edition, although in the meantime the concordance proved useful to a number of Crane scholars. Several years ago I persuaded Robert DeMott to accept responsibility for completely revising the old concordance, a task which he performed diligently and well. But in order to insure accuracy, the hard labor of checking every entry and proofreading the final draft was shared by all.

We are indebted to the American Philosophical Society for funds which enabled us to complete the early version of the concordance; to Professors Arvin Wells and Frank Fieler of Ohio University for their encouragement and financial support of DeMott's revision; to Professor Tetsumaro Hayashi of Ball State University for his valuable advice concerning publication; and to Professor Martin Nurmi and Dean Alan Coogan of Kent State University for funds to prepare the manuscript for publication.

H.L.

WORDS OMITTED OR MERELY ILLUSTRATED

a	don't	myself	they
about	down		this
above		neither	those
across	each	never	though
after	either	no	through
again	even	nor	thus
against	ever	not	till
all	every	now	to
along			too
also	for	of	
although	from	off	under
am		often	until
among	had	on	up
an	has	once	upon
and	have	only	
any	he	or	very
around	her	out	
as	here	over	was
at	him	own	were
away	himself		what
	how	said	when
be	however	say	where
been		saying	whether
before	if	says	which
behind	in	shall	while
below	indeed	she	who
beneath	into	should	whom
between	is	so	whose
both	it	some	why
but	its	such	will (verb)
by	itself		with
		than	within
can	less	that	without
cannot	let	the	would
could	like	their	
couldn't		theirs	yes
	may	them	yet
did	might	then	you
do	more	there	your
does	most	therefore	yours
done	must	these	

ABP	--And Bees of Paradise
AM	Ave Maria (Section I of THE BRIDGE)
AMT	At Melville's Tomb
An	Annunciations
AP	Air Plant
APE	America's Plutonic Ecstasies
At	Atlantis (Section VIII of THE BRIDGE)
Ba	Bathers
BE	The Bridge of Estador
BNOK	By Nilus Once I Knew...
BSEW	Bacardi Spreads the Eagle's Wings
BT	Black Tambourine
B Tow	The Broken Tower
C	C 33
CDB	Carmen de Boheme
CH	Cape Hatteras (Section IV of THE BRIDGE)
Chap	Chaplinesque
CL	Carrier Letter
CS	Cutty Sark (Section III of THE BRIDGE)
Dan	The Dance (From "Powhatan's Daughter," Section II of THE BRIDGE)
EC	Emblems of Conduct
Ech	Echoes
Emp	To the Empress Josephine's Statue
EpH	Episode of Hands
Et	Eternity
F&H I	For the Marriage of Faustus and Helen I
F&H II	For the Marriage of Faustus and Helen II
F&H III	For the Marriage of Faustus and Helen III
Fern	The Fernery
For	Forgetfulness
Fr	Fear
GA	Garden Abstract
GWP	The Great Western Plains
HD	The Harbor Dawn (From "Powhatan's Daughter," Section II of THE BRIDGE)
Hi	The Hive
HR	Havana Rose
Hur	The Hurricane
Id	The Idiot
In	Interludium
Ind	Indiana (From "Powhatan's Daughter," Section II of THE BRIDGE)
Int	Interior
IQ	Island Quarry
IS	In Shadow
IV	Imperator Victus
KW	Key West
LC	Lachrymae Christi
Leg	Legend
Lege	Legende
Len	Lenses
Lib	To Liberty

Loc	Locutions des Pierrots
Ma	March
MC	Modern Craft
Mer	The Mermen
MF	Moment Fugue
MGLL	My Grandmother's Love Letters
Moth	The Moth That God Made Blind
MT	The Mango Tree
NA	A Name For All
NL	North Labrador
NWG	National Winter Garden (From "Three Songs," Section V of THE BRIDGE)
OC	O Carib Isle
O-N	October-November
OS	Old Song
PA	Porphyro in Akron
Par	Paraphrase
Pass	Passage
Past	Pastorale
PB	The Phantom Bark
Per	A Persuasion
Port	To Portapovitch
Pos	Possessions
Post	A Postscript
Ps	Postscript
PU	Praise for an Urn
Purg	Purgatorio
QH	Quaker Hill (Section VI of THE BRIDGE)
Rec	Recitative
Rel	Reliquary
Rep	Reply
Riv	The River (From "Powhatan's Daughter," Section II of THE BRIDGE)
RP	Royal Palm
RR	Repose of Rivers
SC	Southern Cross (From "Three Songs," Section V of THE BRIDGE)
Shak	To Shakespeare
SI	The Sad Indian
SM	Stark Major
SMA	Sunday Morning Apples
TBB	To Brooklyn Bridge (Proem to THE BRIDGE)
TCJ	To the Cloud Juggler
TED	To Emily Dickinson
Tun	The Tunnel (Section VII of THE BRIDGE)
V-1	Voyages I
V-2	Voyages II
V-3	Voyages III
V-4	Voyages IV
V-5	Voyages V
V-6	Voyages VI

Each entry contains a page number, the line using the key word (without end punctuation), an abbreviation of the poem's title, and the number of the line in the poem. Thus the following entry under brow

      23. A leopard ranging always in the brow WM 3

signifies that brow occurs in line 3 of "Wine Menagerie," a line which appears on page 23 of THE COMPLETE POEMS AND SELECTED LETTERS AND PROSE OF HART CRANE, edited by Brom Weber (New York, 1966). Since all key words are listed in strict alphabetical order, inflected forms of a word may well be separated. For example, brown falls between brow and brows while many words and a number of pages separate came and come.

abandoned	89.	Back over Connecticut farms, abandoned pastures CH 57
abating	33.	The abating shadows of our conscript dust F&H III 35
abides	25.	A wind abides the ensign of your will Rec 24
able	174.	An able text, more motion than machines BNOK 10
	181.	No one seemed to be able to get a spark Et 18
abristle	105.	Alight with sticks abristle and cigars QH 32
Absalom	25.	The plummet heart, like Absalom, no stream Rec 20
abscond	169.	Thy drum's gambade, its plunge abscond Hur 13
absence	162.	Thy absence overflows the rose OS 1
absently	68.	A little while gaze absently below Riv 102
absinthe-sipping	133.	Just as absinthe-sipping women shiver through CDB 6
ab-so-loot-lee	151.	and other natural grammarians are ab-so-loot-lee necessary APE 21-22
absolute	48.	More absolute than ever--biding the moon AM 19
absolution	191.	So absolution? Wake pines--but pines wake here Purg 8
absorbing	144.	Absorbing and conveying weariness PA 8
abysmal	95.	And now, as launched in abysmal cupolas of space CH 205
abyss	22.	Sand troughed us in a glittering abyss Pass 33
	50.	Some inmost sob, half-heard, dissuades the abyss AM 39
	112.	Shadowless in that abyss they unaccounting lie Tun 133
acceded	51.	The kindled Crown! acceded of the poles AM 85
accent	27.	The margins of the day, accent the curbs F&H I 10
	41.	Whose accent no farewell can know V-6 32
accept	29.	Accept a lone eye riveted to your plane F&H I 49
accepted	27.	Divided by accepted multitudes F&H I 3
accolade	46.	Thy guerdon...Accolade thou doest bestow TBB 26
accomplished	99.	Insolence. You crept out simmering, accomplished SC 24
account	18.	Account the total of this trembling tabulation Pos 11
	182.	I can't account for him! And true, he stood Et 44
accrete	50.	Starved wide on blackened tides, accrete-- enclose AM 42
accumulate	18.	Accumulate such moments to an hour Pos 10
acetylene	45.	A rip-tooth of the sky's acetylene TBB 22
achieved	170.	Achieved that stillness ultimately best TED 4
acid	104.	Of friendship's acid wine, retarding phlegm QH 12
across	8.	Stretching across a lucid space PU 20
	27.	Across the stacked partitions of the day F&H I 4
	34.	And silent answers crept across the stars AMT 12

across, cont.   45.   And Thee, across the harbor, silver-paced TBB 13
                    56.   From Cyclopean towers across Manhattan waters
                          HD 32
                    66.   They lurk across her, knowing her yonder breast
                          Riv 67
                    74.   Across what bivouacs of thine angered slain
                          Dan 83
                    185. across dawn's broken arc. No; yes...or were
                          they Post 4
act   89.   From which we wake into the dream of act CH 40
                    108. You'll find the garden in the third act dead
                          Tun 8
action   188. Let us strip the desk for action--now we have a
                          horse HR 1
adagios   36.   Adagios of islands, O my Prodigal V-2 14
Adam   89.   Adam and Adam's answer in the forest CH 31
Adam's   89.   Adam and Adam's answer in the forest CH 31
                    171. Nor claim me, either, by Adam's spine--nor rib
                          KW 4
Adams'   105. Ty-five at Adams' auction,--eats the seal QH 44
adaptate   148. To adaptate her methods and deportment Loc 11
add   194. My veins recall and add, revived and sure B Tow 30
A Dios   163. A Dios gracias, grac--I've heard his song
                          Id 14
Adirondacks   72.   Of Adirondacks!--wisped of azure wands Dan 36
adjourned   48.   And greed adjourned,--I bring you back Cathay
                          AM 8
adjustments   11.   We make our meek adjustments Chap 1
admissions   18.   Lacks all but piteous admissions to be split
                          Pos 24
admitted   37.   And so, admitted through black swollen gates
                          V-3 9
adorations   5.   Bowls and cups fill historians with adorations
                          EC 10
adream   178. And leave me half adream upon the main PB 4
adrift   54.   Among distant chiming buoys--adrift. The sky
                          HD 16
                    139. Yet called adrift again at every dawn Lege 4
ads   62.   Tintex--Japalac--Certain-teed Overalls ads
                          Riv 3
                    110. Below the toothpaste and the dandruff ads
                          Tun 74
advance   159. Of districts where cliff, sea and palm advance
                          TCJ 3
advancing   38.   No stream of greater love advancing now V-4 6
advertisements   28.   Stippled with pink and green advertisements
                          F&H I 26
Aegean   144. And the Fjords and the Aegean are remembered
                          PA 16
AEolus   115. Beams yelling AEolus! splintered in the straits
                          At 40

aeons	88.	Those continental folded aeons, surcharged CH 16
	115.	Of inchling aeons silence rivets Troy At 36
aerial	7.	That feed your inquiries with aerial wine SMA 15
AEsop	4.	AEsop, driven to pondering, found BT 5
aetherial	167.	Its frondings sighing in aetherial folds RP 8
affections	148.	The orient moon of my dapper affections Loc 4
afire	40.	Waiting, afire, what name, unspoke V-6 13
aflow	38.	Through clay aflow immortally to you V-4 8
afoot	95.	yes, Walt,/Afoot again, and onward without halt CH 218
Africa	4.	And, in Africa, a carcass quick with flies BT 12
after-glow	140.	Here in the day's after-glow Int 8
afternoon	13.	Out in the late amber afternoon IS 1
	45.	All afternoon the cloud-flown derricks turn TBB 23
	156.	Under the poinciana, of a noon or afternoon OC 23
	179.	a kite high in the afternoon, or in the twilight scanning Len 6
afternoons	157.	Congeal by afternoons here, satin and vacant OC 33
afterwards	64.	And afterwards, who had a colt's eyes--one said Riv 41
	110.	the show she cried a little afterwards but Tun 65
agape	163.	Passed him again...He was alone, agape Id 8
agate	110.	Your eyes like agate lanterns--on and on Tun 73
age	16.	Till age had brought me to the sea RR 5
ageless	48.	Assure us through thy mantle's ageless blue AM 28
agent	105.	To the persuasive suburban land agent QH 34
ages	21.	Died speaking through the ages that you know Pass 19
	89.	"--Recorders ages hence"--ah, syllables of faith CH 43
	95.	Recorders ages hence, yes, they shall hear CH 214
	192.	His fathers took for granted ages since--and so he looms SI 6
agile	116.	The agile precincts of the lark's return At 58
agleam	158.	This Cross, agleam still with a human Face Mer 15
aglitter	56.	Two--three bright window-eyes aglitter, disk HD 33
ago	64.	"It was almost Louisiana, long ago" Riv 45
	68.	Like one whose eyes were buried long ago Riv 119
	130.	Of storm or strain an hour ago Ech 4
	130.	I dream we quarreled long, long ago Ech 12
	151.	that kicked out long ago APE 7

agonized	92.	Lift agonized quittance, tilting from the in-visible brink CH 135
agony	111.	Kiss of our agony thou gatherest Tun 116
	112.	Kiss of our agony Thou gatherest Tun 136
	179.	doors and lips of agony to Len 16
	185.	Friendship agony! words came to me Post 1
ah	89.	"--Recorders ages hence"--ah, syllables of faith CH 43
	148.	Ah, madame! truly it's not right Loc 9
	148.	Ah! the divine infatuation Loc 13
	149.	Ah! without the moon, what white nights Loc 25
ahead	69.	All fades but one thin skyline 'round...Ahead Riv 137
	72.	Grey tepees tufting the blue knolls ahead Dan 39
	89.	O Saunterer on free ways still ahead CH 50
	183.	Doctors shot ahead from the deck in planes Et 57
air	4.	And mingling incantations on the air BT 8
	6.	It trembles as birch limbs webbing the air MGLL 15
	10.	Vivisection of more clamant air SM 6
	17.	Hollowed by air, posts a white paraphrase Par 15
	32.	The mounted, yielding cities of the air F&H III 21
	54.	Ask nothing but this sheath of pallid air HD 20
	73.	And splay tongues thinly busy the blue air Dan 56
	115.	Still wrapping harness to the swarming air At 38
	156.	Sieved upward, white and black along the air OC 25
	174.	Some old Egyptian joke is in the air BNOK 1
	182.	Long tropic roots high in the air, like lace Et 30
	193.	Of that tribunal monarch of the air B Tow 22
air's	168.	Almost no shadow--but the air's thin talk AP 12
aisle	28.	Then I might find your eyes across an aisle F&H I 20
	114.	Onward and up the crystal-flooded aisle At 21
akimbo	133.	Carmen! Akimbo arms and smouldering eyes CDB 17
Akron	144.	Akron, "high place" PA 10
alarm	185.	There were tickets and alarm clocks. There were counters and schedules Post 14
alarms	123.	The honey-wax eyes could find no alarms Moth 39
	138.	Haunt the blank stage with lingering alarms Port 7
	168.	A bird almost--of almost bird alarms AP 4
alas	24.	"Alas,--these frozen billows of your skill WM 38
	99.	Rehearsed hair--docile, alas, from many arms SC 26

alas, cont.	149.	Alas, you know how much I oppose Loc 22
	150.	Alas, there is so little time GWP 11
albatross	93.	Past where the albatross has offered up CH 160
albatross's	38.	Chilled albatross's white immutability V-4 5
albeit	156.	Albeit in a stranger tongue. Tree names, flower names OC 13
alcohol	92.	What alcohol of space...! Remember, Falcon-Ace CH 128
	132.	Drowning cool pearls in alcohol MC 3
alcove	23.	And as the alcove of her jealousy recedes WM 20
alcoves	16.	Flags, weeds. And remembrance of steep alcoves RR 6
alert	75.	Alert, star-triggered in the listening vault Dan 99
alight	105.	Alight with sticks abristle and cigars QH 32
align	46.	How could mere toil align thy choiring strings TBB 30
alike	25.	Alike suspend us from atrocious sums Rec 18
	150.	Alike to stage, equestrian, and pullman GWP 4
all	3.	The only worth all granting Leg 9
	3.	Relentless caper for all those who step Leg 22
	6.	It is all hung by an invisible white hair MGLL 14
	11.	We can evade you, and all else but the heart Chap 17
	16.	And all the singular nestings in the hills RR 13
	16.	And finally, in that memory all things nurse RR 17
	18.	Lacks all but piteous admissions to be split Pos 24
	18.	All but bright stones wherein our smiling plays Pos 29
	26.	All hours clapped dense into a single stride Rec 26
	28.	Reflective conversion of all things F&H I 32
	30.	All relatives, serene and cool F&H II 22
	33.	All stubble streets that have not curved F&H III 27
	36.	All but the pieties of lovers' hands V-2 10
	37.	That must arrest all distance otherwise V-3 10
	38.	All fragrance irrefragibly, and claim V-4 9
	38.	All bright insinuations that my years have caught V-4 21
	38.	The secret oar and petals of all love V-4 25
	39.	In all the argosy of your bright hair I dreamed V-5 19
	48.	Yet lost, all, let this keel one instant yield AM 16
	51.	And all the eddying breath between dost search AM 59

all, cont.	51.	Of all that amplitude that time explores AM 73
	51.	In holy rings all sails charged to the far AM 82
	74.	At last with all that's consummate and free Dan 79
	123.	When the others were blinded by all waking things Moth 27
	125.	Can trace paths tear-wet, and forget all blight C 13
	139.	All, save I Lege 9
	150.	And all unstintingly as to the moon GWP 5
	151.	all america is saying APE 2
	151.	doesn't stink at all APE 19
	162.	Weathers all loneliness OS 12
	163.	Above all reason lifting, halt serene Id 15
	179.	time for these; time for all these, as cattle and birds Len 18
alleys	11.	The moon in lonely alleys make Chap 20
	21.	And wakens alleys with a hidden cough Pass 10
	94.	As vibrantly I following down Sequoia alleys CH 183
	144.	In the streets and alleys PA 14
alley-upward	54.	Comes echoing alley-upward through dim snow HD 9
alluvial	69.	Damp tonnage and alluvial march of days Riv 124
almost	16.	Tyranny; they drew me into hades almost RR 8
	50.	Almost as though the Moor's flung scimitar AM 36
	60.	My mother almost brought me once from church VW 35
	64.	"It was almost Louisiana, long ago" Riv 45
	168.	A bird almost--of almost bird alarms AP 4
	168.	Almost no shadow--but the air's thin talk AP 12
	181.	She almost--even then--got blown across lots Et 5
	182.	Sobbed. Yes, now--it's almost over. For they know Et 42
alms	5.	Alms to the meek the volcano burst EC 3
aloft	56.	The sun, released--aloft with cold gulls hither HD 34
	110.	And Death, aloft,--gigantically down Tun 77
	115.	And you, aloft there--Jason! hesting Shout At 37
	163.	That kite aloft--you should have watched him scan Id 11
alone	13.	To risk alone the light's decline IS 14
	24.	Sparkling alone, within another's will WM 32
	25.	In each the skin alone, and so it is Rec 6
	29.	That world which comes to each of us alone F&H I 48
	38.	Than, singing, this mortality alone V-4 7

alone, cont.	39.	Draw in your head, alone and too tall here V-5 22
	72.	And one star, swinging, take its place, alone Dan 25
	98.	No wraith, but utterly--as still more alone SC 2
	101.	O Magdalene, each comes back to die alone NW 6 26
	109.	Where boxed alone a second, eyes take fright Tun 27
	135.	Yet,--much follows, much endures...Trust birds alone CL 5
	158.	The Cross alone has flown the wave Mer 5
	158.	Leave us, you idols of Futurity--alone Mer 12
	163.	Passed him again...He was alone, agape Id 8
aloud	10.	Scarcely aloud, beyond her door SM 14
alphabet	190.	In wider letters than the alphabet Rel 11
alphabets	174.	From twenty alphabets--we're still unripe BNOK 12
already	12.	Already fallen harvest Past 13
	17.	Your head, unrocking to a pulse, already Par 14
	39.	Already hang, shred ends from remembered stars V-5 7
	39.	Your eyes already in the slant of drifting foam V-5 23
	46.	Already snow submerges an iron year TBB 40
	90.	Already knows the closer clasp of Mars CH 85
	106.	His news already told? Yes, while the heart is wrung QH 61
	109.	Into the slot. The gongs already rattle Tun 30
	182.	Were death predestined! You held your nose al- ready Et 33
altar	46.	O harp and altar, of the fury fused TBB 29
altars	34.	Frosted eyes there were that lifted altars AMT 11
alternate	28.	The press of troubled hands, too alternate F&H I 42
alternating	26.	In alternating bells have you not heard Rec 25
altitude	191.	As one whose altitude at one time was not Purg 21
always	23.	A leopard ranging always in the brow WM 3
	33.	The lavish heart shall always have to leaven F&H III 33
	66.	By iron, iron--always the iron dealt cleavage Riv 87
	68.	Always they smile out eerily what they seem Riv 109
	79.	Good-bye...Good-bye...oh, I shall always wait Ind 63
	100.	Always you wait for someone else though, always NWG 7
	100.	Always and last, before the final ring NWG 9
	116.	Always through blinding cables, to our joy At 76

always, cont.	116.	Always through spiring cordage, pyramids At 78
	164.	Struck free and holy in one Name always NA 12
	176.	Yes, light. And it is always VU 21
	176.	always, always the eternal rainbow VU 22
	176.	And it is always the day, the farewell day unkind VU 23
amaze	94.	Of love's own diametric gaze, of love's amaze CH 188
amazements	30.	New soothings, new amazements F&H II 16
ambassador	32.	You, here beside me, delicate ambassador F&H III 3
amber	13.	Out in the late amber afternoon IS 1
ambiguous	89.	Of the ambiguous cloud. We know the strident rule CH 34
ambushed	156.	Is Commissioner of mildew throughout the ambushed senses OC 21
amenity	140.	O grey and gold amenity Int 3
america	151.	all america is saying APE 2
American	189.	Doctor had said--who was American, also--"You can HR 30
Americans	145.	And some of them "will be Americans" PA 24
amid	167.	Amid the noontide's blazed asperities RP 3
	181.	Where a frantic peacock rummaged amid heaped cans Et 17
ammoniac	90.	Stars prick the eyes with sharp ammoniac proverbs CH 62
amphibian	91.	Behold the dragon's covey--amphibian, ubiquitous CH 88
ample	11.	In slithered and too ample pockets Chap 4
	171.	Out of the valley, past the ample crib KW 2
amplitude	51.	Of all that amplitude that time explores AM 73
amulet	157.	You have given me the shell, Satan,--carbonic amulet OC 34
anagrammatize	156.	And anagrammatize your name)--No, nothing here OC 5
anatomies	24.	New thresholds, new anatomies! Wine talons WM 29
Anchises	33.	Anchises' navel, dripping of the sea F&H III 36
anchored	41.	Hushed willows anchored in its glow V-6 30
	85.	Buntlines tusseling (91 days, 20 hours and anchored!)/Rainbow, Leander CS 73
anchorite	167.	I watched the sun's most gracious anchorite RP 4
ancient	64.	The ancient men--wifeless or runaway Riv 54
	68.	As though you touched hands with some ancient clown Riv 101
	68.	Grimed tributaries to an ancient flow Riv 113
	88.	The ancient names--return home to our own CH 9
	105.	The woodlouse mortgages the ancient deal QH 42
	134.	Yellow, pallid, like ancient lace CDB 28
andante	133.	The andante of smooth hopes and lost regrets CDB 4
	133.	The andante quivers with crescendo's start CDB 9

andantes	147.	The wind plays andantes Per 6
Andean	166.	Andean brain IV 10
anemone	116.	O Answerer of all,--Anemone At 85
anew	92.	Anew CH 131
	191.	I am unraveled, umbilical anew Purg 17
angelic	168.	Angelic Dynamo! Ventriloquist of the Blue AP 13
angels	186.	Where angels beg for doom in ghast distraction Shak 11
angelus	50.	Some Angelus environs the cordage tree AM 55
	106.	In one last angelus lift throbbing throat QH 63
	194.	The angelus of wars my chest evokes B Tow 31
angered	74.	Across what bivouacs of thine angered slain Dan 83
anguish	127.	And I watch, and say, "These the anguish are worth" Hi 8
anguished	24.	Anguished, the wit that cries out of me WM 37
anklets	73.	Fed down your anklets to the sunset's moat Dan 72
annoy	104.	We, who with pledges taste the bright annoy QH 11
anoint	19.	Anoint with innocence,--recall LC 16
anon	69.	Anon tall ironsides up from salt lagoons Riv 135
anonymity	46.	Of anonymity time cannot raise TBB 27
another	48.	That fall back yawning to another plunge AM 12
	50.	For here between two worlds, another, harsh AM 32
	68.	Hitch up your pants and crunch another quid Riv 106
	83.	and sleep another thousand CS 45
another's	24.	Sparkling alone, within another's will WM 32
answer	10.	That hands joined in the dark will answer SM 7
	15.	In answer NL 12
	25.	And gradually white buildings answer day Rec 16
	35.	And in answer to their treble interjections V-1 6
	88.	Our eyes can share or answer--then deflects CH 25
	89.	Adam and Adam's answer in the forest CH 31
	93.	To answer deepest soundings! O, upward from the dead CH 154
	98.	Finally to answer all within one grave SC 12
	109.	This answer lives like verdigris, like hair Tun 47
	114.	So seven oceans answer from their dream At 16
	194.	No answer (could blood hold such a lofty tower B Tow 26
answered	36.	Is answered in the vortex of our grave V-2 24
answerer	116.	O Answerer of all,--Anemone At 85
answering	10.	Still answering her faint good-byes SM 18
answers	34.	And silent answers crept across the stars AMT 12
	92.	Hung low...until a conch of thunder answers CH 120

antagonistic	188.	antagonistic wills--into immunity. Tact, horsemanship HR 24
antarctic	17.	As, when stunned in the antarctic blaze Par 13
	104.	That blends March with August Antarctic skies QH 3
antennae	111.	With antennae toward worlds that glow and sink Tun 110
Anthony	174.	From the sweet jeopardy of Anthony's plight BNOK 7
anthracite	92.	Slit the sky's pancreas of foaming anthracite CH 122
Antillean	185.	Antillean fingers counting my pulse, my love forever Post 16
antiphonal	117.	Whispers antiphonal in azure swing At 96
	193.	Antiphonal carillons launched before B Tow 7
antiquity	105.	The spinster polish of antiquity QH 45
antlers	75.	Do arrows thirst and leap? Do antlers shine Dan 98
Antwerp	82.	"It's S.S. Ala--Antwerp--now remember kid CS 13
anvil	115.	Serenely, sharply up the long anvil cry At 35
anxious	129.	The anxious milk-blood in the veins of the earth An 1
anyhow	109.	anyhow" Tun 56
	109.	And somehow anyhow swing Tun 57
anyone	165.	Anyone but these native high-steppers" BSEW 12
apace	90.	To what fierce schedules, rife of doom apace CH 87
apart	51.	O Thou who sleepest on Thyself, apart AM 57
	169.	But's smithereened apart Hur 4
	181.	Two decks unsandwiched, split sixty feet apart Et 15
	191.	Am I apart--here from you in a land Purg 2
ape	179.	The vigilance of the ape, the repe- Len 14
ape's	25.	While darkness, like an ape's face, falls away Rec 15
apish	171.	Of apish nightmares into steel-strung stone KW 12
a-plenty	165.	Oozing a-plenty. They sat like baking Buddhas BSEW 7
Apollo	190.	The harvest laugh of bright Apollo Rel 4
apostle	5.	The uneven valley graves. While the apostle gave EC 2
	5.	The apostle conveys thought through discipline EC 9
apotheosis	168.	Its apotheosis, at last--the hurricane AP 16
Appalachian	72.	O Appalachian Spring! I gained the ledge Dan 33
apparitional	45.	As apparitional as sails that cross TBB 6
appease	149.	Come now--appease me just a little Loc 35
appetite	177.	Thou canst read nothing except through appetite Rep 1
appetites	18.	Record of rage and partial appetites Pos 26

applause	23.	Applause flows into liquid cynosures WM 7
apple	9.	The apple on its bough is her desire GA 1
	88.	Hearths, there to eat an apple and recall CH 10
apple-lanterns	160.	ripe apple-lanterns gush history, recondite lightnings,/irised MT 12
apples	7.	I have seen the apples there that toss you secrets SMA 13
	7.	Beloved apples of seasonable madness SMA 14
	7.	The apples, Bill, the apples SMA 18
appoint	168.	By what conjunctions do the winds appoint AP 15
appointment	51.	And true appointment from the hidden shoal AM 76
Appomattox	93.	That then from Appomattox stretched to Somme CH 170
apprehensions	18.	Wounded by apprehensions out of speech Pos 19
April	173.	This April morning offers/hurriedly MF 3
April's	40.	Flung into April's inmost day V-6 20
aprons	21.	Aprons rocks, congregates pears Pass 8
Arabian	122.	Conceived in the light of Arabian moons Moth 2
arbiter	32.	Capped arbiter of beauty in this street F&H III 1
arbor-seats	126.	And gilds the silver on the blotched arbor-seats O-N 4
arc	33.	That lowers down the arc of Helen's brow F&H III 29
	94.	Evasive--too--as dayspring's spreading arc to trace is CH 192
	114.	One arc synoptic of all tides below At 10
	185.	across dawn's broken arc. No; yes...or were they Post 4
	185.	Dawn's broken arc! the noon's more furbished room Post 12
arcades	94.	Heard thunder's eloquence through green arcades CH 184
arch	95.	And see! the rainbow's arch--how shimmeringly stands CH 212
	171.	The oar plash, and the meteorite's white arch KW 5
archbeam	149.	Of the archbeam of my cross-legged labours Loc 34
arches	15.	Hugged by plaster-grey arches of sky NL 2
	143.	And you others--follow your arches BE 29
arching	5.	Dolphins still played, arching the horizons EC 16
	114.	Through the bound cable strands, the arching path At 1
	114.	Two worlds of sleep (O arching strands of song) At 20
Arctic	82.	damned white Arctic killed my time CS 21
arenas	21.	In sapphire arenas of the hills Pass 3
argosy	39.	In all the argosy of your bright hair I dreamed V-5 19
argue	22.	"To argue with the laurel," I replied Pass 29
arguing	51.	Who grindest oar, and arguing the mast AM 65

Ariel	85.	a long tack keeping--/Taeping?/Ariel CS 76
	186.	And fail, both! Yet thine Ariel holds his song Shak 12
arise	32.	Of intricate slain numbers that arise F&H III 4
	106.	Arise--yes, take this sheaf of dust upon your tongue QH 62
arm	33.	To memory, or known the ominous lifted arm F&H III 28
armatures	90.	Our hearing momentwise; but fast in whirling armatures CH 69
armchairs	30.	Sit rocked in patent armchairs F&H II 23
armour	106.	That patience that is armour and that shields QH 70
arms	28.	But if I lift my arms it is to bend F&H I 40
	46.	And we have seen night in thine arms TBB 36
	54.	Your cool arms mumurously about me lay HD 24
	56.	arms close; eyes wide, undoubtful HD 28
	70.	She spouted arms; she rose with maize--to die Dan 4
	73.	I heard the hush of lava wrestling your arms Dan 69
	75.	Now is the strong prayer folded in thine arms Dan 103
	99.	Rehearsed hair--docile, alas, from many arms SC 26
	108.	Preparing penguin flexions of the arms Tun 21
	123.	The heat led the moth up in octopus arms Moth 38
	130.	Fresh and fragile, your arms now Ech 9
	133.	Carmen! Akimbo arms and smouldering eyes CDB 17
	138.	Release,--dismiss the passion from your arms Port 5
	152.	immensity in gathered grace; the arms In 3
	168.	Inverted octopus with heavenward arms AP 2
	172.	Yet met the wave again between your arms ABP 2
	181.	With arms in slings, plaster strewn dense with tiles Et 8
aromatic	151.	HEADY!--those aromatic LEMONS! APE 11
aromatically	98.	Climbed by aslant and huddling aromatically SC 19
around	145.	Harry and I, "the gentlemen",--seated around PA 28
aroused	129.	Aroused by some light that had sensed,--ere the shiver An 4
arpeggios	58.	Down gold arpeggios mile on mile unwinds VW 4
arrant	105.	With birthright by blackmail, the arrant page QH 55
arrest	37.	That must arrest all distance otherwise V-3 10
arrow	23.	Speed to the arrow into feathered skies WM 18
	159.	Whose arrow must have pierced you beyond pain TCJ 20
Arrowhead	79.	Whose folks, like mine, came out of Arrowhead Ind 50

arrow's	70.	Greeting they sped us, on the arrow's oath Dan 11
arrows	73.	I could not pick the arrows from my side Dan 66
	75.	Do arrows thirst and leap? Do antlers shine Dan 98
art	116.	Of stars Thou art the stitch and stallion glow At 61
arteries	28.	And now, before its arteries turn dark F&H I 27
articulate	9.	Dumbly articulate in the slant and rise GA 4
as	3.	As silent as a mirror is believed Leg 1
	6.	It trembles as birch limbs webbing the air MGLL 15
	18.	Hidden,--O undirected as the sky Pos 7
	18.	As quiet as you can make a man Pos 17
	21.	So was I turned about and back, much as your smoke Pass 21
	25.	As double as the hands that twist this glass Rec 2
	28.	Lightly as moonlight on the eaves meets snow F&H I 31
	32.	And in other ways than as the wind settles F&H III 8
	39.	As if too brittle or too clear to touch V-5 5
	39.	Nothing so flagless as this piracy V-5 20
	40.	Steadily as a shell secretes V-6 5
	40.	Or as many waters trough the sun's V-6 7
	58.	Macadam, gun-grey as the tunny's belt VW 1
	58.	Firmly as coffee grips the taste,--and away VW 9
	60.	It flashed back at your thrust, as clean as fire VW 25
	62.	breathtaking--as you like it...eh Riv 18
	72.	Fall, Sachem, strictly as the tamarack Dan 48
	90.	As bright as frogs' eyes, giggling in the girth CH 70
	91.	Wounds that we wrap with theorems sharp as hail CH 98
	93.	His last wing-pulse, and downcast as a cup CH 161
	93.	And fraternal massacre! Thou, pallid there as chalk CH 168
	94.	When first I read thy lines, rife as the loam CH 173
	94.	Familiar, thou, as mendicants in public places CH 191
	94.	Evasive--too--as dayspring's spreading arc to trace is CH 192
	95.	And now, as launched in abysmal cupolas of space CH 205
	105.	Must we descend as worm's eye to construe QH 58
	105.	As humbly as a guest who knows himself too late QH 60
	114.	Pouring reply as though all ships at sea At 12

as, cont.

116. As love strikes clear direction for the helm
     At 64
133. Just as absinthe-sipping women shiver through
     CDB 6
135. Between us, voiceless as an uncoiled shell CL 4
137. Forgetfulness is white,--white as a blasted
     tree For 8
139. As a cameo the waves claim again Lege 11
147. As now her heart and mind Per 12
148. Bland as the wide gaze of a Newfoundland Loc 8
159. As you have yielded balcony and room TCJ 15
164. But we must die, as you, to understand NA 8
164. As only they can praise, who build their days
     NA 10
167. Climb up as by communings, year on year RP 5
182. Everything--and lick the grass, as black as
     patent Et 27
191. As one whose altitude at one time was not Purg 21

as though

 39. Infrangible and lonely, smooth as though cast
     V-5 2
 45. As though the sun took step of thee, yet left
     TBB 14
 50. Almost as though the Moor's flung scimitar AM 36
 56. As though to join us at some distant hill HD 37
 68. As though the waters breathed that you might know
     Riv 98
 68. As though you touched hands with some ancient
     clown Riv 101
114. As though a god were issue of the strings At 8
161. In dusk, as though this island lifted, floated
     IQ 8
161. It is at times as though the eyes burned hard
     and glad IQ 12
167. As though it soared suchwise through heaven too
     RP 16
182. Good God! as though his sinking carcass there
     Et 32
193. Dispatches me as though I dropped down the knell
     B Tow 2

ascending   167. Mortality--ascending emerald-bright RP 13
ascends   116. Kinetic of white choiring wings...ascends At 80
ascensions   93. O Walt!--Ascensions of thee hover in me now
                  CH 148

ash   11. A grail of laughter of an empty ash can Chap 21
               60. That flittered from under the ash heap day VW 22
ashes   83. with ashes sifting down CS 27
ask   6. And I ask myself MGLL 16
               33. We did not ask for that, but have survived
                  F&H III 25
               54. Ask nothing but this sheath of pallid air HD 20

ask, cont.	105.	But I must ask slain Iroquois to guide QH 51
	109.	fandaddle daddy don't ask for change--IS THIS Tun 51
	170.	You who desired so much--in vain to ask TED 1
asking	159.	We hold in vision only, asking trace TCJ 2
aslant	98.	Climbed by aslant and huddling aromatically SC 19
asperities	167.	Amid the noontide's blazed asperities RP 3
asphalt	27.	Numbers, rebuffed by asphalt, crowd F&H I 9
assaults	18.	Assaults outright for bolts that linger Pos 6
assemblies	73.	Spears and assemblies: black drums thrusting on Dan 61
assembling	112.	I counted the echoes assembling, one after one Tun 125
assert	159.	Past pleasantries...Assert the ripened dawn TCJ 14
asserts	23.	Asserts a vision in the slumbering gaze WM 4
assessments	8.	And such assessments of the soul PU 12
assigns	116.	Whose canticle fresh chemistry assigns At 74
assortments	108.	Performances, assortments, résumés Tun 1
assuage	164.	We pinion to your bodies to assuage NA 3
assume	29.	White, through white cities passed on to assume F&H I 47
assure	48.	Assure us through thy mantle's ageless blue AM 28
assures	23.	From whom some whispered carillon assures WM 17
astral	88.	Combustion at the astral core--the dorsal change CH 4
astride	112.	A sound of waters bending astride the sky Tun 121
asunder	16.	Asunder RR 11
a-sway	51.	The sea's green crying towers a-sway, Beyond AM 88
Atahualpa	166.	Atahualpa IV 16
athwart	51.	Like ocean athwart lanes of death and birth AM 58
Atlantic	45.	Thy cables breathe the North Atlantic still TBB 24
Atlantis	116.	Atlantis,--hold thy floating singer late At 88
Atlantis Rose	83.	ATLANTIS ROSE drums wreathe the rose CS 43
atom	89.	Seeing himself an atom in a shroud CH 41
atom-withered	123.	And his wings atom-withered,--gone,--left but a leap Moth 47
atone	33.	And spread with bells and voices, and atone F&H III 34
	79.	There's where the stubborn years gleam and atone Ind 55
atrocious	25.	Alike suspend us from atrocious sums Rec 18
attend	54.	Attend the darkling harbor, the pillowed bay HD 12
	162.	More hopes than here attend OS 8
attendance	25.	That yield attendance to one crucial sign Rec 12
attending	110.	Of shoes, umbrellas, each eye attending its shoe, then Tun 87
auction	105.	Ty-five at Adams' auction,--eats the seal QH 44

audible	185.	the audible ransom, ensign of my faith Post 5
aught	167.	Uneaten of the earth or aught earth holds RP 6
augmented	184.	You, who contain augmented tears, explosions Emp 1
August	23.	While August meadows somewhere clasp his brow WM 23
	104.	That blends March with August Antarctic skies QH 3
aunt	64.	"--And when my Aunt Sally Simpson smiled," he drawled Riv 44
aureate	5.	With sulphur and aureate rocks EC 4
aureole	95.	And read thee by the aureole 'round thy head CH 216
auroral	91.	Of pendulous auroral beaches,--satellited wide CH 113
austerities	148.	Because of your perverse austerities Loc 6
authority	68.	O Sheriff, Brakeman and Authority Riv 105
autumn	70.	And in the autumn drouth, whose burnished hands Dan 5
	94.	Gold autumn, captured, crowned the trembling hill CH 186
	139.	And moons of spring and autumn Lege 8
autumnal	106.	Leaf after autumnal leaf/break off,/descend-- descend QH 72
avenue	58.	Van Winkle sweeps a tenement/way down on Avenue A VW 15
avid	105.	Weekenders avid of their turf-won scores QH 29
avoid	108.	Avoid the glass doors gyring at your right Tun 26
awaiting	142.	May slumber yet in the moon, awaiting BE 19
awake	187.	Awake to the cold light Ma 1
aware	60.	And Rip was slowly made aware VW 26
awash	93.	Of tides awash the pedestal of Everest, fail CH 152
awe	36.	Bind us in time, O Seasons clear, and awe V-2 21
awed	133.	"Carmen!," comes awed from wine-hot lips CDB 20
awkward	104.	And they are awkward, ponderous and uncoy QH 9
awnings	31.	Beneath gyrating awnings I have seen F&H II 28
axe	66.	They doze now, below axe and powder horn Riv 88
axle	29.	Bent axle of devotion along companion ways F&H I 50
axle-bound	90.	Of steely gizzards--axle-bound, confined CH 71
axles	144.	O City, your axles need not the oil of song PA 19
axletree	83.	Then you may laugh and dance the axletree CS 41
ay	169.	Ay! Scripture flee'th stone Hur 5
azure	34.	No farther tides...High in the azure steeps AMT 14
	72.	Of Adirondacks!--wisped of azure wands Dan 36
	117.	Whispers antiphonal in azure swing At 96
	159.	Your light lifts whiteness into virgin azure TCJ 5
	194.	In azure circles, widening as they dip B Tow 36
azured	167.	Unshackled, casual of its azured height RP 15

babe's	78.	She cradled a babe's body, riding without rein Ind 34
Bacardi	183.	Drinking Bacardi and talking U.S.A. Et 60
back	6.	To carry back the music to its source MGLL 20
	6.	And back to you again MGLL 21
	21.	The shadows of boulders lengthened my back Pass 13
	21.	So was I turned about and back, much as your smoke Pass 21
	22.	Why are you back here--smiling an iron coffin Pass 28
	24.	"And fold your exile on your back again WM 48
	34.	The calyx of death's bounty giving back AMT 6
	48.	And greed adjourned,--I bring you back Cathay AM 8
	48.	That fall back yawning to another plunge AM 12
	54.	They give it back again. Soft sleeves of sound HD 11
	60.	It flashed back at your thrust, as clean as fire VW 25
	72.	Swooping in eagle feathers down your back Dan 46
	73.	Lie to us,--dance us back the tribal morn Dan 60
	76.	Back on the gold trail--then his lost bones stirred Ind 10
	78.	The long trail back! I huddled in the shade Ind 29
	78.	Perhaps a halfbreed. On her slender back Ind 33
	79.	Come back to Indiana--not too late Ind 61
	89.	Back over Connecticut farms, abandoned pastures CH 57
	93.	That's drained, is shivered back to earth--thy wand CH 162
	98.	To stammer back...It is SC 21
	101.	O Magdalene, each comes back to die alone NWG 26
	101.	Lug us back lifeward--bone by infant bone NWG 28
	109.	Quite unprepared rush naked back to light Tun 28
	110.	In back forks of the chasms of the brain Tun 69
	111.	Back home to children and to golden hair Tun 105
	123.	To the desert,--back,--down,--still lonely he fell Moth 48
	145.	"One month,--I go back rich PA 31
	150.	Indeed, old memories come back to life GWP 15
	151.	but a little BACK DOOR DIGNITY) APE 25
	163.	I hurried by. But back from the hot shore Id 7
	165.	They're back now on that mulching job at Pepper's BSEW 10
	178.	And who trick back the leisured winds again PB 6
	182.	Back at the erstwhile house Et 24
	184.	You, who have looked back to Leda, who have seen the Swan Emp 6
	184.	To wage you surely back to memory Emp 10
	188.	him once before to death's beyond and back again HR 23

bank	84.	<u>Pennies</u> <u>for</u> <u>porpoises</u> <u>that</u> <u>bank</u> <u>the</u> <u>keel</u> CS 59
banked	90.	Capeward, then blading the wind's flank, banked and spun CH 81
	193.	The impasse high with choir. Banked voices slain B Tow 14
banks	94.	White banks of moonlight came descending valleys CH 181
banters	30.	Until somewhere a rooster banters F&H II 14
Baptist	24.	With Baptist John's. Their whispering begins WM 47
bar	23.	Nudges a cannister across the bar WM 22
	50.	Tomorrow's moon will grant us Saltes Bar AM 53
	82.	green glasses, or bar lights made them CS 4
barbaric	138.	Barbaric Prince Igor:--or, blind Pierrot Port 2
barbarous	133.	Disquieting of barbarous fantasy CDB 14
barber	27.	To druggist, barber and tobacconist F&H I 12
bare	50.	Was tumbled from us under bare poles scudding AM 30
	66.	O Nights that brought me to her body bare Riv 72
	111.	The gaunt sky-barracks cleanly now, and bare Tun 103
	182.	Blister the mountain, stripped now, bare of palm Et 26
bared	94.	Around bared teeth of stallions, bloomed that spring CH 172
bargain	33.	Outpacing bargain, vocable and prayer F&H III 48
bark	178.	So dream thy sails, O phantom bark PB 1
baronial	84.	baronial white on lucky blue CS 65
barracudas	165.	"Hell! out there among the barracudas BSEW 5
barren	78.	And barren tears Ind 28
	122.	Their joy with a barren and steely tide Moth 8
barricades	163.	And since, through these hot barricades of green Id 13
barrier	94.	And passed that Barrier that none escapes CH 199
bars	114.	And on, obliquely up bright carrier bars At 17
bartered	16.	How much I would have bartered! the black gorge RR 12
	28.	I would have you meet this bartered blood F&H I 28
basalt	69.	The basalt surface drags a jungle grace Riv 129
base	181.	At the base of the mountain. But the town, the town Et 6
baseball	27.	Across the memoranda, baseball scores F&H I 5
basement	188.	rosy (in their basement basinette)--the Doctor sup- HR 16
basinette	188.	rosy (in their basement basinette)--the Doctor sup- HR 16
baskets	160.	with baskets MT 16
basking	159.	As you raise temples fresh from basking foam TCJ 12
Batabanó	181.	That Havana, not to mention poor Batabanó Et 20

bath	188.	of it, its milk-light regularity above my bath partition HR 10
baths	161.	In Indian baths. At Cuban dusk the eyes IQ 9
battered	169.	Swept, whistling straw! Battered Hur 9
battlements	73.	O yelling battlements,--I, too, was liege Dan 62
battleship	183.	The Presidnet sent down a battleship that baked Et 55
bay	39.	The bay estuaries fleck the hard sky limits V-5 4
	45.	Over the chained bay waters Liberty TBB 4
	54.	Attend the darkling harbor, the pillowed bay HD 12
bayonets	191.	Where are the bayonets that the scorpion may not grow Purg 10
beach	89.	Be still the same as when you walked the beach CH 45
	156.	Near the coral beach--nor zigzag fiddle crabs OC 3
beached	93.	By Hatteras bunched the beached heap of high bravery CH 144
beaches	22.	On unpaced beaches leaned its tongue and drummed Pass 35
	91.	Of pendulous auroral beaches,--satellited wide CH 113
beachward	168.	While beachward creeps the shark-swept Spanish Main AP 14
beacon	172.	Dissolved within a sky of beacon forms ABP 4
beading	46.	Beading thy path--condense eternity TBB 35
beads	83.	then Yucatan selling kitchenware--beads CS 25
	100.	Outspoken buttocks in pink beads NWG 1
beaks	157.	And clenched beaks coughing for the surge again OC 31
beams	115.	Beams yelling AEolus! splintered in the straits At 40
bear	12.	If, dusty, I bear Past 11
	25.	Reciting pain or glee, how can you bear Rec 4
	64.	The last bear, shot drinking in the Dakotas Riv 24
beard	58.	And Captain Smith, all beard and certainty VW 11
	64.	Spreading dry shingles of a beard Riv 51
bearing	115.	Pacific here at time's end, bearing corn At 51
bearings	90.	The bearings glint,--O murmurless and shined CH 73
bears	37.	Infinite consanguinity it bears V-3 1
beat	17.	Of a steady winking beat between Par 1
	29.	That beat, continuous, to hourless days F&H I 51
	34.	Beat on the dusty shore and were obscured AMT 4
	93.	Has beat a song, O Walt,--there and beyond CH 163
	100.	And the lewd trounce of a final muted beat NWG 23
	137.	That, freed from beat and measure, wanders For 2
	182.	I beat the dazed mule toward the road. He got that far Et 48
beaten	109.	Our tongues recant like beaten weather vanes Tun 46

beating	40.	Its beating leagues of monotone V-6 6
	82.	got to beating time..."A whaler once CS 17
beatitude	116.	To wrapt inception and beatitude At 75
beats	35.	The sun beats lightning on the waves V-1 7
beautiful	83.	"O life's a geyser--beautiful--my lungs CS 35
	141.	Deep hand that lay in his,--seemed beautiful EpH 17
beauty	32.	Capped arbiter of beauty in this street F&H III 1
	124.	My eyes have hugged beauty and winged life's brief spell Moth 50
	131.	In silence, beauty blessed and beauty cursed Ba 11
beauty's	142.	How can you tell where beauty's to be found? BE 9
	143.	O Beauty's fool, though you have never BE 25
beavers	16.	Where beavers learn stitch and tooth RR 14
because	164.	Because we are usurpers, and chagrined NA 5
	171.	Because these millions reap a dead conclusion KW 9
become	139.	She has become a pathos Lege 5
bed	17.	One rushing from the bed at night Par 3
	69.	The River lifts itself from its long bed Riv 139
	70.	There was a bed of leaves, and broken play Dan 13
	108.	Finger your knees--and wish yourself in bed Tun 9
	141.	Around the thick bed of the wound EpH 12
	146.	The spindles at the foot of the bed PA 55
	174.	Come, search the marshes for a friendly bed BNOK 3
bedlamite	45.	A bedlamite speeds to thy parapets TBB 18
bedroom	146.	Bedroom occupation PA 60
bees	8.	And miss the dry sound of bees PU 19
	138.	Or, Daphnis, move among the bees with Chloe Port 4
	172.	By the dove filled, and bees of Paradise ABP 10
before	54.	Serenely now, before day claims our eyes HD 23
	61.	Before I had left the window. It VW 39
	73.	Dance, Maquokeeta! snake that lives before Dan 57
	123.	As his blindness before had frozen in Hell Moth 46
	142.	No one has ever walked there before BE 2
	142.	I had never seen a hand before BE 14
	142.	Where no one has ever been before BE 17
	143.	Nor the Gods that danced before you BE 27
	171.	O, steel and stone! But gold was, scarcity before KW 13
	179.	And there is, as Mr. Budge explained before his Len 11
	193.	Antiphonal carillons launched before B Tow 7
beg	186.	Where angels beg for doom in ghast distraction Shak 11
begging	182.	along the roads, begging for buzzards, vultures Et 34
begin	54.	As winch engines begin throbbing on some deck HD 7
	100.	Her silly snake rings begin to mount, surmount NWG 19

begins	24.	With Baptist John's. Their whispering begins WM 47
	100.	When all the fireworks blare, begins NWG 10
	100.	Some cheapest echo of them all--begins NWG 12
begun	12.	Summer scarcely begun Past 18
	74.	Of his own fate, I saw thy change begun Dan 76
behind	48.	Once more behind us....It is morning there AM 14
	64.	Behind/My father's cannery works I used to see Riv 52
	76.	Then, though we'd buried him behind us, far Ind 9
being	104.	Than grass and snow, and their own inner being QH 5
	170.	Being, of all, least sought for: Emily, hear TED 5
	176.	Yes, I being VU 1
beleaguer	25.	Let the same nameless gulf beleaguer us Rec 17
believe	68.	I could believe he joked at heaven's gate Riv 110
believed	3.	As silent as a mirror is believed Leg 1
	3.	Is believed Leg 19
Belle Isle	41.	Still fervid covenant, Belle Isle V-6 25
	41.	Belle Isle, white echo of the oar V-6 28
bellies	23.	Wear me in crescents on their bellies. Slow WM 6
	84.	scarfed of foam, their bellies veered green esplanades CS 68
	142.	Bellies and estuaries of warehouses BE 5
bellows	111.	Whose hideous laughter is a bellows mirth Tun 107
bell-rope	193.	The bell-rope that gathers God at dawn B Tow 1
bells	26.	In alternating bells have you not heard Rec 25
	33.	And spread with bells and voices, and atone F&H III 34
	34.	And wrecks passed without sound of bells AMT 5
	36.	And onward, as bells off San Salvador V-2 11
	102.	From the popcorn bells Va 10
	191.	So ring the church bells here in Mexico Purg 18
	193.	The bells, I say, the bells break down their tower B Tow 9
belly	28.	The limbs and belly, when rainbows spread F&H I 34
	36.	Her undinal vast belly moonward bends V-2 4
	100.	All but her belly buried in the floor NWG 22
beloved	7.	Beloved apples of seasonable madness SMA 14
below	66.	They doze now, below axe and powder horn Riv 88
	69.	Meeting the Gulf, hosannas silently below Riv 143
	88.	With sweetness below derricks, chimneys, tunnels CH 17
	123.	When below him he saw what his whole race had shunned Moth 42

below, cont.	147.	Below the wind Per 9
	156.	Below the palsy that one eucalyptus lifts OC 6
	161.	Where the straight road would seem to ply below the stone, that fierce IQ 4
belt	58.	Macadam, gun-grey as the tunny's belt VW 1
	61.	Macadam, gun-grey as the tunny's belt VW 41
	91.	Hell's belt springs wider into heaven's plumed side CH 92
	132.	And bolts herself within a jewelled belt MC 6
belts	90.	Is stropped to the slap of belts on booming spools, spurred CH 66
	142.	A mesh of belts down into it, made me think BE 13
bemused	162.	Bemused at waking, spend OS 6
bend	28.	But if I lift my arms it is to bend F&H I 40
bending	111.	Wheels off. The train rounds, bending to a scream Tun 92
	112.	A sound of waters bending astride the sky Tun 121
bends	3.	Bends no more than the still Leg 5
	36.	Her undinal vast belly moonward bends V-2 4
	72.	Steep, inaccessible smile that eastward bends Dan 34
benediction	92.	The benediction of the shell's deep, sure reprieve CH 133
bent	29.	Bent axle of devotion along companion ways F&H I 50
	36.	Pass superscription of bent foam and wave V-2 18
	45.	With multitudes bent toward some flashing scene TBB 10
	78.	Bent westward, passing on a stumbling jade Ind 31
	133.	Bent wings, and Carmen with her flaunts through the gloom CDB 22
benzine	19.	Whitely, while benzine LC 1
bequeath	34.	The dice of drowned men's bones he saw bequeath AMT 2
	36.	Bequeath us to no earthly shore until V-2 23
bequeaths	114.	Beyond whose frosted capes the moon bequeaths At 19
Bert Williams	62.	in the guaranteed corner--see Bert Williams what Riv 5
beshrouded	54.	Gongs in white surplices, beshrouded wails HD 4
beside	7.	Put them again beside a pitcher with a knife SMA 16
	14.	Beside her and her fernery, is to follow Fern 4
	32.	You, here beside me, delicate ambassador F&H III 3
	54.	And you beside me, blessed now while sirens HD 21
	109.	And down beside the turnstile press the coin Tun 29
	129.	The moans of travail of one dearest beside me An 7
	185.	their ribbon miles, beside the railroad ties Post 8

bespeak   109. of cities you bespeak Tun 32
best   72. Know, Maquokeeta, greeting; know death's best
                       Dan 47
                  74. On paths thou knewest best to claim her by
                       Dan 88
                 159. The moon's best lover,--guide us by a sleight
                       TCJ 10
                 170. Achieved that stillness ultimately best   TED 4
bestirring   133. Carmen! Bestirring hope and lipping eyes CDB 18
bestow   46. Thy guerdon...Accolade thou dost bestow TBB 26
                 152. thyself, bestow to thee In 6
bestows   173. In bunches sorted freshly--/and bestows MF 4
betrayed   20. Betrayed stones slowly speak LC 32
betrays   133. The tapestry betrays a finger through CDB 11
better   28. Imminent in his dream, none better knows F&H I 29
                 108. A walk is better underneath the L a brisk Tun 19
between   50. For here between two worlds, another, harsh AM 32
                  51. And all the eddying breath between dost search
                       AM 59
                  70. Now lie incorrigibly what years between Dan 12
                  90. What marathons new-set between the stars CH 83
                 172. Yet met the wave again between your arms ABP 2
bewilderment   50. Bewilderment and mutiny heap whelming AM 34
beyond   9. Beyond the grass and shadows at her feet GA 12
                  10. Scarcely aloud, beyond her door SM 14
                  12. An image beyond this Past 12
                  16. At gulf gates...There, beyond the dykes RR 21
                  24. Beyond the wall, whose severed head floats by
                       WM 46
                  25. The bridge swings over salvage, beyond wharves
                       Rec 23
                  29. Beyond their million brittle, bloodshot eyes
                       F&H I 46
                  33. The substance drilled and spent beyond repair
                       F&H III 43
                  33. The imagination spans beyond despair F&H III 47
                  35. You must not cross nor ever trust beyond it V-1 13
                  40. Beyond siroccos harvesting V-6 17
                  51. Thy purpose--still one shore beyond desire AM 87
                  51. The sea's green crying towers a-sway, Beyond
                       AM 88
                  66. Have dreamed beyond the print that bound her name
                       Riv 73
                  73. That casts his pelt, and lives beyond! Sprout,
                       horn Dan 58
                  75. We danced, O Brave, we danced beyond their farms
                       Dan 101
                  93. Thou, there beyond CH 157
                  93. Has beat a song, O Walt,--there and beyond CH 163
                  94. Beyond all sesames of science was thy choice
                       CH 201

beyond, cont.	109.	Beyond extinction, surcease of the bone Tun 48
	114.	Beyond whose frosted capes the moon bequeaths At 19
	159.	Whose arrow must have pierced you beyond pain TCJ 20
	167.	Forever fruitless, and beyond that yield RP 9
	173.	Beyond the roses that no flesh can pass MF 8
	188.	him once before to death's beyond and back again HR 23
biassed	51.	And biassed by full sails, meridians reel AM 86
bicarbonated	92.	Thine eyes bicarbonated white by speed, O Skygak, see CH 124
bicep	171.	Concur with wrist and bicep. In the moon KW 6
bide	158.	Though why they bide here, only hell that's sacked Mer 2
bidest	169.	Thou bidest wall nor floor, Lord Hur 18
bideth	169.	Nought stayeth, nought now bideth Hur 3
biding	48.	More absolute than ever--biding the moon AM 19
	69.	Patience! and you shall reach the biding place Riv 131
big	166.	Big guns again IV 1
	166.	Big guns again IV 8
	166.	Big guns again IV 15
bile	24.	Invent new dominoes of love and bile WM 39
Bill	7.	The apples, Bill, the apples SMA 18
billow	111.	The sod and billow breaking,--lifting ground Tun 120
billows	24.	"Alas,--these frozen billows of your skill WM 38
bind	20.	No longer bind. Some sentient cloud LC 30
	36.	Bind us in time, O Seasons clear, and awe V-2 21
	64.	Bind town to town and dream to ticking dream Riv 27
	95.	Wherewith to bind us throbbing with one voice CH 202
	170.	Needs more than wit to gather, love to bind TED 11
binds	19.	Immaculate venom binds LC 8
	115.	To kneeling wave, one song devoutly binds At 55
biography	21.	Compiles a too well-known biography Pass 22
biplane	90.	O sinewy silver biplane, nudging the wind's withers CH 77
birch	6.	It trembles as birch limbs webbing the air MGLL 15
	73.	A birch kneels. All her whistling fingers fly Dan 49
Birch Hill	105.	Wait for the postman driving from Birch Hill QH 54
bird	89.	Through surf, its bird note there a long time falling CH 47
	137.	Forgetfulness is like a bird whose wings are reconciled For 3
	137.	A bird that coasts the wind unwearyingly For 5
	168.	A bird almost--of almost bird alarms AP 4

birdless	83.	have you seen Popocatepetl--birdless mouth CS 26
bird-note	131.	But there is no sound,--not even a bird-note Ba 5
birds	48.	"The Great White Birds!" (O Madre María, still AM 26
	135.	Yet,--much follows, much endures...Trust birds alone CL 5
	179.	time for these; time for all these, as cattle and birds Len 18
bird-wit	64.	Strange bird-wit, like the elemental gist Riv 37
birth	15.	No birth, no death, no time nor sun NL 11
	51.	Like ocean athwart lanes of death and birth AM 58
	93.	Of love and hatred, birth,--surcease of nations CH 146
	111.	Or the muffled slaughter of a day in birth Tun 108
	122.	But over one moth's eyes were tissues at birth Moth 17
	133.	And dies on fire's birth in each man's heart CDB 10
	189.	happiness which is your own from birth HR 35
birthright	105.	With birthright by blackmail, the arrant page QH 55
bison	76.	And bison thunder rends my dreams no more Ind 5
biting	115.	Pick biting way up towering looms that press At 27
bitten	110.	Whose body smokes along the bitten rails Tun 67
bivouacs	74.	Across what bivouacs of thine angered slain Dan 83
black	4.	The interests of a black man in a cellar BT 1
	4.	The black man, forlorn in the cellar BT 9
	16.	How much I would have bartered! the black gorge RR 12
	18.	That through its black foam has no eyes Pos 8
	21.	See where the red and black Pass 17
	24.	Between black tusks the roses shine WM 28
	37.	And so, admitted through black swollen gates V-3 9
	40.	My eyes pressed black against the prow V-6 11
	72.	Siphoned the black pool from the heart's hot root Dan 44
	73.	Spears and assemblies: black drums thrusting on Dan 61
	78.	Her eyes, strange for an Indian's, were not black Ind 35
	99.	All night the water combed you with black SC 23
	114.	From black embankments, moveless soundings hailed At 15
	122.	That emerge black and vermeil from yellow cocoons Moth 4
	122.	So they sleep in the shade of black palm-bark at noon Moth 13

black, cont.	123.	Though a black god to him in a dizzying light Moth 34
	131.	Shimmering over a black mountain-spear Ba 3
	156.	Sieved upward, white and black along the air OC 25
	165.	"Pablo and Pedro, and black Serafin BSEW 1
	182.	Everything--and lick the grass, as black as patent Et 27
blacken	133.	Their brown eyes blacken, and the blue drop hue CDB 8
blackened	50.	Starved wide on blackened tides, accrete-- enclose AM 42
black-eyed	145.	With four tiny black-eyed girls around her PA 34
blackmail	105.	With birthright by blackmail, the arrant page QH 55
blackness	112.	The blackness somewhere gouged glass on a sky Tun 128
Black Prince	84.	Thermopylae, Black Prince, Flying Cloud through Sunda CS 67
blade	39.	Together in one merciless white blade V-5 3
	115.	Sidelong with flight of blade on tendon blade At 28
blading	90.	Capeward, then blading the wind's blank, banked and spun CH 81
blame	11.	What blame to us if the heart live on Chap 18
blamed	33.	Blamed bleeding hands extend and thresh the height F&H III 46
blameless	132.	O blameless shyness;--innocence dissolute MC 4
bland	148.	Bland as the wide gaze of a Newfoundland Loc 8
blank	111.	Blank windows gargle signals through the roar Tun 99
	138.	Haunt the blank stage with lingering alarms Port 7
blanket	72.	That blanket of the skies: the padded foot Dan 42
	191.	But rather like a blanket than a quilt Purg 14
blankness	54.	Somewhere out there in blankness steam HD 13
blare	100.	When all the fireworks blare, begins NWG 10
	112.	Lunged past, with one galvanic blare stove up the River Tun 124
blast	179.	the buzz of saw mills, the crunch and blast of quarries Len 2
blasted	137.	Forgetfulness is white,--white as a blasted tree For 8
blaze	17.	As, when stunned in that antarctic blaze Par 13
	94.	Panis Angelicus! Eyes tranquil with the blaze CH 187
	122.	She will flush their hid wings in the evening to blaze Moth 15
blazed	167.	Amid the noontide's blazed asperities RP 3
bleached	35.	Fondle your shells and sticks, bleached V-1 11

bled	72.	Until, immortally, it bled into the dawn Dan 27
	105.	Dead rangers bled their comfort on the snow QH 50
Bleecker	18.	In Bleecker Street, still trenchant in a void Pos 18
	102.	Crap-shooting gangs in Bleecker reign Va 20
bleed	159.	With snore of thunder, crowding us to bleed TCJ 7
	168.	The needles and hack-saws of cactus bleed AP 9
bleeding	3.	Bleeding eidolon!) and yet again Leg 16
	18.	Tossed on these horns, who bleeding dies Pos 23
	33.	Blamed bleeding hands extend and thresh the height F&H III 46
	127.	Up the chasm-walls of my bleeding heart Hi 1
	141.	The gash was bleeding, and a shaft of sun EpH 5
bleeds	117.	That bleeds infinity--the orphic strings At 91
blendings	64.	Time's rendings, time's blendings they contrue Riv 35
blends	104.	That blends March with August Antarctic skies QH 3
blent	74.	Like one white meteor, sacrosanct and blent Dan 78
	147.	The hills lie curved and blent Per 11
bless	170.	Dared dignify the labor, bless the quest TED 3
blessed	54.	And you beside me, blessed now while sirens HD 21
	131.	In silence, beauty blessed and beauty cursed Ba 11
blessing	33.	To saturate with blessing and dismay F&H III 30
blest	30.	Blest excursion! this ricochet F&H II 5
blew	181.	From the world outside, but some rumor blew Et 19
blight	125.	Can trace paths tear-wet, and forget all blight C 13
	158.	Of every blight and ingenuity Mer 3
blind	18.	Upon the page whose blind sum finally burns Pos 25
	64.	Ohio, Indiana--blind baggage Riv 33
	66.	Blind fists of nothing, humpty-dumpty clods Riv 61
	89.	The circle, blind crucible of endless space CH 29
	90.	In oilrinsed circles of blind ecstasy CH 74
	122.	Blind only in day, but remembering that soon Moth 14
	123.	But they burned thinly blind like an orange peeled white Moth 40
	138.	Barbaric Prince Igor:--or, blind Pierrot Port 2
	176.	The window weight throbs in its blind VU 19
blinded	40.	Thy derelict and blinded guest V-6 12
	123.	When the others were blinded by all waking things Moth 27
blinding	116.	Always through blinding cables, to our joy At 76
blindly	61.	It flickered through the snow screen, blindly VW 37

blindness	123.	As his blindness before had frozen in Hell Moth 46
bliss	177.	Seek bliss then, brother, in my moment's shame Rep 6
blister	182.	Blister the mountain, stripped now, bare of palm Et 26
blistered	165.	That thin and blistered...just a rotten shell BSEW 4
blithe	40.	Creation's blithe and petalled word V-6 21
	84.	Blithe Yankee vanities, turreted sprites, winged CS 54
	152.	hast known....And blithe In 17
blizzards	66.	Trains sounding the long blizzards out--I heard Riv 74
bloated	168.	The lizard's throat, held bloated for a fly AP 7
blocks	82.	or left you several blocks away CS 7
	108.	Ten blocks or so before? But you find yourself Tun 20
blond	56.	The window goes blond slowly. Frostily clears HD 31
	169.	Whip sea-kelp screaming on blond Hur 15
blonde	100.	You pick your blonde out neatly through the smoke NWG 6
blood	19.	First blood. From flanks unfended LC 11
	24.	Until my blood dreams a receptive smile WM 33
	28.	I would have you meet this bartered blood F&H I 28
	33.	Gathered the voltage of blown blood and vine F&H III 38
	38.	Mutual blood, transpiring as foreknown V-4 19
	98.	It is blood to remember; it is fire SC 20
	168.	But this,--defenseless, thornless, sheds no blood AP 11
	179.	And there is work, blood, suet and sweat,--the rigamarole Len 9
	194.	The steep encroachments of my blood left me B Tow 25
	194.	No answer (could blood hold such a lofty tower B Tow 26
bloodshot	29.	Beyond their million brittle, bloodshot eyes F&H I 46
bloody	93.	What memories of vigils, bloody, by that Cape CH 166
bloom	74.	O stream by slope and vineyard--into bloom Dan 96
bloomed	84.	that bloomed in the spring--Heave, weave CS 56
	94.	Around bared teeth of stallions, bloomed that spring CH 172
blooms	140.	How love blooms like a tardy flower Int 7
blossoms	156.	Let fiery blossoms clot the light, render my ghost OC 24
blotched	126.	And gilds the silver on the blotched arbor-seats O-N 4
blowing	25.	Its drums and darkest blowing leaves ignore Rec 10

blown	33.	Gathered the voltage of blown blood and vine F&H III 38
	181.	She almost--even then--got blown across lots Et 5
bludgeon	91.	Is baited by marauding circles, bludgeon flail CH 96
blue	9.	Holding her to the sky and its quick blue GA 9
	32.	The tensile boughs, the nimble blue plateaus F&H III 20
	38.	Blue latitudes and levels of your eyes V-4 23
	48.	Assure us through thy mantle's ageless blue AM 28
	51.	Into thy steep savannahs, burning blue AM 63
	66.	Snow-silvered, sumac-stained or smoky blue Riv 68
	70.	Your hair's keen crescent running, and the blue Dan 19
	72.	Grey tepees tufting the blue knolls ahead Dan 39
	73.	And splay tongues thinly busy the blue air Dan 56
	79.	Oh, hold me in those eyes' engaging blue Ind 54
	84.	baronial white on lucky blue CS 65
	122.	Countless rubies and tapers in the oasis' blue haze Moth 16
	123.	And without one cloud-car in that wide meshless blue Moth 35
	123.	Which blue tides of cool moons were slow shaken and sunned Moth 44
	133.	With shimmering blue from the bowl in Circe's hall CDB 7
	133.	Their brown eyes blacken, and the blue drop hue CDB 8
	135.	With surging gentleness; and the blue stone CL 7
	148.	For snaring the poor world in a blue funk Loc 12
	168.	Angelic Dynamo! Ventriloquist of the Blue AP 13
blue-eyed	102.	O blue-eyed Mary with the claret scarf Va 7
blue's	91.	The blue's cloud-templed districts unto ether CH 90
	156.	Until it meets the blue's comedian host OC 26
bluet	28.	That winks above it, bluet in your breasts F&H I 38
blue-writ	94.	Blue-writ and odor-firm with violets, 'til CH 176
bluffs	72.	Over how many bluffs, tarns, streams I sped Dan 37
blurs	9.	Of branch on branch above her, blurs her eyes GA 5
blush	15.	Or left you with the faintest blush NL 6
	28.	At your deep blush, when ecstasies thread F&H I 33
	160.	Let them return, saying you blush again for the great MT 1
boast	104.	The jest is too sharp to be kindly?) boast QH 14

boat	72.	I left my sleek boat nibbling margin grass Dan 28
	181.	To Havana on the first boat through. They groaned Et 13
	181.	But was there a boat? By the wharf's old site you saw Et 14
bobbin-bound	90.	Power's script,--wound, bobbin-bound, refined CH 65
bodies	24.	Poor streaked bodies wreathing up and out WM 26
	35.	Spry cordage of your bodies to caresses V-1 14
	164.	We pinion to your bodies to assuage NA 3
	183.	Sliding everywhere. Bodies were rushed into graves Et 51
boding	72.	And knew myself within some boding shade Dan 38
body	28.	Inevitable, the body of the world F&H I 36
	37.	Your body rocking V-3 14
	66.	They know a body under the wide rain Riv 64
	66.	(O Nights that brought me to her body bare Riv 72
	66.	Dead echoes! But I knew her body there Riv 78
	78.	She cradled a babe's body, riding without rein Ind 34
	110.	Whose body smokes along the bitten rails Tun 67
bolder	78.	I held you up--I suddenly the bolder Ind 41
boldest	94.	And it was thou who on the boldest heel CH 194
bolting	110.	Bolting outright somewhere above where streets Tun 88
bolts	18.	Assaults outright for bolts that linger Pos 6
	132.	And bolts herself within a jewelled belt MC 6
Bombay	88.	Or how the priests walked--slowly through Bombay CH 12
bonds	184.	The slit eclipse of moon in palm-lit bonds Emp 4
bone	73.	To rainbows currying each pulsant bone Dan 63
	101.	Lug us back lifeward--bone by infant bone NWG 28
	109.	Beyond extinction, surcease of the bone Tun 48
	169.	Rescindeth flash from bone Hur 7
	171.	Need I presume the same fruit of my bone KW 10
bones	34.	The dice of drowned man's bones he saw bequeath AMT 2
	69.	Over De Soto's bones the freighted floors Riv 132
	76.	Back on the gold trail--then his lost bones stirred Ind 10
bony	82.	weakeyed watches sometimes snooze--" his bony hands CS 16
book	21.	A thief beneath, my stolen book in hand Pass 27
	22.	He closed the book. And from the Ptolemies Pass 32
books	141.	That knew a grip for books and tennis EpH 9
	145.	And hitch yourself up to your book PA 41
booming	90.	Is stropped to the slap of belts on booming spools, spurred CH 66
boon	145.	As down she knelt for heaven's grace and boon PA 44

Booneville	64.	"There's no place like Booneville though, Buddy" Riv 46
bootleg	105.	In bootleg roadhouses where the gin fizz QH 35
borage	20.	Borage of death have cleared my tongue LC 28
borders	40.	Green borders under stranger skies V-6 4
	104.	One's glance could cross the borders of three states QH 26
born	68.	Down, down--born pioneers in time's despite Riv 112
	122.	There are butterflies born in mosaic date-vases Moth 3
borne	5.	And where was finally borne a chosen hero EC 14
	25.	Borne cleft to you, and brother in the half Rec 8
	68.	The Ohio merging,--borne down Tennessee Riv 95
bosoms	125.	The transcient bosoms from the thorny tree C 7
boss	102.	Keep smiling the boss away Va 3
	166.	That defunct boss IV 14
bottle	4.	Gnats toss in the shadow of a bottle BT 3
bottom	35.	The bottom of the sea is cruel V-1 16
bouffe	30.	This crashing opéra bouffe F&H II 4
bough	9.	The apple on its bough is her desire GA 1
	9.	The bough has caught her breath up, and her voice GA 3
boughs	20.	Lean long from sable, slender boughs LC 37
	32.	The tensile boughs, the nimble blue plateaus F&H III 20
	75.	The serpent with the eagle in the boughs Dan 104
	136.	An imagined garden grey with sundered boughs Ps 6
	160.	tisms wrench the golden boughs. Leaves spatter dawn MT 7
bought	165.	Bought a launch last week. It might as well BSEW 2
bouillon	90.	Into the bulging bouillon, harnessed jelly of the stars CH 67
boulders	21.	The shadows of boulders lengthened my back Pass 13
	169.	Lord, e'en boulders now outleap Hur 10
bound	66.	Have dreamed beyond the print that bound her name Riv 73
	93.	Thou bringest tally, and a pact, new bound CH 155
	114.	Through the bound cable strands, the arching path At 1
	122.	They had scorned him, so humbly low, bound there and tied Moth 23
	157.	For slow evisceration bound like those huge terrapin OC 28
bounty	34.	The calyx of death's bounty giving back AMT 6
bow	140.	The world at last, must bow and win Int 11
bowels	151.	"how are my bowels today?" and APE 3

Bowery	84.	he lunged up Bowery way while the dawn CS 50
bowing	58.	And Rip Van Winkle bowing by the way VW 12
bowl	133.	With shimmering blue from the bowl in Circe's hall CDB 7
bowls	5.	Bowls and cups fill historians with adorations EC 10
bows	150.	And Fifi's bows and poodle ease GWP 6
box	60.	So memory, that strikes a rhyme out of a box VW 30
boxed	109.	Where boxed alone a second, eyes take fright Tun 27
boy	7.	A boy runs with a dog before the sun, straddling SMA 9
	76.	As once my womb was torn, my boy, when you Ind 6
	163.	The boy straggling under those mimosas, daft Id 2
	179.	And the idiot boy by the road, with carbonated eyes, laugh- Len 4
bracket	17.	But from its bracket how can the tongue tell Par 9
brain	66.	Screamed redskin dynasties that fled the brain Riv 77
	100.	And while legs waken salads in the brain NWG 5
	110.	The phonographs of hades in the brain Tun 58
	110.	In back forks of the chasms of the brain Tun 69
	166.	Andean brain IV 10
brain's	25.	The brain's disk shivered against lust. Then watch Rec 14
brake	182.	Out of the bamboo brake through howling, sheeted light Et 40
brake-beam	68.	Dan Midland--jolted from the cold brake-beam Riv 111
brakeman	68.	O Sheriff, Brakeman and Authority Riv 105
branch	9.	Of branch on branch above her, blurs her eyes GA 5
	50.	An herb, a stray branch among salty teeth AM 51
branches	136.	And broken branches, wistful and unmended Ps 7
Brandywine	7.	In the valley where you live/(called Brandywine) SMA 12
brass	12.	Bronze and brass. The wind Past 9
brave	75.	We danced, O Brave, we danced beyond their farms Dan 101
bravery	93.	By Hatteras bunched the beached heap of high bravery CH 144
brazen	30.	Brazen hypnotics glitter here F&H II 1
break	106.	Leaf after autumnal leaf/break off,/descend-- descend QH 72
	140.	And even should the world break in Int 9
	193.	The bells, I say, the bells break down their tower B Tow 9
breakers	94.	Of praries, yet like breakers cliffward leaping CH 174

breakfasters	68.	And Pullman breakfasters slide glistening steel Riv 89
breaking	25.	Twin shadowed halves: the breaking second holds Rec 5
	111.	The sod and billow breaking,--lifting ground Tun 120
	141.	Bunches of new green breaking a hard turf EpH 19
breaks	106.	Breaks us and saves, yes, breaks the heart, yet yields QH 69
breast	35.	Too lichen-faithful from too wide a breast V-1 15
	37.	Resigns a breast that every wave enthrones V-3 4
	38.	And widening noon within your breast for gathering V-4 20
	40.	And harbor of the phoenix' breast V-6 10
	66.	They lurk across her, knowing her yonder breast Riv 67
	145.	And threw warm gules on Madeline's fair breast PA 43
	170.	And plundered momently in every breast TED 8
breasts	15.	Upon your glittering breasts NL 7
	28.	That winks above it, bluet in your breasts F&H I 38
	74.	Her hair's warm sibilance. Her breasts are fanned Dan 95
	123.	Swinging in spirals round the fresh breasts of day Moth 30
breath	9.	The bough has caught her breath up, and her voice GA 3
	20.	Lift up in lilac-emerald breath the grail LC 40
	33.	Who dare not share with us the breath released F&H III 42
	39.	Your breath sealed by the ghosts I do not know V-5 24
	48.	For I have seen now what no perjured breath AM 5
	51.	And all the eddying breath between dost search AM 59
	94.	Our Meistersinger, thou set breath in steel CH 193
	114.	Complighted in one vibrant breath made cry At 13
	156.	Coils and withdraws. So syllables want breath OC 16
	167.	And tendril till our deathward breath is sealed RP 11
	171.	There is no breath of friends and no more shore KW 15
	178.	The hot fickle wind, the breath of males PB 11
	184.	Love and the breath of faith, momentous bride Emp 13
breathe	45.	Thy cables breathe the North Atlantic still TBB 24

breathed	68.	As though the waters breathed that you might know Riv 98
breathing	94.	Set trumpets breathing in each clump and grass tuft--'til CH 185
breathless	30.	Know, Olympians, we are breathless F&H II 7
breathtaking	62.	breathtaking--as you like it...eh Riv 18
bred	79.	Kentucky bred Ind 52
breed	89.	For you, the panoramas and this breed of towers CH 48
breeze	68.	Maybe the breeze will lift the River's musk Riv 97
	84.	Fins whip the breeze around Japan CS 60
breezes	32.	Who hurried the hill breezes, spouting malice F&H III 14
bridal	70.	And bridal flanks and eyes hid tawny pride Dan 16
bride	70.	There was a veil upon you, Pocahontas, bride Dan 14
	74.	And see'st thy bride immortal in the maize Dan 84
	184.	Love and the breath of faith, momentous bride Emp 13
bridge	25.	The bridge swings over salvage, beyond wharves Rec 23
	38.	Whose circles bridge, I know, (from palms to the severe V-4 4
	84.	I started walking home across the Bridge CS 53
	94.	Of that great Bridge, our Myth, whereof I sing CH 196
	115.	Bridge, lifting night to cycloramic crest At 43
	116.	Unspeakable Thou Bridge to Thee, O Love At 83
	117.	One Song, one Bridge of Fire! Is it Cathay At 93
	142.	Walk high on the bridge of Estador BE 1
	142.	High on the bridge of Estador BE 16
bridges	32.	On the sixteen thrifty bridges of the city F&H III 9
brief	124.	My eyes have hugged beauty and winged life's brief spell Moth 50
briefly	32.	That waited faintly, briefly and in vain F&H III 18
bright	3.	Until the bright logic is won Leg 17
	15.	Have you no memories, O Darkly Bright NL 8
	18.	All but bright stones wherein our smiling plays Pos 29
	35.	Bright striped urchins flay each other with sand V-1 2
	38.	Bright staves of flowers and quills to-day as I V-4 15
	38.	All bright insinuations that my years have caught V-4 21
	39.	In all the argosy of your bright hair I dreamed V-5 19

bright, cont.	40.	Where icy and bright dungeons lift V-6 1
	56.	Two--three bright window-eyes aglitter, disk HD 33
	84.	those bright designs the trade winds drive CS 57
	84.	Bright skysails ticketing the Line, wink round the Horn CS 61
	89.	Sea eyes and tidal, undenying, bright with myth CH 58
	90.	As bright as frogs' eyes, giggling in the girth CH 70
	91.	O bright circumferences, heights employed to fly CH 93
	104.	We, who with pledges taste the bright annoy QH 11
	108.	Out of the Square, the Circle burning bright Tun 25
	114.	And on, obliquely up bright carrier bars At 17
	116.	Through the bright drench and fabric of our veins At 68
	128.	And the fire-wood glow is bright Fr 2
	133.	Bright peacocks drink from flame-pots by the wall CDB 5
	135.	Set in the tryst-ring has but worn more bright CL 8
	158.	And ponder the bright stains that starred this Throne Mer 14
	176.	bright with myth...Such VU 16
	190.	The harvest laugh of bright Apollo Rel 4
brightening	123.	The sun saw a ruby brightening ever, that flew Moth 36
brighter	186.	And laughter, burnished brighter than our fate Shak 8
brilliant	35.	O brilliant kids, frisk with your dog V-1 10
brine-caked	157.	Each daybreak on the wharf, their brine-caked eyes OC 29
bring	48.	The word I bring, O you who reined my suit AM 3
	48.	And greed adjourned,--I bring you back Cathay AM 8
	111.	O Genoese, do you bring mother eyes and hands Tun 104
	125.	From penitence must needs bring pain C 10
	180.	The sea wall. Bring her no robes yet Lib 9
	188.	Cruz--to bring--to take--to mix--to ransom-- to de- HR 14
bringest	93.	Thou bringest tally, and a pact, new bound CH 155
brink	92.	Lift agonized quittance, tilting from the invis- ible brink CH 135
brinking	111.	O cruelly to inoculate the brinking dawn Tun 109
brisk	108.	A walk is better underneath the L a brisk Tun 19

bristle	91.	Bristle the heights above a screeching gale to hover CH 105
British	84.	British repartees, skil-/ful savage sea girls CS 55
brittle	29.	Beyond their million brittle, bloodshot eyes F&H I 46
	39.	As if too brittle or too clear to touch V-5 5
	156.	Deliberate, gainsay death's brittle crypt. Meanwhile OC 14
Broadway	60.	nor there. He woke and swore he'd seen Broadway VW 28
broke	22.	Memory, committed to the page, had broke Pass 37
	94.	With June the mountain laurel broke through green CH 177
broken	8.	I cannot see that broken brow PU 18
	10.	At doors and stone with broken eyes SM 20
	12.	Broken into smoky panels Past 3
	70.	There was a bed of leaves, and broken play Dan 13
	125.	And with it song of minor, broken strain C 11
	136.	And broken branches, wistful and unmended Ps 7
	185.	across dawn's broken arc. No; yes...or were they Post 4
	185.	Dawn's broken arc! the noon's more furbished room Post 12
	193.	Of broken intervals...And I, their sexton slave B Tow 12
	193.	And so it was I entered the broken world B Tow 17
BRONX	151.	maidenhairferns, and the BRONX APE 18
bronze	12.	Bronze and brass. The wind Past 9
	21.	In the bronze gongs of my cheeks Pass 14
brook's	64.	The river's minute by the far brook's year Riv 30
brooks	62.	WIRES OR EVEN RUNning brooks connecting ears Riv 16
brother	25.	Borne cleft to you, and brother in the half Rec 8
	62.	brother--all over--going west--young man Riv 2
	177.	Where brother passes brother without sight Rep 3
	177.	Seek bliss then, brother, in my moment's shame Rep 6
	177.	So sleep, dear brother, in my fame, my shame un-done Rep 12
brotherhood	93.	Of living brotherhood CH 156
brothers	90.	Two brothers in their twinship left the dune CH 79
brother-thief	33.	O brother-thief of time, that we recall F&H III 40
brought	16.	Till age had brought me to the sea RR 5
	60.	My mother almost brought me once from church VW 35

brought, cont.	66.	O Nights that brought me to her body bare Riv 72
	78.	Knew that mere words could not have brought us nearer Ind 42
	183.	The roads were being cleared, injured brought in Et 53
brow	8.	I cannot see that broken brow PU 18
	23.	A leopard ranging always in the brow WM 3
	23.	While August meadows somewhere clasp his brow WM 23
	33.	That lowers down the arc of Helen's brow F&H III 29
	68.	But drift in stillness, as from Jordan's brow Riv 115
	130.	In opal pools beneath your brow Ech 11
brown	6.	That they are brown and soft MGLL 10
	70.	O Princess whose brown lap was virgin May Dan 15
	133.	Their brown eyes blacken, and the blue drop hue CDB 8
	133.	Of whispering tapestry, brown with old fringe CDB 23
	191.	And I have no decision--is it green or brown Purg 15
brows	51.	Of knowledge,--round thy brows unhooded now AM 84
	70.	Mythical brows we saw retiring--loth Dan 9
	75.	Of dusk?--And are her perfect brows to thine Dan 100
bruised	17.	Among bruised roses on the papered wall Par 16
brush	4.	Fox brush and sow ear top his grave BT 7
	110.	To brush some new presentiment of pain Tun 62
brushed	27.	The mind is brushed by sparrow wings F&H I 8
brutal	156.	Brutal necklaces of shells around each grave OC 10
bubbles	105.	Bubbles in time to Hollywood's new love-nest pageant QH 36
buckled	99.	The Cross, a phantom, buckled--dropped below the dawn SC 28
buckwheat	21.	Casual louse that tissues the buckwheat Pass 7
bud	123.	The florescence, the power he felt bud at the time Moth 26
Buddhas	158.	Buddhas and engines serve us undersea Mer 1
	165.	Oozing a-plenty. They sat like baking Buddhas BSEW 7
Buddy	64.	"There's no place like Booneville though, Buddy" Riv 46
budge	179.	Budge Len 20
	182.	The mule stumbled, staggered. I somehow couldn't budge Et 35
build	5.	But only to build memories of spiritual gates EC 17
	24.	Build freedom up about me and distill WM 30

build, cont.	164.	As only they can praise, who build their days NA 10
	180.	On this strange shore I build Lib 2
building	45.	Shedding white rings of tumult, building high TBB 3
	181.	The only building not sagging on its knees Et 10
buildings	25.	And gradually white buildings answer day Rec 16
builds	194.	And builds, within, a tower that is not stone B Tow 33
built	25.	Built floor by floor on shafts of steel that grant Rec 19
	191.	Exile is thus a purgatory--not such as Dante built Purg 13
bulging	90.	Into the bulging bouillon, harnessed jelly of the stars CH 67
bump	174.	Or let us bump heads in some lowly shed BNOK 4
bunch	144.	A bunch of smoke-ridden hills PA 11
bunched	90.	In coiled precision, bunched in mutual glee CH 72
	93.	By Hatteras bunched the beached heap of high bravery CH 144
bunches	141.	Bunches of new green breaking a hard turf EpH 19
	173.	In bunches sorted freshly--/and bestows MF 4
bundle	110.	Bursts from a smoldering bundle far behind Tun 68
bundle-wise	142.	Tied bundle-wise with cords of smoke BE 6
buntlines	85.	Buntlines tusseling (91 days, 20 hours and anchored!) Rainbow, Leander CS 73
buoys	54.	Among distant chiming buoys--adrift. The sky HD 16
burden	162.	The burden of the rose will fade OS 9
buried	68.	Like one whose eyes were buried long ago Riv 119
	76.	Then, though we'd buried him behind us, far Ind 9
	100.	All but her belly buried in the floor NWG 22
burlesque	101.	Then you, the burlesque of our lust--and faith NWG 27
burned	21.	Dangerously the summer burned Pass 11
	123.	But they burned thinly blind like an orange peeled white Moth 40
	123.	A little time only, for sight burned as deep Moth 45
	161.	It is at times as though the eyes burned hard and glad IQ 12
burning	3.	This cleaving and this burning Leg 11
	51.	Into thy steep savannahs, burning blue AM 63
	83.	the star floats burning in a gulf of tears CS 44
	108.	Out of the Square, the Circle burning bright Tun 25
burnished	70.	And in the autumn drouth, whose burnished hands Dan 5
	186.	And laughter, burnished brighter than our fate Shak 8
burns	18.	Upon the page whose blind sum finally burns Pos 25

burns, cont.	132.	This burns and is not burnt.... My modern love were MC 11
burnt	110.	A burnt match skating in a urinal Run 60
	132.	This burns and is not burnt.... My modern love were MC 11
burr	64.	One said, excising a last burr from his vest Riv 47
burrowing	150.	Burrowing in silk is not their way GWP 13
burst	5.	Alms to the meek the volcano burst EC 3
	111.	Burst suddenly in rain.... The gongs recur Tun 89
bursting	7.	Bursting on the winter of the world SMA 7
bursts	110.	Bursts from a smoldering bundle far behind Tun 68
bury	137.	Or bury the Gods For 10
bush	146.	To find the only rose on the bush PA 51
bushels	21.	In moonlit bushels Pass 9
business	145.	Roumanian business man PA 37
busy	73.	And splay tongues thinly busy the blue air Dan 56
	187.	busy still? For something still Ma 14
butterflies	122.	There are butterflies born in mosaic date-vases Moth 3
	141.	Like wings of butterflies EpH 14
buttocks	100.	Outspoken buttocks in pink beads NWG 1
buying	145.	Using the latest ice-box and buying Fords PA 25
buys	105.	Table that Powitzky buys for only nine- QH 43
buzz	179.	the buzz of saw mills, the crunch and blast of quarries Len 2
buzzard-circleted	73.	And buzzard-circleted, screamed from the stake Dan 65
buzzards	182.	along the roads, begging for buzzards, vultures Et 34

cable	114.	Through the bound cable strands, the arching path At 1
cables	39.	The cables of our sleep so swiftly filed V-5 6
	45.	Thy cables breathe the North Atlantic still TBB 24
	116.	Always through blinding cables, to our joy At 76
caboose-like	64.	Caboose-like they go ruminating through Riv 32
cactus	168.	The needles and hack-saws of cactus bleed AP 9
Caesar	95.	Thou, Vedic Caesar, to the greensward knelt CH 204
Cairo	68.	Southward, near Cairo passing, you can see Riv 94
calendars	74.	Though other calendars now stack the sky Dan 86
call	10.	Will laugh and call your name; while you SM 17
	98.	Whatever call--falls vainly on the wave SC 8
	100.	And shall we call her whiter than the snow NWG 13
	111.	Umbilical to call--and straightway die Tun 114
	114.	And through that cordage, threading with its call At 9
	115.	Silvery the rushing wake, surpassing call At 39
	191.	(They ring too obdurately here to need my call) Purg 19
called	7.	In the valley where you live/(called Brandywine) SMA 12
	78.	A dream called Eldorado was his town Ind 21
	139.	Yet called adrift again at every dawn Lege 4
calls	12.	Her calls, her enthusiasms Past 5
calm	34.	Then in the circuit calm of one vast coil AMT 9
calmly	173.	The syphilitic selling violets calmly and daisies MF 1
calyx	34.	The calyx of death's bounty giving back AMT 6
came	48.	And lowered. And they came out to us crying AM 25
	76.	And glistening through the sluggard freshets came Ind 18
	79.	Whose folks, like mine, came out of Arrowhead Ind 50
	94.	White banks of moonlight came descending valleys CH 181
	122.	Never came light through that honey-thick glaze Moth 20
	131.	She came in such still water, and so nursed Ba 10
	185.	Friendship agony! words came to me Post 1
cameo	139.	As a cameo the waves claim again Lege 11
campaniles	193.	Pagodas, campaniles with reveilles outleaping B Tow 15
can	11.	A grail of laughter of an empty ash can Chap 21
	64.	"--For early trouting." Then peering in the can Riv 48
	163.	One hand dealt out a kite string, a tin can Id 9
	179.	tomato can Len 8
canal	83.	"I ran a donkey engine down there on the Canal CS 23

cancel	176.	that cancel all your kindness. Forthright VU 10
cancelled	104.	Through mapled vistas, cancelled reservations QH 24
	186.	Is justice that has cancelled earthly chains Shak 14
cane	11.	More than the pirouettes of any pliant cane Chap 15
cannery	64.	Behind/My father's cannery works I used to see Riv 52
cannister	23.	Nudges a cannister across the bar WM 22
canoe	70.	I left the village for dogwood. By the canoe Dan 17
cans	181.	Where a frantic peacock rummaged amid heaped cans Et 17
canst	177.	Thou canst read nothing except through appetite Rep 1
canters	30.	Rhythmic ellipses lead into canters F&H II 13
canticle	116.	Whose canticle fresh chemistry assigns At 74
canto	176.	The silver strophe...the canto VU 15
cantos	90.	The gleaming cantos of unvanquished space CH 76
canyoned	89.	Of canyoned traffic...Confronting the Exchange CH 54
canyons	70.	She ran the neighing canyons all the spring Dan 3
	193.	Oval encyclicals in canyons heaping B Tow 13
cape	88.	the mammoth saurian/ghoul, the eastern/Cape CH 2
	91.	Hast splintered space CH 116
	92.	Zodiacs, dashed/(now nearing fast the Cape!) CH 141
	93.	What memories of vigils, bloody, by that Cape CH 166
caper	3.	Relentless caper for all those who step Leg 22
cape's	40.	Red kelson past the cape's wet stone V-6 8
	95.	Above the Cape's ghoul-mound, O joyous seer CH 213
capes	88.	But we, who round the capes, the promontories CH 6
	94.	Years of the Modern! Propulsions toward what capes CH 197
	114.	Beyond whose frosted capes the moon bequeaths At 19
capeward	90.	Capeward, then blading the wind's flank, banked and spun CH 81
capped	32.	Capped arbiter of beauty in this street F&H III 1
captain	58.	And Captain Smith, all beard and certainty VW 11
	156.	But where is the Captain of this doubloon isle OC 17
captive	29.	You found in final chains, no captive then F&H I 45
capture	25.	Regard the capture here, O Janus-faced Rec 1
	148.	Now that she has fled the capture Loc 15
captured	88.	The captured fume of space foams in our cars CH 20

captured, cont.	94.	Gold autumn, captured, crowned the trembling hill CH 186
car	109.	and rivers.... In the car Tun 34
	111.	Thunder is galvothermic here below.... The car Tun 91
caravan	45.	A jest falls from the speechless caravan TBB 20
caravel	48.	Slowly the sun's red caravel drops light AM 13
carbonated	179.	And the idiot boy by the road, with carbonated eyes, laugh- Len 4
carbonic	157.	You have given me the shell, Satan,--carbonic amulet OC 34
carcass	4.	And, in Africa, a carcass quick with flies BT 12
	182.	Good God! as though his sinking carcass there Et 32
car-change	61.	Keep hold of that nickel for car-change, Rip VW 43
cards	30.	Splayed like cards from a loose hand F&H II 12
care	184.	Your generosity dispose relinquishment and care Emp 11
carefully	156.	Squared off so carefully. Then OC 11
caress	177.	That hate is but the vengeance of a long caress Rep 9
caressed	184.	Have kissed, caressed the model of the hurricane Emp 2
caresses	35.	Spry cordage of your bodies to caresses V-1 14
Carib	36.	O minstrel galleons of Carib fire V-2 22
	156.	His Carib mathematics web the eyes' baked lenses OC 22
Caribbean	184.	Deny me not in this sweet Caribbean dawn Emp 5
	184.	Leave, leave that Caribbean praise to me Emp 8
caribou	75.	And when the caribou slant down for salt Dan 97
carillon	23.	From whom some whispered carillon assures WM 17
	102.	It's high carillon Va 9
carillons	193.	Antiphonal carillons launched before B Tow 7
Carmen	133.	Carmen! Akimbo arms and smouldering eyes CDB 17
	133.	Carmen! Bestirring hope and lipping eyes CDB 18
	133.	Carmen whirls, and music swirls and dips CDB 19
	133.	"Carmen!," comes awed from wine-hot lips CDB 20
	133.	Bent wings, and Carmen with her flaunts through the gloom CDB 22
Carmen's	134.	And some dream still of Carmen's mystic face CDB 27
carnage	37.	Presumes no carnage, but this single change V-3 16
carpet	138.	Vault on the opal carpet of the sun Port 1
carried	16.	The willows carried a slow sound RR 1
carrier	114.	And on, obliquely up bright carrier bars At 17
carrion	183.	The morrow's dawn was dense with carrion hazes Et 50
carry	6.	To carry back the music to its source MGLL 20
	192.	Their shadows even--now can't carry him SI 8
cars	144.	Until you feel the weight of many cars PA 6

carve	91.	Of rancorous grenades whose screaming petals carve us CH 97
casement	145.	"Full on this casement shone the wintry moon PA 42
Casey Jones	64.	My Old Kentucky Home and Casey Jones Riv 39
casque	50.	And record of more, floating in a casque AM 29
cast	39.	Infrangible and lonely, smooth as though cast V-5 2
	104.	Even to cast upon the seasons fleeting QH 7
	157.	Slagged of the hurricane--I, cast within its flow OC 32
casts	73.	That casts his pelt, and lives beyond! Sprout, horn Dan 58
casual	21.	Casual louse that tissues the buckwheat Pass 7
	167.	Unshackled, casual of its azured height RP 15
cataracts	73.	Flame cataracts of heaven in seething swarms Dan 71
catastrophes	30.	Above the deft catastrophes of drums F&H II 26
catch	70.	I learned to catch the trout's moon whisper; I Dan 22
catchword	156.	Without a turnstile? Who but catchword crabs OC 18
catharsis	151.	catharsis from gin-daisies as well as APE 17
Cathay	48.	And greed adjourned,--I bring you back Cathay AM 8
	115.	In myriad syllables,--Psalm of Cathay At 47
	117.	One Song, one Bridge of Fire! Is it Cathay At 93
cathedral	102.	Cathedral Mary,/shine Va 24
	193.	Of a spent day--to wander the cathedral lawn B Tow 3
Catskill	60.	a Catskill daisy chain in May VW 29
cattle	179.	time for these; time for all these, as cattle and birds Len 18
	185.	after the western desert and the later cattle country Post 10
caught	9.	The bough has caught her breath up, and her voice GA 3
	38.	All bright insinuations that my years have caught V-4 21
	100.	A caught slide shows her sandstone grey between NWG 16
	111.	O caught like pennies beneath soot and steam Tun 115
	193.	The stars are caught and hived in the sun's ray B Tow 8
caustic	3.	Then, drop by caustic drop, a perfect cry Leg 20
cavalcade	91.	They, cavalcade on escapade, shear Cumulus CH 110
cavil	17.	That shall not rouse, how faint the crow's cavil Par 12
Cayman	165.	Luckily the Cayman schooner streaks BSEW 8

change, cont.	110.	For Gravesend Manor change at Chambers Street Tun 83
	173.	Fall mute and sudden (dealing change/for lilies) MF 7
changed	39.	And changed..."There's V-5 13
channel	108.	Channel the congresses, nightly sessions Tun 3
Chan's	48.	The Chan's great continent.... Then faith, not fear AM 21
chant	19.	Chant pyramids LC 15
chanting	64.	<u>Some Sunny Day</u>. I heard a road-gang chanting so Riv 40
chaos	129.	Then high cries from great chasms of chaos out- drawn An 8
chapter	34.	A scattered chapter, livid hieroglyph AMT 7
charge	92.	Thou hast there in thy wrist a Sanskrit charge CH 129
charged	51.	In holy rings all sails charged to the far AM 82
charities	167.	Green rustlings, more-than-regal charities RP 1
charity	50.	Yet yield thy God's, thy Virgin's charity AM 48
Charley	66.	John, Jake or Charley, hopping the slow freight Riv 59
charmed	34.	Its lashings charmed and malice reconciled AMT 10
charms	190.	Charms that each by each refuse the clinch Rel 9
charred	20.	From charred and riven stakes, O LC 43
	132.	Charred at a stake in younger times than ours MC 12
charter	78.	It had no charter but a promised crown Ind 23
chasms	110.	In back forks of the chasms of the brain Tun 69
	129.	Then high cries from great chasms of chaos out- drawn An 8
chasm-walls	127.	Up the chasm-walls of my bleeding heart Hi 1
cheapest	100.	Some cheapest echo of them all--begins NWG 12
checked	183.	The fever was checked. I stood a long time in Mack's talking Et 58
cheek	28.	The white wafer cheek of love, or offers words F&H I 30
	58.	There was Priscilla's cheek close in the wind VW 10
cheeks	21.	In the bronze gongs of my cheeks Pass 14
chemistry	116.	Whose canticle fresh chemistry assigns At 74
cherub	188.	cherub watchman--tiptoeing the successive patio bal- HR 7
chest	194.	The angelus of wars my chest evokes B Tow 31
chestnut	72.	Smoke swirling through the yellow chestnut glade Dan 40
chevron	48.	The first palm chevron the first lighted hill AM 24
chewing-gum	160.	When you sprouted Paradise a discard of chewing- gum took place. Up jug to musical, hanging jug just gay MT 3-4

Cheyenne	64.	To Cheyenne tagging...Maybe Kalamazoo Riv 34
chicken	62.	Minstrels when you steal a chicken just Riv 6
child	66.	Each seemed a child, like me, on a loose perch Riv 57
	137.	Or an old house in a forest,--or a child For 7
childhood	66.	Holding to childhood like some termless play Riv 58
children	111.	Back home to children and to golden hair Tun 105
	163.	Fumbling his sex. That's why those children laughed Id 4
chill	45.	How many dawns, chill from his rippling rest TBB 1
	170.	Leaves Ormus rubyless, and Ophir chill TED 13
	193.	From pit to crucifix, feet chill on steps from hell B Tow 4
chilled	38.	Chilled albatross's white immutability V-4 5
chime	19.	While chime LC 19
	191.	And what hours they forget to chime I'll know Purg 20
chimes	24.	Wherein new purities are snared; where chimes WM 34
	115.	The vernal strophe chimes from deathless strings At 56
chiming	54.	Among distant chiming buoys--adrift. The sky HD 16
chimney	187.	is it this that keeps the chimney Ma 13
chimneys	88.	With sweetness below derricks, chimneys, tunnels CH 17
chimney-sooted	21.	And hug, chimney-sooted heart of man Pass 20
Chinamen	181.	Wires in the streets and Chinamen up and down Et 7
chisel	169.	Milk-bright, Thy chisel wind Hur 6
chiselled	91.	This tournament of space, the threshed and chiselled height CH 95
chisels	179.	furnaces, chisels and ploughs Len 3
Chloe	138.	Or, Daphnis, move among the bees with Chloe Port 4
choice	94.	Beyond all sesames of science was thy choice CH 201
	193.	But not for long to hold each desperate choice B Tow 20
choir	115.	Of deepest day--O Choir, translating time At 44
	133.	There is a sweep,--a shattering,--a choir CDB 13
	193.	The impasse high with choir. Banked voices slain B Tow 14
choring	46.	(How could mere toil align thy choiring strings TBB 30
	116.	Kinetic of white choiring wings...ascends At 80
choked	69.	The Passion spreads in wide tongues, choked and slow Riv 142
	132.	Even, sank in love and choked with flowers MC 10
chorea	179.	chorea took him away--there is the Nine of Len 12
choristers	91.	Up-chartered choristers of their own speeding CH 109

chose	5.	The wanderer later chose this spot of rest EC 12
	72.	I took the portage climb, then chose Dan 29
chosen	5.	And where was finally borne a chosen hero EC 14
Christmas	145.	Twinkling like little Christmas trees PA 35
	160.	Great-grandmother. It's all like Christmas MT 2
chrysalis	116.	In single chrysalis the many twain At 60
chrysanthemums	13.	Confused among chrysanthemums IS 2
church	60.	My mother almost brought me once from church VW 35
	191.	So ring the church bells here in Mexico Purg 18
churned	98.	The mind is churned to spittle, whispering hell SC 17
churning	40.	And ocean rivers, churning, shift V-6 3
cider	104.	While we who press the cider mill, regarding them QH 10
	191.	I dream the too-keen cider--the too-soft snow Purg 9
cigarettes	133.	On smoky tongues of sweetened cigarettes CDB 2
cigars	105.	Alight with sticks abristle and cigars QH 32
cinch	100.	The world's one flagrant, sweating cinch NWG 4
	176.	And the fingernails that cinch such VU 5
	190.	Rhyme from the same Tau (closing cinch by cinch) Rel 6
cinder	60.	The cinder pile at the end of the backyard VW 17
cinders	179.	pebbles among cinders in the road through a twice-opened Len 7
cinemas	45.	I think of cinemas, panoramic sleights TBB 9
cinquefoil	104.	Hostelry--floor by floor to cinquefoil dormer QH 18
ciphers	90.	What ciphers risen from prophetic script CH 82
cipher-script	115.	What cipher-script of time no traveller reads At 30
Circe's	133.	With shimmering blue from the bowl in Circe's hall CDB 7
circle	89.	The circle, blind crucible of endless space CH 29
	108.	Out of the Square, the Circle burning bright Tun 25
	122.	On that circle of paradise cool in the night Moth 19
circles	38.	Whose circles bridge, I know, (from palms to the severe V-4 4
	73.	The oak grove circles in a crash of leaves Dan 50
	90.	In oilrinsed circles of blind ecstasy CH 74
	91.	Is baited by marauding circles, bludgeon flail CH 96
	130.	Are circles of cool roses,--so Ech 10
	163.	In such infernal circles round his door Id 5
	194.	In azure circles, widening as they dip B Tow 36
circuit	34.	Then in the circuit calm of one vast coil AMT 9
	66.	And past the circuit of the lamp's thin flame Riv 71

circuits	10.	After the daily circuits of its glare SM 8
circular	115.	And still the circular, indubitable frieze
		At 53
circumferences	91.	O bright circumferences, heights employed to fly
		CH 93
circumflex	149.	Oh, by the infinite circumflex Loc 33
circumstance	73.	Surpassed the circumstance, danced out the siege
		Dan 64
Cirrus	91.	Lay siege and hurdle Cirrus down the skies CH 111
citadel	172.	Where cliff and citadel--all verily ABP 3
citadels	88.	Below grey citadels, repeating to the stars CH 8
cities	29.	White, through white cities passed on to assume
		F&H I 47
	32.	The mounted, yielding cities of the air F&H III 21
	83.	teased remnants of the skeletons of cities CS 30
	109.	of cities you bespeak Tun 32
	116.	Sustained in tears the cities are endowed At 70
city	16.	After the city that I finally passed RR 18
	32.	On the sixteen thrifty bridges of the city
		F&H III 9
	69.	Throb past the City storied of three thrones
		Riv 133
	112.	And this thy harbor, O my City, I have driven
		under Tun 129
	134.	Morning: and through the foggy city gate CDB 25
	144.	O City, your axles need not the oil of song PA 19
city's	18.	The city's stubborn lives, desires Pos 22
	46.	The City's fiery parcels all undone TBB 39
claim	38.	All fragrance irrefragibly, and claim V-4 9
	40.	I cannot claim: let thy waves rear V-6 14
	50.	And later hurricanes may claim more pawn AM 31
	74.	On paths thou knewest best to claim her by
		Dan 88
	139.	As a cameo the waves claim again Lege 11
	140.	We claim, and none may know Int 6
	159.	But do not claim a friend like him again
		TCJ 19
	171.	Nor claim me, either, by Adam's spine--nor rib
		KW 4
claims	54.	Serenely now, before day claims our eyes HD 23
	78.	Of claims to stake Ind 24
	184.	Who claims a devout concentration Emp 9
clamant	10.	Vivisection of more clamant air SM 6
clamour	188.	clamour of incessant shutters, trundle doors,
		and the HR 6
clamped	163.	Its course, though he'd clamped midnight to noon
		sky Id 12
clap	164.	Names we have, even, to clap on the wind NA 7
clapped	26.	All hours clapped dense into a single stride
		Rec 26
	163.	The other tilted, peeled end clapped to eye Id 10
claret	102.	O blue-eyed Mary with the claret scarf Va 7

clarion	95.	On clarion cylinders pass out of sight CH 208
clasp	23.	While August meadows somewhere clasp his brow WM 23
	90.	Already knows the closer clasp of Mars CH 85
clause	106.	That triple-noted clause of moonlight QH 67
claws	127.	Humanity pecks, claws, sobs and climbs Hi 2
clay	38.	Through clay aflow immortally to you V-4 8
	76.	In golden syllables loosed from the clay Ind 19
	88.	To that deep wonderment, our native clay CH 14
clay-cold	170.	Else tears heap all within one clay-cold hill TED 14
clays	69.	And roots surrendered down of moraine clays Riv 126
clean	60.	It flashed back at your thrust, as clean as fire VW 25
	142.	Clean on the shore some wreck of dreams BE 21
cleanly	111.	The gaunt sky-barracks cleanly now, and bare Tun 103
clear	36.	Bind us in time, O Seasons clear, and awe V-2 21
	39.	Meticulous, past midnight in clear rime V-5 1
	39.	As if too brittle or too clear to touch V-5 5
	46.	Only in darkness is thy shadow clear TBB 38
	48.	Till dawn should clear that dim frontier, first seen AM 20
	116.	As love strikes clear direction for the helm At 64
	170.	O sweet, dead Silencer, most suddenly clear TED 6
	180.	Eyes widely planted, clear, yet small Lib 11
cleared	20.	Borage of death have cleared my tongue LC 28
	50.	Palos again,--a land cleared of long war AM 54
	183.	The roads were being cleared, injured brought in Et 53
clears	56.	The window goes blond slowly. Frostily clears HD 31
	88.	Relapsing into silence, while time clears CH 22
cleavage	66.	By iron, iron--always the iron dealt cleavage Riv 87
cleaving	3.	This cleaving and this burning Leg 11
cleft	25.	Borne cleft to you, and brother in the half Rec 8
	39.	Too, into that godless cleft of sky V-5 16
	193.	In wounds pledged once to hope--cleft to despair B Tow 24
clemencies	19.	Distilling clemencies,--worms' LC 21
clenched	157.	And clenched beaks coughing for the surge again OC 31
clever	17.	Above the feet the clever sheets Par 5
cliff	40.	Like a cliff swinging or a sail V-6 19
	89.	Of you--the theme that's statured in the cliff CH 49
	159.	Of districts where cliff, sea and palm advance TCJ 3
	172.	Where cliff and citadel--all verily ABP 3

cliffward	94.	Of prairies, yet like breakers cliffward leaping CH 174
climb	48.	Here waves climb into dusk on gleaming mail AM 9
	72.	I took the portage climb, then chose Dan 29
	123.	And he ventured the desert,--his wings took the climb Moth 28
	152.	that heavens climb to measure, thus In 10
	167.	Climb up as by communings, year on year RP 5
climbed	98.	Climbed by aslant and huddling aromatically SC 19
climbing	16.	And mammoth turtles climbing sulphur dreams RR 9
	76.	The morning glory, climbing the morning long Ind 1
climbs	127.	Humanity pecks, claws, sobs and climbs Hi 2
clinch	100.	Invite the necessary cloudy clinch NWG 2
	190.	Charms that each by each refuse the clinch Rel 9
clip	91.	Wings clip the last peripheries of light CH 102
clipper	84.	clipper dreams indelible and ranging CS 64
clock	8.	The insistent clock commented on PU 14
clocks	185.	There were tickets and alarm clocks. There were counters and schedules Post 14
clods	66.	Blind fists of nothing, humpty-dumpty clods Riv 61
close	36.	Close round one instant in one floating flower V-2 20
	38.	Shall they not stem and close in our own steps V-4 14
	56.	arms close; eyes wide, undoubtful HD 28
	58.	There was Priscilla's cheek close in the wind VW 10
	76.	As I close mine Ind 4
	160.	lean bandits crouch: and dusk is close MT 9
	162.	Such words as it were vain to close OS 3
closed	4.	Mark tardy judgment on the world's closed door BT 2
	22.	He closed the book. And from the Ptolemies Pass 32
closer	90.	Already knows the closer clasp of Mars CH 85
closes	76.	Closes before the dusk, furls in its song Ind 3
closing	190.	Rhyme from the same Tau (closing cinch by cinch) Rel 6
closures	75.	In cobalt desert closures made our vows Dan 102
clot	156.	Let fiery blossoms clot the light, render my ghost OC 24
clothes	181.	The old woman and I foraged some drier clothes Et 2
cloud	18.	The pure possession, the inclusive cloud Pos 27
	20.	No longer bind. Some sentient cloud LC 30

cloud, cont.	51.	And Teneriffe's garnet--flamed it in a cloud AM 70
	64.	High in a cloud of merriment, recalled Riv 43
	72.	A distant cloud, a thunder-bud--it grew Dan 41
	89.	Of the ambiguous cloud. We know the strident rule CH 34
	89.	Man hears himself an engine in a cloud CH 42
	130.	Over the hill a last cloud dips Ech 5
cloud-belfries	92.	Cloud-belfries, banging while searchlights, like fencers CH 121
cloud-car	123.	And without one cloud-car in that wide meshless blue Moth 35
cloud-flown	45.	All afternoon the cloud-flown derricks turn TBB 23
clouds	5.	Where marble clouds support the sea EC 13
cloud-sprockets	160.	from emerald cloud-sprockets. Fat final prophets with MT 8
cloud-templed	91.	The blue's cloud-templed districts unto ether CH 90
cloudy	100.	Invite the necessary cloudy clinch NWG 2
clover	123.	The moat of the desert was melting from clover Moth 31
clown	48.	Of clown nor sage can riddle or gainsay AM 6
	68.	As though you touched hands with some ancient clown Riv 101
clucked	30.	Where cuckoos clucked to finches F&H II 25
clue	64.	Though they'll confess no rosary nor clue Riv 29
clump	94.	Set trumpets breathing in each clump and grass tuft--'til CH 185
clung	135.	A dove's wings clung about my heart last night CL 6
cluster	159.	What you may cluster 'round the knees of space TCJ 1
clustering	54.	While myriad snowy hands are clustering at the panes HD 25
clustrous	94.	And filled the forest with what clustrous sheen CH 178
coal	23.	Painted emulsion of snow, eggs, yarn, coal, manure WM 10
coasting	112.	Lights, coasting, left the oily tympanum of waters Tun 127
coasts	137.	A bird that coasts the wind unwearyingly For 5
coastwise	88.	While rises in the west the coastwise range, slowly the hushed land CH 3
cobalt	75.	In cobalt desert closures made our vows Dan 102
cobblestone	116.	Inventions that cobblestone the heart At 82
cobwebbed	104.	At sunset with a silent, cobwebbed patience QH 22
cocoa-nut	122.	Among cocoa-nut palms of a far oasis Moth 1
cocoons	122.	That emerge black and vermeil from yellow cocoons Moth 4

coffee	58.	Firmly as coffee grips the taste,--and away VW 9
coffin	22.	"Why are you back here--smiling an iron coffin Pass 28
cognate	193.	My word I poured. But was it cognate, scored B Tow 21
Cognizance	116.	O Thou steeled Cognizance whose leap commits At 57
coil	34.	Then in the circuit calm of one vast coil AMT 9
	99.	Water rattled that stinging coil, your SC 25
	112.	Tossed from the coil of ticking towers.... Tomorrow Tun 130
coiled	90.	In coiled precision, bunched in mutual glee CH 72
coils	156.	Coils and withdraws. So syllables want breath OC 16
coin	109.	And down beside the turnstile press the coin Tun 29
	190.	Return the mirage on a coin that spells Rel 16
coins	24.	Each chamber, transept, coins some squint WM 24
cold	56.	The sun, released--aloft with cold gulls hither HD 34
	68.	Dan Midland--jolted from the cold brake-beam Riv 111
	178.	Have kept no faith but wind, the cold stream PB 10
	187.	Awake to the cold light Ma 1
cold-hushed	15.	Cold-hushed, there is only the shifting of moments NL 9
collapsed	100.	We wait that writhing pool, her pearls collapsed NWG 21
collapses	11.	And yet these fine collapses are not lies Chap 14
cologne	33.	A goose, tobacco and cologne F&H III 31
Colorado	76.	We found God lavish there in Colorado Ind 15
colored	151.	that make your colored syrup fairly APE 12
colors	74.	That drops his legs and colors in the sun Dan 74
colt's	64.	And afterwards, who had a colt's eyes--one said Riv 41
Columbus Circle	108.	Up Times Square to Columbus Circle lights Tun 2
combed	99.	All night the water combed you with black SC 23
combustion	88.	Combustion at the astral core--the dorsal change CH 4
	92.	In guerrilla sleights, trapped in combustion gyr- CH 139
come	13.	"Come, it is too late,--too late IS 13
	15.	"Has no one come here to win you NL 5
	18.	Whose heart is fire shall come,--the white wind rase Pos 28
	79.	Come back to Indiana--not too late Ind 61
	148.	Come now, when will they restore me Loc 3

come, cont.	149.	Doesn't someone come to turn the knob Loc 28
	149.	Come now--appease me just a little Loc 35
	150.	Indeed, old memories come back to life GWP 15
	160.	Maggy, come on MT 17
	172.	I had come all the way here from the sea ABP 1
	174.	Come, search the marshes for a friendly bed BNOK 3
	177.	Shall come to you through wounds prescribed by swords Rep 8
comedian	156.	Until it meets the blue's comedian host OC 26
comes	9.	And so she comes to dream herself the tree GA 7
	29.	That world which comes to each of us alone F&H I 48
	54.	Comes echoing alley-upward through dim snow HD 9
	101.	O Magdalene, each comes back to die alone NWG 26
	133.	"Carmen!," comes awed from wine-hot lips CDB 20
comfort	105.	Dead rangers bled their comfort on the snow QH 50
coming	62.	Mazda--and the telegraphic night coming on Thomas Riv 9
	145.	And his wife, like a mountain, coming in PA 33
commemorating	5.	Dull lips commemorating spiritual gates EC 11
commented	8.	The insistent clock commented on PU 14
commerce	62.	SCIENCE--COMMERCE and the HOLYGHOST Riv 13
commissioner	156.	Is Commissioner of mildew throughout the ambushed senses OC 21
committed	22.	Memory, committed to the page, had broke Pass 37
commits	116.	O Thou steeled Cognizance whose leap commits At 57
commodious	194.	The commodious, tall decorum of that sky B Tow 39
communicant	152.	communicant and speeding new In 14
communings	167.	Climb up as by communings, year on year RP 5
companion	29.	Bent axle of devotion along companion ways F&H I 50
company	146.	Could get away from the company PA 50
	193.	To trace the visionary company of love, its voice B Tow 18
compass	34.	Compass, quadrant and sextant contrive AMT 13
competence	24.	This competence--to travel in a tear WM 31
competent	93.	The competent loam, the probable grass,--travail CH 151
compiles	21.	Compiles a too well-known biography Pass 22
complete	5.	And radio the complete laws to the people EC 8
	36.	Complete the dark confessions her veins spell V-2 15
complighted	114.	Complighted in one vibrant breath made cry At 13
composed	14.	The zigzags fast around dry lips composed Fern 5
compulsion	20.	Compulsion of the year, O Nazarene LC 36

conceding	40.	Conceding dialogue with eyes V-6 23
conceive	189.	tern's mastery that you can conceive, that you can HR 33
conceived	122.	Conceived in the light of Arabian moons Moth 2
concentration	184.	Who claims a devout concentration Emp 9
conch	92.	Hung low...until a conch of thunder answers CH 120
conclamant	116.	And justified conclamant with ripe fields At 71
conclusion	171.	Because these millions reap a dead conclusion KW 9
concur	171.	Concur with wrist and bicep. In the moon KW 6
condense	46.	Beading thy path--condense eternity TBB 35
condensed	111.	Condensed, thou takest all--shrill ganglia Tun 117
condor	93.	Hermetically past condor zones, through zenith havens CH 159
confess	64.	Though they'll confess no rosary nor clue Riv 29
confession	191.	The landscape of confession--and if confession Purg 7
confessions	36.	Complete the dark confessions her veins spell V-2 15
confidence	176.	stir your confidence VU 13
confined	90.	Of steely gizzards--axle-bound, confined CH 71
conflicting	186.	Conflicting, purposeful yet outcry vain Shak 4
confronting	89.	Of canyoned traffic...Confronting the Exchange CH 54
confused	13.	Confused among chrysanthemums IS 2
confusion	171.	As draws them toward a doubly mocked confusion KW 11
confusions	14.	I have known myself a nephew to confusions Fern 8
congeal	157.	Congeal by afternoons here, satin and vacant OC 33
congregates	21.	Aprons rocks, congregates pears Pass 8
congresses	108.	Channel the congresses, nightly sessions Tun 3
conjugate	92.	To conjugate infinity's dim marge CH 130
conjunctions	168.	By what conjunctions do the winds appoint AP 15
connais	145.	"Connais tu le pays...?" PA 45
Connecticut	89.	Back over Connecticut farms, abandoned pastures CH 57
connecting	62.	WIRES OR EVEN RUNning brooks connecting ears Riv 16
conquest	35.	They have contrived a conquest for shell shucks V-1 3
conquerers	184.	You did not die for conquerers at your side Emp 14
consanguinity	37.	Infinite consanguinity it bears V-3 1
conscience	111.	The conscience navelled in the plunging wind Tun 113
	149.	That my conscience sees double Loc 30
	171.	Where gold has not been sold and conscience tinned KW 16

consciousness	95.	To course that span of consciousness thou'st named CH 209
consript	33.	The abating shadows of our conscript dust F&H III 35
conscripted	23.	I am conscripted to their shadows' glow WM 8
consented	141.	Consented,--and held out EpH 3
consolations	11.	Contented with such random consolations Chap 2
constant	3.	Shall string some constant harmony Leg 21
	22.	Under the constant wonder of your eyes Pass 31
	136.	And mist that is more constant than your vows Ps 8
construe	64.	Time's rendings, time's blendings they construe Riv 35
	105.	Must we descend as worm's eye to construe QH 58
consumes	89.	Flickers a moment, consumes us in its smile CH 36
consummate	74.	At last with all that's consummate and free Dan 79
consummately	51.	Within whose primal scan consummately AM 67
consummations	142.	Far consummations of the tides to throw BE 20
contain	184.	You, who contain augmented tears, explosions Emp 1
contented	11.	Contented with such random consolations Chap 2
continent	48.	The Chan's great continent.... Then faith, not fear AM 21
continental	88.	Those continental folded aeons, surcharged CH 16
continual	41.	Which rainbows twine continual hair V-6 27
continues	6.	And so I stumble. And the rain continues on the roof MGLL 25
continuous	29.	That beat, continuous, to hourless days F&H I 51
contrive	34.	Compass, quadrant and sextant contrive AMT 13
contrived	35.	They have contrived a conquest for shell shucks V-1 3
controls	186.	Engrave such hazards as thy might controls Shak 3
converge	62.	watching the tail lights wizen and converge, slip- Riv 22
	117.	Sidereal phalanxes, leap and converge At 92
conversion	28.	Reflective conversion of all things F&H I 32
conveying	144.	Absorbing and conveying weariness PA 8
conveys	5.	The apostle conveys thought through discipline EC 9
conviviality	177.	But finally knows conviviality Rep 4
convoy	91.	By convoy planes, moonferrets that rejoin thee CH 114
convoying	27.	Convoying divers dawns on every corner F&H I 11
convulsive	88.	Of energy--convulsive shift of sand CH 5
cool	10.	Lies cool upon her--not yet pain SM 12
	27.	Virginal perhaps, less fragmentary, cool F&H I 15

corymbulous	32.	In corymbulous formations of mechanics F&H III 13
cotted	181.	For cotted negroes, bandaged to be taken Et 12
cough	21.	And wakens alleys with a hidden cough Pass 10
coughing	157.	And clenched beaks coughing for the surge again OC 31
counsel	48.	To you, too, Juan Perez, whose counsel fear AM 7
count	24.	And count some dim inheritance of sand WM 42
	28.	Those hands of yours that count the nights F&H I 25
	64.	But some men take their liquor slow--and count Riv 28
	156.	I count these nacreous frames of tropic death OC 9
	192.	Sad heart, the gymnast of inertia, does not count SI 1
counted	38.	Whose counted smile of hours and days, suppose V-4 1
	112.	I counted the echoes assembling, one after one Tun 125
counterpane	10.	Beneath the green silk counterpane SM 10
	145.	Pull down the hotel counterpane PA 40
counters	185.	There were tickets and alarm clocks. There were counters and schedules Post 14
counting	50.	Isaiah counting famine on this lee AM 50
	185.	Antillean fingers counting my pulse, my love forever Post 16
	194.	And through whose pulse I hear, counting the strokes B Tow 29
countless	122.	Countless rubies and tapers in the oasis' blue haze Moth 16
country	185.	after the western desert and the later cattle country Post 10
	191.	My country, O my land, my friends Purg 1
	191.	That I prefer to country or to town Purg 16
countrymen	191.	And all my countrymen I see rush toward one stall Purg 12
courage	188.	courage were germicides to him.... Poets may not HR 25
course	95.	To course that span of consciousness thou'st named CH 209
	163.	Its course, though he'd clamped midnight to noon sky Id 12
	181.	Of course, there too Et 23
cove	168.	Thrust parching from a palm-bole hard by the cove AP 3
covenant	41.	Still fervid covenant, Belle Isle V-6 25
cover	91.	Surely no eye that Sunward Escadrille can cover CH 106
coverings	5.	For joy rides in stupendous coverings EC 5

crevice	4.	And a roach spans a crevice in the floor BT 4
crib	171.	Out of the valley, past the ample crib KW 2
cried	110.	the show she cried a little afterwards but Tun 65
cries	7.	From whiteness that cries defiance to the snow SMA 8
	10.	Than yours, in cries, in ecstasies SM 23
	24.	Anguished, the wit that cries out of me WM 37
	129.	Then high cries from great chasms of chaos out-drawn An 8
	180.	Out of the seagull cries and wind Lib 1
crime-sheets	108.	With tabloid crime-sheets perched in easy sight Tun 10
crimson	126.	With crimson feathers whips away the mists O-N 2
crisp	148.	My crisp soul will be flooded by a langour Loc 7
crocus	36.	Salute the crocus lustres of the stars V-2 12
cross	35.	You must not cross nor ever trust beyond it V-1 13
	45.	As apparitional as sails that cross TBB 6
	98.	I wanted you...The embers of the Cross SC 18
	99.	The Cross, a phantom, buckled--dropped below the dawn SC 28
	104.	One's glance could cross the borders of three states QH 26
	158.	The Cross alone has flown the wave Mer 5
	158.	But since the Cross sank, much that's warped and cracked Mer 6
	158.	This Cross, agleam still with a human Face Mer 15
	166.	The Dollar from the Cross IV 7
	188.	me "the True Cross"--let us remember the Doctor and HR 3
cross-legged	149.	Of the archbeam of my cross-legged labours Loc 34
cross-line	144.	It dwindles at each cross-line PA 5
crouch	160.	lean bandits crouch: and dusk is close MT 9
crowd	27.	Numbers, rebuffed by asphalt, crowd F&H I 9
	162.	Such tears as crowd the dream OS 4
crowding	159.	With snore of thunder, crowding us to bleed TCJ 7
crown	51.	The kindled Crown! acceded of the poles AM 85
	78.	It had no charter but a promised crown Ind 23
	104.	Faces--loose panes crown the hill and gleam QH 21
	167.	A fountain at salute, a crown in view RP 14
crowned	94.	Gold autumn, captured, crowned the trembling hill CH 186
crowns	14.	In crowns less grey--O merciless tidy hair Fern 10
crow's	17.	That shall not rouse, how faint the crow's cavil Par 12

crows	66.	And re-descend with corn from querulous crows Riv 84
crucial	25.	That yield attendance to one crucial sign Rec 12
crucible	89.	The circle, blind crucible of endless space CH 29
crucifix	193.	From pit to crucifix, feet chill on steps from hell B Tow 4
cruel	35.	The bottom of the sea is cruel V-1 16
cruelly	51.	Cruelly with love thy parable of man AM 60
	111.	O cruelly to inoculate the brinking dawn Tun 109
crumble	35.	And their fingers crumble fragments of baked weed V-1 4
	98.	Eyes crumble at its kiss. Its long-drawn spell SC 15
crumbled	188.	crumbled palace in the square--the typhus in a trap HR 12
crumbs	24.	"Rise from the dates and crumbs. And walk away WM 44
crunch	68.	Hitch up your pants and crunch another quid Riv 106
	179.	the buzz of saw mills, the crunch and blast of quarries Len 2
crust	25.	I crust a plate of vibrant mercury Rec 7
crutches	173.	His eyes--/like crutches hurtled against glass MF 6
cry	3.	Then, drop by caustic drop, a perfect cry Leg 20
	39.	Are overtaken. Now no cry, no sword V-5 10
	46.	Prayer of pariah, and the lover's cry TBB 32
	76.	Yielded your first cry at the prairie's door Ind 7
	114.	Complighted in one vibrant breath made cry At 13
	115.	Serenely, sharply up the long anvil cry At 35
crying	48.	And lowered. And they came out to us crying AM 25
	51.	The sea's green crying towers a-sway, Beyond AM 88
	66.	Papooses crying on the wind's long mane Riv 76
crypt	89.	Gleam from the great stones of each prison crypt CH 53
	156.	Deliberate, gainsay death's brittle crypt. Meanwhile OC 14
crystal	123.	To yellow,--to crystal,--a sea of white spray Moth 32
	193.	Whose thigh embronzes earth, strikes crystal Word B Tow 23
crystal-flooded	114.	Onward and up the crystal-flooded aisle At 21
Cuban	161.	In Indian baths. At Cuban dusk the eyes IQ 9
	181.	And Cuban doctors, troopers, trucks, loose hens Et 9

cycloramic	115.	Bridge, lifting night to cycloramic crest At 43
Cydalise	148.	That I nurse for Cydalise Loc 14
cylinders	95.	On clarion cylinders pass out of sight CH 208
cynosures	23.	Applause flows into liquid cynosures WM 7
cypresses	16.	Where cypresses shared the noon's RR 7
Czars	105.	Here three hours from the semaphores, the Czars QH 30

dapper	148.	The orient moon of my dapper affections Loc 4
dare	33.	Who dare not share with us the breath released F&H III 42
	136.	I should not dare to let you in again Ps 4
dared	170.	Dared dignify the labor, bless the quest TED 3
dark	4.	Wanders in some mid-kingdom, dark, that lies BT 10
	10.	That hands joined in the dark will answer SM 7
	28.	And now, before its arteries turn dark F&H I 27
	36.	Complete the dark confessions her veins spell V-2 15
	50.	Dark waters onward shake the dark prow free AM 56
	56.	dark/drink the dawn HD 29
	66.	Time like a serpent down her shoulder, dark Riv 79
darkest	25.	Its drums and darkest blowing leaves ignore Rec 10
darkling	54.	Attend the darkling harbor, the pillowed bay HD 12
darkling	15.	Have you no memories, O Darkly Bright NL 8
	32.	That narrows darkly into motor dawn F&H III 2
darkness	14.	To darkness through a wreath of sudden pain Fern 6
	25.	While darkness, like an ape's face, falls away Rec 15
	46.	Only in darkness is thy shadow clear TBB 38
dark-skinned	144.	The dark-skinned Greeks grin at each other PA 13
darts	16.	With scalding unguents spread and smoking darts RR 19
dashed	92.	Zodiacs, dashed/(now nearing fast the Cape!) CH 141
dashing	169.	Sky-seethe, dense heaven dashing Hur 16
dates	24.	"Rise from the dates and crumbs. And walk away WM 44
date-vases	122.	There are butterflies born in mosaic date-vases Moth 3
dawn	32.	That narrows darkly into motor dawn F&H III 2
	37.	Upon the steep floor flung from dawn to dawn V-3 17
	40.	Till dawn should clear that dim frontier, first seen AM 20
	56.	dark/drink the dawn HD 29
	72.	Until, immortally, it bled into the dawn Dan 27
	84.	he lunged up Bowery way while the dawn CS 50
	91.	Tellurian wind-sleuths on dawn patrol CH 103
	99.	The Cross, a phantom, buckled--dropped below the dawn SC 28
	111.	O cruelly to inoculate the brinking dawn Tun 109

dawn, cont.	123.	And lo, in that dawn he was pierroting over Moth 29
	129.	Hush! these things were all heard before dawn An 9
	131.	The dawn, a shell's pale lining restlessly Ba 2
	139.	Yet called adrift again at every dawn Lege 4
	144.	Greeting the dawn PA 1
	159.	Past pleasantries...Assert the ripened dawn TCJ 14
	160.	tisms wrench the golden boughs. Leaves spatter dawn MT 7
	162.	On skies that gild thy remote dawn OS 7
	182.	One ours, and one, a stranger, creeping up with dawn Et 39
	183.	The morrow's dawn was dense with carrion hazes Et 50
	184.	Deny me not in this sweet Caribbean dawn Emp 5
	185.	Remember the lavender lilies of that dawn Post 7
	193.	The bell-rope that gathers God at dawn B Tow 1
dawn's	185.	across dawn's broken arc. No; yes...or were they Post 4
	185.	Dawn's broken arc! the noon's more furbished room Post 12
dawns	27.	Convoying divers dawns on every corner F&H I 11
	45.	How many dawns, chill from his rippling rest TBB 1
day	25.	And gradually white buildings answer day Rec 16
	27.	Across the stacked partitions of the day F&H I 4
	27.	The margins of the day, accent the curbs F&H I 10
	40.	Flung into April's inmost day V-6 20
	45.	Till elevators drop us from our day TBB 8
	48.	Into the Queen's great heart that doubtful day AM 4
	54.	Sing to us, stealthily weave us into day HD 22
	54.	Serenely now, before day claims our eyes HD 23
	58.	It is the same hour though a later day VW 6
	60.	That flittered from under the ash heap day VW 22
	60.	After day whenever your stick discovered VW 23
	60.	One day in spring my father took to me VW 33
	108.	Someday by heart you'll learn each famous sight Tun 6
	111.	Or the muffled slaughter of a day in birth Tun 108
	115.	Of deepest day--O Choir, translating time At 44
	122.	Blind only in day, but remembering that soon Moth 14
	123.	Swinging in spirals round the fresh breasts of day Moth 30
	135.	And with the day, distance again expands CL 3

day, cont.	146.	One summer day in a little town PA 47
	152.	again round one more fairest day In 21
	176.	And it is always the day, the farewell day unkind VU 23
	193.	Of a spent day--to wander the cathedral lawn B Tow 3
daybreak	157.	Each daybreak on the wharf, their brine-caked eyes OC 29
day's	129.	Of the first moth's descent--day's predestiny An 5
	140.	Here in the day's after-glow Int 8
	158.	And smoking racks for penance when day's done Mer 10
days	29.	That beat, continuous, to hourless days F&H I 51
	33.	Laugh out the meager penance of their days F&H III 41
	38.	Whose counted smile of hours and days, suppose V-4 1
	64.	"Jesus! Oh I remember watermelon days!" And sped Riv 42
	69.	Damp tonnage and alluvial march of days Riv 124
	85.	Buntlines tusseling (91 days, 20 hours and anchored!) Rainbow, Leander CS 73
	89.	Now the eagle dominates our days, is jurist CH 33
	150.	The world moves by so fast these days GWP 12
	164.	As only they can praise, who build their days NA 10
	172.	Yes, tall, inseparably our days ABP 7
	186.	Of all our days, being pilot,--tempest, too Shak 5
	192.	Hours, days--and scarcely sun and moon SI 2
dayspring's	94.	Evasive--too--as dayspring's spreading arc to trace is CH 192
dazed	182.	I beat the dazed mule toward the road. He got that far Et 48
dead	8.	Of what the dead keep, living still PU 11
	12.	A few picked, the rest dead Past 20
	39.	Where nothing turns but dead sands flashing V-5 17
	66.	Dead echoes! But I knew her body there Riv 78
	93.	To answer deepest soundings! O, upward from the dead CH 154
	105.	The resigned factions of the dead preside QH 49
	105.	Dead rangers bled their comfort on the snow QH 50
	108.	You'll find the garden in the third act dead Tun 8
	110.	The platform hurries along to a dead stop Tun 84
	156.	Across the feet of the dead, laid in white sand OC 2

dead, cont.	170.	O sweet, dead Silencer, most suddenly clear TED 6
	171.	Because these millions reap a dead conclusion KW 9
	180.	A dead sailor that knew Lib 6
	182.	And fell dead or dying, but it didn't so much matter Et 49
deaf	39.	Can strangle this deaf moonlight? For we V-5 9
	174.	This hieroglyph is no dumb, deaf mistake BNOK 13
deal	105.	The woodlouse mortgages the ancient deal QH 42
dealing	173.	Fall mute and sudden (dealing change/for lilies) MF 7
dealt	66.	By iron, iron--always the iron dealt cleavage Riv 87
	88.	The songs that gypsies dealt us at Marseille CH 11
	163.	One hand dealt out a kite string, a tin can Id 9
dear	174.	Dear lady--the poet said--release your hair BNOK 2
	177.	So sleep, dear brother, in my fame, my shame undone Rep 12
	190.	Will hold it--wear the keepsake, dear, of time Rel 15
dearest	129.	The moans of travail of one dearest beside me An 7
death	10.	The lover's death, how regular SM 1
	10.	Walk now, and note the lover's death SM 21
	15.	No birth, no death, no time nor sun NL 11
	20.	Borage of death have cleared my tongue LC 28
	28.	The earth may glide diaphanous to death F&H I 39
	30.	While titters hailed the groans of death F&H II 27
	36.	Hasten, while they are true,--sleep, death, desire V-2 19
	37.	and where death, if shed V-3 15
	40.	More savage than the death of kings V-6 15
	51.	Like ocean athwart lanes of death and birth AM 58
	110.	And Death, aloft,--gigantically down Tun 77
	115.	But who, through smoking pyres of love and death At 31
	156.	I count these nacreous frames of tropic death OC 9
	156.	The wind that knots itself in one great death OC 15
	182.	Were death predestined! You held your nose already Et 33
	184.	Thy death is sacred to all those who share Emp 12
	188.	death around white teeth HR 28
	190.	What is death without a ditch Rel 3
deathless	115.	The vernal strophe chimes from deathless strings At 56

death's	34.	The calyx of death's bounty giving back AMT 6
	72.	Know, Maquokeeta, greeting; know death's best
		Dan 47
	104.	But I have seen death's stare in slow survey
		QH 27
	116.	Whose fell unshadow is death's utter wound
		At 66
	156.	Deliberate, gainsay death's brittle crypt.
		Meanwhile OC 14
	188.	him once before to death's beyond and back again
		HR 23
death-strife	94.	But knows it leastwise as death-strife?--O, some-
		thing green CH 200
deathward	167.	And tendril till our deathward breath is sealed
		RP 11
debris	93.	dispersion...into mashed and shapeless debris
		CH 143
decanters	23.	Then glozening decanters that reflect the street
		WM 5
decimals	21.	The dozen particular decimals of time Pass 25
decision	191.	And I have no decision--is it green or brown
		Purg 15
decisive	174.	Decisive grammar given unto queens BNOK 9
deck	54.	As winch engines begin throbbing on some deck
		HD 7
	183.	Doctors shot ahead from the deck in planes
		Et 57
decks	92.	Regard the moving turrets! From grey decks
		CH 118
	98.	Windswept guitars on lonely decks forever SC 11
	181.	Two decks unsandwiched, split sixty feet apart
		Et 15
decline	13.	To risk alone the light's decline IS 14
decorum	194.	The commodious, tall decorum of that sky B Tow 39
deduct	188.	Cruz--to bring--to take--to mix--to ransom--to de-
		duct--to cure.... The rats played ring around the
		HR 14-15
deeds	56.	your hands within my hands are deeds HD 26
deep	28.	At your deep blush, when ecstasies thread
		F&H I 33
	88.	To that deep wonderment, our native clay CH 14
	92.	The benediction of the shell's deep, sure reprieve
		CH 133
	123.	A little time only, for sight burned as deep
		Moth 45
	141.	Deep hand that lay in his,--seemed beautiful
		EpH 17
	159.	The green preëmption of the deep seaweed TCJ 8
deepest	93.	To answer deepest soundings! O, upward from the
		dead CH 154
	115.	Of deepest day--O Choir, translating time At 44
deeply	142.	Do not think too deeply, and you'll find BE 7

Deep River	68.	And hum Deep River with them while they go Riv 103
defends	190.	Something of sand and sun the Nile defends Rel 17
defenseless	168.	But this,--defenseless, thornless, sheds no blood AP 11
defer	25.	Defer though, revocation of the tears Rec 11
defiance	7.	From whiteness that cries defiance to the snow SMA 8
deflect	39.	Can fasten or deflect this tidal wedge V-5 11
deflects	88.	Our eyes can share or answer--then deflects CH 25
deft	30.	Above the deft catastrophes of drums F&H II 26
defunct	166.	That defunct boss IV 14
Deity's	116.	Forever Deity's glittering Pledge, O Thou At 73
	116.	Of silver sequel, Deity's young name At 79
delayed	188.	...delayed, and struck--again, again. Only the May- HR 19
deliberate	156.	Deliberate, gainsay death's brittle crypt. Meanwhile OC 14
deliberation	184.	I own it still--that sure deliberation Emp 7
delicate	8.	Delicate riders of the storm PU 8
	32.	You, here beside me, delicate ambassador F&H III 3
delirium	50.	Yet no delirium of jewels! O Fernando AM 46
	126.	In delirium O-N 7
delivered	8.	His thoughts, delivered to me PU 5
delivery	177.	All this that balks delivery through words Rep 7
delta	16.	The monsoon cut across the delta RR 20
deltaed	73.	Of lightning deltaed down your saber hair Dan 54
delve	33.	Delve upward for the new and scattered wine F&H III 39
demands	128.	But hold me...somewhere I heard demands Fr 7
demeanors	36.	As her demeanors motion well or ill V-2 9
demented	111.	Demented, for a hitching second, humps; then Tun 96
Democrat	82.	Democrat--I know what time it is--No CS 19
demure	159.	Disclose your lips, O Sun, nor long demure TCJ 6
demurring	111.	Daemon, demurring and eventful yawn Tun 106
denial	149.	A stiff denial to postures Loc 23
dense	26.	All hours clapped dense into a single stride Rec 26
	169.	Sky-seethe, dense heaven dashing Hur 16
	176.	the dense mine of the orchid, split in two VU 4
	181.	With arms in slings, plaster strewn dense with tiles Et 8
	183.	The morrow's dawn was dense with carrion hazes Et 50

denser	70.	Disturbed and destined, into denser green Dan 10
deny	110.	Shaking, did you deny the ticket, Poe Tun 82
	184.	Deny me not in this sweet Caribbean dawn Emp 5
deposits	11.	As the wind deposits Chap 3
depth	88.	Whose depth of red, eternal flesh of Pocahontas CH 15
	92.	Ing, dance the curdled depth/down whizzing CH 140
deportment	148.	To adaptate her methods and deportment Loc 11
derelict	40.	Thy derelict and blinded guest V-6 12
derision	98.	Furrow of all our travel--trailed derision SC 14
derricks	45.	All afternoon the cloud-flown derricks turn TBB 23
	88.	With sweetness below derricks, chimneys, tunnels CH 17
descend	46.	Unto us lowliest sometime sweep, descend TBB 43
	105.	Must we descend as worm's eye to construe QH 58
	106.	Leaf after autumnal leaf/break off,/descend--descend QH 72
descending	94.	White banks of moonlight came descending valleys CH 181
descent	129.	Of the first moth's descent,--day's predestiny An 5
descried	170.	The harvest you descried and understand TED 10
desert	75.	In cobalt desert closures made our vows Dan 102
	123.	And he ventured the desert,--his wings took the climb Moth 28
	123.	The moat of the desert was melting from clover Moth 31
	123.	To the desert,--back,--down,--still lonely he fell Moth 48
	125.	Of dreaming on the desert white C 4
	185.	after the western desert and the later cattle country Post 10
designs	84.	those bright designs the trade winds drive CS 57
desire	9.	The apple on its bough is her desire GA 1
	36.	Hasten, while they are true,--sleep, death, desire V-2 19
	51.	Thy purpose--still one shore beyond desire AM 87
desired	170.	You who desired so much--in vain to ask TED 1
desires	18.	The city's stubborn lives, desires Pos 22
desk	188.	Let us strip the desk for action--now we have a horse HR 1
De Soto's	69.	Over De Soto's bones the freighted floors Riv 132
despair	33.	The imagination spans beyond despair F&H III 47
	106.	Love from despair--when love foresees the end QH 71
	138.	Despair until the moon by tears be won Port 3
	193.	In wounds pledged once to hope--cleft to despair B Tow 24

desperate	17.	The pillow--how desperate is the light Par 11
	190.	With desperate propriety, whose name is writ Rel 10
	193.	But not for long to hold each desperate choice B Tow 20
despite	68.	Down, down,--born pioneers in time's despite Riv 112
	108.	And watch the curtain lift in hell's despite Tun 7
despondencies	148.	True, I nibble at despondencies Loc 17
destined	70.	Disturbed and destined, into denser green Dan 10
destiny	74.	And saw thee dive to kiss that destiny Dan 77
	105.	That unfolds a new destiny to fill QH 56
destroy	176.	destroy the sky. To VU 12
destruction	32.	Who drove speediest destruction F&H III 12
devils	186.	Swears high in Hamlet's throat, and devils throng Shak 10
devotion	29.	Bent axle of devotion along companion ways F&H I 50
devout	184.	Who claims a devout concentration Emp 9
devoutly	115.	To kneeling wave, one song devoutly binds At 55
dew	68.	From tunnel into field--iron strides the dew Riv 90
	106.	While high from dim elm-chancels hung with dew QH 66
dial	13.	Over the garden dial distill IS 6
dialogue	40.	Conceding dialogue with eyes V-6 23
diametric	94.	Of love's own diametric gaze, of love's amaze CH 188
diapason	36.	Take this Sea, whose diapason knells V-2 6
diaphonous	28.	The earth may glide diaphanous to death F&H I 39
diastole	17.	Systole, diastole spokes-of-a-wheel Par 2
dice	34.	The dice of drowned men's bones he saw bequeath AMT 2
didja	109.	swing on it, why didja Tun 54
die	70.	She spouted arms; she rose with maize--to die Dan 4
	70.	But, watching, saw that fleet young crescent die Dan 24
	101.	O Magdalene, each comes back to die alone NWG 26
	104.	Though they should thin and die on last year's stubble QH 8
	111.	Umbilical to call--and straightway die Tun 114
	112.	Unceasing with some Word that will not die Tun 122
	112.	Or shall the hands be drawn away, to die Tun 135
	164.	But we must die, as you, to understand NA 8
	179.	die Len 23
	184.	You did not die for conquerers at your side Emp 14

died	21.	Died speaking through the ages that you know Pass 19
dies	18.	Tossed on these horns, who bleeding dies Pos 23
	133.	And dies on fire's birth in each man's heart CDB 10
dig	109.	to dig in the field--travlin the town--too Tun 43
digging	35.	Gaily digging and scattering V-1 5
dignify	170.	Dared dignify the labor, bless the quest TED 3
dignity	151.	but a little BACK DOOR DIGNITY APE 25
dim	24.	And count some dim inheritance of sand WM 42
	48.	Till dawn should clear that dim frontier, first seen AM 20
	54.	Comes echoing alley-upward through dim snow HD 9
	70.	He holds the twilight's dim, perpetual throne Dan 8
	79.	Down the dim turnpike to the river's edge Ind 57
	88.	Where each sees only his dim past reversed CH 27
	92.	To conjugate infinity's dim marge CH 130
	106.	While high from dim elm-chancels hung with dew QH 66
	111.	To spoon us out more liquid than the dim Tun 111
	124.	Dim eyes;--a tongue that cannot tell Moth 52
dimensional	28.	There is the world dimensional for those untwisted by the love of things irreconcilable F&H I 16
dinner	188.	And during the wait over dinner at La Diana the HR 29
dinasaur	88.	Imponderable the dinosaur/sinks slow CH 1
Dionysus	20.	Dionysus, Thy LC 44
dip	45.	The seagull's wings shall dip and pivot him TBB 2
	194.	In azure circles, widening as they dip B Tow 36
dipped	33.	The hands Erasmus dipped in gleaming tides F&H III 37
dipping	31.	Dipping here in this cultivated storm F&H II 36
dips	130.	Over the hill a last cloud dips Ech 5
	133.	Carmen whirls, and music swirls and dips CDB 19
direction	18.	That steals softly direction Pos 2
	116.	As love strikes clear direction for the helm At 64
direst	18.	One moment in sacrifice (the direst) Pos 4
Dirigible	91.	While Cetus-like, O thou Dirigible, enormous Lounger CH 112
disappears	130.	And disappears, as I should go Ech 6
discard	51.	Yielding by inference and discard, faith AM 75
	160.	When you sprouted Paradise a discard of chewing- MT 3

discipline	5.	The apostle conveys thought through discipline EC 9
disclose	159.	Disclose your lips, O Sun, nor long demure TCJ 6
disclosed	45.	Never disclosed, but hastened to again TBB 11
discovered	60.	After day whenever your stick discovered VW 23
discovering	148.	To the sole end of discovering Loc 19
disgrace	105.	Who holds the lease on time and on disgrace QH 46
disk	18.	I hold it up against a disk of light Pos 20
	25.	The brain's disk shivered against lust. Then watch Rec 14
	56.	Two--three bright window-eyes aglitter, disk HD 33
dismay	33.	To saturate with blessing and dismay F&H III 30
dismiss	138.	Release,--dismiss the passion from your arms Port 5
disown	171.	To skies impartial, that do not disown me KW 3
dispatches	193.	Dispatches me as though I dropped down the knell B Tow 2
dispersed	54.	Far strum of fog horns...signals dispersed in veils HD 5
dispersion	93.	dispersion...into mashed and shapeless debris CH 143
dispose	184.	Your generosity dispose relinquishment and care Emp 11
disposition	51.	This disposition that thy night relates AM 77
disquieting	133.	Disquieting of barbarous fantasy CDB 14
dissolute	132.	O blameless shyness;--innocence dissolute MC 4
dissolve	19.	Dissolve all but the windows of the mills LC 3
dissolved	172.	Dissolved within a sky of beacon forms ABP 4
dissuades	50.	Some inmost sob, half-heard, dissuades the abyss AM 39
distance	37.	That must arrest all distance otherwise V-3 10
	135.	And with the day, distance again expands CL 3
distances	66.	Wail into distances I knew were hers Riv 75
	176.	distances leap landward without VU 17
distant	18.	I know the screen, the distant flying taps Pos 12
	54.	Among distant chiming buoys--adrift. The sky HD 16
	56.	As though to join us at some distant hill HD 37
	72.	A distant cloud, a thunder-bud--it grew Dan 41
distill	13.	Over the garden dial distill IS 6
	24.	Build freedom up about me and distill WM 30
distilling	19.	Distilling clemencies,--worms' LC 21
distills	54.	Cool feathery fold, suspends, distills HD 17
distinctly	33.	Distinctly praise the years, whose volatile F&H III 45
distraction	186.	Where angels beg for doom in ghast distraction Shak 11
districts	91.	The blue's cloud-templed districts unto ether CH 90

districts, cont.	159.	Of districts where cliff, sea and palm advance TCJ 3
disturbed	70.	Disturbed and destined, into denser green Dan 10
ditch	190.	What is death without a ditch Rel 3
dive	74.	And saw thee dive to kiss that destiny Dan 77
	111.	Taking the final level for the dive Tun 93
divers	27.	Convoying divers dawns on every corner F&H I 11
dives	126.	Dives through the filter of trellises O-N 3
divided	27.	Divided by accepted multitudes F&H I 3
divides	21.	Where the cedar leaf divides the sky Pass 1
divine	31.	The incunabula of the divine grotesque F&H II 29
	148.	Ah! the divine infatuation Loc 13
dizzying	123.	Though a black god to him in a dizzying night Moth 34
docile	99.	Rehearsed hair--docile, alas, from many arms SC 26
	104.	They keep that docile edict of the Spring QH 2
doctor	188.	me "The True Cross"--let us remember the Doctor and HR 3
	188.	rosy (in their basement basinette)--the Doctor sup- HR 16
	188.	records spurred the Doctor into something nigh those HR 21
	189.	Doctor had said--who was American, also--"You can- HR 30
doctor's	188.	the Doctor's rat trap. Where? Somewhere in Vera HR 13
doctors	181.	And Cuban doctors, troopers, trucks, loose hens Et 9
	183.	Doctors shot ahead from the deck in planes Et 57
	188.	be doctors, but doctors are rare poets when roses leap HR 26
dog	7.	A boy runs with a dog before the sun, straddling SMA 9
	35.	O brilliant kids, frisk with your dog V-1 10
Doge's	50.	Like pearls that whisper through the Doge's hands AM 45
dogwood	70.	I left the village for dogwood. By the canoe Dan 17
dollar	166.	The Dollar from the Cross IV 7
dolphins	5.	Dolphins still played, arching the horizons EC 16
domain	148.	Among the flowers of her domain Loc 18
domed	66.	Under the Ozarks, domed by Iron Mountain Riv 81
dominates	89.	Now the eagle dominates our days, is jurist CH 33
dominoes	24.	Invent new dominoes of love and bile WM 39
Don	182.	The weather's in their noses. There's Don-- but that one, white Et 43
donkey	83.	"I ran a donkey engine down there on the Canal CS 23

doom	11.	Dally the doom of that inevitable thumb Chap 10
	90.	To what fierce schedules, rife of doom apace CH 87
	92.	Thou sowest doom thou hast nor time nor chance CH 126
	116.	And like an organ, Thou, with sound of doom At 62
	176.	with all their zest for doom VU 8
	186.	Where angels beg for doom in ghast distraction Shak 11
	189.	doom...must therefore loose yourself within a pat- HR 32
door	4.	Mark tardy judgment on the world's closed door BT 2
	10.	Scarcely aloud, beyond her door SM 14
	76.	Yielded your first cry at the prairie's door Ind 7
	83.	"--that spiracle!" he shot a finger out the door CS 34
	100.	We flee her spasm through a fleshless door NWG 24
	111.	Elbows and levers, guard and hissing door Tun 90
	145.	Played ragtime and dances before the door PA 38
	151.	but a little BACK DOOR DIGNITY APE 25
	163.	In such infernal circles round his door Id 5
	169.	Thou ridest to the door, Lord Hur 17
doors	10.	At doors and stone with broken eyes SM 20
	108.	Avoid the glass doors gyring at your right Tun 26
	179.	doors and lips of agony to Len 16
	188.	clamour of incessant shutters, trundle doors, and the HR 6
	188.	conies with a typical pistol--trying to muffle doors HR 8
doorway	61.	It forsook her at the doorway, it was gone VW 38
dormer	104.	Hostelry--floor by floor to cinquefoil dormer QH 18
dorsal	88.	Combustion at the astral core--the dorsal change CH 4
dost	51.	And all the eddying breath between dost search AM 59
	74.	Lo, through what infinite seasons dost thou gaze Dan 82
	91.	On fleeing balconies as thou dost glide CH 115
	93.	With vast eternity, dost wield the rebound seed CH 150
doth	116.	O Thou whose radiance doth inherit me At 87
dotting	66.	With racetrack jargon,--dotting immensity Riv 66
double	25.	As double as the hands that twist this glass Rec 2
	149.	That my conscience sees double Loc 30
doubloon	156.	But where is the Captain of this doubloon isle OC 17

doubly   171. As draws them towards a doubly mocked confusion
                      KW 11

doubtful   48. Into the Queen's great heart that doubtful day
                      AM 4

dough   27. Too much the baked and labeled dough   F&H I 2

dove   172. By the dove filled, and bees of Paradise   ABP 10

dove's   129. The sound of a dove's flight waved over the lawn
                      An 6
                135. A dove's wings clung about my heart last night
                      CL 6

downcast   93. His last wing-pulse, and downcast as a cup
                      CH 161

downstairs   30. And you may fall downstairs with me   F&H II 18

downy   91. War's fiery kennel masked in downy offings
                      CH 94

doze   66. They doze now, below axe and powder horn
                      Riv 88

dozen   21. The dozen particular decimals of time   Pass 25

drag   50. The jellied weeds that drag the shore,--perhaps
                      AM 52

dragged   110. And when they dragged your retching flesh
                      Tun 79

dragon's   91. Behold the dragon's covey--amphibian, ubiquitous
                      CH 88

drags   23. Sharp to the windowpane guile drags a face   WM 19
                 69. The basalt surface drags a jungle grace   Riv 129

drained   93. That's drained, is shivered back to earth--thy
                      wand   CH 162

draw   39. Draw in your head, alone and too tall here   V-5 22
                 39. Draw in your head and sleep the long way home
                      V-5 25

drawled   64. "--And when my Aunt Sally Simpson smiled," he
                      drawled   Riv 44

drawn   112. Or shall the hands be drawn away, to die   Tun 135
                147. She has drawn her hands away   Per 5

draws   171. As draws them towards a doubly mocked confusion
                      KW 11

dream   9. And so she comes to dream herself the tree   GA 7
                 28. Imminent in his dream, none better knows
                      F&H I 29
                 54. They meet you listening midway in your dream
                      HD 2
                 64. Bind town to town and dream to ticking dream
                      Riv 27
                 69. The River, spreading, flows--and spends your
                      dream   Riv 120
                 69. Poised wholly on its dream, a mustard glow
                      Riv 140
                 74. Her speechless dream of snow, and stirred again
                      Dan 90
                 78. A dream called Eldorado was his town   Ind 21
                 89. Dream cancels dream in this new realm of fact
                      CH 39

dream, cont.	89.	From which we wake into the dream of act CH 40
	104.	See them, like eyes that still uphold some dream QH 23
	109.	like a pigeon's muddy dream--potatoes Tun 42
	114.	So seven oceans answer from their dream At 16
	130.	I dream we quarreled long, long ago Ech 12
	134.	And some dream still of Carmen's mystic face CDB 27
	162.	Such tears as crowd the dream OS 4
	178.	So dream thy sails, O phantom bark PB 1
	178.	Their vanity, and dream no land in vain PB 8
	180.	Or must we rend our dream Lib 13
	191.	I dream the too-keen cider--the too-soft snow Purg 9
dreamed	39.	In all the argosy of your bright hair I dreamed V-5 19
	66.	Have dreamed beyond the print that bound her name Riv 73
	164.	I dreamed that all men dropped their names, and sang NA 9
dreamer	131.	A dreamer might see these, and wake to hear Ba 4
dreaming	46.	Vaulting the sea, the prairies' dreaming sod TBB 42
	125.	Of dreaming on the desert white C 4
dreams	16.	And mammoth turtles climbing sulphur dreams RR 9
	24.	Until my blood dreams a receptive smile WM 33
	56.	Under the mistletoe of dreams, a star HD 36
	76.	And bison thunder rends my dreams no more Ind 5
	82.	O Stamboul Rose--dreams weave the rose CS 10
	84.	clipper dreams indelible and ranging CS 64
	142.	Clean on the shore some wreck of dreams BE 21
	176.	the terrible puppet of my dreams, shall VU 2
drench	100.	Pearls whip her hips, a drench of whirling strands NWG 18
	116.	Through the bright drench and fabric of our veins At 68
drew	12.	The sun drew out Past 7
	16.	Tyranny; they drew me into hades almost RR 8
	72.	Within,--I heard it; 'til its rhythm drew Dan 43
dried	21.	The rain dried without odour Pass 15
drier	181.	The old woman and I foraged some drier clothes Et 2
drift	68.	But drift in stillness, as from Jordan's brow Riv 115
	167.	Drift coolly from that tower of whispered light RP 2
drifted	70.	Drifted how many hours I never knew Dan 23
drifting	39.	Your eyes already in the slant of drifting foam V-5 23
drilled	33.	The substance drilled and spent beyond repair F&H III 43

drink	56.	dark/drink the dawn HD 29
	133.	Bright peacocks drink from flame-pots by the wall CDB 5
drinking	64.	The last bear, shot drinking in the Dakotas Riv 24
	183.	Drinking Bacardi and talking U.S.A. Et 60
drinks	69.	The Mississippi drinks the farthest dale Riv 127
dripping	33.	Anchises' navel, dripping of the sea F&H III 36
drive	84.	those bright designs the trade winds drive CS 57
driven	4.	AEsop, driven to pondering, found BT 5
	112.	And this thy harbor, O my City, I have driven under Tun 129
driving	105.	Wait for the postman driving from Birch Hill QH 54
droop	136.	Though fountains droop in waning light and pain Ps 2
drop	3.	Then, drop by caustic drop, a perfect cry Leg 20
	45.	Till elevators drop us from our day TBB 8
	76.	But you who drop the scythe to grasp the oar Ind 11
	112.	Here at the waters' edge the hands drop memory Tun 132
	133.	Their brown eyes blacken, and the blue drop hue CDB 8
	159.	Wrap us and lift us; drop us then, returned TCJ 17
dropped	99.	The Cross, a phantom, buckled--dropped below the dawn SC 28
	164.	I dreamed that all men dropped their names, and sang NA 9
	193.	Dispatches me as though I dropped down the knell B Tow 2
drops	48.	Slowly the sun's red caravel drops light AM 13
	74.	That drops his legs and colors in the sun Dan 74
drouth	70.	And in the autumn drouth, whose burnished hands Dan 5
drove	32.	Who drove speediest destruction F&H III 12
drown	83.	snarling stone--green--drums--drown CS 32
drowned	34.	The dice of drowned men's bones he saw bequeath AMT 2
	99.	Light drowned the lithic trillions of your spawn SC 29
	146.	The stars are drowned in a slow rain PA 56
	178.	That I thy drowned man may speak again PB 2
drowning	9.	Drowning the fever of her hands in sunlight GA 10
	132.	Drowning cool pearls in alcohol MC 3
druggist	27.	To druggist, barber and tobacconist F&H I 12
drummed	22.	On unpaced beaches leaned its tongue and drummed Pass 35
drum's	169.	Thy drum's gambade, its plunge abscond Hur 13
drums	25.	Its drums and darkest blowing leaves ignore Rec 10

drums, cont.	30.	Above the deft catastrophes of drums F&H II 26
	73.	Spears and assemblies: black drums thrusting on Dan 61
	83.	O Stamboul Rose--drums weave CS 22
	83.	snarling stone--green--drums--drown CS 32
	83.	ATLANTIS ROSE drums wreathe the rose CS 43
	115.	From gulfs unfolding, terrible of drums At 41
drunken	54.	Or a drunken stevedore's howl and thud below HD 8
dry	8.	And miss the dry sound of bees PU 19
	14.	The zigzags fast around dry lips composed Fern 5
	64.	Spreading dry shingles of a beard Riv 51
	156.	Patrols the dry groins of the underbrush OC 19
	161.	This dry road silvering toward the shadow of the quarry IQ 11
	165.	"By just in time, and lifts 'em high and dry BSEW 9
	181.	And a funnel high and dry up near the park Et 16
due	183.	And treated, it seemed. In due time Et 54
dugs	152.	from thine open dugs shall still the sun In 20
dull	5.	Dull lips commemorating spiritual gates EC 11
	11.	Facing the dull squint with what innocence Chap 12
dumb	174.	This hieroglyph is no dumb, deaf mistake BNOK 13
dumbly	9.	Dumbly articulate in the slant and rise GA 4
dun	142.	Lapped under it,--or the dun BE 4
dune	90.	Two brothers in their twinship left the dune CH 79
dungeons	40.	Where icy and bright dungeons lift V-6 1
during	188.	And during the wait over dinner at La Diana the HR 29
dusk	48.	Here waves climb into dusk on gleaming mail AM 9
	68.	And if it's summer and the sun's in dusk Riv 96
	75.	Of dusk?--And are her perfect brows to thine Dan 100
	76.	Closes before the dusk, furls in its song Ind 3
	160.	lean bandits crouch: and dusk is close MT 9
	161.	In dusk, as though this island lifted, floated IQ 8
	161.	In Indian baths. At Cuban dusk the eyes IQ 9
dust	28.	Weeps in inventive dust for the hiatus F&H I 37
	33.	The abating shadows of our conscript dust F&H III 35
	106.	Arise--yes, take this sheaf of dust upon your tongue QH 62
	115.	Eyes stammer through the pangs of dust and steel At 52
	144.	In the dust of a road PA 23
dusty	12.	If, dusty, I bear Past 11
	34.	Beat on the dusty shore and were obscured AMT 4

dusty, cont.	188.	through the lofty, dusty glass--<u>Cortez</u>--<u>Cortez</u>-- his HR 11
dwindle	187.	their glistenings dwindle Ma 6
dwindles	144.	It dwindles at each cross-line PA 5
dying	182.	When the storm was dying. And Sarah saw them, too Et 41
	182.	And fell dead or dying, but it didn't so much matter Et 49
dykes	16.	At gulf gates...There, beyond the dykes RR 21
dynamo	168.	Angelic Dynamo! Ventriloquist of the Blue AP 13
dynamos	90.	Of dynamos, where hearing's leash is strummed CH 64
dynasties	66.	Screamed redskin dynasties that fled the brain Riv 77

eagle	72.	Swooping in eagle feathers down your back Dan 46
	75.	The serpent with the eagle in the boughs Dan 104
	89.	Now the eagle dominates our days, is jurist CH 33
	117.	The serpent with the eagle in the leaves At 95
eagle-bright	92.	Now eagle-bright, now/quarry-hid, twist-/-ing, sink with CH 136
eagles	192.	And--backwards--is it thus the eagles fly SI 10
eaglet's	66.	And space, an eaglet's wing, laid on her hair Riv 80
ear	4.	Fox brush and sow ear top his grave BT 7
earlier	58.	Times earlier, when you hurried off to school VW 5
early	64.	"--For early trouting." Then peering in the can Riv 48
	78.	But we,--too late, too early, howsoever Ind 25
	94.	O, early following thee, I searched the hill CH 175
ears	62.	WIRES OR EVEN RUNning brooks connecting ears Riv 16
	88.	The captured fume of space foams in our ears CH 20
	133.	The pulse is in the ears, the heart is higher CDB 15
earth	20.	Of earth again LC 41
	28.	The earth may glide diaphanous to death F&H I 39
	93.	That's drained, is shivered back to earth--thy wand CH 162
	129.	The anxious milk-blood in the veins of the earth An 1
	167.	Uneaten of the earth or aught earth holds RP 6
	168.	A milk of earth when stricken off the stalk AP 10
	191.	Here quakes of earth make houses fall Purg 11
	193.	Whose thigh embronzes earth, strikes crystal Word B Tow 23
	194.	Unseals her earth, and lifts love in its shower B Tow 40
earthly	36.	Bequeath us to no earthly shore until V-2 23
	186.	Is justice that has cancelled earthly chains Shak 14
ease	12.	For ease or resolution Past 17
	150.	And Fifi's bows and poodle ease GWP 6
East	112.	And to be.... Here by the River that is East Tun 131
	144.	North-bound, and East and West PA 7
eastern	50.	Take of that eastern shore, this western sea AM 47
	88.	the mammoth saurian/ghoul, the eastern/Cape CH 2
Easters	95.	Toward endless terminals, Easters of speeding light CH 206

eastings	84.	locked in wind-humours, ran their eastings down CS 69
eastward	72.	Steep, inaccessible smile that eastward bends Dan 34
easy	108.	With tabloid crime-sheets perched in easy sight Tun 10
eat	88.	Hearths, there to eat an apple and recall CH 10
eatage	66.	Such pilferings make up their timeless eatage Riv 85
eats	105.	Ty-five at Adams' auction,--eats the seal QH 44
	105.	What eats the pattern with ubiquity QH 47
eaves	28.	Lightly as moonlight on the eaves meets snow F&H I 31
echo	26.	Forgive me for an echo of these things Rec 27
	41.	Belle Isle, white echo of the oar V-6 28
	100.	Some cheapest echo of them all--begins NWG 12
echoes	6.	Old keys that are but echoes MGLL 18
	66.	Dead echoes! But I knew her body there Riv 78
	112.	I counted the echoes assembling, one after one Tun 125
	193.	O terraced echoes prostrate on the plain B Tow 16
echoing	54.	Comes echoing alley-upward through dim snow HD 9
eclipse	184.	The slit eclipse of moon in palm-lit bonds Emp 4
ecstasy	90.	In oilrinsed circles of blind ecstasy CH 74
ecstasies	10.	Than yours, in cries, in ecstasies SM 23
	28.	At your deep blush, when ecstasies thread F&H I 33
eddied	54.	Flurried by keen fifings, eddied HD 15
eddying	51.	And all the eddying breath between dost search AM 59
edelweiss	94.	And Klondike edelweiss of occult snows CH 180
Eden	51.	Of Eden and the enchained Sepulchre AM 62
	191.	Of Eden--and the dangerous tree--are these Purg 6
edge	79.	Down the dim turnpike to the river's edge Ind 57
	112.	Here at the waters' edge the hands drop memory Tun 132
edges	136.	Glitters on the edges of wet ferns Ps 3
edict	104.	They keep that docile edict of the Spring QH 2
Ediford	62.	a Ediford--and whistling down the tracks Riv 10
e'en	169.	Lord, e'en boulders now outleap Hur 10
eerily	68.	Always they smile out eerily what they seem Riv 109
eggs	23.	Painted emulsion of snow, eggs, yarn, coal, manure WM 10
Egyptian	174.	Some old Egyptian joke is in the air BNOK 1
	174.	An old Egyptian jest has cramped the tape BNOK 5
eh	62.	breathtaking--as you like it...eh Riv 18

eidolon	3.	Bleeding eidolon!) and yet again Leg 16
elbow	11.	Or warm torn elbow coverts Chap 8
elbows	111.	Elbows and levers, guard and hissing door Tun 90
eldest	111.	Locution of the eldest star, and pack Tun 112
Eldorado	78.	A dream called Eldorado was his town Ind 21
elegiac	93.	As thou at junctions elegiac, there, of speed CH 149
element	142.	A soul, an element in it all BE 8
elemental	64.	Strange bird-wit, like the elemental gist Riv 37
elements	35.	By time and the elements; but there is a line V-1 12
elephantine	167.	And the grey trunk, that's elephantine, rear RP 7
elevators	45.	Till elevators drop us from our day TBB 8
eleven	102.	Pay-check at eleven Va 2
	102.	Gone seven--gone eleven Va 5
Elizabeth	6.	Elizabeth MGLL 7
ellipses	30.	Rhythmic ellipses lead into canters F&H II 13
elm-chancels	106.	While high from dim elm-chancels hung with dew QH 66
Elohim	51.	Elohim, still I hear thy sounding heel AM 80
eloquence	94.	Heard thunder's eloquence through green arcades CH 184
else	11.	We can evade you, and all else but the heart Chap 17
	100.	Always you wait for someone else though, always NWG 7
	170.	Else tears heap all within one clay-cold hill TED 14
'em	165.	"By just in time, and lifts 'em high and dry BSEW 9
embankments	114.	--From black embankments, moveless soundings hailed At 15
embassy	34.	An embassy. Their numbers as he watched AMT 3
embers	98.	I wanted you...The embers of the Cross SC 18
embrace	69.	No embrace opens but the stinging sea Riv 138
embronzes	193.	Whose thigh embronzes earth, strikes crystal Word B Tow 23
emerald	100.	Sprayed first with ruby, then with emerald sheen NWG 14
	160.	from emerald cloud-sprockets. Fat final prophets with MT 8
emerald-bright	167.	Mortality--ascending emerald-bright RP 13
emerge	91.	Wheeled swiftly, wings emerge from larval-silver hangars CH 99
	122.	That emerge black and vermeil from yellow cocoons Moth 4
Emily	106.	Of pain that Emily, that Isadora knew QH 65
	170.	Being, of all, least sought for: Emily, hear TED 5

emperies	48.	O where our Indian emperies lie revealed AM 15
empire	64.	An empire wilderness of freight and rails Riv 56
	89.	Not this our empire yet, but labyrinth CH 51
employed	91.	O bright circumferences, heights employed to fly CH 93
emptier	111.	And somewhat emptier than before Tun 95
empty	11.	A grail of laughter of an empty ash can Chap 21
	32.	On rifts of torn and empty houses F&H III 16
	101.	Yet, to the empty trapeze of your flesh NWG 25
	125.	About the empty heart of night C 2
emulsion	23.	(Painted emulsion of snow, eggs, yarn, coal, manure WM 10
enchained	51.	Of Eden and the enchained Selupchre AM 62
encinctured	116.	Within whose lariat sweep encinctured sing At 59
enclose	50.	Starved wide on blackened tides, accrete--enclose AM 42
encroachments	194.	The steep encroachments of my blood left me B Tow 25
encyclicals	193.	Oval encyclicals in canyons heaping B Tow 13
end	24.	Has followed you. Though in the end you know WM 41
	60.	The cinder pile at the end of the backyard VW 17
	79.	(Or will you be a ranger to the end Ind 62
	106.	Love from despair--when love foresees the end QH 71
	115.	Pacific here at time's end, bearing corn At 51
	148.	To the sole end of discovering Loc 19
	163.	The other tilted, peeled end clapped to eye Id 10
endear	78.	Will still endear her Ind 44
ended	136.	Mine is a world foregone though not yet ended Ps 5
endless	89.	The circle, blind crucible of endless space CH 29
	95.	Toward endless terminals, Easters of speeding light CH 206
	170.	Yet fed your hunger like an endless task TED 2
endlessly	28.	With steel and soil to hold you endlessly F&H I 43
endow	180.	How I endow her, standing Lib 4
endowed	116.	Sustained in tears the cities are endowed At 70
ends	12.	Ends in this latter muffled Past 8
	39.	Already hang, shred ends from remembered stars V-5 7
endures	135.	Yet,--much follows, much endures...Trust birds alone CL 5
energy	88.	Of energy--convulsive shift of sand CH 5
enforces	11.	The game enforces smirks; but we have seen Chap 19

engaged	188.	metaphysics that are typhoid plus and had engaged HR 22
engaging	79.	Oh, hold me in those eyes' engaging blue Ind 54
engine	83.	"I ran a donkey engine down there on the Canal CS 23
	89.	Man hears himself an engine in a cloud CH 42
	165.	Their engine stalled. No oars, and leaks BSEW 6
engines	54.	As winch engines begin throbbing on some deck HD 7
	95.	Vast engines outward veering with seraphic grace CH 207
	158.	Buddhas and engines serve us undersea Mer 1
engrave	186.	Engrave such hazards as thy might controls Shak 3
	193.	And swing I know not where. Their tongues engrave B Tow 10
enormous	91.	While Cetus-like, O thou Dirigible, enormous Lounger CH 112
	92.	Enormous repercussive list-/-ings down CH 137
enough	6.	There is even room enough MGLL 5
	6.	"Are your fingers long enough to play MGLL 17
	6.	Is the silence strong enough MGLL 19
	165.	--Yes, patent-leather shoes hot enough to fry BSEW 11
enrich	125.	O Materna! to enrich thy gold head C 8
ensanguined	117.	Like spears ensanguined of one tolling star At 90
ensign	25.	A wind abides the ensign of your will Rec 24
	185.	the audible ransom, ensign of my faith Post 5
entered	16.	The pond I entered once and quickly fled RR 15
	193.	And so it was I entered the broken world B Tow 17
entering	18.	And I, entering, take up the stone Pos 16
enterprise	11.	Our obsequies are, in a way, no enterprise Chap 16
enthrones	37.	Resigns a breast that every wave enthrones V-3 4
enthusiasms	12.	Her calls, her enthusiasms Past 5
entrainments	21.	(I had joined the entrainments of the wind Pass 12
entrances	84.	swinging summer entrances to cooler hells CS 48
	186.	Through torrid entrances, past icy poles Shak 1
environs	50.	Some Angelus environs the cordage tree AM 55
	176.	environs VU 6
envy	122.	And rings macrocosmic won envy as thrall Moth 22
	164.	Our envy of your freedom--we must maim NA 4

equal	26.	And let us walk through time with equal pride Rec 28
equally	171.	To heaven or hades--to an equally frugal noon KW 8
equanimity	30.	With perfect grace and equanimity F&H II 19
equestrian	150.	Alike to stage, equestrian, and pullman GWP 4
equivocations	27.	Smutty wings flash out equivocations F&H I 7
erased	139.	And even my vision will be erased Lege 10
Erasmus	33.	The hands Erasmus dipped in gleaming tides F&H III 37
ere	129.	Aroused by some light that had sensed,--ere the shiver An 4
	131.	But they are wrong.... Ere man was given sight Ba 9
Erie	62.	Erie it ain't for miles around a Riv 8
erstwhile	182.	Back at the erstwhile house Et 24
Escadrille	91.	Surely no eye that Sunward Escadrille can cover CH 106
escalator	110.	The intent escalator lifts a serenade Tun 85
escapade	91.	They, cavalcade on escapade, shear Cumulus CH 110
escape	174.	The keyboard no more offers an escape BNOK 6
escapes	94.	And passed that Barrier that none escapes CH 199
escarpments	116.	With white escarpments swinging into light At 69
escorts	73.	Wrapped in that fire, I saw more escorts wake Dan 67
escutcheoned	92.	Lead-perforated fuselage, escutcheoned wings CH 134
esplanades	84.	--scarfed of foam, their bellies veered green esplanades CS 68
Estador	142.	Walk high on the bridge of Estador BE 1
	142.	High on the bridge of Estador BE 16
estuaries	39.	The bay estuaries fleck the hard sky limits V-5 4
	142.	Bellies and estuaries of warehouses BE 5
eternal	32.	We know, eternal gunman, our flesh remembers F&H III 19
	88.	Whose depth of red, eternal flesh of Pocahontas CH 15
	176.	always, always the eternal rainbow VU 22
eternity	15.	Into eternity NL 4
	36.	--And yet this great wink of eternity V-2 1
	46.	Beading thy path--condense eternity TBB 35
	93.	With vast eternity, dost wield the rebound seed CH 150
	170.	When singing that Eternity possessed TED 7
	182.	Of screaming rain--Eternity Et 46
eternity's	177.	That rises on eternity's long willingness Rep 11
ether	91.	The blue's cloud-templed districts unto ether CH 90

eucalyptus	156.	Below the palsy that one eucalyptus lifts OC 6
evade	11.	We can evade you, and all else but the heart Chap 17
	68.	And few evade full measure of their fate Riv 108
evasive	94.	Evasive--too--as dayspring's spreading arc to trace is CH 192
Eve	98.	Eve! Magdalene!/or Mary, you SC 7
	98.	O simian Venus, homeless Eve SC 9
	99.	Yes, Eve--wraith of my unloved seed SC 27
	149.	For Eve, Gioconda and Dalila Loc 32
even	32.	We even F&H III 11
	94.	Stood up and flung the span on even wing CH 195
	192.	--Their shadows even--now can't carry him SI 8
evening	13.	Nor has the evening long to wait IS 15
	21.	The evening was a spear in the ravine Pass 23
	27.	Until the graduate opacities of evening F&H I 13
	28.	And yet, suppose some evening I forgot F&H I 17
	70.	First moth of evening take wing stealthily Dan 20
	90.	Where spouting pillars spoor the evening sky CH 60
	122.	She will flush their hid wings in the evening to blaze Moth 15
	139.	Like a shell surrendered to evening sands Lege 3
	179.	In the focus of the evening there is this island with Len 1
eventful	111.	Daemon, demurring and eventful yawn Tun 106
eventual	28.	I meet you, therefore, in that eventual flame F&H I 44
Everest	93.	Of tides awash the pedestal of Everest, fail CH 152
everlasting	8.	The everlasting eyes of Pierrot PU 3
	143.	The everlasting eyes of Pierrot BE 31
evermore	110.	Probing through you--toward me, O evermore Tun 78
Everpresence	117.	So to thine Everpresence, beyond time At 89
everything	182.	Everything--and lick the grass, as black as patent Et 27
	182.	Everything gone--or strewn in riddled grace Et 29
everywhere	183.	Sliding everywhere. Bodies were rushed into graves Et 51
evil	176.	evil smile. And, as for me VU 18
evisceration	157.	For slow evisceration bound like those huge terrapin OC 28
evokes	194.	The angelus of wars my chest evokes B Tow 31
except	177.	Thou canst read nothing except through appetite Rep 1
Exchange	89.	Of canyoned traffic...Confronting the Exchange CH 54
excising	64.	One said, excising a last burr from his vest Riv 47

exclaim	38.	In this expectant, still exclaim receive V-4 24
	108.	walking down--exclaim Tun 14
excursion	30.	Blest excursion! this ricochet F&H II 5
exile	8.	That mingled in such exile guise PU 2
	24.	"--And fold your exile on your back again WM 48
	48.	That made me exile in her streets, stood me AM 18
	191.	Exile is thus a purgatory--not such as Dante built Purg 13
exit	100.	(Then rush the nearest exit through the smoke NWG 8
exist	100.	Her eyes exist in swivellings of her teats NWG 17
expands	135.	And with the day, distance again expands CL 3
expectant	38.	In this expectant, still exclaim receive V-4 24
explained	179.	And there is, as Mr. Budge explained before his Len 11
exploded	157.	Sere of the sun exploded in the sea OC 35
explores	51.	Of all that amplitude that time explores AM 73
explosion	7.	And poise them full and ready for explosion SMA 17
explosions	184.	You, who contain augmented tears, explosions Emp 1
expose	159.	Expose vaunted validities that yawn TCJ 13
express	62.	imagine--while an EXpress makes time like Riv 12
	110.	Somewhere above Fourteenth TAKE THE EXPRESS Tun 61
extend	33.	Blamed bleeding hands extend and thresh the height F&H III 46
extending	179.	ing or extending a phallus through the grating, --talking to Len 5
extinction	109.	Beyond extinction, surcease of the bone Tun 48
extinguish	176.	partition. To extinguish what I have of faith VU 20
extra	100.	Of bandy eyes.... No extra mufflings here NWG 3
eye	29.	Accept a lone eye rivited to your plane F&H I 49
	91.	Surely no eye that Sunward Escadrille can cover CH 106
	105.	Must we descend as worm's eye to construe OH 58
	110.	Of shoes, umbrellas, each eye attending its shoe, then Tun 87
	163.	The other tilted, peeled end clapped to eye Id 10
	194.	The matrix of the heart, lift down the eye B Tow 37
eyeless	66.	Where eyeless fish curvet a sunken fountain Riv 83

eyes

8. The everlasting eyes of Pierrot   PU 3
9. Of branch on branch above her, blurs her eyes
    GA 5
10. At doors and stone with broken eyes   SM 20
14. Seldom, now, meet a mirror in her eyes   Fern 2
18. That through its black foam has no eyes   Pos 8
19. Had galvanized the eyes   LC 18
19. Thy Nazarene and tinder eyes   LC 26
20. Names peeling from Thine eyes   LC 33
22. Under the constant wonder of your eyes   Pass 31
23. Narrowing the mustard scansions of the eyes
    WM 2
23. Her eyes, unmake an instant of the world   WM 13
23. Octagon, sapphire transepts round the eyes
    WM 16
25. Such eyes at search or rest you cannot see
    Rec 3
28. Then I might find your eyes across an aisle
    F&H I 20
29. Beyond their million brittle, bloodshot eyes
    F&H I 46
34. Frosted eyes there were that lifted altars
    AMT 11
38. Portending eyes and lips and making told   V-4 12
38. Blue latitudes and levels of your eyes   V-4 23
39. Your eyes already in the slant of drifting foam
    V-5 23
40. Of swimmers their lost morning eyes   V-6 2
40. My eyes pressed black against the prow   V-6 11
40. Conceding dialogue with eyes   V-6 23
45. Then, with inviolate curve, forsake our eyes
    TBB 5
45. Foretold to other eyes on the same screen   TBB 12
50. Series on series, infinite,--till eyes   AM 41
54. Serenely now, before day claims our eyes   HD 23
56. arms close; eyes wide, undoubtful   HD 28
64. And afterwards, who had a colt's eyes--one said
    Riv 41
66. Youngsters with eyes like fjords, old reprobates
    Riv 65
68. Like one whose eyes were buried long ago   Riv 119
70. And bridal flanks and eyes hid tawny pride
    Dan 16
78. Her eyes, strange for an Indian's, were not black
    Ind 35
79. And you're the only one with eyes like him
    Ind 51
82. His eyes pressed through green grass   CS 3
82. so--/shine--/GREEN--/eyes   CS 5
88. Our eyes can share or answer--then deflects
    CH 25

eyes, cont.

89. Wherein your eyes, like the Great Navigator's without ship CH 52
89. Sea eyes and tidal, undenying, bright with myth CH 58
90. Stars prick the eyes with sharp ammoniac proverbs CH 62
90. As bright as frogs' eyes, giggling in the girth CH 70
90. Stars scribble on our eyes the frosty sagas CH 75
91. While Iliads glimmer through eyes raised in pride CH 91
92. Thine eyes bicarbonated white by speed, O Skygak, see CH 124
92. To reckon--as thy stilly eyes partake CH 127
93. The stars have grooved our eyes with old persuasions CH 145
94. Panis Angelicus! Eyes tranquil with the blaze CH 187
98. Eyes crumble at its kiss. Its long-drawn spell SC 15
100. Of bandy eyes.... No extra mufflings here NWG 3
100. Her eyes exist in swivellings of her teats NWG 17
104. Perspective never withers from their eyes QH 1
104. See them, like eyes that still uphold some dream QH 23
109. Where boxed alone a second, eyes take fright Tun 27
110. Your eyes like agate lanterns--on and on Tun 73
110. --And did their riding eyes right through your side Tun 75
110. And did their eyes like unwashed platters ride Tun 76
111. O Genoese, do you bring mother eyes and hands Tun 104
115. Sheerly the eyes, like seagulls stung with rime At 25
115. Eyes stammer through the pangs of dust and steel At 52
122. That their land is too gorgeous to free their eyes wide Moth 6
122. But over one moth's eyes were tissues at birth Moth 17
123. The honey-wax eyes could find no alarms Moth 39
124. My eyes have hugged beauty and winged life's brief spell Moth 50
124. Dim eyes;--a tongue that cannot tell Moth 52
132. Ophelia had such eyes; but she MC 9
133. Their brown eyes blacken, and the blue drop hue CDB 8

eyes, cont.   133.   And stretches up through mortal eyes to see
                          CDB 16
                   133.   Carmen! Akimbo arms and smouldering eyes
                          CDB 17
                   133.   Carmen! Bestirring hope and lipping eyes
                          CDB 18
                   141.   The two men smiled into each other's eyes
                          EpH 24
                   143.   The everlasting eyes of Pierrot BE 31
                   148.   Your eyes, those pools with soft rushes Loc 1
                   157.   Each daybreak on the wharf, their brine-caked
                          eyes OC 29
                   161.   In Indian baths. At Cuban dusk the eyes IQ 9
                   161.   --It is at times as though the eyes burned hard
                          and glad IQ 12
                   162.   So eyes that mind thee fair and gone OS 5
                   172.   Sea gardens lifted rainbow-wise through eyes
                          ABP 5
                   173.   His eyes--/like crutches hurtled against glass
                          MF 6
                   177.   And here we join eyes in that sanctity Rep 2
                   179.   And the idiot boy by the road, with carbonated
                          eyes, laugh- Len 4
                   180.   Eyes widely planted, clear, yet small Lib 11

eyes'   79.   Oh, hold me in those eyes' engaging blue Ind 54
                   156.   His Carib mathematics web the eyes' baked lenses
                          OC 22

fabric	116.	Through the bright drench and fabric of our veins At 68
fabulous	34.	This fabulous shadow only the sea keeps AMT 16
face	8.	It was a kind and northern face PU 1
	20.	Thy face LC 42
	23.	Sharp to the windowpane guile drags a face WM 19
	25.	While darkness, like an ape's face, falls away Rec 15
	134.	And some dream still of Carmen's mystic face CDB 27
	158.	--This Cross, agleam still with a human Face Mer 15
	163.	My trespass vision shrinks to face his wrong Id 16
faces	104.	Faces--loose panes crown the hill and gleam QH 21
	108.	Refractions of the thousand theatres, faces Tun 4
	109.	of other faces, also underground Tun 38
	191.	Where all your gas lights--faces--sputum gleam Purg 3
facing	11.	Facing the dull squint with what innocence Chap 12
facsimile	23.	Whose skin, facsimile of time, unskeins WM 15
fact	89.	Dream cancels dream in this new realm of fact CH 39
faction	186.	Thou wieldest with such tears that every faction Shak 9
factions	105.	The resigned factions of the dead preside QH 49
factory	141.	And as the fingers of the factory owner's son EpH 8
	141.	And factory sounds and factory thoughts EpH 20
fade	162.	The burden of the rose will fade OS 9
fades	69.	All fades but one thin skyline 'round...Ahead Riv 137
fail	93.	Of tides awash the pedestal of Everest, fail CH 152
	111.	Impassioned with some song we fail to keep Tun 118
	186.	--And fail, both! Yet thine Ariel holds his song Shak 12
faint	10.	Still answering her faint good-byes SM 18
	17.	That shall not rouse, how faint the crow's cavil Par 12
faintest	15.	Or left you with the faintest blush NL 6
faintly	32.	That waited faintly, briefly and in vain F&H III 18
fair	145.	And threw warm gules on Madeline's fair breast PA 43
	162.	So eyes that mind thee fair and gone OS 5

fairest	152.	again round one more fairest day In 21
fairly	151.	that make your colored syrup fairly APE 12
faith	48.	--The Chan's great continent.... Then faith, not fear AM 21
	51.	Yielding by inference and discard, faith AM 75
	89.	"--Recorders ages hence"--ah, syllables of faith CH 43
	101.	Then you, the burlesque of our lust--and faith NWG 27
	104.	Much of our store of faith in other men QH 15
	171.	Here has my salient faith annealed me KW 1
	176.	partition. To extinguish what I have of faith VU 20
	178.	Have kept no faith but wind, the cold stream PB 10
	184.	Love and the breath of faith, momentous bride Emp 13
	185.	the audible ransom, ensign of my faith Post 5
	185.	Yet seldom was there faith in the heart's right kindness Post 13
faithful	7.	That are your rich and faithful strength of line SMA 3
	151.	to india, o ye faithful APE 24
faithfully	32.	Who faithfully, yourself, will fall too soon F&H III 7
faithfuls	159.	Of quarts to faithfuls--surely smuggled home TCJ 11
fakes	100.	Each other--turquoise fakes on tinselled hands NWG 20
Falcon-Ace	92.	What alcohol of space...! Remember, Falcon-Ace CH 128
fall	7.	The leaves will fall again sometime and fill SMA 1
	13.	Twilight, stiller than shadows, fall IS 12
	30.	And you may fall downstairs with me F&H II 18
	32.	Who faithfully, yourself, will fall too soon F&H III 7
	48.	That fall back yawning to another plunge AM 12
	50.	Found more than flesh to fathom in its fall AM 37
	72.	--Fall, Sachem, strictly as the tamarack Dan 48
	173.	Fall mute and sudden (dealing change/for lilies) MF 7
	191.	Here quakes of earth make houses fall Purg 11
fallen	12.	Already fallen harvest Past 13
falling	3.	In the white falling flakes Leg 7
	89.	Through surf, its bird note there a long time falling CH 47
	159.	The falling wonder of a rainbow's trance TCJ 4
falls	24.	While darkness, like an ape's face, falls away Rec 15
	45.	A jest falls from the speechless caravan TBB 20

farewells	115.	Like hails, farewells--up planet-sequined heights At 33
farm	78.	You were the first--before Ned and this farm Ind 47
farms	75.	We danced, O Brave, we danced beyond their farms Dan 101
	89.	Back over Connecticut farms, abandoned pastures CH 57
Far Rockaway	58.	Leaps from Far Rockaway to Golden Gate VW 2
	61.	Leaps from Far Rockaway to Golden Gate VW 42
farther	34.	No farther tides...High in the azure steeps AMT 14
	105.	Me farther than scalped Yankees knew to go QH 52
	185.	toward something far, now farther than ever away Post 6
	192.	Farther than his sun-shadow--farther than wings SI 7
farthest	69.	The Mississippi drinks the farthest dale Riv 127
fast	14.	The zigzags fast around dry lips composed Fern 5
	90.	Our hearing momentwise; but fast in whirling armatures CH 69
	92.	Zodiacs, dashed/(now nearing fast the Cape!) CH 141
	150.	The world moves by so fast these days GWP 12
	151.	the nation's lips are thin and fast APE 14
fasten	39.	Can fasten or deflect this tidal wedge V-5 11
fat	160.	from emerald cloud-sprockets. Fat final prophets with MT 8
fatal	38.	Must first be lost in fatal tides to tell V-4 16
fate	68.	And few evade full measure of their fate Riv 108
	74.	Of his own fate, I saw thy change begun Dan 76
	186.	And laughter, burnished brighter than our fate Shak 8
father	60.	One day in spring my father took to me VW 33
	69.	You are your father's father, and the stream Riv 122
	76.	Your father knew Ind 8
father's	64.	Behind/My father's cannery works I used to see Riv 52
	69.	You are your father's father, and the stream Riv 122
	78.	As long as Jim, your father's memory, is warm Ind 45
fathers	192.	His fathers took for granted ages since--and so he looms SI 6
fathom	50.	Found more than flesh to fathom in its fall AM 37
fault	149.	And it's your fault that I'm this way Loc 29

fear	9.	She has no memory, nor fear, nor hope GA 11
	32.	Let us unbind our throats of fear and pity F&H III 10
	48.	To you, too, Juan Perez, whose counsel fear AM 7
	48.	--The Chan's great continent.... Then faith, not fear AM 21
feasts	25.	Look steadily--how the wind feasts and spins Rec 13
feathered	23.	Speed to the arrow into feathered skies WM 18
feathers	72.	Swooping in eagle feathers down your back Dan 46
	126.	With crimson feathers whips away the mists O-N 2
feathery	54.	Cool feathery fold, suspends, distills HD 17
	184.	Gathered and made musical in feathery fronds Emp 3
fed	73.	Fed down your anklets to the sunset's moat Dan 72
	170.	Yet fed your hunger like an endless task TED 2
feed	7.	That feed your inquiries with aerial wine SMA 15
	68.	For you, too, feed the River timelessly Riv 107
feel	111.	And yet, like Lazarus, to feel the slope Tun 119
	144.	Until you feel the weight of many cars PA 6
feeling	151.	feeling them in every way and APE 4
feet	9.	Beyond the grass and shadows at her feet GA 12
	17.	Above the feet the clever sheets Par 5
	51.	The orbic wake of thy once whirling feet AM 79
	72.	Feet nozzled wat'ry webs of upper flows Dan 31
	156.	Across the feet of the dead, laid in white sand OC 2
	181.	Two decks unsandwiched, split sixty feet apart Et 15
	193.	From pit to crucifix, feet chill on steps from hell B Tow 4
fell	116.	Whose fell unshadow is death's utter wound At 66
	123.	To the desert,--back,--down,--still lonely he fell Moth 48
	141.	Fell lightly, warmly, down into the wound EpH 7
	182.	And fell dead or dying, but it didn't so much matter Et 49
felt	123.	The florescence, the power he felt bud at the time Moth 26
	132.	Surely she must have felt MC 8
	145.	And we overpayed them because we felt like it PA 39
feminine	18.	And the mercy, feminine, that stays Pos 14
fencers	92.	Cloud-belfries, banging, while searchlights, like fencers CH 121
Fernandez' Hotel	181.	Fernandez' Hotel, was requisitioned into pens Et 11

Fernando	50.	--Yet no delirium of jewels! O Fernando AM 46
fernery	14.	Beside her and her fernery, is to follow Fern 4
ferns	136.	Glitters on the edges of wet ferns Ps 3
fertile	156.	To the white sand I may speak a name, fertile OC 12
fever	9.	Drowning the fever of her hands in sunlight GA 10
	183.	The fever was checked. I stood a long time in Mack's talking Et 58
fervid	41.	Still fervid covenant, Belle Isle V-6 25
few	12.	A few picked, the rest dead Past 20
	68.	And few evade full measure of their fate Riv 108
fibre	60.	Some sunning inch of unsuspecting fibre VW 24
fickle	178.	--The hot fickle wind, the breath of males PB 11
fiddle	156.	Near the coral beach--nor zigzag fiddle crabs OC 3
fiddlers	145.	And some Sunday fiddlers PA 36
field	68.	From tunnel into field--iron strides the dew Riv 90
	109.	to dig in the field--travlin the town--too Tun 43
fields	51.	Hushed gleaming fields and pendant seething wheat AM 83
	116.	And justified conclamant with ripe fields At 71
	141.	Flickering in sunlight over summer fields EpH 15
fierce	90.	To what fierce schedules, rife of doom apace CH 87
	161.	Where the straight road would seem to ply below the stone, that fierce IQ 4
fiery	46.	The City's fiercy parcels all undone TBB 39
	91.	War's fiery kennel masked in downy offings CH 94
	156.	Let fiery blossoms clot the light, render my ghost OC 24
fifings	54.	--Flurried by keen fifings, eddied HD 15
Fifi's	150.	And Fifi's bows and poodle ease GWP 6
fifty-nine	78.	Won nothing out of fifty-nine--those years Ind 26
fights	144.	The Greek grins and fights with the Swede PA 15
figs	102.	Where green figs gleam Va 13
figures	45.	Some page of figures to be filed away TBB 7
file	114.	White tempest nets file upward, upward ring At 22
filed	39.	The cables of our sleep so swiftly filed V-5 6
	45.	Some page of figures to be filed away TBB 7

fill	5.	Bowls and cups fill historians with adorations EC 10
	7.	The leaves will fall again sometime and fill SMA 1
	105.	That unfolds a new destiny to fill QH 56
filled	94.	And filled the forest with what clustrous sheen CH 178
	172.	By the dove filled, and bees of Paradise ABP 10
fills	8.	Into the smoky spring that fills PU 22
filter	10.	Filter in to us before we waken SM 4
	126.	Dives through the filter of trellises O-N 3
fin	164.	With fin and hoof, with wing and sweetened fang NA 11
final	11.	We will sidestep, and to the final smirk Chap 9
	29.	You found in final chains, no captive then F&H I 45
	64.	As final reckonings of fire and snow Riv 36
	100.	Always and last, before the final ring NWG 9
	100.	And the lewd trounce of a final muted beat NWG 23
	111.	Taking the final level for the dive Tun 93
	160.	from emerald cloud-sprockets. Fat final prophets with MT 8
	185.	at last shyly. My only final friends Post 2
finale	133.	Finale leaves in silence to replume CDB 21
finally	5.	And where was finally borne a chosen hero EC 14
	16.	And finally, in that memory all things nurse RR 17
	16.	After the city that I finally passed RR 18
	18.	Upon the page whose blind sum finally burns Pos 25
	98.	Finally to answer all within one grave SC 12
	177.	But finally knows conviviality Rep 4
finches	30.	Where cuckoos clucked to finches F&H II 25
find	10.	Will find the street, only to look SM 19
	11.	For we can still love the world, who find Chap 5
	17.	May find the record wedged in his soul Par 4
	28.	Then I might find your eyes across an aisle F&H I 20
	108.	You'll find the garden in the third act dead Tun 8
	108.	Ten blocks or so before? But you find yourself Tun 20
	123.	The honey-wax eyes could find no alarms Moth 39
	142.	Do not think too deeply, and you'll find BE 7
	146.	To find the only rose on the bush PA 51
fine	11.	And yet these fine collapses are not lies Chap 14
	105.	What cunning neighbors history has in fine QH 41

finger	83.	"--that spiracle!" he shot a finger out the door CS 34
	108.	Finger your knees--and wish yourself in bed Tun 9
	133.	The tapestry betrays a finger through CDB 11
	141.	One finger from the others EpH 4
	158.	Here where we finger moidores of spent grace Mer 13
fingernail	176.	And the fingernail that cinch such VU 5
fingers	6.	"Are your fingers long enough to play MGLL 17
	9.	She is prisoner of the tree and its green fingers GA 6
	35.	And their fingers crumble fragments of baked weed V-1 4
	73.	A birch kneels. All her whistling fingers fly Dan 49
	141.	And as the fingers of the factory owner's son EpH 8
	141.	As his taut, spare fingers wound the gauze EpH 11
	143.	When your fingers spread among stars BE 28
	185.	Antillean fingers counting my pulse, my love forever Post 16
fins	84.	Fins whip the breeze around Japan CS 60
	115.	Slit and propelled by glistening fins of light At 26
fire	18.	Whose heart is fire shall come,--the white wind rase Pos 28
	32.	Repeated play of fire--no hypogeum F&H III 23
	36.	O minstrel galleons of Carib fire V-2 22
	50.	Sun-cusped and zoned with modulated fire AM 44
	52.	Te Deum laudamus/O Thou Hand of Fire AM 90
	60.	It flashed back at your thrust, as clean as fire VW 25
	64.	As final reckonings of fire and snow Riv 36
	64.	He trod the fire down pensively and grinned Riv 50
	73.	Wrapped in that fire, I saw more escorts wake Dan 67
	98.	High, cool,/wide from the slowly smoldering fire SC 5
	98.	It is blood to remember; it is fire SC 20
	112.	O Hand of Fire/gatherest Tun 137
	117.	--One Song, one Bridge of Fire! Is it Cathay At 93
firecat	76.	The pebbles sang, the firecat slunk away Ind 17
fire-gall	74.	Totem and fire-gall, slumbering pyramid Dan 85
fire's	133.	And dies on fire's birth in each man's heart CDB 10
fires	181.	Was halfway under water with fires Et 21
fire-wood	128.	And the fire-wood glow is bright Fr 2

fireworks	100.	When all the fireworks blare, begins NWG 10
firmly	58.	Firmly as coffee grips the taste,--and away VW 9
first	19.	First blood. From flanks unfended LC 11
	38.	Must first be lost in fatal tides to tell V-4 16
	48.	Till dawn should clear that dim frontier, first seen AM 20
	48.	The first palm chevron the first lighted hill AM 24
	70.	First moth of evening take wing stealthily Dan 20
	74.	There, where the first and last gods keep thy tent Dan 80
	76.	Yielded your first cry at the prairie's door Ind 7
	78.	You were the first--before Ned and this farm Ind 47
	94.	When first I read thy lines, rife as the loam CH 173
	94.	Not greatest, thou,--not first, nor last,--but near CH 189
	100.	Sprayed first with ruby, then with emerald sheen NWG 14
	129.	Of the first moth's descent,--day's predestiny An 5
	160.	spiders yoked you first,--silking of shadows good under-/drawers for owls MT 5
	181.	To Havana on the first boat through. They groaned Et 13
first-born	78.	First-born, remember Ind 48
first-plucked	160.	First-plucked before and since the Flood, old hypno- MT 6
fish	66.	Where eyeless fish curvet a sunken fountain Riv 83
fishes	149.	And my heart fishes in troubled water Loc 31
fissures	110.	In interborough fissures of the mind Tun 71
fists	66.	Blind fists of nothing, humpty-dumpty clods Riv 61
fixed	18.	For this fixed stone of lust Pos 9
fizz	105.	In bootleg roadhouses where the gin fizz QH 35
fjords	66.	Youngsters with eyes like fjords, old reprobates Riv 65
	144.	And the Fjords and the Aegean are remembered PA 16
flagless	39.	Nothing so flagless as this piracy V-5 20
flagrant	100.	The world's one flagrant, sweating cinch NWG 4
flags	16.	Flags, weeds. And remembrance of steep alcoves RR 6
flail	91.	Is baited by marauding circles, bludgeon flail CH 96

flaked	94.	Cowslip and shad-blow, flaked like tethered foam CH 171
flakes	3.	In the white falling flakes Leg 7
flaking	16.	I heard wind flaking sapphire, like this summer RR 22
flame	3.	Imploring flame. And tremorous Leg 6
	20.	And their undimming lattices of flame LC 34
	24.	Before some flame of gaunt repose a shell WM 35
	28.	I meet you, therefore, in that eventual flame F&H I 44
	66.	And past the circuit of the lamp's thin flame Riv 71
	73.	Flame cataracts of heaven in seething swarms Dan 71
flamed	51.	And Teneriffe's garnet--flamed it in a cloud AM 70
flame-pots	133.	Bright peacocks drink from flame-pots by the wall CDB 5
flank	90.	Capeward, then blading the wind's flank, banked and spun CH 81
flanks	19.	First blood. From flanks unfended LC 11
	70.	And bridal flanks and eyes hid tawny pride Dan 16
flare	126.	In a mad orange flare O-N 9
flash	27.	Smutty wings flash out equivocations F&H I 7
	89.	A flash over the horizon--shifting gears CH 37
flashed	60.	It flashed back at your thrust, as clean as fire VW 25
	188.	watches at least--the lighthouse flashed... whirled HR 18
flashing	39.	Where nothing turns but dead sands flashing V-5 17
	45.	With multitudes bent toward some flashing scene TBB 10
	62.	and no more sermons windows flashing roar Riv 17
flat	131.	Flat lily petals to the sea's white throat Ba 7
	161.	Flat prison slabs there at the marble quarry IQ 2
Flatbush	109.	Flatbush--on the fourth of July Tun 41
flattering	152.	(no instinct flattering vainly now In 8
flaunt	131.	Only simple ripples flaunt, and stroke, and float Ba 6
flaunts	133.	Bent wings, and Carmen with her flaunts through the gloom CDB 22
flay	35.	Bright striped urchins flay each other with sand V-1 2
fleck	39.	The bay estuaries fleck the hard sky limits V-5 4
fleckless	114.	Transparent meshes--fleckless the gleaming staves At 6
fled	16.	The pond I entered once and quickly fled RR 15

fled, cont.	66.	Screamed redskin dynasties that fled the brain Riv 77
	115.	Sheened harbor lanterns backward fled the keel At 50
	148.	Now that she has fled the capture Loc 15
fledged	90.	The soul, by naphtha fledged into new reaches CH 84
	91.	There, meaningful, fledged as the Pleiades CH 107
flee	100.	We flee her spasm through a fleshless door NWG 24
	164.	Moonmoth and grasshopper that flee our page NA 1
fleece	7.	The fleece of nature with those purposes SMA 2
fleeing	22.	"Am justified in transience, fleeing Pass 30
	91.	On fleeing balconies as thou dost glide CH 115
fleet	70.	But, watching, saw that fleet young crescent die Dan 24
flee'th	169.	Ay! Scripture flee'th stone Hur 5
fleeting	104.	Even to cast upon the seasons fleeting QH 7
flesh	18.	Through a thousand nights the flesh Pos 5
	32.	We know, eternal gunman, our flesh remembers F&H III 19
	50.	Found more than flesh to fathom in its fall Am 37
	70.	The swift red flesh, a winter king Dan 1
	88.	Whose depth of red, eternal flesh of Pocahontas CH 15
	101.	Yet, to the empty trapeze of your flesh NWG 25
	110.	And when they dragged your retching flesh Tun 79
	116.	Sight, sound and flesh Thou leadest from time's realm At 63
	132.	Though I have touched her flesh of moons MC 1
	169.	Rescindeth flesh from bone Hur 7
	173.	Beyond the roses that no flesh can pass MF 8
	186.	Are lifted from torn flesh with human rue Shak 7
fleshless	100.	We flee her spasms through a fleshless door NWG 24
flew	123.	The sun saw a ruby brightening ever, that flew Moth 36
flexions	108.	Preparing penguin flexions of the arms Tun 21
flicker	114.	Sibylline voices flicker, waveringly stream At 7
flickered	61.	It flickered through the snow screen, blindly VW 37
flickering	28.	Still flickering with those prefigurations F&H I 21
	73.	Flickering, sprint up the hill groins like a tide Dan 68
	141.	Flickering in sunlight over summer fields EpH 15
flickers	89.	Flickers a moment, consumes us in its smile CH 36
flies	4.	And, in Africa, a carcass quick with flies BT 12

flight   91. Taut motors surge, space-gnawing, into flight
                      CH 100
                 93. Glacial sierras and the flight of ravens   CH 158
                114. Upward, veering with light, the flight of strings
                      At 2
                115. Sidelong with flight of blade on tendon blade
                      At 28
                129. The sound of a dove's flight waved over the lawn
                      An 6
flings   15. Flings itself silently   NL 3
                194. As flings the question true?)--or is it she
                      B Tow 27
flint   73. Now snaps the flint in every tooth; red fangs
                      Dan 55
                190. And the flint tooth of Sagittarius   Rel 5
flittered   60. That flittered from under the ash heap day
                      VW 22
float   131. Only simple ripples flaunt, and stroke, and
                      float Ba 6
floated   161. In dusk, as though this island lifted, floated
                      IQ 8
floating   36. Close round one instant in one floating flower
                      V-2 20
                 41. --Unfolded floating dias before   V-6 26
                 50. And record of more, floating in a casque   AM 29
                 69. A liquid theme that floating niggers swell
                      Riv 123
                116. Atlantis,--hold thy floating singer late   At 88
                159. Or tempest--in a silver, floating plume   TCJ 16
floats   24. Beyond the wall, whose severed head floats by
                      WM 46
                 83. the star floats burning in a gulf of tears
                      CS 44
flocks   20. Of tears flocks through the tendoned loam   LC 31
flood   17. When systematic morn shall sometime flood
                      Par 10
                160. First-plucked before and since the Flood, old
                      hypno-   MT 6
flooded   148. My crisp soul will be flooded by a langour
                      Loc 7
floods   36. Of rimless floods, unfettered leewardings   V-2 2
                126. Floods the grape-hung night   O-N 10
floor   4.   And a roach spans a crevice in the floor   BT 4
                 10. Until you reach the muffled floor   SM 16
                 25. Build floor by floor on shafts of steel that
                      grant   Rec 19
                 30. White shadows slip across the floor   F&H II 11
                 37. Upon the steep floor flung from dawn to dawn
                      V-3 17
                100. --All but her belly buried in the floor   NWG 22
                104. Hostelry--floor by floor to cinquefoil dormer
                      QH 18

floor, cont.   111.   Lets go....   Toward corners of the floor
                             Tun 97
                      169.   Thou bidest wall nor floor, Lord   Hur 18
floors   69.   Over De Soto's bones the freighted floors
                             Riv 132
Floral Park   109.   at Floral Park   Tun 40
florescence   123.   The florescence, the power he felt bud at the
                             time Moth 26
flow   68.   Grimed tributaries to an ancient flow Riv 113
                       69.   Tortured with history, its one will--flow
                             Riv 141
                      130.   Jade-green with sunlight, melt and flow Ech 2
                      157.   Slagged of the hurricane--I, cast within its
                             flow OC 32
flower   36.   Close round one instant in one floating flower
                             V-2 20
                      116.   Thy pardon for this history, whitest Flower
                             At 84
                      140.   How love blooms like a tardy flower Int 7
                      156.   Albeit in a stranger tongue. Tree names, flower
                             names OC 13
                      170.   --Truly no flower yet withers in your hand TED 9
flowers   38.   Bright staves of flowers and quills to-day as I
                             V-4 15
                       60.   Or splits a random smell of flowers through glass
                             VW 31
                      132.   Even, sank in love and choked with flowers
                             MC 10
                      148.   Among the flowers of her domain Loc 18
flown   158.   The Cross alone has flown the wave Mer 5
flows   23.   Applause flows into liquid cynosures WM 7
                       69.   The River, spreading, flows--and spends your
                             dream Riv 120
                       69.   And flows within itself, heaps itself free
                             Riv 136
                       72.   Feet nozzled wat'ry webs of upper flows Dan 31
flung   37.   Upon the steep floor flung from dawn to dawn
                             V-3 17
                       40.   Flung into April's inmost day V-6 20
                       50.   Almost as though the Moor's flung scimitar AM 36
                       94.   Stood up and flung the span on even wing CH 195
flurried   54.   --Flurried by keen fifings, eddied HD 15
flush   122.   She will flush their hid wings in the evening to
                             blaze Moth 15
                      141.   The unexpected interest made his flush EpH 1
fly   73.   A birch kneels. All her whistling fingers fly
                             Dan 49
                       91.   O bright circumferences, heights employed to fly
                             CH 93
                      168.   The lizard's throat, held bloated for a fly AP 7
                      192.   And--backwards--is it thus the eagles fly SI 10
flying   18.   I know the screen, the distant flying taps
                             Pos 12

Flying Cloud	84.	Thermopylae, Black Prince, Flying Cloud through Sunda CS 67
foam	18.	That through its black foam has no eyes Pos 8
	36.	Pass superscription of bent foam and wave V-2 18
	39.	Your eyes already in the slant of drifting foam V-5 23
	73.	And stag teeth foam about the raven throat Dan 70
	84.	--scarfed of foam, their bellies veared green esplanades CS 68
	94.	Cowslip and shad-blow, flaked like tethered foam CH 171
	131.	They say that Venus shot through foam to light Ba 8
	159.	As you raise temples fresh from basking foam TCJ 12
foaming	92.	Slit the sky's pancreas of foaming anthracite CH 122
foams	88.	The captured fume of space foams in our ears CH 20
focus	88.	Our lenses, lifts a focus, resurrects CH 23
	179.	In the focus of the evening there is this island with Len 1
fog	54.	Far strum of fog horns...signals dispersed in veils HD 5
	56.	The fog leans one last moment on the sill HD 35
	180.	And must they overcome the fog Lib 12
foggy	134.	Morning: and through the foggy city gate CDB 25
fog-insulated	54.	The long, tired sounds, fog-insulated noises HD 3
fold	24.	"--And fold your exile on your back again WM 48
	35.	The waves fold thunder on the samd V-1 8
	54.	Cool feathery fold, suspends, distills HD 17
folded	75.	Now is the strong prayer folded in thine arms Dan 103
	88.	Those continental folded aeons, surcharged CH 16
folds	167.	Its frondings sighing in aetherial folds RP 8
folks	79.	Whose folks, like mine, came out of Arrowhead Ind 50
follow	5.	Orators follow the universe EC 7
	14.	Beside her and her fernery, is to follow Fern 4
	143.	And you others--follow your arches BE 29
	190.	And pocket us who, somehow, do not follow Rel 7
followed	24.	Has followed you. Though in the end you know WM 41
	158.	Has followed in its name, has heaped its grave Mer 7
following	94.	O, early following thee, I searched the hill CH 175
	94.	As vibrantly I following down Sequoia alleys CH 183

follows	133.	The slit, soft-pulling: -- -- -- and music follows cue CDB 12
	135.	Yet,--much follows, much endures...Trust birds alone CL 5
fond	188.	my thoughts, my humble, fond rememberances of the HR 4
fondle	35.	Fondle your shells and sticks, bleached V-1 11
food	128.	The food has a warm and tempting smell Fr 3
fool	12.	I can only query, "Fool Past 14
	143.	O Beauty's fool, though you have never BE 25
foot	30.	Glee shifts from foot to foot F&H II 2
	72.	That blanket of the skies: the padded foot Dan 42
	146.	The spindles at the foot of the bed PA 55
	156.	The tarantula rattling at the lily's foot OC 1
foraged	181.	The old woman and I foraged some drier clothes Et 2
forbidden	152.	from sleep forbidden now and wide In 12
forceps	23.	Regard the forceps of the smile that takes her WM 11
ford	79.	Perhaps I'll hear the mare's hoofs to the ford Ind 58
Fords	145.	Using the latest ice-box and buying Fords PA 25
foregone	136.	Mine is a world foregone though not yet ended Ps 5
foreknown	38.	Mutual blood, transpiring as foreknown V-4 19
foresees	106.	Love from despair--when love foresees the end QH 71
forest	56.	a forest shudders in your hair HD 30
	89.	Adam and Adam's answer in the forest CH 31
	94.	And filled the forest with what clustrous sheen CH 178
	137.	Or an old house in a forest,--or a child For 7
foretold	45.	Foretold to other eyes on the same screen TBB 12
forever	64.	Hobo-trekkers that forever search Riv 55
	98.	Windswept guitars on lonely decks forever SC 11
	116.	Forever Deity's glittering Pledge, O Thou At 73
	167.	Forever fruitless, and beyond that yield RP 9
	185.	Antillean fingers counting my pulse, my love forever Post 16
forget	125.	Can trace paths tear-wet, and forget all blight C 13
	141.	Suddenly he seemed to forget the pain EpH 2
	143.	Seen them again, you won't forget BE 26
	191.	And what hours they forget to chime I'll know Purg 20
forgetfulness	137.	Forgetfulness is like a song For 1
	137.	Forgetfulness is like a bird whose wings are reconciled For 3
	137.	Forgetfulness is rain at night For 6
	137.	Forgetfulness is white,--white as a blasted tree For 8

forgetfulness	137.	I can remember much forgetfulness For 11
forget-me-nots	102.	Forget-me-nots at windowpanes Va 22
forgive	26.	Forgive me for an echo of these things Rec 27
forgot	28.	And yet, suppose some evening I forgot F&H I 17
	58.	And Rip forgot the office hours,/and he forgot the pay VW 14
	82.	stepped out--forgot to look at you CS 6
forgotten	70.	Where prayers, forgotten, streamed the mesa sands Dan 7
forked	90.	Toward what? The forked crash of split thunder parts CH 68
forking	18.	I, turning, turning on smoked forking spires Pos 21
forks	110.	In back forks of the chasms of the brain Tun 69
forlorn	4.	The black man, forlorn in the cellar BT 9
form	7.	Spontaneities that form their independent orbits SMA 10
	125.	And he tended with far truths he would form C 6
formulations	32.	In corymbulous formations of mechanics F&H III 13
former	104.	Long tiers of windows staring out toward former QH 20
forms	172.	Dissolved within a sky of beacon forms ABP 4
forsake	45.	Then, with inviolate curve, forsake our eyes TBB 5
forsaken	191.	Like something left, forsaken--here am I Purg 4
forsook	61.	It forsook her at the doorway, it was gone VW 38
forth	127.	And reaping, have mercy and love issued forth Hi 6
forthright	176.	that cancel all your kindness. Forthright VU 10
fostering	152.	and fostering In 5
fought	178.	As they were fought--and wooed? They now but stoke PB 7
found	4.	AEsop, driven to pondering, found BT 5
	21.	Touching an opening laurel, I found Pass 26
	29.	You found in final chains, no captive then F&H I 45
	50.	Found more than flesh to fathom in its fall AM 37
	70.	With mineral wariness found out the stone Dan 6
	76.	We found God lavish there in Colorado Ind 15
	142.	How can you tell where beauty's to be found BE 9
	172.	I found ABP 6
fountain	66.	Where eyeless fish curvet a sunken fountain Riv 83
	167.	A fountain at salute, a crown in view RP 14
fountains	19.	Perpetual fountains, vines LC 25

freight	64.	An empire wilderness of freight and rails Riv 56
	66.	John, Jake or Charley, hopping the slow freight Riv 59
freighted	69.	Over De Soto's bones the freighted floors Riv 132
fresh	14.	--So, while fresh sunlight splinters humid green Fern 7
	35.	Above the fresh ruffles of the surf V-1 1
	105.	Fresh from the radio in the old Meeting House QH 37
	116.	Whose canticle fresh chemistry assigns At 74
	123.	Swinging in spirals round the fresh breasts of day Moth 30
	159.	As you raise temples fresh from basking foam TCJ 12
	174.	Have levers for,--stampede it with fresh type BNOK 11
freshen	19.	Thorns freshen on the year's LC 10
freshened	85.	at Java Head freshened the nip CS 70
freshets	76.	And glistening through the sluggard freshets came Ind 18
freshly	173.	In bunches sorted freshly--/and bestows MF 4
friend	58.	"Is this Sleepy Hollow, friend--?" And he VW 13
	79.	You, Larry, traveller--/stranger,/son,/--my friend Ind 64
	159.	But do not claim a friend like him again TCJ 19
friendly	174.	Come, search the marshes for a friendly bed BNOK 3
Friends	105.	Who saw the Friends there ever heard before QH 40
friends	128.	Friends! No,--it is not fright Fr 6
	171.	There is no breath of friends and no more shore KW 15
	185.	at last shyly. My only final friends Post 2
	191.	My country, O my land, my friends Purg 1
friendship	185.	Friendship agony! words came to me Post 1
friendship's	104.	Of friendship's acid wine, retarding phlegm QH 12
frieze	115.	And still the circular, indubitable frieze At 53
fright	106.	Yes, whip-poor-will, unhusks the heart of fright QH 68
	109.	Where boxed alone a second, eyes take fright Tun 27
	128.	Friends! No,--it is not fright Fr 6
fringe	133.	Of whispering tapestry, brown with old fringe CDB 23
Frisco	84.	to Frisco, Melbourne... CS 62
frisk	35.	O brilliant kids, frisk with your dog V-1 10

frogs'	90.	As bright as frogs' eyes, giggling in the girth CH 70
frondings	167.	Its frondings sighing in aetherial folds RP 8
fronds	184.	Gathered and made musical in feathery fronds Emp 3
front	146.	In the front yard PA 52
frontier	48.	Till dawn should clear that dim frontier, first seen AM 20
	68.	They win no frontier by their wayward plight Riv 114
frontiers	83.	I saw the frontiers gleaming of his mind CS 37
	83.	or are there frontiers--running sands sometimes CS 38
frosted	34.	Frosted eyes there were that lifted altars AMT 11
	114.	Beyond whose frosted capes the moon bequeaths At 19
frostily	56.	The window goes blond slowly. Frostily clears HD 31
frosty	90.	Stars scribble on our eyes the frosty sagas CH 75
frown	31.	We cannot frown upon her as she smiles F&H II 35
frozen	24.	"Alas,--these frozen billows of your skill WM 38
	39.	One frozen trackless smile...What words V-5 8
	123.	As his blindness before had frozen in Hell Moth 46
frugal	171.	To heaven or hades--to an equally frugal noon KW 8
fruit	171.	Need I presume the same fruit of my bone KW 10
	184.	Nor that fruit of mating which is widowed pride Emp 15
fruitless	167.	Forever fruitless, and beyond that yield RP 9
fry	165.	--Yes, patent-leather shoes hot enough to fry BSEW 11
full	7.	And poise them full and ready for explosion SMA 17
	51.	And biassed by full sails, meridians reel AM 86
	68.	And few evade full measure of their fate Riv 108
	145.	"Full on this casement shone the wintry moon PA 42
fumbling	163.	Fumbling his sex. That's why those children laughed Id 4
fume	88.	The captured fume of space foams in our ears CH 20
funk	148.	For snaring the poor world in a blue funk Loc 12
funnel	178.	For who shall lift head up to funnel smoke PB 5
	181.	And a funnel high and dry up near the park Et 16
furbished	185.	Dawn's broken arc! the noon's more furbished room Post 12
furious	74.	O, like the lizard in the furious noon Dan 73
furls	76.	Closes before the dusk, furls in its song Ind 3

furnaces   179. furnaces, chisels and ploughs Len 3
furrow   98. Furrow of all our travel--trailed derision
                      SC 14
further   72. A further valley-shed; I could not stop Dan 30
furtive   13. Her furtive lace and misty hair IS 5
fury   11. Recesses for it from the fury of the street
                      Chap 7
                 46. O harp and altar, of the fury fused TBB 29
fuse   115. And synergy of waters ever fuse, recast At 46
fused   46. O harp and altar, of the fury fused TBB 29
fuselage   92. Lead-perforated fuselage, escutcheoned wings
                      CH 134
futile   122. At night like a grain of sand, futile and dried
                      Moth 24
futurity   158. Leave us, you idols of Futurity--alone Mer 12

gaiety	11.	And through all sound of gaiety and quest Chap 22
gaily	35.	Gaily digging and scattering V-1 5
gain	189.	yield to--by which also you win and gain mastery and HR 34
gained	72.	O Appalachian Spring! I gained the ledge Dan 33
gains	152.	with langour such as gains In 2
	186.	And that serenity that Prospero gains Shak 13
gainsay	48.	Of clown nor sage can riddle or gainsay AM 6
	156.	Deliberate, gainsay death's brittle crypt. Meanwhile OC 14
gale	90.	Warping the gale, the Wright windwrestlers veered CH 80
	91.	Bristle the heights above a screeching gale to hover CH 105
galleons	36.	O minstrel galleons of Carib fire V-2 22
galleries	83.	and galleries, galleries of watergutted lava CS 31
gallows	158.	Gallows and guillotines to hail the sun Mer 9
galvanic	112.	Lunged past, with one galvanic blare stove up the River Tun 124
galvanized	19.	Had galvanized the eyes LC 18
galvothermic	111.	Thunder is galvothermic here below.... The car Tun 91
gambade	169.	Thy drum's gambade, its plunge abscond Hur 13
game	11.	The game enforces smirks; but we have seen Chap 19
Ganges	51.	The glistening seignories of Ganges swim AM 68
gangs	102.	Crap-shooting gangs in Bleecker reign Va 20
garden	13.	Over the garden dial distill IS 6
	108.	You'll find the garden in the third act dead Tun 8
	136.	An imagined garden grey with sundered boughs Ps 6
gardened	31.	Among slim skaters of the gardened skies F&H II 37
gardenless	98.	Unwedded, stumbling gardenless to grieve SC 10
gardens	172.	Sea gardens lifted rainbow-wise through eyes ABP 5
Gargantua	8.	And, of Gargantua, the laughter PU 4
	143.	Or, of Gargantua, the laughter BE 32
gargle	111.	Blank windows gargle signals through the roar Tun 99
garland	40.	Some splintered garland for the seer V-6 16
garnet	51.	And Teneriffe's garnet--flamed it in a cloud AM 70
garter	60.	Garter snakes under...And the monoplanes VW 19
gas	191.	Where all your gas lights--faces--sputum gleam Purg 3
gaseous	92.	See scouting griffons rise through gaseous crepe CH 119

gash	141.	The gash was bleeding, and a shaft of sun EpH 5
	142.	Yet a gash with sunlight jerking through BE 12
gate	68.	I could believe he joked at heaven's gate Riv 110
	105.	Our love of all we touch, and take it to the Gate QH 59
	109.	you don't like my gate why did you Tun 53
	134.	Morning: and through the foggy city gate CDB 25
	179.	this gate of Len 27
gates	5.	Luring the living into spiritual gates EC 6
	5.	Dull lips commemorating spiritual gates EC 11
	5.	But only to build memories of spiritual gates EC 17
	16.	At gulf gates...There, beyond the dykes RR 21
	37.	And so, admitted through black swollen gates V-3 9
gather	147.	It is to gather kindnesses Per 3
	170.	Needs more than wit to gather, love to bind TED 11
gathered	33.	Gathered the voltage of blown blood and vine F&H III 38
	152.	immensity in gathered grace; the arms In 3
	184.	Gathered and made musical in feathery fronds Emp 3
gatherest	111.	Kiss of our agony thou gatherest Tun 116
	112.	Kiss of our agony Thou gatherest Tun 136
	112.	O Hand of Fire/gatherest Tun 137
gathering	38.	And widening noon within your breast for gathering V-4 20
gathers	193.	The bell-rope that gathers God at dawn B Tow 1
gaunt	24.	Before some flame of gaunt repose a shell WM 35
	111.	The gaunt sky-barracks cleanly now, and bare Tun 103
gauntlets	92.	Giddily spiralled/gauntlets, upturned, unlooping CH 138
gauze	141.	As his taut, spare fingers wound the gauze EpH 11
gave	5.	The uneven valley graves. While the apostle gave EC 2
gay	76.	Waved Seminary Hill a gay good-bye Ind 14
	160.	gum took place. Up jug to musical, hanging jug just gay MT 4
gaze	23.	Asserts a vision in the slumbering gaze WM 4
	36.	The seal's wide spindrift gaze toward paradise V-2 25
	68.	--A little while gaze absently below Riv 102
	74.	Lo, through what infinite seasons dost thou gaze Dan 82
	78.	And like twin stars. They seemed to shun the gaze Ind 37

giddily   92.   Giddily spiralled/gauntlets, upturned, unloop-
                         ing   CH 138
gigantic   90.   Under the looming stacks of the gigantic power
                         house   CH 61
gigantically   110.   And Death, aloft,--gigantically down   Tun 77
giggling   90.   As bright as frogs' eyes, giggling in the girth
                         CH 70
gild   162.   On skies that gild thy remote dawn   OS 7
gilded   78.   But gilded promise, yielded to us never   Ind 27
gilds   126.   And gilds the silver on the blotched arbor-seats
                         O-N 4
gimleted   62.   ping gimleted and neatly out of sight   Riv 23
gin   105.   In bootleg roadhouses where the gin fizz   QH 35
gin-daisies   151.   catharsis from gin-daisies as well as   APE 17
Gioconda   148.   When one isn't the real Gioconda   Loc 10
                  149.   For Eve, Gioconda and Dalila   Loc 32
girded   172.   Inexorable and girded with your praise   ABP 9
girder   45.   Down Wall, from girder into street noon leaks
                         TBB 21
girdle   6.   In the loose girdle of soft rain   MGLL 4
girdles   98.   And lifts her girdles from her, one by one   SC 4
girls   109.   girls all shaping up--it used to be   Tun 45
                  145.   With four tiny black-eyed girls around her
                         PA 34
girth   90.   As bright as frogs' eyes, giggling in the girth
                         CH 70
                  129.   That strives long and quiet to sever the girth
                         An 2
gist   64.   Strange bird-wit, like the elemental gist   Riv 37
give   54.   They give it back again. Soft sleeves of sound
                         HD 11
                   90.   New latitudes, unknotting, soon give place   CH 86
                  128.   Pile on the logs.... Give me your hands   Fr 5
                  150.   They will give three hurrahs   GWP 3
given   131.   But they are wrong.... Ere man was given sight
                         Ba 9
                  157.   You have given me the shell, Satan,--carbonic
                         amulet   OC 34
                  174.   Decisive grammar given unto queens   BNOK 9
giving   34.   The calyx of death's bounty giving back   AMT 6
gizzards   90.   Of steely gizzards--axle-bound, confined   CH 71
glacial   93.   Glacial sierras and the flight of ravens   CH 158
glacier   70.   Who squired the glacier woman down the sky   Dan 2
glad   100.   Least tearful and least glad (who knows her
                         smile?)   NWG 15
                  161.   --It is at times as though the eyes burned hard
                         and glad   IQ 12
glade   72.   Smoke swirling through the yellow chestnut glade
                         Dan 40
glance   104.   One's glance could cross the borders of three
                         states   QH 26
glare   10.   After the daily circuits of its glare   SM 8

glass	25.	As double as the hands that twist this glass Rec 2
	60.	Or splits a random smell of flowers through glass VW 31
	108.	Avoid the glass doors gyring at your right Tun 26
	112.	The blackness somewhere gouged glass on a sky Tun 128
	145.	Setting down a glass and saying PA 30
	150.	Noses pressed against the glass GWP 17
	173.	His eyes--/like crutches hurtled against glass MF 6
	188.	through the lofty, dusty glass-Cortez--Cortez-- his HR 11
glasses	82.	--green glasses, or bar lights made them CS 4
glaze	122.	Never came light through that honey-thick glaze Moth 20
glazed	182.	Leather, which the rimed white wind had glazed Et 28
gleam	79.	There's where the stubborn years gleam and atone Ind 55
	89.	Gleam from the great stones of each prison crypt CH 53
	102.	Where green figs gleam Va 13
	104.	Faces--loose panes crown the hill and gleam QH 21
	162.	From every petal gleam OS 2
	191.	Where all your gas lights--faces--sputum gleam Purg 3
gleaming	33.	The hands Erasmus dipped in gleaming tides F&H III 37
	48.	Here waves climb into dusk on gleaming mail AM 9
	51.	Hushed gleaming fields and pendant seething wheat AM 83
	76.	His gleaming name Ind 20
	83.	I saw the frontiers gleaming of his mind CS 37
	90.	The gleaming cantos of unvanquished space CH 76
	114.	Transparent meshes--fleckless the gleaming staves At 6
glee	25.	Reciting pain or glee, how can you bear Rec 4
	30.	Glee shifts from foot to foot F&H II 2
	90.	In coiled precision, bunched in mutual glee CH 72
glide	28.	The earth may glide diaphanous to death F&H I 39
	68.	And Pullman breakfasters glide glistening steel Riv 89
	91.	On fleeing balconies as thou dost glide CH 115
glimmer	91.	While Iliads glimmer through eyes raised in pride CH 91
	115.	Some trillion whispering hammers glimmer Tyre At 34

glimpse	88.	A periscope to glimpse what joys or pain CH 24
glint	90.	The bearings glint,--O murmurless and shined CH 73
glistening	51.	The glistening seignories of Ganges swim AM 68
	68.	And Pullman breakfasters glide glistening steel Riv 89
	76.	And glistening through the sluggard freshets came Ind 18
	115.	Slit and propelled by glistening fins of light At 26
glistenings	187.	their glistenings dwindle Ma 6
glitter	30.	Brazen hypnotics glitter here F&H II 1
glittered	141.	That glittered in and out among the wheels EpH 6
glittering	15.	Upon your glittering breasts NL 7
	22.	Sand troughed us in a glittering abyss Pass 33
	116.	Forever Deity's glittering Pledge, O Thou At 73
glitters	136.	Glitters on the edges of wet ferns Ps 3
gloom	133.	Bent wings, and Carmen with her flaunts through the gloom CDB 22
	140.	Silence and gentle gloom Int 4
glories	8.	Of glories proper to the time PU 16
glow	23.	--I am conscripted to their shadows' glow WM 8
	41.	Hushed willows anchored in its glow V-6 30
	69.	Poised wholly on its dream, a mustard glow Riv 140
	111.	With antennae toward worlds that glow and sink Tun 110
	116.	Of stars Thou art the stitch and stallion glow At 61
	128.	And the fire-wood glow is bright Fr 2
	130.	And warmer with a redder glow Ech 8
glowing	29.	One inconspicuous, glowing orb of praise F&H I 52
glozening	23.	Then glozening decanters that reflect the street WM 5
gnats	4.	Gnats toss in the shadow of a bottle BT 3
go	64.	Caboose-like they go ruminating through Riv 32
	68.	And hum Deep River with them while they go Riv 103
	95.	Not soon, nor suddenly,--no, never to let go CH 219
	105.	Me farther than scalped Yankees knew to go QH 52
	108.	and go Tun 12
	111.	Lets go.... Toward corners of the floor Tun 97
	130.	And disappears, as I should go Ech 6
	144.	I will go and pitch quoits with old men PA 22
	145.	"One month,--I go back rich PA 31
	177.	Go then, unto thy turning and thy blame Rep 5
goat	151.	for the one goat (unsqueezable APE 6
	161.	And did not take the goat path quivering to the right IQ 13
gobs	183.	New York with the gobs, Guantanamo, Norfolk Et 59

God		
	46.	And of the curveship lend a myth to God TBB 44
	76.	We found God lavish there in Colorado Ind 15
	98.	God--your namelessness. And the wash SC 22
	169.	Lord God, while summits crashing Hur 14
	182.	Good God! as though his sinking carcass there Et 32
	193.	The bell-rope that gathers God at dawn B Tow 1
god	114.	As though a god were issue of the strings At 8
	123.	Though a black god to him in a dizzying night Moth 34
goddess	40.	To the lounged goddess when she rose V-6 22
godless	39.	Too, into that godless cleft of sky V-5 16
God's	50.	Yet yield thy God's, thy Virgin's charity AM 48
Gods	137.	Or bury the Gods For 10
	143.	Nor the Gods that danced before you BE 27
gods	66.	The old gods of the rain lie wrapped in pools Riv 82
	74.	There, where the first and last gods keep thy tent Dan 80
goes	56.	The window goes blond slowly. Frostily clears HD 31
	56.	Turns in the waking west and goes to sleep HD 38
	152.	partitions in thee--goes In 13
going	62.	brother--all over--going west--young man Riv 2
	78.	Yes, Larry, now you're going to sea, remember Ind 46
	102.	Mary (what are you going to do Va 4
gold	8.	Still, having in mind gold hair PU 17
	25.	Wrenched gold of Nineveh;--yet leave the tower Rec 22
	33.	For golden, or the shadow of gold hair F&H III 44
	58.	Down gold arpeggios mile on mile unwinds VW 4
	76.	Back on the gold trail--then his lost bones stirred Ind 10
	79.	Where gold is true Ind 56
	94.	Gold autumn, captured, crowned the trembling hill CH 186
	125.	O Materna! to enrich thy gold head C 8
	126.	Now gold and purple scintillate O-N 5
	127.	Mercy, white milk, and honey, gold love Hi 7
	140.	O grey and gold amenity Int 3
	171.	O, steel and stone! But gold was, scarcity before KW 13
	171.	Where gold has not been sold and conscience tinned KW 16
golden	33.	For golden, or the shadow of gold hair F&H III 44
	76.	In golden syllables loosed from the clay Ind 19
	102.	Let down your golden hair Va 16

golden, cont.	111.	Back home to children and to golden hair Tun 105
	160.	tisms wrench the golden boughs. Leaves spatter dawn MT 7
Golden Gate	58.	Leaps from Far Rockaway to Golden Gate VW 2
	61.	Leaps from Far Rockaway to Golden Gate VW 42
gold-shod	33.	Three-winged and gold-shod prophecies of heaven F&H III 32
golf	105.	Of golf, by twos and threes in plaid plusfours QH 31
gone	61.	It forsook her at the doorway, it was gone VW 38
	102.	Gone seven--gone eleven Va 5
	123.	And his wings atom-withered,--gone,--left but a leap Moth 47
	162.	So eyes that mind thee fair and gone OS 5
	182.	Everything gone--or strewn in riddled grace Et 29
gongs	21.	In bronze gongs of my cheeks Pass 14
	54.	Gongs in white surplices, beshrouded wails HD 4
	109.	Into the slot. The gongs already rattle Tun 30
	111.	Burst suddenly in rain.... The gongs recur Tun 89
good	32.	Of wave or rock was good against one hour F&H III 24
	82.	I'm not much good at time any more keep CS 15
	160.	spiders yoked you first,--silking of shadows good under-/drawers for owls MT 5
	182.	Good God! as though his sinking carcass there Et 32
good-bye	76.	Waved Seminary Hill a gay good-bye Ind 14
	79.	Good-bye...Good-bye...oh, I shall always wait Ind 63
good-byes	10.	Still answering her faint good-byes SM 18
goose	33.	A goose, tobacco and cologne F&H III 31
gorge	16.	How much I would have bartered! the black gorge RR 12
gorgeous	122.	That their land is too gorgeous to free their eyes wide Moth 6
got	28.	The fare and transfer, yet got by that way F&H I 18
	61.	Have you got your "Times" VW 44
	82.	got to beating time..."A whaler once CS 17
	83.	in Panama--got tired of that CS 24
	181.	She almost--even then--got blown across lots Et 5
	182.	I beat the dazed mule toward the road. He got that far Et 48
gouged	112.	The blackness somewhere gouged glass on a sky Tun 128
grace	30.	With perfect grace and equanimity F&H II 19
	69.	The basalt surface drags a jungle grace Riv 129

grace, cont.   95. Vast engines outward veering with seraphic
                         grace   CH 207
                   145. As down she knelt for heaven's grace and boon
                         PA 44
                   152. immensity in gathered grace; the arms   In 3
                   158. Here where we finger moidores of spent grace
                         Mer 13
                   182. Everything gone--or strewn in riddled grace
                         Et 29
gracious   167. I watched the sun's most gracious anchorite
                         RP 4
gradually   25. And gradually white buildings answer day   Rec 16
graduate   27. Until the graduate opacities of evening   F&H I 13
grail   11. A grail of laughter of an empty ash can   Chap 21
                    20. Lift up in lilac-emerald breath the grail   LC 40
grain   122. At night like a grain of sand, futile and dried
                         Moth 24
grammar   174. Decisive grammar given unto queens   BNOK 9
grammarians   151. and other natural grammarians are ab-   APE 21
grandmother   6. Yet I would lead my grandmother by the hand
                         MGLL 23
granite   114. Up the index of night, granite and steel   At 5
grant   25. Built floor by floor on shafts of steel that
                         grant   Rec 19
                    50. Tomorrow's moon will grant us Saltes Bar   AM 53
granted   192. His fathers took for granted ages since--and so
                         he looms   SI 6
grantest   48. One ship of these thou grantest safe returning
                         AM 27
granting   3. The only worth all granting   Leg 9
grape-hung   126. Floods the grape-hung night   O-N 10
grasp   76. But you who drop the scythe to grasp the oar
                         Ind 11
grass   9. Beyond the grass and shadows at her feet   GA 12
                    72. I left my sleek boat nibbling margin grass
                         Dan 28
                    74. And winds across the llano grass resume   Dan 94
                    82. His eyes pressed through green grass   CS 3
                    93. The competent loam, the probable grass,--travail
                         CH 151
                    94. Set trumpets breathing in each clump and grass
                         tuft--'till   CH 185
                   104. Than grass and snow, and their own inner being
                         QII 5
                   117. Now pity steeps the grass and rainbows ring
                         At 94
                   182. Everything--and lick the grass, as black as
                         patent   Et 27
grasshopper   164. Moonmoth and grasshopper that flee our page
                         NA 1
grating   179. ing or extending a phallus through the grating,
                         --talking to   Len 5

Greek	144.	The Greek grins and fights with the Swede PA 15
Greeks	144.	The dark-skinned Greeks grin at each other PA 13
green	9.	She is prisoner of the tree and its green fingers GA 6
	10.	Beneath the green silk counterpane SM 10
	13.	She hears my step behind the green IS 11
	14.	--So, while sunlight splinters humid green Fern 7
	28.	Stippled with pink and green advertisements F&H I 26
	40.	Green borders under stranger skies V-6 4
	51.	The sea's green crying towers a-sway, Beyond AM 88
	70.	Disturbed and destined, into denser green Dan 10
	82.	His eyes pressed through green grass CS 3
	82.	--green glasses, or bar lights made them CS 4
	82.	so--/shine--/GREEN--/eyes CS 5
	83.	snarling stone--green--drums--drown CS 32
	84.	--scarfed of foam, their bellies veered green esplanades CS 68
	94.	With June the mountain laurel broke through green CH 177
	94.	Heard thunder's eloquence through green arcades CH 184
	94.	But knows it leastwise as death-strife?--O, something green CH 200
	102.	Where green figs gleam Va 13
	141.	Bunches of new green breaking a hard turf EpH 19
	159.	The green preëmption of the deep seaweed TCJ 8
	163.	And since, through these hot barricades of green Id 13
	167.	Green rustlings, more-than-regal charities RP 1
	191.	And I have no decision--is it green or brown Purg 15
greenery	129.	Of greenery.... Below the roots, a quickening shiver An 3
greensward	95.	Thou, Vedic Caesar, to the greensward knelt CH 204
greet	30.	Greet naively--yet intrepidly F&H II 15
greeted	150.	Pathetic yelps have sometimes greeted GWP 16
greeting	51.	Who sendest greeting by the corposant AM 69
	70.	Greeting they sped us, on the arrow's oath Dan 11
	72.	Know, Maquokeeta, greeting; know death's best Dan 47
	144.	Greeting the dawn PA 1
grenades	91.	Of rancorous grenades whose screaming petals carve us CH 97
grew	72.	A distant cloud, a thunder-bud--it grew Dan 41

guaranteed	62.	in the guaranteed corner--see Bert Williams what Riv 5
guard	17.	Lie guard upon the integers of life Par 6
	111.	Elbows and levers, guard and hissing door Tun 90
guerdon	46.	Thy guerdon...Accolade thou doest bestow TBB 26
guerilla	92.	In guerilla sleights, trapped in combustion gyr- CH 139
guest	40.	--Thy derelict and blinded guest V-6 12
	105.	As humbly as a guest who knows himself too late QH 60
guide	105.	But I must ask slain Iroquois to guide QH 51
	159.	The moon's best lover,--guide us by a sleight TCJ 10
guile	23.	Sharp to the windowpane guile drags a face WM 19
	140.	With jealous threat and guile Int 10
guillotines	158.	Gallows and guillotines to hail the sun Mer 9
guilty	31.	The siren of the springs of guilty song F&H II 31
guise	8.	That mingled in such exile guise PU 2
guitars	98.	Windswept guitars on lonely decks forever SC 11
gules	145.	And threw warm gules on Madeline's fair breast PA 43
gulf	16.	At gulf gates...There, beyond the dykes RR 21
	25.	Let the same nameless gulf beleaguer us Rec 17
	38.	Vastly now parting gulf on gulf of wings V-4 3
	69.	Meeting the Gulf, hosannas silently below Riv 143
	83.	the star floats burning in a gulf of tears CS 44
gulfs	115.	From gulfs unfolding, terrible of drums At 41
gulls	56.	The sun, released--aloft with cold gulls hither HD 34
gun-grey	58.	Macadam, gun-grey as the tunny's belt VW 1
	61.	Macadam, gun-grey as the tunny's belt VW 41
gunman	32.	religious gunman F&H III 6
	32.	We know, eternal gunman, our flesh remembers F&H III 19
guns	166.	Big guns again IV 1
	166.	Big guns again IV 8
	166.	Big guns again IV 15
gush	160.	ripe apple-lanterns gush history, recondite lightnings,/irised MT 12
gusted	72.	One white veil gusted from the very top Dan 32
gusting	181.	After it was over, though still gusting balefully Et 1
gymnast	192.	Sad heart, the gymnast of inertia, does not count SI 1
gypsies	88.	The songs that gypsies dealt us at Marseille CH 11
gypsy	134.	A gypsy wagon wiggles, striving straight CDB 26
gyrating	31.	Beneath gyrating awnings I have seen F&H II 28

hack-saws	168.	The needles and hack-saws of cactus bleed AP 9
hades	16.	Tyranny; they drew me into hades almost RR 8
	110.	The phonographs of hades in the brain Tun 58
	171.	To heaven or hades--to an equally frugal noon KW 8
hail	91.	Wounds that we wrap with theorems sharp as hail CH 98
	158.	Gallows and guillotines to hail the sun Mer 9
hailed	30.	While titters hailed the groans of death F&H II 27
	114.	From black embankments, moveless soundings hailed At 15
hails	30.	Through snarling hails of melody F&H II 10
	115.	Like hails, farewells--up planet-sequined heights At 33
hair	6.	It is all hung by an invisible white hair MGLL 14
	8.	Still, having in mind gold hair PU 17
	13.	Her furtive lace and misty hair IS 5
	14.	In crowns less grey--O merciless tidy hair Fern 10
	23.	Percussive sweat is spreading to his hair. Mallets WM 12
	33.	For golden, or the shadow of gold hair F&H III 44
	39.	In all the argosy of your bright hair I dreamed V-5 19
	41.	Which rainbows twine continual hair V-6 27
	56.	a forest shudders in your hair HD 30
	66.	And space, an eaglet's wing, laid on her hair Riv 80
	73.	Of lightning deltaed down your saber hair Dan 54
	99.	Rehearsed hair--docile, alas, from many arms SC 26
	102.	Let down your golden hair Va 16
	109.	This answer lives like verdigris, like hair Tun 47
	111.	Wop washerwoman, with the bandaged hair Tun 101
	111.	Back home to children and to golden hair Tun 105
	174.	Dear lady--the poet said--release your hair BNOK 2
	180.	Hair mocked by the sea, her lover Lib 5
hair's	70.	Your hair's keen crescent running, and the blue Dan 19
	74.	Her hair's warm sibilance. Her breasts are fanned Dan 95
half	25.	Borne cleft to you, and brother in the half Rec 8
	79.	I'm standing still, I'm old, I'm half of stone Ind 53

half, cont.   109. FOURTEENTH? it's half past six she said--if
                         Tun 52
                   178. And leave me half adream upon the main PB 4
halfbreed   78. Perhaps a halfbreed. On her slender back Ind 33
half-covered   54. Immemorially the window, the half-covered chair
                         HD 19
half-heard   50. Some inmost sob, half-heard, dissuades the abyss
                         AM 39
half-hour's   68. You have a half-hour's wait at Siskiyou Riv 92
half-riant   28. Half-riant before the jerky window frame
                         F&H I 23
halfway   181. Was halfway under water with fires Et 21
hall   61. Did not return with the kiss in the hall VW 40
                   133. With shimmering blue from the bowl in Circe's
                         hall CDB 7
halo   104. Through the rich halo that they do not trouble
                         QH 6
                   122. Their mother, the moon, marks a halo of light
                         Moth 10
halt   95. yes, Walt,/Afoot again, and onward without halt
                         CH 218
                   163. Above all reason lifting, halt serene   Id 15
halves   25. Twin shadowed halves: the breaking second
                         holds Rec 5
Hamlet's   186. Swears high in Hamlet's throat, and devils throng
                         Shak 10
hammers   115. Some trillion whispering hammers glimmer Tyre
                         At 34
                   183. Without ceremony, while hammers pattered in
                         town Et 52
hand   6. Yet I would lead my grandmother by the hand
                         MGLL 23
                    18. And the key, ready to hand--sifting Pos 3
                    21. A thief beneath, my stolen book in hand Pass 27
                    30. Splayed like cards from a loose hand F&H II 12
                    39. Knowing I cannot touch your hand and look
                         V-5 15
                    52. Te Deum laudamus/O Thou Hand of Fire AM 90
                    93. And this, thine other hand, upon my heart
                         CH 164
                    95. My hand/in yours,/Walt Whitman--/so CH 220
                   112. O Hand of Fire/gatherest Tun 137
                   124. These things I have:--a withered hand Moth 51
                   141. Deep hand that lay in his,--seemed beautiful
                         EpH 17
                   141. Were banished from him by that larger, quieter
                         hand EpH 21
                   142. I had never seen a hand before BE 14
                   142. And the hand was thick and heavily warted BE 15
                   163. One hand dealt out a kite string, a tin can
                         Id 9
                   164. And take the wing and scar it in the hand NA 6
                   170. --Truly no flower yet withers in your hand
                         TED 9

hand, cont.	186.	A hand moves on the page! Who shall again Shak 2
hands	9.	Drowning the fever of her hands in sunlight GA 10
	10.	That hands joined in the dark will answer SM 7
	17.	Involves the hands in purposeless repose Par 8
	25.	As double as the hands that twist this glass Rec 2
	28.	Those hands of yours that count the nights F&H I 25
	28.	The press of troubled hands, too alternate F&H I 42
	33.	The hands Erasmus dipped in gleaming tides F&H III 37
	33.	Blamed bleeding hands extend and thresh the height F&H III 46
	36.	All but the pieties of lovers' hands V-2 10
	37.	The sea lifts, also, reliquary hands V-3 8
	37.	Permit me voyage, love, into your hands V-3 19
	50.	Like pearls that whisper through the Doge's hands AM 45
	54.	While myriad snowy hands are clustering at the panes HD 25
	56.	your hands within my hands are deeds HD 26
	68.	As though you touched hands with some ancient clown Riv 101
	70.	And in the autumn drouth, whose burnished hands Dan 5
	82.	weakeyed watches sometimes snooze--" his bony hands CS 16
	95.	What heritage thou'st signalled to our hands CH 211
	100.	Each other--turquoise fakes on tinselled hands NWG 20
	110.	Your trembling hands that night through Baltimore Tun 80
	111.	O Genoese, do you bring mother eyes and hands Tun 104
	112.	Here at the waters' edge the hands drop memory Tun 132
	112.	Or shall the hands be drawn away, to die Tun 135
	128.	Pile on the logs.... Give me your hands Fr 5
	135.	My hands have not touched water since your hands CL 1
	141.	His own hands seemed to him EpH 13
	142.	I have heard hands praised for what they made BE 10
	142.	I have heard hands praised for line on line BE 11
	147.	She has drawn her hands away Per 5
	152.	to spread; the hands to yield their shells In 4
hang	39.	Already hang, shred ends from remembered stars V-5 7

hangars	91.	Wheeled swiftly, wings emerge from larval-silver hangars CH 99
hanging	115.	We left the haven hanging in the night At 49
	160.	gum took place. Up jug to musical, hanging jug just gay MT 4
happiness	189.	happiness which is your own from birth.["] HR 35
harbor	38.	The harbor shoulders to resign in mingling V-4 18
	40.	And harbor of the phoenix' breast V-6 10
	45.	And Thee, across the harbor, silver-paced TBB 13
	54.	Attend the darkling harbor, the pillowed bay HD 12
	112.	And this thy harbor, O my City, I have driven under Tun 129
	115.	Sheened harbor lanterns backward fled the keel At 50
	180.	They have not seen her in this harbor Lib 10
hard	39.	The bay estuaries fleck the hard sky limits V-5 4
	141.	Bunches of new green breaking a hard turf EpH 19
	161.	--It is at times as though the eyes burned hard and glad IQ 12
	168.	Thrust parching from a palm-bole hard by the cove AP 3
hare	4.	Heaven with the tortoise and the hare BT 6
harmonic	30.	Where, by strange harmonic laws F&H II 21
harmony	3.	Shall string some constant harmony Leg 21
harness	115.	Still wrapping harness to the swarming air At 38
harnessed	90.	Into the bulging bouillon, harnessed jelly of the stars CH 67
harp	46.	O harp and altar, of the fury fused TBB 29
Harry	145.	Harry and I, "the gentlemen",--seated around PA 28
harsh	50.	For here between two worlds, another, harsh AM 32
harvest	12.	Already fallen harvest Past 13
	170.	The harvest you descried and understand TED 10
	190.	The harvest laugh of bright Apollo Rel 4
harvesting	40.	Beyond siroccos harvesting V-6 17
harvests	116.	Revolving through their harvests in sweet torment At 72
hash	146.	And a hash of noises is slung up from the street PA 57
hast	91.	--Hast splintered space! CH 116
	92.	Thou sowest doom thou hast nor time nor chance CH 126
	92.	Thou hast there in thy wrist a Sanskrit charge CH 129
	93.	Hast kept of wounds, O Mourner, all that sum CH 169

hast, cont.	94.	But thou, <u>Panis Angelicus</u>, hast thou not seen CH 198
hasten	36.	And hasten while her penniless rich palms V-2 17
	36.	Hasten, while they are true,--sleep, death, desire V-2 19
hastened	45.	Never disclosed, but hastened to again TBB 11
hat	108.	Then let you reach your hat Tun 11
hate	177.	That hate is but the vengeance of a long caress Rep 9
	186.	Sheets that mock lust and thorns that scribble hate Shak 6
hatred	93.	Of love and hatred, birth,--surcease of nations CH 146
Hatteras	93.	By Hatteras bunched the beached heap of high bravery CH 144
haunt	138.	Haunt the blank stage with lingering alarms Port 7
Havana	181.	To Havana on the first boat through. They groaned Et 13
	181.	That Havana, not to mention poor Batabanó Et 20
haven	115.	We left the haven hanging in the night At 49
havens	93.	Hermetically past condor zones, through zenith havens CH 159
hawk's	105.	So, must we from the hawk's far stemming view QH 57
hazards	132.	She hazards jet; wears tiger-lilies MC 5
	186.	Engrave such hazards as thy might controls Shak 3
haze	78.	Until she saw me--when their violet haze Ind 39
	122.	Countless rubies and tapers in the oasis' blue haze Moth 16
hazes	183.	The morrow's dawn was dense with carrion hazes Et 50
he	34.	The dice of drowned men's bones he saw bequeath AMT 2
	34.	An embassy. Their numbers as he watched AMT 3
	60.	<u>that he</u>, <u>Van Winkle</u>, <u>was not here</u> VW 27
	64.	He trod the fire down pensively and grinned Riv 50
	84.	--he lunged up Bowery way while the dawn CS 50
	123.	But once though, he learned of that span of his wings Moth 25
	123.	To the desert,--back,--down,--still lonely he fell Moth 40
	125.	And he tended with far truths he would form C 6
	163.	Once when he shouted, stretched in ghastly shape Id 6
	163.	Passed him again...He was alone, agape Id 8
	192.	He does not know the new hum in the sky SI 9

head   7. In that ripe nude with head/reared SMA 5
                17. Your head, unrocking to a pulse, already
                     Par 14
                24. Beyond the wall, whose severed head floats by
                     WM 46
                39. Draw in your head, alone and too tall here
                     V-5 22
                39. Draw in your head and sleep the long way home
                     V-5 25
                95. And read thee by the aureole 'round thy head
                     CH 216
               110. Whose head is swinging from the swollen strap
                     Tun 66
               125. O Materna! to enrich thy gold head C 8
               163. With squint lanterns in his head, and it's
                     likely Id 3
               178. For who shall lift head up to funnel smoke PB 5
headland   91. To hedge the seaboard, wrap the headland, ride
                     CH 89
headlight   62. a headlight rushing with the sound--can you
                     Riv 11
heads   82. and rum was Plato in our heads CS 12
               174. Or let us bump heads in some lowly shed BNOK 4
heady   151. HEADY!--those aromatic LEMONS APE 11
healed   194. What I hold healed, original now, and pure
                     B Tow 32
heap   23. What is it in this heap the serpent pries WM 14
                50. Bewilderment and mutiny heap whelming AM 34
                60. That flittered from under the ash heap day VW 22
                93. By Hatteras bunched the beached heap of high
                     bravery CH 144
               170. Else tears heap all within one clay-cold hill
                     TED 14
heaped   158. Has followed in its name, has heaped its grave
                     Mer 7
               181. Where a frantic peacock rummaged amid heaped
                     cans Et 17
heaping   193. Oval encyclicals in canyons heaping B Tow 13
heaps   69. And flows within itself, heaps itself free
                     Riv 136
hear   22. What fountains did I hear? what icy speeches
                     Pass 36
                35. And could they hear me I would tell them V-1 9
                51. Elohim, still I hear thy sounding heel AM 80
                68. You will not hear it as the sea; even stone
                     Riv 116
                79. Perhaps I'll hear the mare's hoofs to the ford
                     Ind 58
                92. Toward thee, O Corsair of the typhoon,--pilot,
                     hear CH 123
                95. Recorders ages hence, yes, they shall hear
                     CH 214

hear, cont.	125.	But you who hear the lamp whisper thru night C 12
	131.	A dreamer might see these, and wake to hear Ba 4
	170.	Being, of all, least sought for: Emily, hear TED 5
	180.	The virgin. They laugh to hear Lib 3
	194.	And through whose pulse I hear, counting the strokes B Tow 29
heard	11.	Have heard a kitten in the wilderness Chap 23
	16.	I heard wind flaking sapphire, like this summer RR 22
	21.	I heard the sea Pass 2
	26.	In alternating bells have you not heard Rec 25
	64.	Some Sunny Day. I heard a road-gang chanting so Riv 40
	66.	Trains sounding the long blizzards out--I heard Riv 74
	72.	Within,--I heard it; 'til its rhythm drew Dan 43
	73.	I heard the hush of lava wrestling your arms Dan 69
	76.	Knew not, nor heard Ind 12
	89.	Near Paumanok--your lone patrol--and heard the wraith CH 46
	94.	Heard thunder's eloquence through green arcades CH 184
	105.	Who saw the Friends there ever heard before QH 40
	128.	But hold me...somewhere I heard demands Fr 7
	129.	Hush! these things were all heard before dawn An 9
	142.	I have heard hands praised for what they made BE 10
	142.	I have heard hands praised for line on line BE 11
	163.	A Dios gracias, grac--I've heard his song Id 14
	193.	Have you not heard, have you not seen that corps B Tow 5
hearing	48.	Nigh surged me witless.... Hearing the surf near AM 22
	90.	Our hearing momentwise; but fast in whirling armatures CH 69
	147.	Hearing the wind Per 2
hearing's	90.	Of dynamos, where hearing's leash is strummed CH 64
hears	13.	She hears my step behind the green IS 11
	89.	Man hears himself an engine in a cloud CH 42
heart	11.	We can evade you, and all else but the heart Chap 17
	11.	What blame to us if the heart live on Chap 18
	18.	Whose heart is fire shall come,--the white wind rase Pos 28

heart, cont.	21.	And hug, chimney-sooted heart of man Pass 20
	25.	The plummet heart, like Absalom, no stream Rec 20
	33.	The lavish heart shall always have to leaven F&H III 33
	48.	Into the Queen's great heart that doubtful day AM 4
	50.	Laughter, and shadow cuts sleep from the heart AM 35
	52.	And kingdoms/naked in the/trembling heart AM 89
	93.	And this, thine other hand, upon my heart CH 164
	106.	His news already told? Yes, while the heart is wrung QH 61
	106.	Yes, whip-poor-will, unhusks the heart of fright QH 68
	106.	Breaks us and saves, yes, breaks the heart, yet yields QH 69
	108.	Someday by heart you'll learn each famous sight Tun 6
	116.	Inventions that cobblestone the heart At 82
	125.	About the empty heart of night C 2
	127.	Up the chasm-walls of my bleeding heart Hi 1
	127.	Of the hive of the world that is my heart Hi 4
	133.	And dies on fire's birth in each man's heart CDB 10
	133.	The pulse is in the ears, the heart is higher CDB 15
	135.	A dove's wings clung about my heart last night CL 6
	147.	As now her heart and mind Per 12
	149.	And my heart fishes in troubled water Loc 31
	169.	Lord, Lord, Thy swifting heart Hur 2
	192.	Sad heart, the gymnast of inertia, does not count SI 1
	194.	The matrix of the heart, lift down the eye B Tow 37
hearths	88.	Hearths, there to eat an apple and recall CH 10
heart's	72.	--Siphoned the black pool from the heart's hot root Dan 44
	185.	Yet seldom was there faith in the heart's right kindness Post 13
heat	10.	Not yet is there that heat and sober SM 5
	123.	The heat led the moth up in octopus arms Moth 38
heave	84.	that bloomed in the spring--Heave, weave CS 56
heaven	4.	Heaven with the tortoise and the hare BT 6
	33.	Three-winged and gold-shod prophecies of heaven F&H III 32
	46.	And obscure as that heaven of the Jews TBB 25
	73.	Flame cataracts of heaven in seething swarms Dan 71

heaven, cont.	167.	As though it soared suchwise through heaven too RP 16
	169.	Sky-seethe, dense heaven dashing Hur 16
	171.	To heaven or hades--to an equally frugal noon KW 8
	173.	On every purchaser/(of heaven perhaps) MF 5
	194.	(Not stone can jacket heaven)--but slip B Tow 34
heaven's	51.	White toil of heaven's cordons, mustering AM 81
	68.	I could believe he joked at heaven's gate Riv 110
	91.	Hell's belt spring wider into heaven's plumed side CH 92
	115.	Of heaven's meditation, yoking wave At 54
	145.	As down she knelt for heaven's grace and boon PA 44
heavens	98.	Of lower heavens,--/vaporous scars SC 6
	152.	that heavens climb to measure, thus In 10
heavenward	168.	Inverted octopus with heavenward arms AP 2
heavily	142.	And the hand was thick and heavily warted BE 15
he'd	163.	Its course, though he'd clamped midnight to noon sky Id 12
hedge	91.	To hedge the seaboard, wrap the headland, ride CH 89
heed	189.	not heed the negative,--so might go on to un- deserved HR 31
heel	51.	Elohim, still I hear thy sounding heel AM 80
	94.	And it was thou who on the boldest heel CH 194
height	33.	Blamed bleeding hands extend and thresh the height F&H III 46
	91.	This tournament of space, the threshed and chiselled height CH 95
	92.	But first, here at this height receive CH 132
	104.	Portholes the ceilings stack their stoic height QH 19
	167.	Unshackled, casual of its azured height RP 15
heights	91.	O bright circumferences, heights employed to fly CH 93
	91.	Bristle the heights above a screeching gale to hover CH 105
	93.	But who has held the heights more sure than thou CH 147
	115.	Like hails, farewells--up planet-sequined heights At 33
hoir	31.	That we are heir to: she is still so young F&H II 34
held	78.	I held you up--I suddenly the bolder Ind 41
	93.	But who has held the heights more sure than thou CH 147
	141.	Consented,--and held out EpH 3
	168.	The lizard's throat, held bloated for a fly AP 7
	182.	Were death predestined! You held your nose already Et 33

Helen	28.	To you who turned away once, Helen, knowing F&H I 41
Helen's	33.	That lowers down the arc of Helen's brow F&H III 29
	180.	Not even Helen's fame Lib 7
helix	91.	With razor sheen they zoom each rapid helix CH 108
hell	98.	The mind is churned to spittle, whispering hell SC 17
	123.	As his blindness before had frozen in Hell Moth 46
	158.	Though why they bide here, only hell that's sacked Mer 2
	165.	"Hell! out there among the barracudas BSEW 5
	193.	From pit to crucifix, feet chill on steps from hell B Tow 4
hell's	91.	Hell's belt springs wider into heaven's plumed side CH 92
	108.	And watch the curtain lift in hell's despite Tun 7
hells	84.	swinging summer entrances to cooler hells CS 48
helm	114.	The loft of vision, palladium helm of stars At 24
	116.	As love strikes clear direction for the helm At 64
hence	89.	"--Recorders ages hence"--ah, syllables of faith CH 43
	95.	Recorders ages hence, yes, they shall hear CH 214
henceforth	10.	Henceforth her memory is more SM 22
hens	181.	And Cuban doctors, troopers, trucks, loose hens Et 9
her	7.	Into a realm of swords, her purple shadow SMA 6
	9.	The apple on its bough is her desire GA 1
	10.	Henceforth her memory is more SM 22
	13.	Her parasol, a pale balloon IS 3
	14.	The lights that travel on her spectacles Fern 1
	23.	Her eyes, unmake an instant of the world WM 13
	23.	And as the alcove of her jealousy recedes WM 20
	31.	Let us take her on the incandescent wax F&H II 32
	36.	Her undinal vast belly moonward bends V-2 4
	36.	As her demeanors motion well or ill V-2 9
	36.	In these poinsettia meadows of her tides V-2 13
	36.	Complete the dark confessions her veins spell V-2 15
	36.	Mark how her turning shoulders wind the hours V-2 16
	36.	And hasten while her penniless rich palms V-2 17
	66.	They lurk across her, knowing her yonder breast Riv 67

her, cont.	74.	Her speechless dream of snow, and stirred again Dan 90
	100.	A caught slide shows her sandstone grey between NWG 16
	100.	We flee her spasm through a fleshless door NWG 24
	139.	Rounds off my memory of her Lege 2
	147.	She has drawn her hands away Per 5
	147.	As now her heart and mind Per 12
	180.	How I endow her, standing Lib 4
	194.	Unseals her earth, and lifts love in its shower B Tow 40
herb	50.	An herb, a stray branch among salty teeth AM 51
here	50.	For here between two worlds, another, harsh AM 32
	50.	This third, of water, tests the word; lo, here AM 33
	60.	that he, Van Winkle, was not here VW 27
	112.	And to be.... Here by the River that is East Tun 131
	112.	Here at the waters' edge the hands drop memory Tun 132
	156.	And anagrammatize your name)--No, nothing here OC 5
	191.	So ring the church bells here in Mexico Purg 18
	191.	(They ring too obdurately here to need my call Purg 19
heritage	95.	What heritage thou'st signalled to our hands CH 211
hermetically	93.	Hermetically past condor zones, through zenith havens CH 159
hero	5.	And where was finally borne a chosen hero EC 14
herself	9.	And so she comes to dream herself the tree GA 7
	132.	And bolts herself within a jewelled belt MC 6
Hesperus	89.	Left Hesperus mirrored in the lucid pool CH 32
hesting	115.	And you, aloft there--Jason! hesting Shout At 37
hiatus	28.	Weeps in inventive dust for the hiatus F&H I 37
hid	70.	And bridal flanks and eyes hid tawny pride Dan 16
	74.	Thy freedom is her largesse, Prince, and hid Dan 87
	122.	She will flush their hid wings in the evening to blaze Moth 15
hidden	18.	Hidden,--O undirected as the sky Pos 7
	21.	And wakens alleys with a hidden cough Pass 10
	51.	And true appointment from the hidden shoal AM 76
hideous	111.	Whose hideous laughter is a bellows mirth Tun 107
hieroglyph	34.	A scattered chapter, livid hieroglyph AMT 7

hieroglyph, cont. 174. This hieroglyph is no dumb, deaf mistake BNOK 13
high   34. No farther tides...High in the azure steeps
                        AMT 14
                   45. Shedding white rings of tumult, building high
                        TBB 3
                   64. High in a cloud of merriment, recalled Riv 43
                   74. High unto Labrador the sun strikes free Dan 89
                   93. By Hatteras bunched the beached heap of high
                        bravery CH 144
                   98. High, cool,/wide from the slowly smouldering
                        fire SC 5
                  102. It's high carillon Va 9
                  102. O Mary, leaning from the high wheat tower Va 15
                  102. High in the noon of May Va 17
                  104. High from the central cupola, they say QH 25
                  106. While high from dim elm-chancels hung with dew
                        QH 66
                  129. Then high cries from great chasms of chaos
                        outdrawn An 8
                  142. Walk high on the bridge of Estador BE 1
                  142. High on the bridge of Estador BE 16
                  144. Akron, "high place" PA 10
                  165. "By just in time, and lifts 'em high and dry
                        BSEW 9
                  179. a kite high in the afternoon, or in the twi-
                        light scanning Len 6
                  181. And a funnel high and dry up near the park
                        Et 16
                  182. Long tropic roots high in the air, like lace
                        Et 30
                  186. Swears high in Hamlet's throat, and devils
                        throng Shak 10
                  191. And are these stars--the high plateau--the
                        scents Purg 5
                  193. The impasse high with choir. Banked voices
                        slain B Tow 14
higher   133. The pulse is in the ears, the heart is higher
                        CDB 15
highest   25. The highest tower,--let her ribs palisade
                        Rec 21
highsteppers   105. A welcome to highsteppers that no mouse QH 39
                  165. Anyone but these native high-steppers BSEW 12
hill   8. The slant moon on the slanting hill PU 9
                   19. Are trillion on the hill LC 13
                   32. Who hurried the hill breezes, spouting malice
                        F&H III 14
                   48. The first palm chevron the first lighted hill
                        AM 24
                   56. As though to join us at some distant hill HD 37
                   68. Straddles the hill, a dance of wheel on wheel
                        Riv 91
                   73. Flickering, sprint up the hill groins like a
                        tide Dan 68

hill, cont.	94.	O, early following thee, I searched the hill CH 175
	94.	Gold autumn, captured, crowned the trembling hill CH 186
	104.	Faces--loose panes crown the hill and gleam QH 21
	130.	Over the hill a last cloud dips Ech 5
	143.	The slant moon with the slanting hill BE 24
	170.	Else tears heap all within one clay-cold hill TED 14
hills	16.	And all the singular nestings in the hills RR 13
	21.	In sapphire arenas of the hills Pass 3
	66.	From pole to pole across the hills, the states Riv 63
	89.	Across the hills where second timber strays CH 56
	144.	Rumbling over the hills PA 9
	144.	A bunch of smoke-ridden hills PA 11
	144.	Among rolling Ohio hills PA 12
	147.	The hills lie curved and blent Per 11
him	45.	The seagull's wings shall dip and pivot him TBB 2
	84.	Outside a wharf truck nearly ran him down CS 49
	122.	They had scorned him, so humbly low, bound there and tied Moth 23
	123.	Though a black god to him in a dizzying night Moth 34
	141.	His own hands seemed to him EpH 13
	159.	But do not claim a friend like him again TCJ 19
	163.	Passed him again...He was alone, agape Id 8
	163.	That kite aloft--you should have watched him scan Id 11
	188.	him once before to death's beyond and back again HR 23
	192.	--Their shadows even--now can't carry him SI 8
himself	3.	Spends out himself again Leg 13
	89.	Seeing himself an atom in a shroud CH 41
	89.	Man hears himself an engine in a cloud CH 42
	105.	As humbly as a guest who knows himself too late QH 60
	157.	Let not the pilgrim see himself again OC 27
hips	100.	Pearls whip her hips, a drench of whirling strands NWG 18
his	4.	Fox brush and sow ear top his grave BT 7
	8.	His thoughts, delivered to me PU 5
	23.	Percussive sweat is spreading to his hair. Mallets WM 12
	23.	While August meadows somewhere clasp his brow WM 23
	28.	Imminent in his dream, none better knows F&H I 29
	45.	How many dawns, chill from his rippling rest TBB 1

his, cont.	64.	One said, excising a last burr from his vest Riv 47
	76.	His gleaming name Ind 20
	122.	And had not his pinions with signs mystical Moth 21
	123.	But once though, he learned of that span of his wings Moth 25
	123.	And he ventured the desert,--his wings took the climb Moth 28
	125.	And vented his long mellowed wines C 3
	141.	As his taut, spare fingers wound the gauze EpH 11
	163.	With squint lanterns in his head, and it's likely Id 3
	163.	Fumbling his sex. That's why those children laughed Id 4
	163.	In such infernal circles round his door Id 5
	163.	A Dios gracias, grac--I've heard his song Id 14
	163.	My trespass vision shrinks to face his wrong Id 16
	166.	Peace from his Mystery IV 12
	186.	--And fail, both! Yet thine Ariel holds his song Shak 12
	192.	The warp is in the woof--and his keen vision SI 3
	192.	Spells what his tongue has had--and only that SI 4
hissing	111.	Elbows and levers, guard and hissing door Tun 90
historians	5.	Bowls and cups fill historians with adorations EC 10
history	69.	Tortured with history, its one will-flow Riv 141
	105.	What cunning neighbors history has in fine QH 41
	114.	Their labyrinthine mouths of history At 11
	116.	Thy pardon for this history, whitest Flower At 84
	160.	ripe apple-lanterns gush history, recondite lightnings, irised MT 12
hitch	68.	Hitch up your pants and crunch another quid Riv 106
	145.	And hitch yourself up to your book PA 41
hitching	111.	Demented, for a hitching second, humps; then Tun 96
hither	56.	The sun, released--aloft with cold gulls hither HD 34
hive	127.	Of the hive of the world that is my heart Hi 4
hived	193.	The stars are caught and hived in the sun's ray B Tow 8

hiving	108.	Be minimum, then, to swim the hiving swarms Tun 24
hobo-trekkers	64.	Hobo-trekkers that forever search Riv 55
hold	16.	And willows could not hold more stady sound RR 23
	18.	I hold it up against a disk of light Pos 20
	28.	With steel and soil to hold you endlessly F&H I 43
	61.	Keep hold of that nickel for car-change, Rip VW 43
	79.	Oh, hold me in those eyes' engaging blue Ind 54
	116.	Now while thy petals spend the suns about us, hold At 86
	116.	Atlantis,--hold thy floating singer late At 88
	128.	But hold me...somewhere I heard demands Fr 7
	159.	We hold in vision only, asking trace TCJ 2
	190.	Will hold it--wear the keepsake, dear, of time Rel 15
	193.	But not for long to hold each desperate choice B Tow 20
	194.	No answer (could blood hold such a lofty tower B Tow 26
	194.	What I hold healed, original now, and pure B Tow 32
holding	9.	Holding her to the sky and its quick blue GA 9
	66.	Holding to childhood like some termless play Riv 58
holds	25.	Twin shadowed halves: the breaking second holds Rec 5
	41.	The imaged Word, it is, that holds V-6 29
	70.	He holds the twilight's dim, perpetual throne Dan 8
	105.	Who holds the lease on time and on disgrace QH 46
	167.	Uneaten of the earth or aught earth holds RP 6
	186.	--And fail, both! Yet thine Ariel holds his song Shak 12
hollowed	17.	Hollowed by air, posts a white paraphrase Par 15
Hollywood's	105.	Bubbles in time to Hollywood's new love-nest pageant QH 36
holocaust	51.	Subscribest holocaust of ships, O Thou AM 66
Holofernes'	24.	Stepping over Holofernes' shins WM 45
holy	51.	In holy rings all sails charged to the far AM 82
	164.	Struck free and holy in one Name always NA 12
Holyghost	62.	SCIENCE--COMMERCE and the HOLYGHOST Riv 13
home	39.	Draw in your head and sleep the long way home V-5 25
	62.	RADIO ROARS IN EVERY HOME WE HAVE THE NORTHPOLE Riv 14
	84.	I started walking home across the Bridge CS 53
	88.	The ancient names--return home to our own CH 9

host	128.	The host, he says that all is well Fr 1
	145.	A table of raisin-jack and wine, our host PA 29
	156.	Until it meets the blue's comedian host OC 26
hostelry	104.	Hostelry--floor by floor to cinquefoil dormer QH 18
hot	72.	--Siphoned the black pool from the heart's hot root Dan 44
	163.	I hurried by. But back from the hot shore Id 7
	163.	And since, through these hot barricades of green Id 13
	165.	--Yes, patent-leather shoes hot enough to fry BSEW 11
	167.	Of sweat the jungle presses with hot love RP 10
	178.	--The hot fickle wind, the breath of males PB 11
hotel	145.	Pull down the hotel counterpane PA 40
hour	18.	Accumulate such moments to an hour Pos 10
	32.	Of wave or rock was good against one hour F&H III 24
	37.	Wide from your side, whereto this hour V-3 7
	38.	Madly meeting logically in this hour V-4 10
	58.	--It is the same hour though a later day VW 6
	130.	Of storm or strain an hour ago Ech 4
	140.	Wide from the world, a stolen hour Int 5
hourless	29.	That beat, continuous, to hourless days F&H I 51
hours	70.	Drifted how many hours I never knew Dan 23
	26.	All hours clapped dense into a single stride Rec 26
	36.	Mark how her turning shoulders wind the hours V-2 16
	38.	Whose counted smile of hours and days, suppose V-4 1
	58.	And Rip forgot the office hours,/and he forgot the pay VW 14
	85.	Buntlines tusseling (91 days, 20 hours and anchored!)/Rainbow, Leander CS 73
	105.	Here three hours from the semaphores, the Czars QH 30
	181.	For some hours since--all wireless down Et 22
	191.	And what hours they forget to chime I'll know Purg 20
	192.	Hours, days--and scarcely sun and moon SI 2
house	90.	Under the looming stacks of the gigantic power house CH 61
	137.	Or an old house in a forest,--or a child For 7
	181.	And left the house, or what was left of it Et 3
	182.	Back at the erstwhile house Et 24

houses	32.	On rifts of torn and empty houses F&H III 16
	191.	Here quakes of earth make houses fall Purg 11
hover	91.	Bristle the heights above a screeching gale to hover CH 105
	93.	O Walt!--Ascensions of thee hover in me now CH 148
how	45.	How many dawns, chill from his rippling rest TBB 1
	46.	(How could mere toil align thy choiring strings TBB 30
	95.	And see! the rainbow's arch--how shimmeringly stands CH 212
	142.	How can you tell where beauty's to be found BE 9
	151.	"how are my bowels today?" and APE 3
	192.	How more?--but the lash, lost vantage--and the prison SI 5
howl	54.	Or a drunken stevedore's howl and thud below HD 8
howling	182.	Out of the bamboo brake through howling, sheeted light Et 40
howsoever	78.	But we,--too late, too early, howsoever Ind 25
huddled	78.	The long trail back! I huddled in the shade Ind 29
huddling	98.	Climbed by aslant and huddling aromatically SC 19
hue	133.	Their brown eyes blacken, and the blue drop hue CDB 8
hug	21.	And hug, chimney-sooted heart of man Pass 20
huge	157.	For slow evisceration bound like those huge terrapin OC 28
hugged	15.	Hugged by plaster-grey arches of sky NL 2
	124.	My eyes have hugged beauty and winged life's brief spell Moth 50
hum	68.	And hum Deep River with them while they go Riv 103
	123.	And the torrid hum of great wings was his song Moth 41
	192.	He does not know the new hum in the sky SI 9
human	158.	--This Cross, agleam still with a human Face Mer 15
	186.	Are lifted from torn flesh with human rue Shak 7
humanity	127.	Humanity pecks, claws, sobs and climbs Hi 2
humble	188.	my thoughts, my humble, fond remembrances of the HR 4
humbly	105.	As humbly as a guest who knows himself too late QH 60
	122.	They had scorned him, so humbly low, bound there and tied Moth 23
humid	14.	So, while fresh sunlight splinters humid green Fern 7

hummed	90.	New verities, new inklings in the velvet hummed CH 63
humming	114.	With silver terraces the humming spars At 23
humps	111.	Demented, for a hitching second, humps; then Tun 96
humpty-dumpty	66.	Blind fists of nothing, humpty-dumpty clods Riv 61
hung	92.	Hung low...until a conch of thunder answers CH 120
	106.	While high from dim elm-chancels hung with dew QH 66
hunger	170.	Yet fed your hunger like an endless task TED 2
hungry	62.	three men, still hungry on the tracks, ploddingly Riv 21
	187.	willows, a little hungry Ma 11
hunted	124.	I have hunted long years for a spark in the sand Moth 49
hurdle	91.	Lay siege and hurdle Cirrus down the skies CH 111
hurdy-gurdy	58.	Listen! the miles a hurdy-gurdy grinds VW 3
hurled	193.	An instant in the wind (I know not whither hurled) B Tow 19
hurrahs	150.	They will give three hurrahs GWP 3
hurricane	157.	Slagged of the hurricane--I, cast within its flow OC 32
	168.	Its apotheosis, at last--the hurricane AP 16
	184.	Have kissed, caressed the model of the hurricane Emp 2
hurricanes	50.	And later hurricanes may claim more pawn AM 31
hurried	32.	Who hurried the hill breezes, spouting malice F&H III 14
	58.	Times earlier, when you hurried off to school VW 5
	163.	I hurried by. But back from the hot shore Id 7
hurriedly	173.	This April morning offers/hurriedly MF 3
hurries	110.	The platform hurries along to a dead stop Tun 84
hurry	61.	And hurry along, Van Winkle--it's getting late VW 45
hurtled	173.	His eyes--/like crutches hurtled against glass MF 6
hurtling	91.	Each plane a hurtling javelin of winged ordnance CH 104
hush	73.	I heard the hush of lava wrestling your arms Dan 69
	129.	Hush! these things were all heard before dawn An 9
hushed	41.	Hushed willows anchored in its glow V-6 30
	51.	Hushed gleaming fields and pendant seething wheat AM 83
	68.	Is not more hushed by gravity...But slow Riv 117
	88.	While rises in the west the coastwise range, slowly the hushed land CH 3

hyacinths	173.	By the subway news-stand knows/how hyacinths MF 2
hypnotics	30.	Brazen hypnotics glitter here F&H II 1
hypnotisms	160.	First-plucked before and since the Flood, old hypno-/tisms wrench the golden boughs. Leaves spatter dawn MT 6-7
hypogeum	32.	Repeated play of fire--no hypogeum F&H III 23

I, cont.

30. O, I have known metallic paradises F&H II 24
31. Beneath gyrating awnings I have seen F&H II 28
35. And could they hear me I would tell them V-1 9
37. While ribboned water lanes I wind V-3 5
38. I know as spectrum of the sea and pledge V-4 2
38. Whose circles bridge, I know, (from palms to the
     severe V-4 4
38. Bright staves of flowers and quills to-day as I
     V-4 15
39. Knowing I cannot touch your hand and look V-5 15
39. In all the argosy of your bright hair I dreamed
     V-5 19
39. Your breath sealed by the ghosts I do not know
     V-5 24
40. I cannot claim: let thy waves rear V-6 14
45. I think of cinemas, panoramic sleights TBB 9
46. Under thy shadow by the piers I waited TBB 37
48. The word I bring, O you who reined my suit AM 3
48. For I have seen now what no perjured breath
     AM 5
48. And greed adjourned,--I bring you back Cathay
     AM 8
48. I thought of Genoa; and this truth, now proved
     AM 17
48. I, wonder-breathing, kept the watch,--saw AM 23
51. Elohim, still I hear thy sounding heel AM 80
60. And once only, as I recall VW 36
61. Before I had left the window. It VW 39
64. Some Sunny Day. I heard a road-gang chanting
     so Riv 40
64. Behind/My father's cannery works I used to see
     Riv 52
66. --As I have trod the rumorous midnights, too
     Riv 70
66. Trains sounding the long blizzards out--I heard
     Riv 74
66. Wail into distances I knew were hers Riv 75
66. --Dead echoes! But I knew her body there Riv 78
68. I could believe he joked at heaven's gate
     Riv 110
70. I left the village for dogwood. By the canoe
     Dan 17
70. Tugging below the mill-race, I could see Dan 18
70. I learned to catch the trout's moon whisper; I
     Dan 22
70. Drifted how many hours I never knew Dan 23
72. I took the portage climb, then chose Dan 29
72. A further valley-shed; I could not stop Dan 30
72. O Appalachian Spring! I gained the ledge Dan 33
72. Over how many bluffs, tarns, streams I sped
     Dan 37
72. Within,--I heard it; 'til its rhythm drew Dan 43

I, cont.

imploring	3.	Imploring flame. And tremorous Leg 6
imponderable	88.	Imponderable the dinosaur/sinks slow CH 1
imprisoned	178.	Imprisoned never, no[,] not soot &[?] steam PB 12
impromptu	149.	That seem too much impromptu Loc 24
improved	21.	I was promised an improved infancy Pass 4
impulse	93.	Not less than thou in pure impulse inbred CH 153
inaccessible	72.	Steep, inaccessible smile that eastward bends Dan 34
inaudible	19.	Inaudible whistle, tunneling LC 22
inbred	93.	Not less than thou in pure impulse inbred CH 153
Inca	166.	Imperator Inca IV 17
incandescent	31.	Let us take her on the incandescent wax F&H II 32
incantations	4.	And mingling incantations on the air BT 8
incarnate	38.	In signature of the incarnate word V-4 17
inception	116.	To wrapt inception and beatitude At 75
incessant	188.	clamour of incessant shutters, trundle doors, and the HR 6
incessantly	37.	Light wrestling there incessantly with light V-3 12
inch	60.	Some sunning inch of unsuspecting fibre VW 24
inchling	115.	Of inchling aeons silence rivets Troy At 36
incision	122.	On their own small oasis, ray-cut, an incision Moth 11
incites	98.	Incites a yell. Slid on that backward vision SC 16
inclusive	18.	The pure possession, the inclusive cloud Pos 27
incognizable	51.	Inquisitor! incognizable Word AM 61
inconspicuous	29.	One inconspicuous, glowing orb of praise F&H I 52
incorrigibly	70.	Now lie incorrigibly what years between Dan 12
incunabula	31.	The incunabula of the divine grotesque F&H II 29
indeed	150.	Indeed, old memories come back to life GWP 15
indelible	84.	clipper dreams indelible and ranging CS 64
independent	7.	Spontaneities that form their independent orbits SMA 10
index	11.	That slowly chafes its puckered index toward us Chap 11
	114.	Up the index of night, granite and steel At 5
India	174.	It knows its way through India--tropic shake BNOK 14
india	151.	to india, o ye faithful APE 24
Indian	48.	O where our Indian emperies lie revealed AM 15
	161.	In Indian baths. At Cuban dusk the eyes IQ 9
Indiana	64.	Ohio, Indiana--blind baggage Riv 33
	79.	Come back to Indiana--not too late Ind 61
Indian's	78.	Her eyes, strange for an Indian's, were not black Ind 35
Indian-summer-sun	126.	Indian-summer-sun O-N 1

Indies	185.	and a paralytic woman on an island of the Indies Post 15
indubitable	115.	And still the circular, indubitable frieze At 53
inertia	192.	Sad heart, the gymnast of inertia, does not count SI 1
inevitable	11.	Dally the doom of that inevitable thumb Chap 10
	28.	Inevitable, the body of the world F&H I 36
inexorable	172.	Inexorable and girded with your praise ABP 9
infancy	21.	I was promised an improved infancy Pass 4
infant	101.	Lug us back lifeward--bone by infant bone NWG 28
infatuation	148.	Ah! the divine infatuation Loc 13
inference	51.	Yielding by inference and discard, faith AM 75
infernal	163.	In such infernal circles round his door Id 5
infinite	37.	Infinite consanguinity it bears V-3 1
	50.	Series on series, infinite,--till eyes AM 41
	74.	Lo, through what infinite seasons dost thou gaze Dan 82
	149.	Oh, by the infinite circumflex Loc 33
infinity	89.	But that star-glistered salver of infinity CH 28
	89.	Walt, tell me, Walt Whitman, if infinity CH 44
	117.	That bleeds infinity--the orphic strings At 91
infinity's	92.	To conjugate infinity's dim marge CH 130
inflections	36.	Laughing the wrapt inflections of our love V-2 5
infrangible	39.	Infrangible and lonely, smooth as though cast V-5 2
ingenuity	149.	What nightmares rich with ingenuity Loc 26
	158.	Of every blight and ingenuity Mer 3
inherit	116.	(O Thou whose radiance doth inherit me At 87
inheritance	24.	And count some dim inheritance of sand WM 42
inheritances	8.	I see now, were inheritances PU 7
injured	183.	The roads were being cleared, injured brought in Et 53
inklings	90.	New verities, new inklings in the velvet hummed CH 63
inmost	40.	Flung into April's inmost day V-6 20
	50.	Some inmost sob, half-heard, dissuades the abyss AM 39
inner	104.	Than grass and snow, and their own inner being QH 5
innocence	11.	Facing the dull squint with what innocence Chap 12
	19.	Anoint with innocence,--recall LC 16
	132.	O blameless shyness;--innocence dissolute MC 4
inoculate	111.	O cruelly to inoculate the brinking dawn Tun 109
inquire	25.	Inquire this much-exacting fragment smile Rec 9
inquiries	7.	That feed your inquiries with aerial wine SMA 15
inquisitor	51.	Inquisitor! incognizable Word AM 61

inseparably	172.	Yes, tall, inseparably our days ABP 7
inside	19.	(Inside the sure machinery LC 4
	127.	Up the inside, and over every part Hi 3
insinuations	38.	All bright insinuations that my years have caught V-4 21
insistent	8.	The insistent clock commented on PU 14
insistently	54.	Insistently through sleep--a tide of voices HD 1
insolence	99.	Insolence. You crept out simmering, accomplished SC 24
instant	23.	Her eyes, unmake an instant of the world WM 13
	36.	Close round one instant in one floating flower V-2 20
	48.	Yet lost, all, let this keel one instant yield AM 16
	193.	An instant in the wind (I know not whither hurled B Tow 19
instantaneous	89.	Of wings imperious...Space, instantaneous CH 35
instinct	152.	(no instinct flattering vainly now In 8
instruments	64.	Keen instruments, strung to a vast precision Riv 26
integers	17.	Lie guard upon the integers of life Par 6
	95.	New integers of Roman, Viking, Celt CH 203
intent	110.	The intent escalator lifts a serenade Tun 85
interborough	110.	In interborough fissures of the mind Tun 71
interest	141.	The unexpected interest made him flush EpH 1
interests	4.	The interests of a black man in a cellar BT 1
interjections	35.	And in answer to their treble interjections V-1 6
interminably	83.	interminably/long since somebody's nickel--stopped--/playing CS 46
intervals	193.	Of broken intervals...And I, their sexton slave B Tow 12
intrepidly	30.	Greet naïvely--yet intrepidly F&H II 15
intricate	32.	Of intricate slain numbers that arise F&H III 4
intrinsic	116.	Swift peal of secular light, intrinsic Myth At 65
introduce	30.	That cornets introduce at every turn F&H II 17
invariably	23.	Invariably when wine redeems the sight WM 1
invent	24.	Invent new dominoes of love and bile WM 39
inventions	116.	Inventions that cobblestone the heart At 82
inventive	28.	Weeps in inventive dust for the hiatus F&H I 37
inverted	168.	Inverted octopus with heavenward arms AP 2
inviolably	38.	For islands where must lead inviolably V-4 22
inviolate	45.	Then, with inviolate curve, forsake our eyes TBB 5
invisible	6.	It is all hung by an invisible white hair MGLL 14
	48.	Invisible valves of the sea,--locks, tendons AM 10

invisible, cont.	92.	Lift agonized quittance, tilting from the invisible brink CH 135
invite	100.	Invite the necessary cloudy clinch NWG 2
involves	17.	Involves the hands in purposeless repose Par 8
inwraps	13.	Of stars inwraps her parasol IS 10
iridescent	98.	And this long wake of phosphor,/iridescent SC 13
iridescently	116.	O River-throated--iridescently upborne At 67
irised	160.	ripe apple-lanterns gush history, recondite lightnings, irised MT 12
iron	22.	"Why are you back here--smiling an iron coffin Pass 28
	46.	Already snow submerges an iron year TBB 40
	66.	By iron, iron--always the iron dealt cleavage Riv 87
	68.	From tunnel into field--iron strides the dew Riv 90
	141.	As well as one for iron and leather EpH 10
Iron Mountain	66.	Under the Ozarks, domed by Iron Mountain Riv 81
ironsides	69.	(Anon tall ironsides up from salt lagoons Riv 135
Iroquois	105.	But I must ask slain Iroquois to guide QH 51
irreconcilable	28.	There is the world dimensional for those untwisted by the love of things irreconcilable F&H I 16
	143.	Of things irreconcilable BE 23
irrefragibly	38.	All fragrance irrefragibly, and claim V-4 9
Isadora	106.	Of pain that Emily, that Isadora knew QH 65
Isaiah	50.	Isaiah counting famine on this lee AM 50
island	161.	In dusk, as though this island lifted, floated IQ 8
	179.	In the focus of the evening there is this island with Len 1
	185.	and a paralytic woman on an island of the Indies Post 15
islands	36.	Adagios of islands, O my Prodigal V-2 14
	38.	For islands where must lead inviolably V-4 22
isle	156.	But where is the Captain of this doubloon isle OC 17
issue	114.	As though a god were issue of the strings At 8
issued	127.	And reaping, have mercy and love issued forth Hi 6
I've	163.	A Dios gracias, grac--I've heard his song Id 14
ivory	131.	Two ivory women by a milky sea Ba 1

jacket	194.	(Not stone can jacket heaven)--but slip B Tow 34
jade	78.	Bent westward, passing on a stumbling jade Ind 31
jade-green	130.	Jade-green with sunlight, melt and flow Ech 2
Jake	66.	John, Jake or Charley, hopping the slow freight Riv 59
Janus-faced	25.	Regard the capture here, O Janus-faced Rec 1
Japalac	62.	Tintex--Japalac--Certain-teed Overalls ads Riv 3
Japan	84.	Fins whip the breeze around Japan CS 60
jargon	66.	With racetrack jargon,--dotting immensity Riv 66
jars	168.	Is pulmonary to the wind that jars AP 5
Jason	115.	And you, aloft there--Jason! hesting Shout At 37
Java Head	85.	at Java Head freshened the nip CS 70
javelin	91.	Each plane a hurtling javelin of winged ordnance CH 104
jealous	140.	With jealous threat and guile Int 10
jealousy	23.	And as the alcove of her jealousy recedes WM 20
jellied	50.	The jellied weeds that drag the shore,--perhaps AM 52
jelly	90.	Into the bulging bouillon, harnessed jelly of the stars CH 67
jeopardy	174.	From the sweet jeapardy of Anthony's plight BNOK 7
jerking	142.	Yet a gash with sunlight jerking through BE 12
jerky	28.	Half-riant before the jerky window frame F&H I 23
jest	45.	A jest falls from the speechless caravan TBB 20
	104.	The jest is too sharp to be kindly?) boast QH 14
	174.	An old Eqyptian jest has cramped the tape BNOK 5
Jesus	64.	"Jesus! Oh I remember watermelon days!" And sped Riv 42
jet	132.	She hazards jet; wears tiger-lilies MC 5
jewelled	132.	And bolts herself within a jewelled belt MC 6
jewelleries	122.	Where are set all the myriad jewelleries of night Moth 12
jewels	50.	--Yet no delirium of jewels! O Fernando AM 46
Jews	46.	And obscure as that heaven of the Jews TBB 25
Jim	78.	As long as Jim, your father's memory, is warm Ind 45
	79.	And since then--all that's left to me of Jim Ind 49
Jimmy	109.	"Let's have a pencil Jimmy--living now Tun 39
job	165.	They're back now on that mulching job at Pepper's BSEW 10
jogged	82.	in the nickel-in-the-slot piano jogged CS 8
John	66.	John, Jake or Charley, hopping the slow freight Riv 59

John's	24.	With Baptist John's. Their whispering begins WM 47
join	56.	As though to join us at some distant hill HD 37
	177.	And here we join eyes in that sanctity Rep 2
joined	10.	That hands joined in the dark will answer SM 7
	21.	(I had joined the entrainments of the wind Pass 12
joke	174.	Some old Egyptian joke is in the air BNOK 1
joked	68.	I could believe he joked at heaven's gate Riv 110
jokes	185.	and other gratuities, like porters[,] jokes, roses Post 11
jolted	68.	Dan Midland--jolted from the cold brake-beam Riv 111
Jordan's	68.	But drift in stillness, as from Jordan's brow Riv 115
journey	15.	That journey toward no Spring NL 10
joy	5.	For joy rides in stupendous coverings EC 5
	116.	Always through blinding cables, to our joy At 76
	122.	Their joy with a barren and steely tide Moth 8
joyous	95.	Above the Cape's ghoul-mound, O joyous seer CH 213
joys	88.	A periscope to glimpse what joys or pain CH 24
Juan Perez	48.	To you, too, Juan Perez, whose counsel fear AM 7
judgment	4.	Mark tardy judgment on the world's closed door BT 2
jug	160.	gum took place. Up jug to musical, hanging jug just gay MT 4
July	109.	Flatbush--on the fourth of July Tun 41
junctions	93.	As thou at junctions elegiac, there, of speed CH 149
June	38.	The chancel port and portion of our June V-4 13
	94.	With June the mountain laurel broke through green CH 177
jungle	69.	The basalt surface drags a jungle grace Riv 129
	167.	Of sweat the jungle presses with hot love RP 10
jurist	89.	Now the eagle dominates our days, is jurist CH 33
just	62.	Minstrels when you steal a chicken just Riv 6
	133.	Just as absinthe-sipping women shiver through CDB 6
	160.	gum took place. Up jug to musical, hanging jug just gay MT 4
	165.	That thin and blistered...just a rotten shell BSEW 4
	165.	"By just in time, and lifts 'em high and dry BSEW 9
justice	186.	Is justice that has cancelled earthly chains Shak 14
justified	22.	"Am justified in transience, fleeing Pass 30
	116.	And justified conclamant with ripe fields At 71

Kalamazoo	64.	To Cheyenne tagging...Maybe Kalamazoo Riv 34
keel	48.	Yet lost, all, let this keel one instant yield AM 16
	84.	<u>Pennies</u> <u>for</u> <u>porpoises</u> <u>that</u> <u>bank</u> <u>the</u> <u>keel</u> CS 59
	115.	Sheened harbor lanterns backward fled the keel At 50
keen	54.	--Flurried by keen fifings, eddied HD 15
	64.	Keen instruments, strung to a vast precision Riv 26
	70.	Your hair's keen crescent running, and the blue Dan 19
	192.	The warp is in the woof--and his keen vision SI 3
keep	8.	Of what the dead keep, living still PU 11
	61.	Keep hold of that nickel for car-change, Rip VW 43
	74.	There, where the first and last gods keep thy tent Dan 80
	79.	Write me from Rio...and you'll keep your pledge Ind 59
	82.	I'm not much good at time any more keep CS 15
	82.	I ought to keep time and get over it--I'm a CS 18
	102.	Keep smiling the boss away Va 3
	104.	They keep that docile edict of the Spring QH 2
	111.	Impassioned with some song we fail to keep Tun 118
keeping	85.	a long tack keeping--/<u>Taeping</u>?/<u>Ariel</u> CS 76
keeps	34.	This fabulous shadow only the sea keeps AMT 16
	187.	is it this that keeps the chimney Ma 13
keepsake	190.	Will hold it--wear the keepsake, dear, of time Rel 15
kelson	40.	Red kelson past the cape's wet stone V-6 8
kennel	91.	War's fiery kennel masked in downy offings CH 94
Kentucky	79.	Kentucky bred Ind 52
kept	48.	I, wonder-breathing, kept the watch,--saw AM 23
	64.	"--But I kept on the tracks." Possessed, re- signed Riv 49
	93.	Hast kept of wounds, O Mourner, all that sum CH 169
	178.	Have kept no faith but wind, the cold stream PB 10
key	18.	And the key, ready to hand--sifting Pos 3
	66.	Yet they touch something like a key perhaps Riv 62
keyboard	174.	The keyboard no more offers an escape BNOK 6
keys	6.	Old keys that are but echoes MGLL 18
kick	83.	steel--silver--kick the traces--and know CS 42
kicked	151.	that kicked out long ago APE 7
kid	82.	"It's S.S. <u>Ala</u>--Antwerp--now remember kid CS 13
kids	35.	O brilliant kids, frisk with your dog V-1 10

knees, cont.	159.	What you may cluster 'round the knees of space TCJ 1
	181.	The only building not sagging on its knees Et 10
knell	193.	Dispatches me as though I dropped down the knell B Tow 2
knells	36.	Take this Sea, whose diapason knells V-2 6
knelt	95.	Thou, Vedic Caesar, to the greensward knelt CH 204
	145.	As down she knelt for heaven's grace and boon PA 44
knew	66.	Wail into distances I knew were hers Riv 75
	66.	--Dead echoes! But I knew her body there Riv 78
	70.	Drifted how many hours I never knew Dan 23
	72.	--And knew myself within some boding shade Dan 38
	76.	Your father knew Ind 8
	76.	Knew not, nor heard Ind 12
	78.	Knew that mere words could not have brought us nearer Ind 42
	105.	Me farther than scalped Yankees knew to go QH 52
	106.	Of pain that Emily, that Isadora knew QH 65
	141.	That knew a grip for books and tennis EpH 9
	174.	And then it pleads again, "I wish I knew BNOK 16
	180.	A dead sailor that knew Lib 6
	190.	As though we knew (those who are variants Rel 8
knewest	74.	On paths thou knewest best to claim her by Dan 88
knife	7.	Put them again beside a pitcher with a knife SMA 16
knife-like	122.	To horizons which knife-like would only mar Moth 7
knob	149.	Doesn't someone come to turn the knob Loc 28
knolls	72.	Grey tepees tufting the blue knolls ahead Dan 39
knot	141.	And as the bandage knot was tightened EpH 23
knots	141.	The knots and notches,--many in the wide EpH 16
	156.	The wind that knots itself in one great death OC 15
know	11.	A famished kitten on the step, and know Chap 6
	18.	I know the screen, the distant flying taps Pos 12
	21.	Died speaking through the ages that you know Pass 19
	24.	Has followed you. Though in the end you know WM 41
	30.	Know, Olympians, we are breathless F&H II 7
	32.	We know, eternal gunman, our flesh remembers F&H III 19

know, cont.	38.	I know as spectrum of the sea and pledge V-4 2
	38.	Whose circles bridge, I know, (from palms to the severe V-4 4
	39.	Your breath sealed by the ghosts I do not know V-5 24
	41.	Whose accent no farewell can know V-6 32
	66.	--They know a body under the wide rain Riv 64
	68.	--As though the waters breathed that you might know Riv 98
	72.	Know, Maquokeeta, greeting; know death's best Dan 47
	79.	I know your word Ind 60
	82.	Democrat--I know what time it is--No CS 19
	82.	I don't want to know what time it is--that CS 20
	83.	steel--silver--kick the traces--and know CS 42
	84.	torch of hers you know 52
	89.	Of the ambiguous cloud. We know the strident rule CH 34
	140.	We claim, and none may know Int 6
	142.	I do not know what you'll see,--your vision BE 18
	149.	Alas, you know how much I oppose Loc 22
	150.	And yet they know the tomahawk GWP 14
	179.	know, Mr. Len 19
	182.	Sobbed. Yes, now--it's almost over. For they know Et 42
	191.	And what hours they forget to chime I'll know Purg 20
	192.	He does not know the new hum in the sky SI 9
	193.	And swing I know not where. Their tongues engrave B Tow 10
	193.	An instant in the wind (I know not whither hurled B Tow 19
knowing	28.	To you who turned away once, Helen, knowing F&H I 41
	39.	Knowing I cannot touch your hand and look V-5 15
	66.	They lurk across her, knowing her yonder breast Riv 67
	88.	Or to read you, Walt,--knowing us in thrall CH 13
knowledge	51.	Of knowledge,--round thy brows unhooded now AM 84
known	14.	I have known myself a nephew to confusions Fern 8
	30.	O, I have known metallic paradises F&H II 24
	33.	To memory, or known the ominous lifted arm F&H III 28
	152.	hast known.... And blithe In 17
knows	28.	Imminent in his dream, none better knows F&H I 29

knows, cont.

90. Already knows the closer clasp of Mars   CH 85
94. But knows it leastwise as death-strife?--O,
    something green   CH 200
100. Least tearful and least glad (who knows her
     smile   NWG 15
105. As humbly as a guest who knows himself too
     late   QH 60
173. By the subway new-stand knows/how hyacinths
     MF 2
174. It knows its way through India--tropic shake
     BNOK 14
177. But finally knows conviviality   Rep 4
187. and knows its waning   Ma 19

lands	62.	and lands sakes! under the new playbill ripped Riv 4
landscape	191.	The landscape of confession--and if confession Purg 7
landward	176.	distances leap landward without VU 17
lanes	37.	While ribboned water lanes I wind V-3 5
	51.	Like ocean athwart lanes of death and birth AM 58
languor	148.	My crisp soul will be flooded by a languor Loc 7
	152.	with languor such as gains In 2
lanterns	110.	Your eyes like agate lanterns--on and on Tun 73
	115.	Sheened harbor lanterns backward fled the keel At 50
	163.	With squint lanterns in his head, and it's likely Id 3
lap	70.	O Princess whose brown lap was virgin May Dan 15
	150.	Whirl by them centred in the lap GWP 7
lapels	84.	A wind worried those wicker-neat lapels, the CS 47
lapped	142.	Lapped under it,--or the dun Be 4
larches	72.	Cupped in the larches of the mountain pass Dan 26
larger	141.	Were banished from him by that larger, quieter hand EpH 21
largesse	74.	Thy freedom is her largesse, Prince, and hid Dan 87
lariat	116.	Within whose lariat sweep encinctured sing At 59
lark	178.	Perhaps as once Will Collins spoke the lark PB 3
lark's	116.	The agile precincts of the lark's return At 58
Larry	78.	Yes, Larry, now you're going to sea, remember Ind 46
	79.	You, Larry, traveller--/stranger,/son,/--my friend Ind 64
larval-silver	91.	Wheeled swiftly, wings emerge from larval-silver hangars CH 99
lash	192.	How more?--but the lash, lost vantage--and the prison SI 5
lashings	34.	Its lashings charmed and malice reconciled AMT 10
last	56.	The fog leans one last moment on the sill HD 35
	64.	The last bear, shot drinking in the Dakotas Riv 24
	64.	One said, excising a last burr from his vest Riv 47
	74.	At last with all that's consummate and free Dan 79
	74.	There, where the first and last gods keep thy tent Dan 80

last, cont.   74. And she is virgin to the last of men Dan 92
                       85. (last trip a tragedy)--where can you be CS 74
                       91. Wings clip the last peripheries of light CH 102
                       93. His last wing-pulse, and downcast as a cup
                            CH 161
                       94. Not greatest, thou,--not first, nor last,--but
                            near CH 189
                      100. Always and last, before the final ring NWG 9
                      104. Though they should thin and die on last year's
                            stubble QH 8
                      106. In one last angelus lift throbbing throat QH 63
                      110. That last night on the ballot rounds, did you
                            Tun 81
                      130. Over the hill a last cloud dips Ech 5
                      135. A dove's wings clung about my heart last night
                            CL 6
                      140. The world, at last, must bow and win Int 11
                      165. Bought a launch last week. It might as well
                            BSEW 2
                      168. Its apotheosis, at last--the hurricane AP 16
                      180. Light the last torch in the wall Lib 8
                      185. at last shyly. My only final friends Post 2
late   13. Out in the late amber afternoon IS 1
                       13. "Come, it is too late,--too late IS 13
                       61. And hurry along, Van Winkle--it's getting
                            late VW 45
                       78. But we,--too late, too early, howsoever Ind 25
                       79. Come back to Indiana--not too late Ind 61
                      105. As humbly as a guest who knows himself too late
                            QH 60
                      116. Atlantis,--hold thy floating singer late At 88
                      147. If she waits late at night Per 1
latent   194. Whose sweet mortality stirs latent power
                            B Tow 28
later   5. The wanderer later chose this spot of rest
                            EC 12
                       50. And later hurricanes may claim more pawn AM 31
                       58. --It is the same hour though a later day VW 6
                      185. after the western desert and the later cattle
                            country Post 10
latest   145. Using the latest ice-box and buying Fords PA 25
latitudes   38. Blue latitudes and levels of your eyes V-4 23
                       90. New latitudes, unknotting, soon give place CH 86
latter   12. Ends in this latter muffled Past 8
lattices   20. And their undimming lattices of flame LC 34
laugh   10. Will laugh and call your name; while you SM 17
                       33. Laugh out the meager penance of their days
                            F&H III 41
                       83. Then you may laugh and dance the axletree CS 41
                      115. Searches the timeless laugh of mythic spears
                            At 32
                      180. The virgin. They laugh to hear Lib 3

laugh, cont.	190.	The harvest laugh of bright Apollo Rel 4
laughed	163.	Fumbling his sex. That's why those children laughed Id 4
laughing	36.	Laughing the wrapt inflections of our love V-2 5
	70.	What laughing chains the water wove and threw Dan 21
	179.	And the idiot boy by the road, with carbonated eyes, laugh-/ing or extending a phallus through the grating,--talking to Len 4-5
laughs	74.	--And laughs, pure serpent, Time itself, and moon Dan 75
laughter	6.	With such a sound of gently pitying laughter MGLL 26
	8.	And, of Gargantua, the laughter PU 4
	11.	A grail of laughter of an empty ash can Chap 21
	50.	Laughter, and shadow cuts sleep from the heart AM 35
	89.	And we have laughter, or more sudden tears CH 38
	111.	Whose hideous laughter is a bellows mirth Tun 107
	135.	No;--nor my lips freed laughter since "farewell CL 2
	143.	Or, of Gargantua, the laughter BE 32
	186.	And laughter, burnished brighter than our fate Shak 8
launch	165.	Bought a launch last week. It might as well BSEW 2
launched	60.	We launched--with paper wings and twisted VW 20
	95.	And now, as launched in abysmal cupolas of space CH 205
	167.	It grazes the horizons, launched above RP 12
	193.	Antiphonal carillons launched before B Tow 7
laurel	21.	Touching an opening laurel, I found Pass 26
	22.	"To argue with the laurel," I replied Pass 29
	94.	With June the mountain laurel broke through green CH 177
lava	73.	I heard the hush of lava wrestling your arms Dan 69
	83.	and galleries, galleries of watergutted lava CS 31
laved	37.	Are laved and scattered with no stroke V-3 6
lavender	185.	Remember the lavender lilies of that dawn Post 7
lavish	33.	The lavish heart shall always have to leaven F&H III 33
	76.	We found God lavish there in Colorado Ind 15
	176.	lavish this on you VU 3

leap, cont.	176.	distances leap landward without VU 17
	188.	be doctors, but doctors are rare poets when roses leap HR 26
leaping	94.	Of prairies, yet like breakers cliffward leaping CH 174
leaps	58.	Leaps from Far Rockaway to Golden Gate VW 2
	61.	Leaps from Far Rockaway to Golden Gate VW 42
learn	16.	Where beavers learn stitch and tooth RR 14
	108.	Someday by heart you'll learn each famous sight Tun 6
learned	3.	It is to be learned Leg 10
	70.	I learned to catch the trout's moon whisper; I Dan 22
	123.	But once though, he learned of that span of his wings Moth 25
lease	105.	Who holds the lease on time and on disgrace QH 46
leash	90.	Of dynamos, where hearing's leash is strummed CH 64
least	100.	Least tearful and least glad (who knows her smile NWG 15
	170.	Being, of all, least sought for: Emily, hear TED 5
	188.	watches at least--the lighthouse flashed... whirled HR 18
leastwise	94.	But knows it leastwise as death-strife?--O, something green CH 200
leather	141.	As well as one for iron and leather EpH 10
	182.	Leather, which the rimed white wind had glazed Et 28
leave	25.	Wrenched gold of Nineveh:--yet leave the tower Rec 22
	130.	Upward again:--they leave no stain Ech 3
	133.	The winers leave too, and the small lamps twinge CDB 24
	158.	Leave us, you idols of Futurity--alone Mer 12
	178.	And leave me half adream upon the main PB 4
	184.	Leave, leave that Caribbean praise to me Emp 8
leaven	33.	The lavish heart shall always have to leaven F&H III 33
leaves	7.	The leaves will fall again sometime and fill SMA 1
	12.	That ritual of sap and leaves Past 6
	35.	Its drums and darkest blowing leaves ignore Rec 10
	70.	There was a bed of leaves, and broken play Dan 13
	73.	The oak grove circles in a crash of leaves Dan 50
	117.	The serpent with the eagle in the leaves At 95
	133.	Finale leaves in silence to replume CDB 21

leaves, cont.	160.	tisms wrench the golden boughs. Leaves spatter dawn MT 7
	170.	Leaves Ormus rubyless, and Ophir chill TED 13
leaving	108.	to twelve upward leaving Tun 15
led	123.	The heat led the moth up in octopus arms Moth 38
Leda	184.	You, who have looked back to Leda, who have seen the Swan Emp 6
ledge	34.	Often beneath the wave, wide from this ledge AMT 1
	72.	O Appalachian Spring! I gained the ledge Dan 33
lee	50.	Isaiah counting famine on this lee AM 50
	85.	and turned and left us on the lee CS 72
leewardings	36.	Of rimless floods, unfettered leewardings V-2 2
left	15.	Or left you with the faintest blush NL 6
	21.	My memory I left in a ravine Pass 6
	23.	An urchin who has left the snow WM 21
	45.	As though the sun took step of thee, yet left TBB 14
	61.	Before I had left the window. It VW 39
	62.	whizzed the Limited--roared by and left Riv 20
	70.	I left the village for dogwood. By the canoe Dan 17
	72.	I left my sleek boat nibbling margin grass Dan 28
	79.	And since then--all that's left to me of Jim Ind 49
	82.	or left you several blocks away CS 7
	85.	and turned and left us on the lee CS 72
	89.	Left Hesperus mirrored in the lucid pool CH 32
	90.	Two brothers in their twinship left the dune CH 79
	112.	Lights, coasting, left the oily tympanum of waters Tun 127
	115.	We left the haven hanging in the night At 49
	123.	And his wings atom-withered,--gone,--left but a leap Moth 47
	181.	And left the house, or what was left of it Et 3
	190.	Who is now left to vary the Sanscrit Rel 12
	191.	Like something left, forsaken--here am I Purg 4
	194.	The steep encroachments of my blood left me B Tow 25
legend	3.	The legend of their youth into the noon Leg 23
legs	74.	That drops his legs and colors in the sun Dan 74
	100.	And while legs waken salads in the brain NWG 5
leisured	178.	And who trick back the leisured winds again PB 6

lemons	151.	HEADY!--those aromatic LEMONS! APE 11
lend	46.	And of the curveship lend a myth to God TBB 44
lengthened	21.	The shadows of boulders lengthened my back Pass 13
lengthening	69.	Ochreous and lynx-barred in lengthening might Riv 130
lenses	88.	Our lenses, lifts a focus, resurrects CH 23
	156.	His Carib mathematics web the eyes' baked lenses OC 22
leopard	23.	A leopard ranging always in the brow WM 3
less	93.	Not less than thou in pure impulse inbred CH 153
let	48.	Yet lost, all, let this keel one instant yeild AM 16
	95.	Not soon, nor suddenly,--no, never to let go CH 219
	102.	Let down your golden hair Va 16
	108.	Then let you reach your hat Tun 11
	108.	As usual, let you--also Tun 13
	136.	I should not dare to let you in again Ps 4
	156.	Let fiery blossoms clot the light, render my ghost OC 24
	157.	Let not the pilgrim see himself again OC 27
	160.	Let them return, saying you blush again for the great MT 1
	174.	Or let us bump heads in some lowly shed BNOK 4
	188.	Let us strip the desk for action--now we have a horse HR 1
let's	109.	"Let's have a pencil Jimmy--living now Tun 39
lets	111.	Lets go.... Toward corners of the floor Tun 97
letters	6.	For the letters of my mother's mother MGLL 6
	190.	In wider letters than the alphabet Rel 11
level	111.	Taking the final level for the dive Tun 93
leveling	16.	That seething, steady leveling of the marshes RR 4
levels	38.	Blue latitudes and levels of your eyes V-4 23
levers	111.	Elbows and levers, guard and hissing door Tun 90
	174.	Have levers for,--stampede it with fresh type BNOK 11
Leviathan	82.	Murmurs of Leviathan he spoke CS 11
levin	74.	Thewed of the levin, thunder-shod and lean Dan 81
levin-lathered	169.	Rock sockets, levin-lathered Hur 11
levin's	92.	How from thy path above the levin's lance CH 125
lewd	100.	And the lewd trounce of a final muted beat NWG 23
liable	6.	And liable to melt as snow MGLL 11
Liberty	45.	Over the chained bay waters Liberty TBB 4
lichen-faithful	35.	Too lichen-faithful from too wide a breast V-1 15

lick	182.	Everything--and lick the grass, as black as patent Et 27
licks	128.	But on the window licks the night Fr 4
	128.	And on the window licks the night Fr 8
lie	17.	Lie guard upon the integers of life Par 6
	48.	O where our Indian emperies lie revealed AM 15
	66.	The old gods of the rain lie wrapped in pools Riv 82
	70.	Now lie incorrigibly what years between Dan 12
	73.	Lie to us,--dance us back the tribal morn Dan 60
	112.	Shadowless in that abyss they unaccounting lie Tun 133
	147.	The hills lie curved and blent Per 11
liege	73.	O yelling battlements,--I, too, was liege Dan 62
lies	4.	Wanders in some mid-kingdom, dark, that lies BT 10
	10.	Lies cool upon her--not yet pain SM 12
	11.	And yet these fine collapses are not lies Chap 14
life	10.	Her mound of undelivered life SM 11
	17.	Lie guard upon the integers of life Par 6
	138.	More real than life, the gestures you have spun Port 6
	150.	Indeed, old memories come back to life GWP 15
	190.	What is our life without a sudden pillow Rel 2
life's	83.	"O life's a geyser--beautiful--my lungs CS 35
	124.	My eyes have hugged beauty and winged life's brief spell Moth 50
lifeward	101.	Lug us back lifeward--bone by infant bone NWG 28
lift	14.	But turning, as you may chance to lift a shade Fern 3
	20.	Lift up in lilac-emerald breath the grail LC 40
	28.	But if I lift my arms it is to bend F&H I 40
	40.	Where icy and bright dungeons lift V-6 1
	68.	Maybe the breeze will lift the River's musk Riv 97
	92.	Lift agonized quittance, tilting from the invisible brink CH 135
	106.	In one last angelus lift throbbing throat QH 63
	108.	And watch the curtain lift in hell's despite Tun 7
	159.	Wrap us and lift us; drop us then, returned TCJ 17
	178.	For who shall lift head up to funnel smoke PB 5
	182.	To lift a stick for pity of his stupor Et 36
	194.	The matrix of the heart, lift down the eye B Tow 37

lifted   33. To memory, or known the ominous lifted arm
                            F&H III 28
                       34. Frosted eyes there were that lifted altars
                            AMT 11
                       46. And we have seen night lifted in thine arms
                            TBB 36
                      161. In dusk, as though this island lifted, floated
                            IQ 8
                      172. Sea gardens lifted rainbow-wise through eyes
                            ABP 5
                      186. Are lifted from torn flesh with human rue
                            Shak 7

lifting   10. With lifting spring and starker SM 2
                      111. The sod and billow breaking,--lifting ground
                            Tun 120
                      115. Bridge, lifting night to cycloramic crest At 43
                      163. Above all reason lifting, halt serene Id 15

lifts   37. The sea lifts, also, reliquary hands V-3 8
                       69. The River lifts itself from its long bed
                            Riv 139
                       88. Our lenses, lifts a focus, resurrects CH 23
                       98. And lifts her girdles from her, one by one SC 4
                      110. The intent escalator lifts a serenade Tun 85
                      156. Below the palsy that one eucalyptus lifts OC 6
                      159. Your light lifts whiteness into virgin azure
                            TCJ 5
                      165. "By just in time, and lifts 'em high and dry
                            BSEW 9
                      194. Unseals her earth, and lifts love in its shower
                            B Tow 40

light   7. Their own perennials of light SMA 11
                       17. The pillow--how desperate is the light Par 11
                       18. I hold it up against a disk of light Pos 20
                       30. A thousand light shrugs balance us F&H II 9
                       37. This tendered theme of you that light V-3 2
                       37. Light wrestling there incessantly with light
                            V-3 12
                       48. Slowly the sun's red caravel drops light AM 13
                       91. Wings clip the last peripheries of light CH 102
                       95. Toward endless terminals, Easters of speeding
                            light CH 206
                       99. Light drowned the lithic trillions of your spawn
                            SC 29
                      109. --Quite unprepared rush naked back to light
                            Tun 28
                      114. Upward, veering with light, the flight of
                            strings At 2
                      115. Slit and propelled by glistening fins of light
                            At 26
                      116. Swift peal of secular light, intrinsic Myth
                            At 65
                      116. With white escarpments swinging into light
                            At 69

like

13. Like a waiting moon, in shadow swims   IS 4
25. While darkness, like an ape's face, falls away
     Rec 15
25. The plummet heart, like Absalom, no stream
     Rec 20
30. Splayed like cards from a loose hand   F&H II 12
32. Like old women with teeth unjubilant   F&H III 17
39. Nothing like this in the world," you say   V-5 14
40. Like a cliff swinging or a sail   V-6 19
50. Like pearls that whisper through the Doge's
     hands   AM 45
51. Like ocean athwart lanes of death and birth
     AM 58
62. imagine--while an EXpress makes time like
     Riv 12
62. breathtaking--as you like it...eh   Riv 18
64. Strange bird-wit, like the elemental gist
     Riv 37
66. Each seemed a child, like me, on a loose perch
     Riv 57
66. Holding to childhood like some termless play
     Riv 58
66. Yet they touch something like a key perhaps
     Riv 62
66. Youngsters with eyes like fjords, old reprobates
     Riv 65
66. Time like a serpent down her shoulder, dark
     Riv 79
68. Like one whose eyes were buried long ago
     Riv 119
73. Flickering, sprint up the hill groins like a
     tide   Dan 68
74. O, like the lizard in the furious noon   Dan 73
74. Like one white meteor, sacrosanct and blent
     Dan 78
78. And like twin stars. They seemed to shun the
     gaze   Ind 37
89. Wherein your eyes, like the Great Navigator's
     without/ship   CH 52
92. Cloud-belfries, banging, while searchlights, like
     fencers   CH 121
94. Cowslip and shad-blow, flaked like tethered foam
     CH 171
94. Of prairies, yet like breakers cliffward leaping
     CH 174
104. See them, like eyes that still uphold some dream
      QH 23
109. like a pigeon's muddy dream--potatoes   Tun 42
109. Our tongues recant like beaten weather vanes
      Tun 46
109. This answer lives like verdigris, like hair
      Tun 47

like, cont.   109.   you don't like my gate why did you   Tun 53
                   110.   Your eyes like agate lanterns--on and on
                          Tun 73
                   110.   And did their eyes like unwashed platters ride
                          Tun 76
                   111.   And yet, like Lazarus, to feel the slope
                          Tun 119
                   115.   Sheerly the eyes, like seagulls stung with rime
                          At 25
                   115.   Like hails, farewells--up planet-sequined heights
                          At 33
                   116.   And like an organ, Thou, with sound of doom
                          At 62
                   117.   Like spears ensanguined of one tolling star
                          At 90
                   122.   At night like a grain of sand, futile and dried
                          Moth 24
                   123.   But they burned thinly blind like an orange
                          peeled white Moth 40
                   134.   Yellow, pallid, like ancient lace CDB 28
                   137.   Forgetfulness is like a song For 1
                   137.   Forgetfulness is like a bird whose wings are
                          reconciled For 3
                   139.   Like a shell surrendered to evening sands
                          Lege 3
                   140.   How love blooms like a tardy flower Int 7
                   141.   Like wings of butterflies EpH 14
                   141.   They were like the marks of wild ponies' play
                          EpH 18
                   145.   And his wife, like a mountain, coming in PA 33
                   145.   Twinkling like little Christmas trees PA 35
                   157.   For slow evisceration bound like those huge
                          terrapin OC 28
                   159.   Like water, undestroyed,--like mist, unburned
                          TCJ 18
                   160.   Great-grandmother. It's all like Christmas MT 2
                   165.   Oozing a-plenty. They sat like baking Buddhas
                          BSEW 7
                   170.   Yet fed your hunger like an endless task TED 2
                   173.   His eyes--/like crutches hurtled against glass
                          MF 6
                   182.   Long tropic roots high in the air, like lace
                          Et 30
                   182.   Like a vast phantom maned by all that memoried/
                          night Et 45
                   185.   and other gratuities, like porters[,] jokes,
                          roses Post 11
                   187.   like a mouse under pussy Ma 10
                   188.   like rats--and too, when rats make rose nozzles
                          of pink HR 27
                   191.   But rather like a blanket than a quilt Purg 14

likely   163.   With squint lanterns in his head, and it's
                       likely   Id 3
lilac   60.   Is it the whip stripped from the lilac tree
                       VW 32
lilac-emerald   20.   Lift up in lilac-emerald breath the grail
                       LC 40
lilies   94.   Potomac lilies,--then the Pontiac rose   CH 179
                173.   Fall mute and sudden (dealing change/for lilies
                       MF 7
                185.   Remember the lavender lilies of that dawn
                       Post 7
lily   131.   Flat lily petals to the sea's white throat
                       Ba 7
lily's   156.   The tarantula rattling at the lily's foot   OC 1
limbs   6.   It trembles as birch limbs webbing the air
                       MGLL 15
                 28.   The limbs and belly, when rainbows spread
                       F&H I 34
Limited   62.   whizzed the Limited--roared by and left   Riv 20
limits   39.   The bay estuaries fleck the hard sky limits
                       V-5 4
                122.   That they only can see when their moon limits
                       vision   Moth 9
line   7.   That are your rich and faithful strength of line
                       SMA 3
                 24.   Remorseless line, minting their separate wills
                       WM 25
                 35.   By time and the elements; but there is a line
                       V-1 12
                 78.   Of all our silent men--the long team line   Ind 38
                 84.   Bright skysails ticketing the Line, wink round
                       the Horn   CS 61
                109.   night after night--the Culver line--the   Tun 44
                142.   I have heard hands praised for line on line   BE 11
lines   94.   When first I read thy lines, rife as the loam
                       CH 173
linger   18.   Assaults outright for bolts that linger   Pos 6
lingering   138.   Haunt the blank stage with lingering alarms
                       Port 7
lining   131.   The dawn, a shell's pale lining restlessly   Ba 2
link   115.   --Tomorrows into yesteryear--and link   At 29
links   109.   "what do you want? getting weak on the links
                       Tun 50
lintel   76.   Over the lintel on its wiry vine   Ind 2
lipping   133.   Carmen! Bestirring hope and lipping eyes
                       CDB 18
lips   5.   Dull lips commemorating spiritual gates   EC 11
                 14.   The zigzags fast around dry lips composed
                       Fern 5
                 38.   Portending eyes and lips and making told   V-4 12
                130.   Silently, now, but that your lips   Ech 7

living, cont.	8.	Of what the dead keep, living still PU 11
	93.	Of living brotherhood! CH 156
	109.	"Let's have a pencil Jimmy--living now Tun 39
lizard	74.	O, like the lizard in the furious noon Dan 73
lizard's	168.	The lizard's throat, held bloated for a fly AP 7
llano	74.	And winds across the llano grass resume Dan 94
lo	50.	This third, of water, tests the word; lo, here AM 33
	74.	Lo, through what infinite seasons dost thou gaze Dan 82
	123.	And lo, in that dawn he was pierroting over Moth 29
	169.	Lo, Lord, Thou ridest Hur 1
loam	20.	Of tears flocks through the tendoned loam LC 31
	93.	The competent loam, the probably grass,--travail CH 151
	94.	When first I read thy lines, rife as the loam CH 173
loaves	183.	Something like two thousand loaves on the way Et 56
lobby	8.	As, perched in the crematory lobby PU 13
locked	84.	locked in wind-humors, ran their eastings down CS 69
locks	48.	Invisible valves of the sea,--locks, tendons AM 10
	179.	tition of the parrot. Locks on Len 15
locution	111.	Locution of the eldest star, and pack Tun 112
loft	45.	Out of some subway scuttle, cell or loft TBB 17
	114.	The loft of vision, palladium helm of stars At 24
lofty	188.	through the lofty, dusty glass--Cortez--Cortez--his HR 11
	194.	No answer (could blood hold such a lofty tower B Tow 26
logic	3.	Until the bright logic is won Leg 17
logically	38.	Madly meeting logically in this hour V-4 10
logs	128.	Pile on the logs.... Give me your hands Fr 5
lone	29.	Accept a lone eye riveted to your plane F&H I 49
	89.	Near Paumanok--your lone patrol--and heard the/ wraith CH 46
loneliness	51.	Utter to loneliness the sail is true AM 64
	139.	The tossing loneliness of many nights Lege 1
	162.	Weathers all loneliness OS 12
lonely	11.	The moon in lonely alleys make Chap 20
	39.	Infrangible and lonely, smooth as though cast V-5 2
	98.	Windswept guitars on lonely decks forever SC 11
	123.	To the desert,--back,--down,--still lonely he fell Moth 48

long

long, cont.   183. The fever was checked. I stood a long time in
                           Mack's/talking Et 58
                     193. But not for long to hold each desperate choice
                           B Tow 20
long-drawn   98. Eyes crumble at its kiss. It's long-drawn
                           spell SC 15
longer   20. No longer bind. Some sentient cloud LC 30
long-scattered   193. Membrane through marrow, my long-scattered score
                           B Tow 11
look   10. Will find the street, only to look SM 19
                      25. Look steadily--how the wind feasts and spins
                           Rec 13
                      39. Knowing I cannot touch your hand and look
                           V-5 15
                      68. Yes, turn again and sniff once more--look see
                           Riv 104
                      82. stepped out--forgot to look at you CS 6
                     146. But look up, Porphyro,--your toes PA 53
looked   32. Plangent over meadows, and looked down
                           F&H III 15
                      78. Of wagon-tenting looked out once and saw Ind 30
                     184. You, who have looked back to Leda, who have seen
                           the Swan Emp 6
looming   90. Under the looming stacks of the gigantic power
                           house CH 61
looms   115. Pick biting way up towering looms that press
                           At 27
                     192. His fathers took for granted ages since--and so
                           he looms SI 6
loose   6. In the loose girdle of soft rain MGLL 4
                      30. Splayed like cards from a loose hand F&H II 12
                      66. Each seemed a child, like me, on a loose perch
                           Riv 57
                     104. Faces--loose panes crown the hill and gleam
                           QH 21
                     181. And Cuban doctors, troopers, trucks, loose hens
                           Et 9
                     189. doom...must therefore loose yourself within a
                           pat- HR 32
loosed   76. In golden syllables loosed from the clay Ind 19
loped   64. Loped under wires that span the mountain stream
                           Riv 25
Lord   169. Lo, Lord, Thou ridest Hur 1
                     169. Lord, Lord, Thy swifting heart Hur 2
                     169. Lord, e'en boulders now outleap Hur 10
                     169. Nor, Lord, may worm outdeep Hur 12
                     169. Lord God, while summits crashing Hur 14
                     169. Thou ridest to the door, Lord Hur 17
                     169. Thou bidest wall nor floor, Lord Hur 18

love, cont.	114.	"Make thy love sure--to weave whose song we ply At 14
	115.	But who, through smoking pyres of love and death At 31
	115.	O Love, thy white, pervasive Paradigm At 48
	116.	As love strikes clear direction for the helm At 64
	116.	Unspeakable Thou Bridge to Thee, O Love At 83
	127.	And reaping, have mercy and love issued forth Hi 6
	127.	Mercy, white milk, and honey, gold love Hi 7
	132.	Even, sank in love and choked with flowers MC 10
	132.	This burns and is not burnt.... My modern love were MC 11
	140.	How love blooms like a tardy flower Int 7
	143.	But some are twisted with the love BE 22
	167.	Of sweat the jungle presses with hot love RP 10
	170.	Needs more than wit to gather, love to bind TED 11
	179.	of wine and mandolines. Midnight; and maybe love Len 10
	184.	Love and the breath of faith, momentous bride Emp 13
	185.	Antillean fingers counting my pulse, my love forever Post 16
	193.	To trace the visionary company of love, its voice B Tow 18
	194.	Unseals her earth, and lifts love in its shower B Tow 40
loved	39.	Slow tyranny of moonlight, moonlight loved V-5 12
love-nest	105.	Bubbles in time to Hollywood's new love-nest pageant QH 36
lover	159.	The moon's best lover,--guide us by a sleight TCJ 10
	180.	Hair mocked by the sea, her lover Lib 5
lover's	10.	The lover's death, how regular SM 1
	10.	Walk now, and note the lover's death SM 21
	46.	Prayer of pariah, and the lover's cry TBB 32
lovers'	36.	All but the pieties of lovers' hands V-2 10
love's	94.	Of loves' own diametric gaze, of love's amaze CH 188
low	64.	Of unwalled winds they offer, singing low Riv 38
	92.	Hung low...until a conch of thunder answers CH 120
	122.	They had scorned him, so humbly low, bound there and tied Moth 23
lower	98.	Of lower heavens,--/vaporous scars SC 6

macadam	58.	Macadam, gun-grey as the tunny's belt VW 1
	61.	Macadam, gun-grey as the tunny's belt VW 41
machine	83.	Or they may start some white machine that sings CS 40
machinery	19.	(Inside the sure machinery LC 4
machines	174.	And able text, more motion than machines BNOK 10
Mack's	183.	The fever was checked. I stood a long time in Mack's talking Et 58
macrocosmic	122.	And rings macrocosmic won envy as thrall Moth 22
mad	126.	In a mad orange flare O-N 9
madame	148.	Ah, madame! truly it's not right Loc 9
made	48.	That made me exile in her streets, stood me AM 18
	60.	And Rip was slowly made aware VW 26
	75.	In cobalt desert closures made our vows Dan 102
	82.	--green glasses, or bar lights made them CS 4
	114.	Complighted in one vibrant breath made cry At 13
	141.	The unexpected interest made him flush EpH 1
	142.	I have heard hands praised for what they made BE 10
	142.	A mesh of belts down into it, made me think BE 13
	165.	Have been made of--well, say paraffin BSEW 3
	184.	Gathered and made musical in feathery fronds Emp 3
	185.	the wren and thrush, made solid print for me Post 3
Madeline's	145.	And threw warm gules on Madeline's fair breast PA 43
mademoiselle	160.	Mademoiselle MT 15
madly	38.	Madly meeting logically in this hour V-4 10
madness	7.	Beloved apples of seasonable madness SMA 14
Madonna	152.	Madonna, natal to thy yielding In 18
Madre	48.	"The Great white Birds!" (O Madre María, still AM 26
Magdalene	98.	Eve! Magdalene!/or Mary, you SC 7
	100.	O Magdalene, each comes back to die alone NWG 26
Maggy	160.	Maggy, come on MT 17
magnetic	30.	Magnetic to their tremolo F&H II 3
maidenhairferns	151.	maidenhairferns, and the BRONX APE 18
mail	40.	Here waves climb into dusk on gleaming mail AM 9
maim	164.	Our envy of your freedom--we must maim NA 4
main	88.	What whisperings of far watches on the main CH 21
	178.	And leave me half adream upon the main PB 4
Main	144.	South Main PA 3

maize	70.	She spouted arms; she rose with maize--to die Dan 4
	74.	And see'st thy bride immortal in the maize Dan 84
make	11.	We make our meek adjustments Chap 1
	11.	The moon in lonely alleys make Chap 20
	18.	As quiet as you can make a man Poss 17
	66.	Such pilferings make up their timeless eatage Riv 85
	108.	Or can't you quite make up your mind to ride Tun 18
	114.	"Make thy love sure--to weave whose song we ply At 14
	151.	that make your colored syrup fairly APE 12
	188.	like rats--and too, when rats make rose nozzles of pink HR 27
	191.	Here quakes of earth make houses fall Purg 11
makes	62.	imagine--while an EXpress makes time like Riv 12
making	38.	Portending eyes and lips and making told V-4 12
males	178.	--The hot fickle wind, the breath of males PB 11
malice	32.	Who hurried the hill breezes, spouting malice F&H III 14
	34.	Its lashings charmed and malice reconciled AMT 10
mallets	23.	Percussive sweat is spreading to his hair. Mallets WM 12
mammoth	16.	And mammoth turtles climbing sulphur dreams RR 9
	88.	the mammoth saurian/ghoul, the eastern/Cape CH 2
man	4.	The interests of a black man in a cellar BT 1
	4.	The black man, forlorn in the cellar BT 9
	18.	As quiet as you can make a man Pos 17
	21.	And hug, chimney-sooted heart of man Pass 20
	51.	Cruelly with love thy parable of man AM 60
	62.	brother--all over--going west--young man Riv 2
	82.	I met a man in South Street, tall CS 1
	89.	Man hears himself an engine in a cloud CH 42
	131.	But they are wrong.... Ere man was given sight Ba 9
	156.	What man, or What OC 20
	178.	That I thy drowned man may speak again PB 2
mandolines	179.	of wine and mandolines. Midnight; and maybe love LEN 10
mane	66.	Papooses crying on the wind's long mane Riv 76
maned	182.	Like a vast phantom maned by all that memoried/ night Et 45
manes	102.	Peonies with pony manes Va 21
Manhattan	56.	From Cyclopean towers across Manhattan waters HD 32
mankind	161.	Against mankind. It is at times IQ 7

man's	93.	Ghoul-mound of man's perversity at balk CH 167
	133.	And dies on fire's birth in each man's heart CDB 10
mantle's	48.	Assure us through thy mantle's ageless blue AM 28
manure	23.	(Painted emulsion of snow, eggs, yarn, coal, manure WM 10
many	40.	Or as many waters through the sun's V-6 7
	45.	How many dawns, chill from his rippling rest TBB 1
	70.	Drifted how many hours I never knew Dan 23
	72.	Over how many bluffs, tarns, streams 1 sped Dan 37
	99.	Rehearsed hair--docile, alas, from many arms SC 26
	132.	Too many palms have grazed her shoulders MC 7
	139.	The tossing loneliness of many nights Lege 1
	141.	The knots and notches,--many in the wide EpH 16
	144.	Until you feel the weight of many cars PA 6
	145.	I ride black horse.... Have many sheep PA 32
mapled	104.	Through mapled vistas, cancelled reservations QH 24
Maquokeeta	72.	Know, Maquokeeta, greeting; know death's best Dan 47
	73.	Dance, Maquokeeta: Pocahontas grieves Dan 52
	73.	Dance, Maquokeeta! snake that lives before Dan 57
mar	122.	To horizons which knife-like would only mar Moth 7
marathons	90.	What marathons new-set between the stars CH 83
marauding	91.	Is baited by marauding circles, bludgeon flail CH 96
marble	5.	Where marble clouds support the sea EC 13
	136.	Though now but marble are the marble urns Ps 1
	161.	Square sheets--they saw the marble only into IQ 1
	161.	Flat prison slabs there at the marble quarry IQ 2
	161.	Profile of marble spiked with yonder IQ 5
	161.	But went on into marble that does not weep IQ 15
march	69.	Damp tonnage and alluvial march of days Riv 124
	171.	That now has sunk I strike a single march KW 7
March	104.	That blends March with August Antarctic skies QH 3
	187.	March Ma 8
mare's	79.	Perhaps I'll hear the mare's hoofs to the ford Ind 58
marge	92.	To conjugate infinity's dim marge CH 130

margin   72. I left my sleek boat nibbling margin grass
                       Dan 28
margins   27. The margins of the day, accent the curbs
                       F&H I 10
Maria   48. "The Great White Birds!" (O Madre María, still
                       AM 26
mariner   34. Monody shall not wake the mariner AMT 15
mark   4. Mark tardy judgment on the world's closed door
                       BT 2
                  36. Mark how her turning shoulders wind the hours
                       V-2 16
marks   122. Their mother, the moon, marks a halo of light
                       Moth 10
                 141. They were like the marks of wild ponies' play
                       EpH 18
marrow   193. Membrane through marrow, my long-scattered
                       score B Tow 11
Mars   90. Already knows the closer clasp of Mars CH 85
Marseille   88. The songs that gypsies dealt us at Marseille
                       CH 11
marshes   16. That seething, steady leveling of the marshes
                       RR 4
                 174. Come, search the marshes for a friendly bed
                       BNOK 3
Mary   98. Eve! Magdalene!/or Mary, you SC 7
                 102. Mary (what are you going to do Va 4
                 102. O blue-eyed Mary with the claret scarf Va 7
                 102. Saturday Mary, mine Va 8
                 102. O Mary, leaning from the high wheat tower
                       Va 15
                 102. Cathedral Mary,/shine Va 24
mashed   93. ....dispersion...into mashed and shapeless debris
                       CH 143
masked   91. War's fiery kennel masked in a downy offings
                       CH 94
massacre   93. And fraternal massacre! Thou, pallid there as
                       chalk CH 168
mast   51. Who grindest oar, and arguing the mast AM 65
mastery   189. tern's mastery that you can conceive, that you
                       can HR 33
                 189. yeild to--by which also you win and gain mastery
                       and HR 34
match   3. Nor to match regrets. For the moth Leg 4
                 110. A burnt match skating in a urinal Tun 60
materna   125. O Materna! to enrich thy gold head C 8
mathematics   156. His Carib mathematics web the eyes' baked
                       lenses OC 22
mating   184. Nor that fruit of mating which is widowed pride
                       Emp 15
matrix   194. The matrix of the heart, lift down the eye
                       B Tow 37

matter	182.	And fell dead or dying, but it didn't so much matter Et 49
May	60.	a <u>Catskill</u> <u>daisy</u> <u>chain</u> <u>in</u> <u>May</u> VW 29
	70.	O Princess whose brown lap was virgin May Dan 15
	102.	High in the noon of May Va 17
	142.	May slumber yet in the moon, awaiting BE 19
Mayans	188.	...delayed, and struck--<u>again</u>, <u>again</u>. Only the May-/ans surely slept--whose references to typhus and whose HR 19-20
maybe	64.	To Cheyenne tagging...Maybe Kalamazoo Riv 34
	68.	Maybe the breeze will lift the River's musk Riv 97
	161.	Palms against the sunset's towering sea, and maybe IQ 6
	179.	of wine and mandolines. Midnight; and maybe love Len 10
Mazda	62.	Mazda--and the telegraphic night coming on Thomas Riv 9
me	8.	His thoughts, delivered to me PU 5
	16.	Till age had brought me to the sea RR 5
	16.	Tyranny; they drew me into hades almost RR 8
	23.	Wear me in crescents on their bellies. Slow WM 6
	24.	Build freedom up about me and distill WM 30
	24.	--Anguished, the wit that cries out of me WM 37
	26.	Forgive me for an echo of these things Rec 27
	30.	And you may fall downstairs with me F&H II 18
	32.	You, here beside me, delicate ambassador F&H III 3
	35.	And could they hear me I would tell them V-1 9
	48.	Be with me, Luis de San Angel, now AM 1
	48.	That made me exile in her streets, stood me AM 18
	48.	Nigh surged me witless.... Hearing the surf near AM 22
	54.	And you beside me, blessed now while sirens HD 21
	60.	One day in spring my father took to me VW 33
	66.	Each seemed a child, like me, on a loose perch Riv 57
	66.	(O Nights that brought me to her body bare Riv 72
	79.	And since then--all that's left to me of Jim Ind 49
	79.	Oh, hold me in those eyes' engaging blue Ind 54
	82.	to put me out at three she sails on time CS 14
	89.	Walt, tell me, Walt Whitman, if infinity CH 44
	93.	O Walt!--Ascensions of thee hover in me now CH 148
	105.	Me farther than scalped Yankees knew to go QH 52

me, cont.   110. Probing through you--toward me, O evermore
                         Tun 78
                   128. Pile on the logs.... Give me your hands Fr 5
                   128. But hold me...somewhere I heard demands Fr 7
                   129. The moans of travail of one dearest beside me
                         An 7
                   142. A mesh of belts down into it, made me think
                         BE 13
                   148. Come now, when will they restore me Loc 3
                   149. Come now--appease me just a little Loc 35
                   157. You have given me the shell, Satan,--carbonic
                         amulet OC 34
                   171. Here has my salient faith annealed me KW 1
                   171. To skies impartial, that do not disown me KW 3
                   171. Nor claim me, either, by Adam's spine--nor rib
                         KW 4
                   176. evil smile. And, as for me VU 18
                   178. And leave me half adream upon the main PB 4
                   184. Deny me not in this sweet Caribbean dawn Emp 5
                   184. Leave, leave that Caribbean praise to me Emp 8
                   185. Friendship agony! words came to me Post 1
                   185. the wren and thrush, made solid print for me
                         Post 3
                   188. me "the True Cross"--let us remember the Doctor
                         and HR 3
                   193. Dispatches me as though I dropped down the knell
                         B Tow 2
                   194. The steep encroachments of my blood left me
                         B Tow 25

mead   16. A sarabande the wind mowed on the mead RR 2
meadows   23. While August meadows somewhere clasp his brow
                         WM 23
                    32. Plangent over meadows, and looked down F&H III 15
                    36. In these poinsettia meadows of her tides V-2 13
meager   33. Laugh out the meager penance of their days
                         F&H III 41
meaningful   91. There, meaningful, fledged as the Pleiades
                         CH 107
meanwhile   156. Deliberate, gainsay death's brittle crypt.
                         Meanwhile OC 14
measure   50. Merges the wind in measure to the waves AM 40
                    68. And few evade full measure of their fate Riv 108
                   137. That, freed from beat and measure, wanders For 2
                   152. that heavens climb to measure, thus Int 10
mechanics   32. In corymbulous formations of mechanics
                         F&H III 13
medicine-man   73. Spark, tooth! Medicine-man, relent, restore
                         Dan 59
meditation   115. Of heaven's meditation, yoking wave At 54
medley   18. And stabbing medley that sways Pos 13
meek   5. Alms to the meek the volcano burst EC 3
                    11. We make our meek adjustments Chap 1

meet	14.	Seldom, now, meet a mirror in her eyes Fern 2
	28.	I would have you meet this bartered blood F&H I 28
	28.	I meet you, therefore, in that eventual flame F&H I 44
	54.	They meet you listening midway in your dream HD 2
	108.	As usual you will meet the scuttle yawn Tun 22
	110.	And why do I often meet your visage here Tun 72
meeting	38.	Madly meeting logically in this hour V-4 10
	69.	Meeting the Gulf, hosannas silently below Riv 143
Meeting House	105.	Fresh from the radio in the old Meeting House QH 37
meets	24.	How much yet meets the treason of the snow WM 43
	28.	Lightly as moonlight on the eaves meets snow F&H I 31
	156.	Until it meets the blue's comedian host OC 26
Meistersinger	94.	Our Meistersinger, thou set breath in steel CH 193
Melbourne	84.	to Frisco, Melbourne CS 62
mellowed	125.	And vented his long mellowed wines C 3
melody	30.	Through snarling hails of melody F&H II 10
melt	6.	And liable to melt as snow MGLL 11
	130.	Jade-green with sunlight, melt and flow Ech 2
melting	123.	The moat of the desert was melting from clover Moth 31
membrane	193.	Membrane through marrow, my long-scattered score B Tow 11
memoranda	27.	Across the memoranda, baseball scores F&H I 5
memoried	182.	Like a vast phantom maned by all that memoried night Et 45
memories	5.	But only to build memories of spiritual gates EC 17
	15.	Have you no memories, O Darkly Bright NL 8
	93.	What memories of vigils, bloody, by that Cape CH 166
	150.	Indeed, old memories come back to life GWP 15
memory	6.	But those of memory MGLL 2
	6.	Yet how much room for memory there is MGLL 3
	9.	She has no memory, nor fear, nor hope GA 11
	10.	Honceforth her memory is more SM 22
	16.	And finally, in that memory all things nurse RR 17
	21.	My memory I left in a ravine Pass 6
	22.	Memory, committed to the page, had broke Pass 37
	33.	To memory, or known the ominous lifted arm F&H III 28
	60.	So memory, that strikes a rhyme out of a box VW 30

memory, cont.	78.	As long as Jim, your father's memory, is warm Ind 45
	112.	Here at the waters' edge the hands drop memory Tun 132
	116.	Migrations that must needs void memory At 81
	139.	Rounds off my memory of her Lege 2
	141.	The two men smiled into each other's eyes EpH 24
	151.	memory serves there is still APE 16
	184.	To wage you surely back to memory Emp 10
Memphis	66.	--Memphis to Tallahassee--riding the rods Riv 60
	68.	Memphis Johnny, Steamboat Bill, Missouri Joe Riv 99
men	62.	three men, still hungry on the tracks, ploddingly Riv 21
	64.	But some men take their liquor slow--and count Riv 28
	64.	The ancient men--wifeless or runaway Riv 54
	74.	And she is virgin to the last of men Dan 92
	78.	Of all our silent men--the long team line Ind 38
	104.	Much of our store of faith in other men QH 15
	144.	I will go and pitch quoits with old men PA 22
	145.	Roumanian business men PA 37
	164.	I dreamed that all men dropped their names, and sang NA 9
mendicants	94.	Familiar, thou, as mendicants in public places CH 191
men's	34.	The dice of drowned men's bones he saw bequeath AMT 2
mention	181.	That Havana, not to mention poor Batabanó Et 20
merciless	14.	In crowns less grey--O merciless tidy hair Fern 10
	39.	Together in one merciless white blade V-5 3
mercury	25.	I crust a plate of vibrant mercury Rec 7
mercy	18.	And the mercy, feminine, that stays Pos 14
	127.	And reaping, have mercy and love issued forth Hi 6
	127.	Mercy, white milk, and honey, gold love Hi 7
mere	46.	(How could mere toil align thy choiring strings TBB 30
	78.	Knew that mere words could not have brought us nearer Ind 42
merges	50.	Merges the wind in measure to the waves AM 40
merging	68.	The Ohio merging,--borne down Tennessee Riv 95
meridians	51.	And biassed by full sails, meridians reel AM 86
merriest	104.	Who would, ourselves, stalk down the merriest ghost QH 16
merriment	64.	High in a cloud of merriment, recalled Riv 43
mesa	70.	Where prayers, forgotten, streamed the mesa sands Dan 7

mesh	142.	A mesh of belts down into it, made me think BE 13
meshes	114.	Transparent meshes--fleckless the gleaming staves At 6
meshless	123.	And without one cloud-car in that wide meshless blue Moth 35
messages	88.	Where strange tongues vary messages of surf CH 7
met	82.	I met a man in South Street, tall CS 1
	172.	Yet met the wave again between your arms ABP 2
metallic	30.	O, I have known metallic paradises F&H II 24
metaphysics	188.	metaphysics that are typhoid plus and had engaged HR 22
meteor	74.	Like one white meteor, sacrosanct and blent Dan 78
meteorite's	171.	The oar plash, and the meteorite's white arch KW 5
methods	148.	To adaptate her methods and deportment Loc 11
meticulous	39.	Meticulous, past midnight in clear rime V-5 1
Mexico	188.	in Mexico.... That night in Vera Cruz--verily for HR 2
	191.	So ring the church bells here in Mexico Purg 18
mid-kingdom	4.	Wanders in some mid-kingdom, dark, that lies BT 10
midnight	39.	Meticulous, past midnight in clear rime V-5 1
	112.	Searching, thumbing the midnight on the piers Tun 126
	163.	Its course, though he'd clamped midnight to noon sky Id 12
	179.	of wine and mandolines. Midnight; and maybe love Len 10
	188.	and the pharos shine--the mid-wind midnight stroke HR 9
midnights	66.	--As I have trod the rumorous midnights, too Riv 70
midway	54.	They meet you listening midway in your dream HD 2
mid-wind	188.	and the pharos shine--the mid-wind midnight stroke HR 9
might	69.	Ochreous and lynx-barred in lengthening might Riv 130
	186.	Engrave such hazards as thy might controls Shak 3
migrations	116.	Migrations that must needs void memory At 81
mildew	156.	Is Commissioner of mildew throughout the ambushed senses OC 21
mile	58.	Down gold arpeggios mile on mile unwinds VW 4
miles	58.	Listen! the miles a hurdy-gurdy grinds VW 3
	62.	Erie it ain't for miles around a Riv 8
	114.	Taut miles of shuttling moonlight syncopate At 3
	185.	their ribbon miles, beside the railroad ties Post 8

milk   127. Mercy, white milk, and honey, gold love Hi 7
                    168. A milk of earth when stricken off the stalk
                          AP 10
milk-blood   129. The anxious milk-blood in the veins of the earth
                          An 1
milk-bright   169. Milk-bright, Thy chisel wind Hur 6
milk-light   188. of its, its milk-light regularity above my bath
                          partition HR 10
milky   131. Two ivory women by a milky sea Ba 1
mill   104. While we who press the cider mill, regarding
                          them QH 10
million   29. Beyond their million brittle, bloodshot eyes
                          F&H I 46
                    102. Pigeons by the million Va 11
millions   171. Because these millions reap a dead conclusion
                          KW 9
mill-race   70. Tugging below the mill-race, I could see Dan 18
mills   19. Dissolve all but the windows of the mills LC 3
                    179. the buzz of saw mills, the crunch and blast of
                          quarries Len 2
mimic   9. Shining suspension, mimic of the sun GA 2
mimosas   163. The boy straggling under those mimosas, daft
                          Id 2
mind   8. Still, having in mind gold hair PU 17
                     27. The mind has shown itself at times F&H I 1
                     27. The mind is brushed by sparrow wings F&H I 8
                     83. I saw the frontiers gleaming of his mind CS 37
                     98. The mind is churned to spittle, whispering hell
                          SC 17
                    108. Or can't you quite make up your mind to ride
                          Tun 18
                    110. In interborough fissures of the mind Tun 71
                    147. As now her heart and mind Per 12
                    162. So eyes that mind thee fair and gone OS 5
                    170. Some reconcilement of remotest mind TED 12
mine   13. But her own words are night's and mine IS 16
                     76. As I close mine Ind 4
                     79. Whose folks, like mine, came out of Arrowhead
                          Ind 50
                    102. Saturday Mary, mine Va 8
                    136. Mine is a world foregone though not yet ended
                          Ps 5
                    149. --Which is to be mine, you say Loc 21
                    176. the dense mine of the orchid, split in two
                          VU 4
mineral   70. With mineral wariness found out the stone Dan 6
mingled   8. That mingled in such exile guise PU 2
mingling   4. And mingling incantations on the air BT 8
                     38. The harbor shoulders to resign in mingling
                          V-4 18
                     40. O rivers mingling toward the sky V-6 9
minimum   108. Be minimum, then, to swim the hiving swarms
                          Tun 24

minor   125. And with it song of minor, broken strain C 11
minstrel   36. O minstrel galleons of Carib fire V-2 22
minstrels   62. Minstrels when you steal a chicken just Riv 6
minting   24. Remorseless line, minting their separate wills
                         WM 25
minute   64. The river's minute by the far brook's year
                         Riv 30
mirage   190. Return the mirage on a coin that spells Rel 16
mirror   3. As silent as a mirror is believed Leg 1
                     3. Unwhispering as a mirror Leg 18
                    14. Seldom, now, meet a mirror in her eyes Fern 2
mirrored   89. Left Hesperus mirrored in the lucid pool CH 32
mirth   111. Whose hideous laughter is a bellows mirth
                         Tun 107
miss   8. And miss the dry sound of bees PU 19
                   160. missus Miss MT 14
Mississippi   69. The Mississippi drinks the farthest dale Riv 127
                    69. Down two more turns the Mississippi pours
                         Riv 134
Missouri   68. Memphis Johnny, Steamboat Bill, Missouri Joe
                         Riv 99
missus   160. missus Miss MT 14
mist   136. And mist that is more constant than your vows
                         Ps 8
                   159. Like water, undestroyed,--like mist, unburned
                         TCJ 18
mistake   174. This hieroglyph is no dumb, deaf mistake BNOK 13
mister   160. O mister Senor MT 13
mistletoe   56. Under the mistletoe of dreams, a star HD 36
mists   126. With crimson feathers whips away the mists
                         O-N 2
misty   13. Her furtive lace and misty hair IS 5
Mizzentop   104. Above them old Mizzentop, palatial white QH 17
mix   188. Cruz--to bring--to take--to mix--to ransom--to
                         de- HR 14
moan   73. The long moan of a dance is in the sky Dan 51
moans   129. The moans of travail of one dearest beside me
                         An 7
moat   73. Fed down your anklets to the sunset's moat
                         Dan 72
                   123. The moat of the desert was melting from clover
                         Moth 31
mock   186. Sheets that mock lust and thorns that scribble
                         hate Shak 6
mocked   171. As draws them towards a doubly mocked confusion
                         KW 11
                   180. Hair mocked by the sea, her lover Lib 5
model   184. Have kissed, caressed the model of the hurricane
                         Emp 2
modern   94. Years of the Modern! Propulsions toward what
                         capes CH 197
                   132. This burns and is not burnt.... My modern love
                         were MC 11

modulated   50. Sun-cusped and zoned with modulated fire AM 44
moidores   158. Here where we finger moidores of spent grace
                      Mer 13
moment   18. One moment in sacrifice (the direst Pos 4
                 56. The fog leans one last moment on the sill HD 35
                 89. Flickers a moment, consumes us in its smile
                      CH 36
                 148. For imminent is that moment when Loc 5
momently   45. Tilting there momently, shrill shirt ballooning
                      TBB 19
                 170. And plundered momently in every breast TED 8
momentous   185. Love and the breath of faith, momentous bride
                      Emp 13
moment's   177. Seek bliss then, brother, in my moment's shame
                      Rep 6
moments   15. Cold-hushed, there is only the shifting of
                      moments NL 9
                 18. Accumulate such moments to an hour Pos 10
momentwise   90. Our hearing momentwise; but fast in whirling
                      arma-/tures CH 69
monarch   193. Of that tribunal monarch of the air B Tow 22
monkey   144. The trowel,--and the monkey wrench PA 18
monody   34. Monody shall not wake the mariner AMT 15
monoliths   114. New octaves trestle the twin monoliths At 18
monoplanes   60. Garter snakes under...And the monoplanes VW 19
monotone   40. Its beating leagues of monotone V-6 6
                 109. underground, the monotone Tun 36
monsoon   16. The monsoon cut across the delta RR 20
month   145. "One month,--I go back rich PA 31
moon   8.   The slant moon on the slanting hill PU 9
                 11. The moon in lonely alleys make Chap 20
                 13. Like a waiting moon, in shadow swims IS 4
                 19. Rinsings from the moon LC 2
                 48. More absolute than ever--biding the moon AM 19
                 50. Tomorrow's moon will grant us Saltes Bar AM 53
                 51. From Moon to Saturn in one sapphire wheel AM 78
                 70. I learned to catch the trout's moon whisper; I
                      Dan 22
                 74. --And laughs, pure serpent, Time itself, and
                      moon Dan 75
                 114. Beyond whose frosted capes the moon bequeaths
                      At 19
                 122. That they only can see when their moon limits
                      vision Moth 9
                 122. Their mother, the moon, marks a halo of light
                      Moth 10
                 126. Then the moon O-N 8
                 138. Despair until the moon by tears be won Port 3
                 142. May slumber yet in the moon, awaiting BE 19
                 143. The slant moon with the slanting hill BE 24
                 145. "Full on this casement shone the wintry moon
                      PA 42

moon, cont.	148.	The orient moon of my dapper affections Loc 4
	149.	Ah! without the moon, what white nights Loc 25
	150.	And all unstintingly as to the moon GWP 5
	171.	Concur with wrist and bicep. In the moon KW 6
	184.	The slit eclipse of moon in palm-lit bonds Emp 4
	192.	Hours, days--and scarcely sun and moon SI 2
moonferrets	91.	By convoy planes, moonferrets that rejoin thee CH 114
moonlight	28.	Lightly as moonlight on the eaves meets snow F&H I 31
	39.	Can strangle this deaf moonlight? For we V-5 9
	39.	Slow tyranny of moonlight, moonlight loved V-5 12
	94.	White banks of moonlight came descending valleys CH 181
	106.	That triple-noted clause of moonlight QH 67
	114.	Taut miles of shuttling moonlight snycopate At 3
moonlit	21.	In moonlit bushels Pass 9
moonmoth	164.	Moonmoth and grasshopper that flee our page NA 1
moon's	159.	The moon's best lover,--guide us by a sleight TCJ 10
moons	122.	Conceived in the light of Arabian moons Moth 2
	123.	Which blue tides of cool moons were slow shaken and sunned Moth 44
	132.	Though I have touched her flesh of moons MC 1
	139.	And moons of spring and autumn Lege 8
moonward	36.	Her undinal vast belly moonward bends V-2 4
Moor's	50.	Almost as though the Moor's flung scimitar AM 36
moraine	69.	And roots surrendered down of moraine clays Riv 126
morn	17.	When systematic morn shall sometime flood Par 10
	73.	Lie to us,--dance us back the tribal morn Dan 60
morning	40.	Of swimmers their lost morning eyes V-6 2
	48.	Once more behind us.... It is morning there AM 14
	76.	The morning glory, climbing the morning long Ind 1
	134.	Morning: and through the foggy city gate CDB 25
	147.	Waiting for morning Per 10
	173.	This April morning offers/hurriedly MF 3
morning glory	76.	The morning glory, climbing the morning long Ind 1
morrow's	183.	The morrow's dawn was dense with carrion hazes Et 50

mortal	133.	And stretches up through mortal eyes to see CDB 16
mortality	38.	Than, singing, this mortality alone V-4 7
	167.	Mortality--ascending emerald-bright RP 13
	194.	Whose sweet mortality stirs latent power B Tow 28
mortgages	105.	The woodlouse mortgages the ancient deal QH 42
mosaic	122.	There are butterflies born in mosaic date-vases Moth 3
moth	3.	Nor to match regrets. For the moth Leg 4
	70.	First moth of evening take wing stealthily Dan 20
	123.	The heat led the moth up in octopus arms Moth 38
mother	6.	For the letters of my mother's mother MGLL 6
	60.	My mother almost brought me once from church VW 35
	111.	O Genoese, do you bring mother eyes and hands Tun 104
	122.	Their mother, the moon, marks a halo of light Moth 10
mother's	6.	For the letters of my mother's mother MGLL 6
moth's	122.	But over one moth's eyes were tissues at birth Moth 17
	129.	Of the first moth's descent,--day's predestiny An 5
motion	36.	As her demeanors motion well or ill V-2 9
	45.	Some motion ever unspent in thy stride TBB 15
	89.	Is sluiced by motion,--subjugated never CH 30
	109.	the overtone of motion Tun 35
	109.	of motion is the sound Tun 37
	174.	An able text, more motion than machines BNOK 10
motionless	137.	Outspread and motionless For 4
motor	32.	That narrows darkly into motor dawn F&H III 2
motors	91.	Taut motors surge, space-gnawing, into flight CH 100
mound	10.	Her mound of undelivered life SM 11
mount	100.	Her silly snake rings begin to mount, surmount NWG 19
mountain	64.	Loped under wires that span the mountain stream Riv 25
	72.	Cupped in the larches of the mountain pass Dan 26
	94.	With June the mountain laurel broke through green CH 177
	145.	And his wife, like a mountain, coming in PA 33
	161.	At the turning of the road around the roots of the/mountain IQ 3
	161.	Wide of the mountain--thence to tears and sleep IQ 14
	181.	At the base of the mountain. But the town, the town Et 6
	182.	Blister the mountain, stripped now, bare of palm Et 26

mountain-spear	131.	Shimmering over a black mountain-spear Ba 3
mounted	32.	The mounted, yielding cities of the air F&H III 21
mourner	93.	Has kept of wounds, O Mourner, all that sum CH 169
mourns	156.	In wrinkled shadows--mourns OC 7
mouse	105.	A welcome to highsteppers that no mouse QH 39
	187.	like a mouse under pussy Ma 10
mouth	83.	have you seen Popocatepetl--birdless mouth CS 26
mouths	114.	Their labyrinthine mouths of history At 11
move	138.	Or, Daphnis, move among the bees with Chloe Port 4
moved	8.	Once moved us toward presentiments PU 10
moveless	114.	--From black embankments, moveless soundings/ hailed At 15
moves	150.	The world moves by so fast these days GWP 12
	186.	A hand moves on the page! Who shall again Shak 2
movie	150.	Of Lottie Honeydew, movie queen GWP 8
moving	92.	Regard the moving turrets! From grey decks CH 118
mowed	16.	A sarabande the wind mowed on the mead RR 2
Mr.	179.	know, Mr. Len 19
Mr. Budge	179.	And there is, as Mr. Budge explained before his Len 11
much	6.	Yet how much room for memory there is MGLL 3
	6.	Through much of what she would not understand MGLL 24
	16.	How much I would have bartered! the black gorge RR 12
	21.	So was I turned about and back, much as your smoke Pass 21
	24.	How much yet meets the treason of the snow WM 43
	27.	Too much the baked and labeled dough F&H I 2
	82.	I'm not much good at time any more keep CS 15
	135.	Yet,--much follows, much endures...Trust birds/ alone CL 5
	137.	I can remember much forgetfulness For 11
	149.	Alas, you know how much I oppose Loc 22
	149.	That seem too much impromptu Loc 24
	150.	And how much more they cannot see GWP 10
	158.	But since the Cross sank, much that's warped and/cracked Mer 6
	170.	You who desired so much--in vain to ask TED 1
	182.	And fell dead or dying, but it didn't so much matter Et 49
much-exacting	25.	Inquire this much-exacting fragment smile Rec 9
muddy	109.	like a pigeon's muddy dream--potatoes Tun 42
	144.	With the stubbornness of muddy water PA 4

muffle	188.	conies with a typical pistol--trying to muffle doors HR 8
muffled	10.	Until you reach the muffled floor SM 16
	12.	Ends in this latter muffled Past 8
	111.	--Or the muffled slaughter of a day in birth Tun 108
mufflings	100.	Of bandy eyes.... No extra mufflings here NWG 3
mulching	165.	They're back now on that mulching job at Pepper's BSEW 10
mule	182.	And somebody's mule steamed, swaying right by the/pump Et 31
	182.	The mule stumbled, staggered. I somehow couldn't budge Et 35
	182.	I beat the dazed mule toward the road. He got that far Et 48
multiplied	122.	Too multiplied even to center his gaze Moth 18
multitudes	27.	Divided by accepted multitudes F&H I 3
	45.	With multitudes bent toward some flashing scene TBB 10
multitudinous	115.	Into what multitudinous Verb the suns At 45
murmurless	90.	The bearings glint,--O murmurless and shined CH 73
murmurously	54.	Your cool arms murmurously about me lay HD 24
murmurs	82.	Murmurs of Leviathan he spoke CS 11
music	6.	To carry back the music to its source MGLL 20
	19.	To music and retrieve what perjuries LC 17
	31.	This music has a reassuring way F&H II 30
	133.	The slit, soft-pulling:---and music follows cue CDB 12
	133.	Carmen whirls, and music swirls and dips CDB 19
musical	160.	gum took place. Up jug to musical, hanging jug just gay MT 4
	184.	Gathered and made musical in feathery fronds Emp 3
musk	68.	Maybe the breeze will lift the River's musk Riv 97
mustard	23.	Narrowing the mustard scansions of the eyes WM 2
	69.	Poised wholly on its dream, a mustard glow Riv 140
mustering	51.	White toil of heaven's cordons, mustering AM 81
mute	132.	Still she sits gestureless and mute MC 2
	173.	Fall mute and sudden (dealing change/for lilies MF 7
muted	100.	And the lewd trounce of a final muted beat NWG 23
mutiny	50.	Bewilderment and mutiny heap whelming AM 34
mutual	38.	Mutual blood, transpiring as foreknown V-4 19
	90.	In coiled precision, bunched in mutual glee CH 72

my

  6. For the letters of my mother's mother   MGLL 6
 13. She hears my step behind the green   IS 11
 21. My memory I left in a ravine   Pass 6
 21. The shadows of boulders lengthened my back
       Pass 13
 21. In the bronze gongs of my cheeks   Pass 14
 21. A thief beneath, my stolen book in hand
       Pass 27
 24. Until my blood dreams a receptive smile   WM 33
 28. But if I lift my arms it is to bend   F&H I 40
 36. Adagios of islands, O my Prodigal   V-2 14
 38. All bright insinuations that my years have caught
       V-4 21
 40. My eyes pressed black against the prow   V-6 11
 48. The word I bring, O you who reined my suit
       AM 3
 56. my tongue upon your throat--singing   HD 27
 60. My mother almost brought me once from church
       VW 35
 64. "--And when my Aunt Sally Simpson smiled," he/
       drawled   Riv 44
 64. Behind my father's cannery works I used to see
       Riv 52
 72. I left my sleek boat nibbling margin grass
       Dan 28
 73. I could not pick the arrows from my side
       Dan 66
 76. And bison thunder rends my dreams no more
       Ind 5
 76. As once my womb was torn, my boy, when you
       Ind 6
 79. You, Larry, traveller--/stranger,/son,/--my
       friend   Ind 64
 82. damned white Arctic killed my time   CS 21
 83. "O life's a geyser--beautiful--my lungs   CS 35
 93. And this, thine other hand, upon my heart
       CH 164
 94. And onward yielding past my utmost year   CH 190
 95. My hand/in yours,/Walt Whitman--/so   CH 220
 99. Yes, Eve--wraith of my unloved seed   SC 27
105. Where are my kinsmen and the patriarch race
       QH 48
112. And this thy harbor, O my City, I have driven
       under   Tun 129
124. My eyes have hugged beauty and winged life's
       brief spell   Moth 50
127. Up the chasm-walls of my bleeding heart   Hi 1
127. Of the hive of the world that is my heart   Hi 4
132. This burns and is not burnt.... My modern love
       were   MC 11
135. My hands have not touched water since your hands
       CL 1

my, cont.   135. No;--nor my lips freed laughter since "farewell
                               CL 2
                         135. A dove's wings clung about my heart last night
                               CL 6
                         139. Rounds off my memory of her Lege 2
                         139. And even my vision will be erased Lege 10
                         144. And put them in my pockets PA 21
                         148. The orient moon of my dapper affections Loc 4
                         148. My crisp soul will be flooded by a langour
                               Loc 7
                         148. Of my lunar sensibility Loc 16
                         149. That my conscience sees double Loc 30
                         149. And my heart fishes in troubled water Loc 31
                         149. Of the archbeam of my cross-legged labours
                               Loc 34
                         151. "how are my bowels today?" and APE 3
                         156. Let fiery blossoms clot the light, render my
                               ghost OC 24
                         163. My trespass vision shrinks to face his wrong
                               Id 16
                         171. Here has my salient faith annealed me KW 1
                         171. Need I presume the same fruit of my bone KW 10
                         174. You've overruled my typewriter tonight BNOK 8
                         176. the terrible puppet of my dreams, shall VU 2
                         177. Seek bliss then, brother, in my moment's shame
                               Rep 6
                         177. So sleep, dear brother, in my fame, my shame un-
                               done Rep 12
                         185. at last shyly. My only final friends Post 2
                         185. the audible ransom, ensign of my faith Post 5
                         185. Antillean fingers counting my pulse, my love
                               forever Post 16
                         188. my thoughts, my humble, fond remembrances of
                               the HR 4
                         188. of it, its milk-light regularity above my bath
                               partition HR 10
                         188. posedly slept, supposedly in #35--thus in my
                               wakeful HR 17
                         190. My wrist in the vestibule of time--who Rel 14
                         191. My country, O my land, my friends Purg 1
                         191. And all my countrymen I see rush toward one
                               stall Purg 12
                         191. (They ring too obdurately here to need my call
                               Purg 19
                         193. Membrane through marrow, my long-scattered score
                               B Tow 11
                         193. My word I poured. But was it cognate, scored
                               B Tow 21
                         194. The steep encroachments of my blood left me
                               B Tow 25
                         194. My veins recall and add, revived and sure
                               B Tow 30

my, cont.	194.	The angelus of wars my chest evokes B Tow 31
My Old Kentucky Home	64.	<u>My</u> <u>Old</u> <u>Kentucky</u> <u>Home</u> and <u>Casey</u> <u>Jones</u> Riv 39
myriad	54.	While myriad snowy hands are clustering at the panes HD 25
	115.	In myriad syllables,--Psalm of Cathay At 47
	122.	Where are set all the myriad jewelleries of night Moth 12
myself	72.	--And knew myself within some boding shade Dan 38
	144.	I will whisper words to myself PA 20
mystery	166.	Peace from his Mystery IV 12
mysterious	108.	Mysterious kitchens.... You shall search them all Tun 5
mystic	134.	And some dream still of Carmen's mystic face CDB 27
mystical	122.	And had not his pinions with signs mystical Moth 21
myth	46.	And of the curveship lend a myth to God TBB 44
	89.	Sea eyes and tidal, undenying, bright with myth CH 58
	94.	Of that great Bridge, our Myth, whereof I sing CH 196
	116.	Swift peal of secular light, intrinsic Myth At 65
	176.	bright with myth...Such VU 16
mythic	115.	Searches the timeless laugh of mythic spears At 32
mythical	70.	Mythical brows we saw retiring--loth Dan 9

nacreous	156.	I count these nacreous frames of tropic death OC 9
naively	30.	Greet naively--yet intrepidly F&H II 15
naked	32.	In whispers, naked of steel F&H III 5
	52.	And kingdoms/naked in the/trembling heart AM 89
	109.	--Quite unprepared rush naked back to light Tun 28
	187.	are naked. Twilights raw Ma 4
name	10.	Will laugh and call your name; while you SM 17
	40.	Waiting, afire, what name, unspoke V-6 13
	62.	Stick your patent name on a signboard Riv 1
	66.	Have dreamed beyond the print that bound her name Riv 73
	76.	His gleaming name Ind 20
	116.	Of silver sequel, Deity's young name At 79
	156.	And anagrammatize your name)--No, nothing here OC 5
	156.	To the white sand I may speak a name, fertile OC 12
	158.	Has followed in its name, has heaped its grave Mer 7
	164.	And still wing on, untarnished of the name NA 2
	164.	Struck free and holy in one Name always NA 12
	190.	With desperate propriety, whose name is writ Rel 10
named	95.	To course that span of consciousness thou'st named CH 209
nameless	25.	Let the same nameless gulf beleaguer us Rec 17
	98.	I wanted you, nameless Woman of the South SC 1
namelessness	98.	God--your namelessness. And the wash SC 22
names	20.	Names peeling from Thine eyes LC 33
	88.	The ancient names--return home to our own CH 9
	156.	Albeit in a stranger tongue. Tree names, flower names OC 13
	164.	Names we have, even, to clap on the wind NA 7
	164.	I dreamed that all men dropped their names, and sang NA 9
naphtha	90.	The soul, by naphtha fledged into new reaches CH 84
narrowing	23.	Narrowing the mustard scansions of the eyes WM 2
narrows	32.	That narrows darkly into motor dawn F&H III 2
nasal	90.	The nasal whine of power whips a new universe CH 59
natal	152.	Madonna, natal to thy yielding In 18
nations	93.	Of love and hatred, birth,--surcease of nations CH 146
nation's	151.	the nation's lips are thin and fast APE 14
native	88.	To that deep wonderment, our native clay CH 14
	165.	Anyone but these native high-steppers BSEW 12

natural	151.	and other natural grammarians are ab- APE 21
nature	7.	The fleece of nature with those purposes SMA 2
navel	33.	Anchises' navel, dripping of the sea F&H III 36
navelled	111.	The conscience navelled in the plunging wind Tun 113
Nazarene	19.	Thy Nazarene and tinder eyes LC 26
	20.	Compulsion of the year, O Nazarene LC 36
near	48.	Nigh surged me witless.... Hearing the surf near AM 22
	89.	Near Paumanok--your lone patrol--and heard the wraith CH 46
	94.	Not greatest, thou,--not first, nor last,--but near CH 189
	156.	Near the coral beach--nor zigzag fiddle crabs OC 3
	181.	And a funnel high and dry up near the park Et 16
nearer	78.	Knew that mere words could not have brought us nearer Ind 42
nearest	100.	(Then rush the nearest exit through the smoke NWG 8
nearing	92.	Zodiacs, dashed/(now nearing fast the Cape CH 141
nearly	84.	Outside a wharf truck nearly ran him down CS 49
nears	185.	as one nears New Orleans, sweet trenches by the train Post 9
neatly	62.	ping gimleted and neatly out of sight Riv 23
	100.	You pick your blonde out neatly through the smoke NWG 6
necessary	100.	Invite the necessary cloudy clinch NWG 2
	151.	so-loot-lee necessary APE 22
necklaces	156.	Brutal necklaces of shells around each grave OC 10
Ned	78.	You were the first--before Ned and this farm Ind 47
need	144.	O City, your axles need not the oil of song PA 19
	171.	Need I presume the same fruit of my bone KW 10
	191.	(They ring too obdurately here to need my call Purg 19
needle	51.	A needle in the sight, suspended north AM 74
needles	168.	The needles and hack-saws of cactus bleed AP 9
needs	116.	Migrations that must needs void memory At 81
	125.	From penitence must needs bring pain C 10
	170.	Needs more than wit to gather, love to bind TED 11
negative	189.	not heed the negative--so might go on to undeserved HR 31
negroes	181.	For cotted negroes, bandaged to be taken Et 12
neighbor	176.	And what about the staunch neighbor tabulations VU 7
neighbors	105.	What cunning neighbors history has in fine QH 41

neighing	70.	She ran the neighing canyons all the spring Dan 3
nephew	14.	I have known myself a nephew to confusions Fern 8
nervosities	31.	Striated with nuances, nervosities F&H II 33
nervous	82.	a nervous shark tooth swung on his chain CS 2
nestings	16.	And all the singular nestings in the hills RR 13
nets	114.	White tempest nets file upward, upward ring At 22
Nevada	150.	Toward lawyers and Nevada GWP 9
never	122.	Never came light through that honey-thick glaze Moth 20
new	24.	New thresholds, new anatomies! Wine talons WM 29
	24.	Wherein new purities are snared; where chimes WM 34
	24.	Invent new dominoes of love and bile WM 39
	30.	New soothings, new amazements F&H II 16
	33.	Delve upward for the new and scattered wine F&H III 39
	62.	and lands sakes! under the new playbill ripped Riv 4
	89.	Dream cancels dream in this new realm of fact CH 39
	90.	The nasal whine of power whips a new universe CH 59
	90.	New verities, new inklings in the velvet hummed CH 63
	90.	The soul, by naphtha fledged into new reaches CH 84
	90.	New latitudes, unknotting, soon give place CH 86
	93.	Thou bringest tally, and a pact, new bound CH 155
	95.	New integers of Roman, Viking, Celt CH 203
	105.	Bubbles in time to Hollywood's new love-nest pageant QH 36
	105.	That unfolds a new destiny to fill QH 56
	110.	To brush some new presentiment of pain Tun 62
	114.	New octaves trestle the twin monoliths At 18
	125.	And wavering shoulders with a new light shed C 9
	141.	Bunches of new green breaking a hard turf EpH 19
	152.	communicant and speeding new In 14
	192.	He does not know the new hum in the sky SI 9
New Avalon Hotel	105.	(Now the New Avalon Hotel) volcanoes roar QH 38
Newfoundland	148.	Bland as the wide gaze of a Newfoundland Loc 8
New Orleans	185.	as one nears New Orleans, sweet trenches by the train Post 9

night, cont.   122. At night like a grain of sand, futile and dried
                        Moth 24
                  123. Though a black god to him in a dizzying night
                        Moth 34
                  125. About the empty heart of night C 2
                  125. But you who hear the lamp whisper thru night
                        C 12
                  126. Floods the grape-hung night O-N 10
                  128. But on the window licks the night Fr 4
                  128. And on the window licks the night Fr 8
                  135. A dove's wings clung about my heart last night
                        CL 6
                  137. Forgetfulness is rain at night For 6
                  147. If she waits late at night Per 1
                  188. in Mexico.... That night in Vera Cruz--verily
                        for HR 2
                  188. great bacteriologist.... The wind that night,
                        the HR 5

nightly   108. Channel the congresses, nightly sessions Tun 3
nightmares   149. What nightmares rich with ingenuity Loc 26
                 171. Of apish nightmares into steel-strung stone
                       KW 12

night's   13. But her own words are night's and mine IS 16
nights   18. Through a thousand nights the flesh Pos 5
                  19. And the nights opening LC 14
                  20. Unstanched and luminous. And as the nights
                       LC 38
                  28. Those hands of yours that count the nights
                       F&H I 25
                  66. (O Nights that brought me to her body bare
                       Riv 72
                  69. Nights turbid, vascular with silted shale
                       Riv 125
                 139. The tossing loneliness of many nights Lege 1
                 149. Ah! without the moon, what white nights Loc 25

Nile   190. Something of sand and sun the Nile defends
                       Rel 17

nimble   32. The tensile boughs, the nimble blue plateaus
                       F&H III 20

Nimbus   85. Nimbus? and you rivals two CS 75
Nine   179. chorea took him away--there is the Nine of
                       Len 12

ninety-five   105. Table that Powitzky buys for only nine-/Ty-
                       five at Adams' auction,--eats the seal QH 43-44

ninety-one   85. Buntlines tusseling (91 days, 20 hours, and
                       anchored!)/Rainbow, Leander CS 73

Nineveh   25. Wrenched gold of Nineveh;--yet leave the tower
                       Rec 22

nip   85. at Java Head freshened the nip CS 70
nodded   78. She nodded--and that smile across her shoulder
                       Ind 43

noises	54.	The long, tired sounds, fog-insulated noises HD 3
	146.	And a hash of noises is slung up from the street PA 57
nomad	64.	Rail-squatters ranged in nomad raillery Riv 53
none	28.	Imminent in his dream, none better knows F&H I 29
	94.	And passed that Barrier that none escapes CH 199
	140.	We claim, and none may know Int 6
noon	3.	The legend of their youth into the noon Leg 23
	38.	And widening noon within your breast for gathering V-4 20
	45.	Down Wall, from girder into street noon leaks TBB 21
	74.	O, like the lizard in the furious noon Dan 73
	102.	High in the noon of May Va 17
	122.	So they sleep in the shade of black palm-bark at noon Moth 13
	145.	I remember one Sunday noon PA 27
	156.	Under the poinciana, of a noon or afternoon OC 23
	160.	under your noon MT 10
	163.	Its course, though he'd clamped midnight to noon sky Id 12
	171.	To heaven or hades--to an equally frugal noon KW 8
noon's	16.	Where cypresses shared the noon's RR 7
	185.	Dawn's broken arc! the noon's more furbished room Post 12
noontide's	167.	Amid the noontide's blazed asperities RP 3
Norfolk	183.	New York with the gobs, Guantanamo, Norfolk Et 59
north	45.	Thy cables breathe the North Atlantic still TBB 24
	51.	A needle in the sight, suspended north AM 74
north-bound	144.	North-bound, and East and West PA 7
northern	8.	It was a kind and northern face PU 1
northpole	62.	RADIO ROARS IN EVERY HOME WE HAVE THE NORTHPOLE Riv 14
northward	72.	And northward reaches in that violet wedge Dan 35
nose	182.	Were death predestined! You held your nose already Et 33
noses	150.	Noses pressed against the glass GWP 17
	182.	The weather's in their noses. There's Don--but that one, white Et 43
notches	141.	The knots and notches,--many in the wide EpH 16
note	10.	Walk now, and note the lover's death SM 21
	89.	Through surf, its bird note there a long time falling CH 47
	106.	Listen, transmuting silence with that stilly note QH 64

nothing	39.	Nothing like this in the world," you say V-5 14
	39.	Where nothing turns but dead sands flashing V-5 17
	39.	Nothing so flagless as this piracy V-5 20
	54.	Ask nothing but this sheath of pallid air HD 20
	66.	Blind fists of nothing, humpty-dumpty clods Riv 61
	78.	Won nothing out of fifty-nine--those years Ind 26
	156.	And anagrammatize your name)--No, nothing here OC 5
	177.	Thou canst read nothing except through appetite Rep 1
nothingness	168.	This tuft that thrives on saline nothingness AP 1
nought	169.	Nought stayeth, nought now bideth Hur 3
now	152.	from sleep forbidden now and wide Int 12
nozzled	72.	Feet nozzled wat'ry webs of upper flows Dan 31
nozzles	188.	like rats--and too, when rats make rose nozzles of pink HR 27
nuances	31.	Striated with nuances, nervosities F&H II 33
nude	7.	In that ripe nude with head/reared SMA 5
nudges	23.	Nudges a cannister across the bar WM 22
	187.	nudges shingles and windows Ma 15
nudging	90.	O sinewy silver biplane, nudging the wind's withers CH 77
nuggets'	78.	It rose up shambling in the nuggets' wake Ind 22
number	188.	posedly slept, supposedly in #35--thus in my wakeful HR 17
numbers	27.	Numbers, rebuffed by asphalt, crowd F&H I 9
	32.	Of intricate slain numbers that arise F&H III 4
	34.	An embassy. Their numbers as he watched AMT 3
nurse	16.	And finally, in that memory all things nurse RR 17
	148.	That I nurse for Cydalise Loc 14
nursed	131.	She came in such still water, and so nursed Ba 10

15. Have you no memories, O Darkly Bright   NL 8
18. Hidden,--O undirected as the sky   Pos 7
20. Compulsion of the year, O Nazarene   LC 36
20. From charred and riven stakes, O   LC 43
25. Regard the capture here, O Janus-faced   Rec 1
30. O, I have known metallic paradises   F&H II 24
33. O brother-thief of time, that we recall
    F&H III 40
35. O brilliant kids, frisk with your dog   V-1 10
36. Adagios of islands, O my Prodigal   V-2 14
36. Bind us in time, O Seasons clear, and awe
    V-2 21
36. O minstrel galleons of Carib fire   V-2 22
40. O rivers mingling toward the sky   V-6 9
46. O harp and altar, of the fury fused   TBB 29
46. O Sleepless as the river under thee   TBB 41
48. The word I bring, O you who reined my suit   AM 3
48. O where our Indian emperies lie revealed   AM 15
48. "The Great White Birds!" (O Madre María still
    AM 26
50. --Yet no delirium of jewels! O Fernando   AM 46
51. O Thou who sleepest on Thyself, apart   AM 57
51. Subscribest holocaust of ships, O Thou   AM 66
52. te Deum laudamus/O Thou Hand of Fire   AM 90
66. (O Nights that brought me to her body bare   Riv 72
68. O Sheriff, Brakeman and Authority   Riv 105
69. O quarrying passion, undertowed sunlight   Riv 128
70. O Princess whose brown lap was virgin May   Dan 15
72. O Appalachian Spring! I gained the ledge   Dan 33
73. O yelling battlements,--I, too, was liege   Dan 62
74. O, like the lizard in the furious noon   Dan 73
74. O stream by slope and vineyard--into bloom
    Dan 96
75. We danced, O Brave, we danced beyond their farms
    Dan 101
83. O Stamboul Rose--drums weave   CS 22
83. Rose of Stamboul O coral Queen   CS 29
83. "O life's a geyser--beautiful--my lungs   CS 35
89. O Saunterer on free ways still ahead   CH 50
90. The bearings glint,--O murmurless and shined
    CH 73
90. O sinewy silver biplane, nudging the wind's
    withers   CH 77
91. O bright circumferences, heights employed to fly
    CH 93
91. While Cetus-like, O thou Dirigible, enormous
    Lounger   CH 112
92. Toward thee, O Corsair of the typhoon,--pilot,
    hear   CH 123
92. Thine eyes bicarbonated white by speed, O
    Skygak, see   CH 124
93. O Walt!--Ascensions of thee hover in me now
    CH 148

O, cont.   171. O, steel and stone! But gold was, scarcity be-
                            fore KW 13
                      178. So dream thy sails, O phantom bark PB 1
                      191. My country, O my land, my friends Purg 1
                      193. O terraced echoes prostrate on the plain
                            B Tow 16

oak   21. That throve through very oak. And had I walked
                            Pass 24
                       73. The oak grove circles in a crash of leaves
                            Dan 50

oak-vizored   94. How speechful on oak-vizored palisades CH 182
oar   38. The secret oar and petals of all love V-4 25
                       41. Belle Isle, white echo of the oar V-6 28
                       51. Who grindest oar, and arguing the mast AM 65
                       76. But you who drop the scythe to grasp the oar
                            Ind 11
                      171. The oar plash, and the meteorite's white arch
                            KW 5

oars   165. Their engine stalled. No oars, and leaks
                            BSEW 6

oasis   122. Among cocoa-nut palms of a far oasis Moth 1
                      122. On their own small oasis, ray-cut, an incision
                            Moth 11

oasis'   122. Countless rubies and tapers in the oasis' blue
                            haze Moth 16

oath   70. Greeting they sped us, on the arrow's oath
                            Dan 11

obdurately   191. (They ring too obdurately here to need my call
                            Purg 19

obliquely   114. And on, obliquely up bright carrier bars At 17
obscure   46. And obscure as that heaven of the Jews TBB 25
obscured   34. Beat on the dusty shore and were obscured AMT 4
obsequies   11. Our obsequies are, in a way, no enterprise
                            Chap 16

occult   94. And Klondike edelweiss of occult snows CH 180
occupation   146. Bedroom occupation PA 60
ocean   40. And ocean rivers, churning, shift V-6 3
                       51. Like ocean athwart lanes of death and birth
                            AM 58

oceans   114. So seven oceans answer from their dream At 16
ochreous   69. Ochreous and lynx-barred in lenghtening might
                            Riv 130

octagon   23. Octagon, sapphire transepts round the eyes
                            WM 16

octaves   114. New octaves trestle the twin monoliths At 18
octopus   123. The heat led the moth up in octopus arms
                            Moth 38
                      168. Inverted octopus with heavenward arms AP 2

odor-firm   94. Blue-writ and odor-firm with violets, 'til
                            CH 176

odour   21. The rain dried without odour Pass 15

offer	64.	Of unwalled winds they offer, singing low Riv 38
	147.	No world can offer Per 4
offered	93.	Past where the albatross has offered up CH 160
offers	28.	The white wafer cheek of love, or offers words F&H I 30
	173.	This April morning offers/hurriedly MF 3
	174.	The keyboard no more offers an escape BNOK 6
office	58.	And Rip forgot the office hours,/and he forgot the pay VW 14
	110.	"But I want service in this office SERVICE Tun 63
offings	91.	War's fiery kennel masked in downy offings CH 94
often	110.	And why do I often meet your visage here Tun 72
ogre	182.	We shoveled and sweated; watched the ogre sun Et 25
oh	64.	"Jesus! Oh I remember watermelon days!" And sped Riv 42
	79.	Good-bye...Good-bye...oh, I shall always wait Ind 63
	149.	Oh, by the infinite circumflex Loc 33
	151.	of something--Oh APE 9
	151.	unbelievably--Oh APE 10
	158.	Oh Mer 8
Ohio	64.	Ohio, Indiana--blind baggage Riv 33
	68.	The Ohio merging,--borne down Tennessee Riv 95
	144.	Among rolling Ohio hills PA 12
oil	144.	O City, your axles need not the oil of song PA 19
oilrinsed	90.	In oilrinsed circles of blind ecstasy CH 74
oily	112.	Lights, coasting, left the oily tympanum of waters Tun 127
old	6.	Old keys that are but echoes MGLL 18
	32.	Like old women with teeth unjubilant F&H III 17
	66.	Youngsters with eyes like fjords, old reprobates Riv 65
	66.	The old gods of the rain lie wrapped in pools Riv 82
	79.	I'm standing still, I'm old, I'm half of stone Ind 53
	93.	The stars have grooved our eyes with old persuasions CH 145
	104.	Above them old Mizzentop, palatial white QH 17
	105.	Fresh from the radio in the old Meeting House QH 37
	133.	Of whispering tapestry, brown with old fringe CDB 23
	137.	Or an old house in a forest,--or a child For 7
	144.	I will go and pitch quoits with old men PA 22
	150.	Indeed, old memories come back to life GWP 15
	160.	First-plucked before and since the Flood, old hypno- MT 6

old, cont.	174.	Some old Egyptian joke is in the air BNOK 1
	174.	An old Eygptian jest has cramped the tape BNOK 5
	178.	Of old there was a promise, and thy sails PB 9
	181.	The old woman and I foraged some drier clothes Et 2
	181.	But was there a boat? By the wharf's old site you saw Et 14
Olympians	30.	Know Olympians, we are breathless F&H II 7
ominous	33.	To memory, or known the ominous lifted arm F&H III 28
once	48.	Once more behind us.... It is morning there AM 14
	51.	The orbic wake of thy once whirling feet AM 79
	60.	My mother almost brought me once from church VW 35
	60.	And once only, as I recall VW 36
	123.	But once though, he learned of that span of his wings Moth 25
	163.	Once when he shouted, stretched in ghastly shape Id 6
one	3.	But only by the one who Leg 12
	15.	"Has no one come here to win you NL 5
	17.	One rushing from the bed at night Par 3
	18.	One moment in sacrifice (the direst Pos 4
	19.	Sluices its one unyielding smile LC 7
	25.	That yield attendance to one crucial sign Rec 12
	29.	One inconspicuous, glowing orb of praise F&H I 52
	32.	Of wave or rock was good against one hour F&H III 24
	34.	Then in the circuit calm of one vast coil AMT 9
	36.	Close round one instant in one floating flower V-2 20
	39.	Together in one merciless white blade V-5 3
	39.	One frozen trackless smile...What words V-5 8
	48.	Yet lost, all, let this keel one instant yield AM 16
	48.	One ship of these thou grantest safe returning AM 27
	51.	From Moon to Saturn in one sapphire wheel AM 78
	51.	Thy purpose--still one shore beyond desire AM 87
	56.	The fog leans one last moment on the sill HD 35
	64.	One said, excising a last burr from his vest Riv 47
	69.	All fades but one thin skyline 'round...Ahead Riv 137
	69.	Tortured with history, its one will--flow Riv 141

one, cont.   79. And you're the only one with eyes like him
                       Ind 51
                  95. Wherewith to bind us throbbing with one voice
                       CH 202
                  98. And lifts her girdles from her, one by one SC 4
                  98. Finally to answer all within one grave SC 12
                 100. The world's one flagrant, sweating cinch NWG 4
                 112. Lunged past, with one galvanic blare stove up
                       the River Tun 124
                 112. I counted the echoes assembling, one after one
                       Tun 125
                 114. One arc synoptic of all tides below At 10
                 114. Complighted in one vibrant breath made cry
                       At 13
                 115. To kneeling wave, one song devoutly binds At 55
                 117. Like spears ensanguined of one tolling star
                       At 90
                 117. --One Song, one Bridge of Fire! Is it Cathay
                       At 93
                 122. But over one moth's eyes were tissues at birth
                       Moth 17
                 123. And without one cloud-car in that wide meshless
                       blue Moth 35
                 129. The moans of travail of one dearest beside me
                       An 7
                 141. One finger from the others EpH 4
                 141. As well as one for iron and leather EpH 10
                 142. No one has ever walked there before BE 2
                 148. When one isn't the real Gioconda Loc 10
                 151. for the one goat (unsqueezable APE 6
                 152. again round one more fairest day Int 21
                 156. Below the palsy that one eucalyptus lifts OC 6
                 156. The wind that knots itself in one great death
                       OC 15
                 163. One hand dealt out a kite string, a tin can
                       Id 9
                 164. Struck free and holy in one Name always NA 12
                 170. Else tears heap all within one clay-cold hill
                       TED 14
                 181. No one seemed to be able to get a spark Et 18
                 182. --One ours, and one, a stranger, creeping up with
                       dawn Et 39
                 185. as one nears New Orleans, sweet trenches by the
                       train Post 9
                 191. And all my countrymen I see rush toward one
                       stall Purg 12
                 191. As one whose altitude at one time was not
                       Purg 21

only   3. The only worth all granting Leg 9
                  3. But only by the one who Leg 12
                  5. But only to build memories of spiritual gates
                       EC 17
                 46. Only in darkness is thy shadow clear TBB 38
                 60. And once only, as I recall VW 36

only, cont.	79.	And you're the only one with eyes like him Ind 51
	88.	Where each sees only his dim past reversed CH 27
	122.	To horizons which knife-like would only mar Moth 7
	122.	That they only can see when their moon limits vision Moth 9
	122.	Blind only in day, but remembering that soon Moth 14
	123.	A little time only, for sight burned as deep Moth 45
	146.	To find the only rose on the bush PA 51
	158.	Though why they bide here, only hell that's sacked Mer 2
	161.	Square sheets--they saw the marble only into IQ 1
	164.	As only they can praise, who build their days NA 10
	192.	Spells what his tongue has had--and only that SI 4
onward	36.	And onward, as bells off San Salvador V-2 11
	50.	Dark waters onward shake the dark prow free AM 56
	94.	And onward yielding past my utmost year CH 190
	95.	yes, Walt,/Afoot again, and onward without halt CH 218
	114.	Onward and up the crystal-flooded aisle At 21
onyx	23.	Against the imitation onyx wainscoting WM 9
oozing	165.	Oozing a-plenty. They sat like baking Buddhas BSEW 7
opacities	27.	Until the graduate opacities of evening F&H I 13
opal	130.	In opal pools beneath your brow Ech 11
	138.	Vault on the opal carpet of the sun Port 1
open	152.	from thine open dugs shall still the sun Int 20
opening	19.	And the nights opening LC 14
	21.	Touching an opening laurel, I found Pass 26
Open Road	95.	The Open Road--thy vision is reclaimed CH 210
opens	69.	No embrace opens but the stinging sea Riv 138
opera	30.	This crashing opera bouffe F&H II 4
Ophelia	132.	Ophelia had such eyes; but she MC 9
Ophir	170.	Leaves Ormus rubyless, and Ophir chill TED 13
opium	84.	Sweet opium and tea, Yo-ho CS 58
	85.	(sweet opium and tea CS 71
oppose	149.	Alas, you know how much I oppose Loc 22
orange	123.	But they burned thinly blind like an orange peeled white Moth 40
	126.	In a mad orange flare O-N 9
orators	5.	Orators follow the universe EC 7
orb	29.	One inconspicuous, glowing orb of praise F&H I 52

orbic	51.	The orbic wake of thy once whirling feet AM 79
orbits	7.	Spontaneities that form their independent orbits SMA 10
orchid	176.	the dense mine of the orchid, split in two VU 4
ordnance	91.	Each plane a hurtling javelin of winged ordnance CH 104
organ	116.	And like an organ, Thou, with sound of doom At 62
orient	148.	The orient moon of my dapper affections Loc 4
original	194.	What I hold healed, original now, and pure B Tow 32
Ormus	170.	Leaves Ormus rubyless, and Ophir chill TED 13
orphic	117.	That bleeds infinity--the orphic strings At 91
other	32.	And in other ways than as the wind settles F&H III 8
	35.	Bright striped urchins flay each other with sand V-1 2
	45.	Foretold to other eyes on the same screen TBB 12
	74.	Though other calendars now stack the sky Dan 86
	93.	And this, thine other hand, upon my heart CH 164
	100.	Each other--turquoise fakes on tinselled hands NWG 20
	104.	These are but cows that see no other thing QH 4
	104.	Much of our store of faith in other men QH 15
	109.	of other faces, also underground Tun 38
	151.	and other natural grammarians are ab- APE 21
	163.	Sheer over to the other side,--for see Id 1
	163.	The other tilted, peeled end clapped to eye Id 10
	185.	and other gratuities, like porters[,] jokes, roses Post 11
others	123.	When the others were blinded by all waking things Moth 27
	141.	One finger from the others EpH 4
	143.	And you others--follow your arches BE 29
	144.	The dark-skinned Greeks grin at each other PA 13
	145.	And others PA 26
other's	141.	The two men smiled into each other's eyes EpH 24
otherwise	37.	That must arrest all distance otherwise V-3 10
ought	82.	I ought to keep time and get over it--I'm a CS 18
	146.	You ought, really, to try to sleep PA 58
our	8.	Touching as well upon our praise PU 15
	11.	Our obsequies are, in a way, no enterprise Chap 16
	18.	All but bright stones wherein our smiling plays Pos 29
	32.	Let us unbind our throats of fear and pity F&H III 10

our, cont.

32. We know, eternal gunman, our flesh remembers
    F&H III 19
33. The abating shadows of our conscript dust
    F&H III 35
36. Laughing the wrapt inflections of our love
    V-2 5
36. Is answered in the vortex of our grave   V-2 24
38. The chancel port and portion of our June
    V-4 13
38. Shall they not stem and close in our own steps
    V-4 14
39. The cables of our sleep so swiftly filed   V-5 6
45. Then, with inviolate curve, forsake our eyes
    TBB 5
51. Urging through night our passage to the Chan
    AM 71
75. In cobalt desert closures made our vows   Dan 102
78. Of all our silent men--the long team line
    Ind 38
88. Our eyes can share or answer--then deflects
    CH 25
101. Then you, the burlesque of our lust--and faith
    NWG 27
111. Kiss of our agony thou gatherest   Tun 116
140. Our pity and a smile   Int 12
164. Moonmoth and grasshopper that flee our page
    NA 1
164. Our envy of your freedom--we must maim   NA 4
167. And tendril till our deathward breath is sealed
    RP 11
172. Yes, tall, inseparably our days   ABP 7
180. Or must we rend our dream   Lib 13

ours

38. And region that is ours to wreathe again   V-4 11
132. Charred at a stake in younger times than ours
    MC 12
182. --One ours, and one, a stranger, creeping up
    with dawn   Et 39

ourselves

104. Who would, ourselves, stalk down the merriest
    ghost   QH 16

outcry

186. Conflicting, purposeful yet outcry vain   Shak 4

outdeep

169. Nor, Lord, may worm outdeep   Hur 12

outdrawn

129. Then high cries from great chasms of chaos
    outdrawn   An 8

outleap

169. Lord, e'en boulders now outleap   Hur 10

outleaping

193. Pagoda, campaniles with reveilles outleaping
    B Tow 15

outpacing

33. Outpacing bargain, vocable and prayer   F&H III 48

outright

18. Assaults outright for bolts that linger   Pos 6
110. Bolting outright somewhere above where streets
    Tun 88

outside

84. Outside a wharf truck nearly ran him down
    CS 49
146. And you were outside as soon as you   PA 49
181. From the world outside, but some rumor blew   Et 19

Pablo	165.	"Pablo and Pedro, and black Serafin BSEW 1
Pacific	115.	Pacific here at time's end, bearing corn At 51
pack	111.	Locution of the eldest star, and pack Tun 112
pact	93.	Thou bringest tally, and a pact, new bound CH 155
padded	72.	That blanket of the skies: the padded foot Dan 42
page	18.	Upon the page whose blind sum finally burns Pos 25
	22.	Memory, committed to the page, had broke Pass 37
	45.	Some page of figures to be filed away TBB 7
	105.	With birthright by blackmail, the arrant page QH 55
	164.	Moonmoth and grasshopper that flee our page NA 1
	186.	A hand moves on the page! Who shall again Shak 2
pageant	105.	Bubbles in time to Hollywood's new love-nest pageant QH 36
pagodas	193.	Pagodas, campaniles with reveilles outleaping B Tow 15
pain	10.	Lies cool upon her--not yet pain SM 12
	14.	To darkness through a wreath of sudden pain Fern 6
	20.	Spell out in palm and pain LC 35
	25.	Reciting pain or glee, how can you bear Rec 4
	78.	But sharp with pain Ind 36
	88.	A periscope to glimpse what joys or pain CH 24
	106.	Of pain that Emily, that Isadora knew QH 65
	110.	To brush some new presentiment of pain Tun 62
	125.	From penitence must needs bring pain C 10
	136.	Though fountains droop in waning light and pain Ps 2
	141.	Suddenly he seemed to forget the pain EpH 2
	159.	Whose arrow must have pierced you beyond pain TCJ 20
painted	23.	(Painted emulsion of snow, eggs, yarn, coal, manure WM 10
palace	188.	crumbled palace in the square--the typhus in a trap HR 12
palatial	104.	Above them old Mizzentop, palatial white QH 17
pale	13.	Her parasol, a pale balloon IS 3
	131.	The dawn, a shell's pale lining restlessly Ba 2
palisade	25.	The highest tower,--let her ribs palisade Rec 21
palisades	94.	How speechful on oak-vizored palisades CH 182
palladium	114.	The loft of vision, palladium helm of stars At 24
pallid	54.	Ask nothing but this sheath of pallid air HD 20
	93.	And fraternal massacre! Thou, pallid there as chalk CH 168

pallid, cont.	134.	Yellow, pallid, like ancient lace CDB 28
palm	20.	Spell out in palm and pain LC 35
	48.	The first palm chevron the first lighted hill AM 24
	159.	Of districts where cliff, sea and palm advance TCJ 3
	182.	Blister the mountain, stripped now, bare of palm Et 26
palm-bark	122.	So they sleep in the shade of black palm-bark at noon Moth 13
palm-bole	168.	Thrust parching from a palm-bole hard by the cove AP 3
palm-lit	184.	The slit eclipse of moon in palm-lit bonds Emp 4
palms	36.	And hasten while her penniless rich palms V-2 17
	38.	Whose circles bridge, I know, (from palms to the severe V-4 4
	122.	Among cocoa-nut palms of a far oasis Moth 1
	132.	Too many palms have grazed her shoulders MC 7
	161.	Palms against the sunset's towering sea, and maybe IQ 6
Palos	50.	Palos again,--a land cleared of long war AM 54
palsy	156.	Below the palsy that one eucalyptus lifts OC 6
Panama	83.	in Panama--got tired of that CS 24
pancreas	92.	Slit the sky's pancreas of foaming anthracite CH 122
pane	130.	Slivers of rain upon the pane Ech 1
panels	12.	Broken into smoky panels Past 3
panes	54.	While myriad snowy hands are clustering at the panes HD 25
	104.	Faces--loose panes crown the hill and gleam QH 21
pangs	115.	Eyes stammer through the pangs of dust and steel At 52
Panis Angelicus	94.	Panis Angelicus! Eyes tranquil with the blaze CH 187
	94.	But thou, Panis Angelicus, hast thou not seen CH 198
	95.	Of pasture-shine, Panis Angelicus CH 217
panoramas	89.	For you, the panoramas and this breed of towers CH 48
panoramic	45.	I think of cinemas, panoramic sleights TBB 9
pants	68.	Hitch up your pants and crunch another quid Riv 106
paper	60.	We launched--with paper wings and twisted VW 20
papered	17.	Among bruised roses on the papered wall Par 16
papooses	66.	Papooses crying on the wind's long mane Riv 76
parable	51.	Cruelly with love thy parable of man AM 60
Paradigm	115.	O Love, thy white, pervasive Paradigm At 48
paradise	36.	The seal's wide spindrift gaze toward paradise V-2 25

paradise, cont.	122.	On that circle of paradise cool in the night Moth 19
	160.	When you sprouted Paradise a discard of chewing- MT 3
paradises	30.	O, I have known metallic paradises F&H II 24
paraffin	165.	Have been made of--well, say paraffin BSEW 3
paralytic	185.	and a paralytic woman on an island of the Indies Post 15
parapets	45.	A bedlamite speeds to thy parapets TBB 18
paraphrase	17.	Hollowed by air, posts a white paraphrase Par 15
parasol	13.	Her parasol, a pale balloon IS 3
	13.	Of stars inwraps her parasol IS 10
parcels	46.	The City's fiery parcels all undone TBB 39
parching	168.	Thrust parching from a palm-bole hard by the cove AP 3
pardon	46.	Vibrant reprieve and pardon thou dost show TBB 28
	116.	Thy pardon for this history, whitest Flower At 84
parentage	105.	Shoulder the curse of sundered parentage QH 53
pariah	46.	Prayer of pariah, and the lover's cry TBB 32
park	181.	And a funnel high and dry up near the park Et 16
parlour	146.	Your mother sang that in a stuffy parlour PA 46
parrot	179.	tition of the parrot. Locks on Len 15
part	127.	Up the inside, and over every part Hi 3
partake	92.	To reckon--as thy stilly eyes partake CH 127
partial	18.	Record of rage and partial appetites Pos 26
particular	21.	The dozen particular decimals of time Pass 25
parting	38.	Vastly now parting gulf on gulf of wings V-4 3
partition	176.	partition. To extinguish what I have of faith VU 20
	188.	of it, its milk-light regularity above my bath partition HR 10
partitions	27.	Across the stacked partitions of the day F&H I 4
	152.	partitions in thee--goes Int 13
parts	90.	Towards what? The forked crash of split thunder parts CH 68
	181.	Parts of the roof reached Yucatan, I suppose Et 4
pass	10.	And she will wake before you pass SM 13
	36.	Pass superscription of bent foam and wave V-2 18
	72.	Cupped in the larches of the mountain pass Dan 26
	95.	On clarion cylinders pass out of sight CH 208
	172.	Pass sunward. We have walked the kindled skies ABP 8
	173.	Beyond the roses that no flesh can pass MF 8
passage	51.	Urging through night our passage to the Chan AM 71

pasture-shine	95.	Of pasture-shine, <u>Panis</u> <u>Angelicus</u> CH 217
patent	30.	Sit rocked in patent armchairs F&H II 23
	62.	Stick your patent name on a signboard Riv 1
	182.	Everything--and lick the grass, as black as patent Et 27
patent-leather	165.	--Yes, patent-leather shoes hot enough to fry BSEW 11
path	46.	Beading thy path--condense eternity TBB 35
	92.	How from thy path above the levin's lance CH 125
	114.	Through the bound cable strands, the arching path At 1
	156.	Side-stilting from the path (that shift, subvert OC 4
	161.	And did not take the goat path quivering to the right IQ 13
pathetic	150.	Pathetic yelps have sometimes greeted GWP 16
pathos	139.	She has become a pathos Lege 5
paths	74.	On paths thou knewest best to claim her by Dan 88
	125.	Can trace paths tear-wet, and forget all blight C 13
patience	69.	Patience! and you shall reach the biding place Riv 131
	104.	At sunset with a silent, cobwebbed patience QH 22
	106.	That patience that is armour and that shields QH 70
patio	188.	cherub watchman--tiptoeing the successive patio bal- HR 7
patriarch	105.	Where are my kinsmen and the patriarch race QH 48
patrol	89.	Near Paumanok--your lone patrol--and heard the wraith CH 46
	91.	Tellurian wind-sleuths on dawn patrol CH 103
patrols	156.	Patrols the dry groins of the underbrush OC 19
pattered	183.	Without ceremony, while hammers pattered in town Et 52
pattern	105.	What eats the pattern with ubiquity QH 47
pattern's	189.	doom...must therefore loose yourself within a pat-/tern's mastery that you can conceive, that you can HR 32-33
Paumanok	89.	Near Paumanok--your lone patrol--and heard the wraith CH 46
pawn	50.	And later hurricanes may claim more pawn AM 31
pay	58.	<u>And</u> <u>Rip</u> <u>forgot</u> <u>the</u> <u>office</u> hours,/<u>and</u> <u>he</u> <u>forgot</u> <u>the</u> <u>pay</u> VW 14
pay-check	102.	Pay-check at eleven Va 2
le pays	145.	"Connais tu le pays PA 45
peace	166.	But peace to thee IV 9
	166.	Peace from his Mystery IV 12
peacock	181.	Where a frantic peacock rummaged amid heaped cans Et 17

peacocks	133.	Bright peacocks drink from flame-pots by the wall CDB 5
peal	116.	Swift peal of secular light, intrinsic Myth At 65
pearls	50.	Like pearls that whisper through the Doge's hands AM 45
	100.	Pearls whip her hips, a drench of whirling strands NWG 18
	100.	We wait that writhing pool, her pearls collapsed NWG 21
	132.	Drowning cool pearls in alcohol MC 3
pears	21.	Aprons rocks, congregates pears Pass 8
pebbles	76.	The pebbles sang, the firecat slunk away Ind 17
	179.	pebbles among cinders in the road through a twice-opened Len 7
	194.	Of pebbles,--visible wings of silence sown B Tow 35
pecks	127.	Humanity pecks, claws, sobs and climbs Hi 2
pedestal	93.	Of tides awash the pedestal of Everest, fail CH 152
pediments	37.	Past whirling pillars and lithe pediments V-3 11
Pedro	165.	"Pablo and Pedro, and black Serafin BSEW 1
peeled	123.	But they burned thinly blind like an orange peeled white Moth 40
	163.	The other tilted, peeled end clapped to eye Id 10
peeling	20.	Names peeling from Thine eyes LC 33
peering	64.	"--For early trouting." Then peering in the can Riv 48
	151.	peering APE 5
pelt	73.	That casts his pelt, and lives beyond! Sprout, horn Dan 58
penance	33.	Laugh out the meager penance of their days F&H III 41
	158.	And smoking racks for penance when day's done Mer 10
pencil	109.	"Let's have a pencil Jimmy--living now Tun 39
pendant	51.	Hushed gleaming fields and pendant seething wheat AM 83
pendulous	91.	Of pendulous auroral beaches,--satellited wide CH 113
penguin	108.	Preparing penguin flexions of the arms Tun 21
peninsula	5.	By a peninsula the wanderer sat and sketched EC 1
penitence	19.	Not penitence LC 23
	125.	From penitence must needs bring pain C 10
pennants	84.	Pennants, parabolas CS 63
pennies	84.	Pennies for porpoises that bank the keel CS 59
	111.	O caught like pennies beneath soot and steam Tun 115

penniless	36.	And hasten while her penniless rich palms V-2 17
pens	181.	Fernandez' Hotel, was requisitioned into pens Et 11
pensively	64.	He trod the fire down pensively and grinned Riv 50
peonies	102.	Peonies with pony manes Va 21
people	5.	And radio the complete laws to the people EC 8
Pepper's	165.	They're back now on that mulching job at Pepper's BSEW 10
perch	66.	Each seemed a child, like me, on a loose perch Riv 57
	168.	Balloons but warily from this throbbing perch AP 8
perched	8.	As, perched in the crematory lobby PU 13
	108.	With tabloid crime-sheets perched in easy sight Tun 10
percussive	23.	Percussive sweat is spreading to his hair. Mallets WM 12
Perennial-Cutty- trophied-Sark	84.	Perennial-<u>Cutty</u>-strophied-<u>Sark</u> CS 66
perennials	7.	Their own perennials of light SMA 11
perfect	3.	Then, drop by caustic drop, a perfect cry Leg 20
	20.	Strike from Thee perfect spheres LC 39
	30.	With perfect grace and equanimity F&H II 19
	75.	Of dusk?--And are her perfect brows to thine Dan 100
perfidies	19.	Twanged red perfidies of spring LC 12
performances	108.	Performances, assortments, résumés Tun 1
perhaps	24.	Tolled once, perhaps, by every tongue in hell WM 36
	27.	Virginal perhaps, less fragmentary, cool F&H I 15
	50.	The jellied weeds that drag the shore,--perhaps AM 52
	66.	Yet they touch something like a key perhaps Riv 62
	78.	Perhaps a halfbread. On her slender back Ind 33
	79.	Perhaps I'll hear the mare's hoofs to the ford Ind 58
	142.	There is a lake, perhaps, with the sun BE 3
	173.	On every purchaser/(of heaven perhaps MF 5
	178.	Perhaps as once Will Collins spoke the lark PB 3
peripheries	91.	Wings clip the last peripheries of light CH 102
periscope	88.	A periscope to glimpse what joys or pain CH 24
perjured	48.	For I have seen now what no perjured breath AM 5
perjuries	19.	To music and retrieve what perjuries LC 17
permit	37.	Permit me voyage, love, into your hands V-3 19

pierroting	123.	And lo, in that dawn he was pierroting over Moth 29
piers	46.	Under thy shadow by the piers I waited TBB 37
	112.	Searching, thumbing the midnight on the piers Tun 126
pieties	36.	All but the pieties of lovers' hands V-2 10
pigeon's	109.	like a pigeon's muddy dream--potatoes Tun 42
pigeons	102.	Pigeons by the million Va 11
pile	60.	The cinder pile at the end of the backyard VW 17
	128.	Pile on the logs.... Give me your hands Fr 5
pilferings	66.	Such pilferings make up their timeless eatage Riv 85
pilgrim	157.	Let not the pilgrim see himself again OC 27
pillars	37.	Past whirling pillars and lithe pediments V-3 11
	90.	Where spouting pillars spoor the evening sky CH 60
pillow	8.	From the white coverlet and pillow PU 6
	17.	The pillow--how desperate is the light Par 11
	190.	What is our life without a sudden pillow Rel 2
pillowed	54.	Attend the darkling harbor, the pillowed bay HD 12
	190.	Pillowed by Rel 13
pilot	92.	Toward thee, O Corsair of the typhoon,--pilot, hear CH 123
	186.	Of all our days, being pilot,--tempest, too Shak 5
pin	24.	Petrushka's valentine pivots on its pin WM 49
pines	191.	So absolution? Wake pines--but pines wake here Purg 8
pinion	164.	We pinion to your bodies to assuage NA 3
pinions	122.	And had not his pinions with signs mystical Moth 21
pink	28.	Stippled with pink and green advertisements F&H I 26
	100.	Outspoken buttocks in pink beads NWG 1
	188.	like rats--and too, when rats make rose nozzles of pink HR 27
pioneers	68.	Down, down--born pioneers in time's despite Riv 112
piracy	39.	Nothing so flagless as this piracy V-5 20
pirouettes	11.	More than the pirouettes of any pliant cane Chap 15
pistol	188.	conies with a typical pistol--trying to muffle doors HR 8
pit	193.	From pit to crucifix, feet chill on steps from hell B Tow 4
pitch	144.	I will go and pitch quoits with old men PA 22
pitcher	7.	Put them again beside a pitcher with a knife SMA 16
piteous	18.	Lacks all but piteous admissions to be split Pos 24

plenitude	50.	--Rush down the plenitude, and you shall see AM 49
pliant	11.	More than the pirouettes of any pliant cane Chap 15
plight	68.	They win no frontier by their wayward plight Riv 114
	174.	From the sweet jeopardy of Anthony's plight BNOK 7
ploddingly	62.	three men, still hungry on the tracks, ploddingly Riv 21
plough	144.	The plough, the sword PA 17
ploughs	179.	furnaces, chisels and ploughs Len 3
plume	159.	Or tempests--in a silver, floating plume TCJ 16
plumed	91.	Hell's belt springs wider into heaven's plumed side CH 92
plummet	25.	The plummet heart, like Absalom, no stream Rec 20
	93.	Is plummet ushered of those tears that start CH 165
plundered	170.	And plundered momently in every breast TED 8
plunge	3.	Realities plunge in silence by Leg 2
	48.	That fall back yawning to another plunge AM 12
	169.	Thy drum's gambade, its plunge abscond Hur 13
plunging	111.	The conscience navelled in the plunging wind Tun 113
plus	188.	metaphysics that are typhoid plus and had engaged HR 22
plusfours	105.	Of golf, by twos and threes in plaid plusfours QH 31
ply	114.	"Make thy love sure--to weave whose song we ply At 14
	161.	Where the straight road would seem to ply below the stone, that fierce IQ 4
Pocahontas	70.	There was a veil upon you, Pocahontas, bride Dan 14
	73.	Dance, Maquokeeta: Pocahontas grieves Dan 52
	88.	Whose depth of red, eternal flesh of Pocahontas CH 15
pocket	190.	And pocket us who, somehow, do not follow Rel 7
pockets	11.	In slithered and too ample pockets Chap 4
	144.	And put them in my pockets PA 21
Poe	110.	Shaking, did you deny the ticket, Poe Tun 82
poet	174.	Dear lady--the poet said--release your hair BNOK 2
poets	188.	courage were germicides to him.... Poets may not HR 25
	188.	be doctors, but doctors are rare poets when roses leap HR 26
poetry's	146.	Even though, in this town, poetry's a PA 59
poinciana	156.	Under the poinciana, of a noon or afternoon OC 23

poinsettia	36.	In these poinsettia meadows of her tides V-2 13
poise	7.	And poise them full and ready for explosion SMA 17
poised	28.	Without recall,--lost yet poised in traffic F&H I 19
	69.	Poised wholly on its dream, a mustard glow Riv 140
pole	66.	From pole to pole across the hills, the states Riv 63
poles	50.	Was tumbled from us under bare poles scudding AM 30
	51.	--The kindled Crown! acceded of the poles AM 85
	186.	Through torrid entrances, past icy poles Shak 1
polish	105.	The spinster polish of antiquity QH 45
pond	16.	The pond I entered once and quickly fled RR 15
ponder	158.	And ponder the bright stains that starred this Throne Mer 14
pondering	4.	AEsop, driven to pondering, found BT 5
ponderous	104.	And they are awkward, ponderous and uncoy QH 9
ponies'	141.	They were like the marks of wild ponies' play EpH 18
Pontiac	94.	Potomac lilies,--then the Pontiac rose CH 179
pony	102.	Peonies with pony manes Va 21
poodle	150.	And Fifi's bows and poodle ease GWP 6
pool	72.	--Siphoned the black pool from the heart's hot root Dan 44
	89.	Left Hesperus mirrored in the lucid pool CH 32
	100.	We wait that writhing pool, her pearls collapsed NWG 21
pooled	112.	How far away the star has pooled the sea Tun 134
pools	66.	The old gods of the rain lie wrapped in pools Riv 82
	148.	Your eyes, those pools with soft rushes Loc 1
poor	24.	Poor streaked bodies wreathing up and out WM 26
	140.	This lamp in our poor room Int 2
	148.	For snaring the poor world in a blue funk Loc 12
	181.	That Havana, not to mention poor Batabanó Et 20
popcorn	102.	From the popcorn bells Va 10
Popocatepetl	83.	have you seen Popocatepetl--birdless mouth CS 26
Porphyro	146.	But look up, Porphyro,--your toes PA 53
porpoises	84.	Pennies for porpoises that bank the keel CS 59
port	38.	The chancel port and portion of our June V-4 13
portage	72.	I took the portage climb, then chose Dan 29
portending	38.	Portending eyes and lips and making told V-4 12
portent	34.	The portent wound in corridors of shells AMT 8
porters	185.	and other gratuities, like porters[,] jokes, roses Post 11

praised	142.	I have heard hands praised for what they made BE 10
prayer	33.	Outpacing bargain, vocable and prayer F&H III 48
	46.	Prayer of pariah, and the lover's cry TBB 32
	75.	Now is the strong prayer folded in thine arms Dan 103
prayers	70.	Where prayers, forgotten, streamed the mesa sands Dan 7
precincts	116.	The agile precincts of the lark's return At 58
precision	64.	Keen instruments, strung to a vast precision Riv 26
	90.	In coiled precision, bunched in mutual glee CH 72
predestined	182.	Were death predestined! You held your nose already Et 33
predestiny	129.	Of the first moth's descent,--day's predestiny An 5
preemption	159.	The green preemption of the deep seaweed TCJ 8
prefer	191.	That I prefer to country or to town Purg 16
preferring	151.	preferring laxatives to wine APE 1
prefigurations	28.	Still flickering with those prefigurations F&H I 21
prepared	18.	As though prepared Pos 15
preparing	108.	Preparing penguin flexions of the arms Tun 21
prescribed	177.	Shall come to you through wounds prescribed by swords Rep 8
presentiment	110.	To brush some new presentiment of pain Tun 62
presentiments	8.	Once moved us toward presentiments PU 10
preside	105.	The resigned factions of the dead preside QH 49
President	183.	The President sent down a battleship that baked Et 55
press	28.	The press of troubled hands, too alternate F&H I 42
	104.	While we who press the cider mill, regarding them QH 10
	109.	And down beside the turnstile press the coin Tun 29
	115.	Pick biting way up towering looms that press At 27
pressed	6.	That have been pressed so long MGLL 8
	40.	My eyes pressed black against the prow V-6 11
	82.	His eyes pressed through green grass CS 3
	150.	Noses pressed against the glass GWP 17
presses	144.	A shift of rubber workers presses down PA 2
	167.	Of sweat the jungle presses with hot love RP 10
presume	171.	Need I presume the same fruit of my bone KW 10
presumes	37.	Presumes no carnage, but this single change V-3 16
prick	90.	Stars prick the eyes with sharp ammoniac proverbs CH 62

pride   -236-

pride	26.	And let us walk through time with equal pride Rec 28
	70.	And bridal flanks and eyes hid tawny pride Dan 16
	91.	While Iliads glimmer through eyes raised in pride CH 91
	184.	Nor that fruit of mating which is widowed pride Emp 15
pries	23.	What is it in this heap the serpent pries WM 14
priests	88.	Or how the priests walked--slowly through Bombay CH 12
primal	51.	Within whose primal scan consummately AM 67
Prince	74.	Thy freedom is her largesse, Prince, and hid Dan 87
Prince Igor	138.	Barbaric Prince Igor:--or, blind Pierrot Port 2
Princess	70.	O Princess whose brown lap was virgin May Dan 15
Prince Street	102.	And Spring in Prince Street Va 12
print	66.	Have dreamed beyond the print that bound her name Riv 73
	185.	the wren and thrush, made solid print for me Post 3
Priscilla's	58.	There was Priscilla's cheek close in the wind VW 10
prison	89.	Gleam from the great stones of each prison crypt CH 53
	161.	Flat prison slabs there at the marble quarry IQ 2
	192.	How more?--but the lash, lost vantage--and the prison SI 5
prisoner	9.	She is prisoner of the tree and its green fingers GA 6
probable	93.	The competent loam, the probable grass,--travail CH 151
probing	110.	Probing through you--toward me, O evermore Tun 78
processioned	36.	Samite sheeted and processioned where V-2 3
Prodigal	28.	Prodigal, yet uncontested now F&H I 22
	36.	Adagios of islands, O my Prodigal V-2 14
	76.	How we, too, Prodigal, once rode off, too Ind 13
prodigal	148.	O prodigal and wholly dilatory lady Loc 2
profile	161.	Profile of marble spiked with yonder IQ 5
promise	78.	But gilded promise, yielded to us never Ind 27
	108.	The subway yawns the quickest promise home Tun 23
	178.	Of old there was a promise, and thy sails PB 9
promised	21.	I was promised an improved infancy Pass 4
	78.	It had no charter but a promised crown Ind 23

pulsant	73.	To rainbows currying each pulsant bone Dan 63
pulse	17.	Your head, unrocking to a pulse, already Par 14
	133.	The pulse is in the ears, the heart is higher CDB 15
	151.	PULSE!--yes, PULSE APE 13
	185.	Antillean fingers counting my pulse, my love forever Post 16
	194.	And through whose pulse I hear, counting the strokes B Tow 29
pump	182.	And somebody's mule steamed, swaying right by the pump Et 31
puppet	176.	the terrible puppet of my dreams, shall VU 2
purchaser	173.	On every purchaser/(of heaven perhaps MF 5
pure	18.	The pure possession, the inclusive cloud Pos 27
	74.	--And laughs, pure serpent, Time itself, and moon Dan 75
	93.	Not less than thou in pure impulse inbred CH 153
	194.	What I hold healed, original now, and pure B Tow 32
purgatory	191.	Exile is thus a purgatory--not such as Dante built Purg 13
purities	24.	Wherein new purities are snared; where chimes WM 34
purple	7.	Into a realm of swords, her purple shadow SMA 6
	126.	Now gold and purple scintillate O-N 5
purpose	51.	Thy purpose--still one shore beyond desire AM 87
purposeful	186.	Conflicting, purposeful yet outcry vain Shak 4
purposeless	17.	Involves the hands in purposeless repose Par 8
purposes	7.	The fleece of nature with those purposes SMA 2
pussy	187.	like a mouse under pussy Ma 10
put	7.	Put them again beside a pitcher with a knife SMA 16
	82.	to put me out at three she sails on time CS 14
	144.	And put them in my pockets PA 21
putting	84.	was putting the Statue of Liberty out--that CS 51
pyramid	74.	Totem and fire-gall, slumbering pyramid Dan 85
pyramids	19.	Chant pyramids LC 15
	116.	Always through spiring cordage, pyramids At 78
pyres	115.	But who, through smoking pyres of love and death At 31

quadrant	34.	Compass, quadrant and sextant contrive AMT 13
quakes	191.	Here quakes of earth make houses fall Purg 11
quarreled	130.	I dream we quarreled long, long ago Ech 12
quarries	179.	the buzz of saw mills, the crunch and blast of quarries Len 2
quarry	161.	Flat prison slabs there at the marble quarry IQ 2
	161.	This dry road silvering toward the shadow of the quarry IQ 11
quarry-hid	92.	Now eagle-bright, now/quarry-hid, twist-/-ing, sink with CH 136
quarrying	69.	O quarrying passion, undertowed sunlight Riv 128
quarts	159.	Of quarts to faithfuls--surely smuggled home TCJ 11
queen	83.	Rose of Stamboul O coral Queen CS 29
	150.	Of Lottie Honeydew, movie queen GWP 8
queen's	48.	Into the Queen's great heart that doubtful day AM 4
queens	174.	Decisive grammar given unto queens BNOK 9
querulous	66.	And re-descend with corn from querulous crows Riv 84
query	12.	I can only query, "Fool Past 14
quest	11.	And through all sound of gaity and quest Chap 22
	170.	Dared dignify the labor, bless the quest TED 3
question	194.	As flings the question true?)--or is it she B Tow 27
quick	4.	And, in Africa, a carcass quick with flies BT 12
	9.	Holding her to the sky and its quick blue GA 9
quickening	129.	Of greenery.... Below the roots, a quickening shiver An 3
quickest	108.	The subway yawns the quickest promise home Tun 23
quickly	16.	The pond I entered once and quickly fled RR 15
quid	68.	Hitch up your pants and crunch another quid Riv 106
quiet	18.	As quiet as you can make a man Pos 17
	129.	That strives long and quiet to sever the girth An 2
	194.	That shrines the quiet lake and swells a tower B Tow 38
quieter	141.	Were banished from him by that larger, quieter hand EpH 21
quills	38.	Bright staves of flowers and quills to-day as I V-4 15
quilt	191.	But rather like a blanket than a quilt Purg 14
quite	39.	"--And never to quite understand!" No V-5 18
	108.	Or can't you quite make up your mind to ride Tun 18
	109.	--Quite unprepared rush naked back to light Tun 28

rainbow-wise	172.	Sea gardens lifted rainbow-wise through eyes ABP 5
raise	46.	Of anonymity time cannot raise TBB 27
	159.	As you raise temples fresh from basking foam TCJ 12
raised	91.	While Iliads glimmer through eyes raised in pride CH 91
raisin-jack	145.	A table of raisin-jack and wine, our host PA 29
ran	70.	She ran the neighing canyons all the spring Dan 3
	83.	"I ran a donkey engine down there on the Canal CS 23
	84.	Outside a wharf truck nearly ran him down CS 49
	84.	locked in wind-humors, ran their eastings down CS 69
rancorous	91.	Of rancorous grenades whose screaming petals carve us CH 97
random	11.	Contented with such random consolations Chap 2
	60.	Or splits a random smell of flowers through glass VW 31
range	88.	While rises in the west the coastwise range, slowly the hushed land CH 3
	89.	Surviving in a world of stocks,--they also range CH 55
ranged	64.	Rail-squatters ranged in nomad raillery Riv 53
ranger	79.	(Or will you be a ranger to the end Ind 62
rangers	105.	Dead rangers bled their comfort on the snow QH 50
ranging	23.	A leopard ranging always in the brow WM 3
	84.	clipper dreams indelible and ranging CS 64
ransom	185.	the audible ransom, ensign of my faith Post 5
	188.	Cruz--to bring--to take--to mix--to ransom--to de- HR 14
rapid	60.	Rubber bands...Recall--recall/the rapid tongues VW 21
	91.	With razor sheen they zoom each rapid helix CH 108
rare	188.	be doctors, but doctors are rare poets when roses leap HR 26
rase	18.	Whose heart is fire shall come,--the white wind rase Pos 28
rat	188.	the Doctors rat trap. Where? Somewhere in Vera HR 13
rather	191.	But rather like a blanket than a quilt Purg 14
rats	188.	duct--to cure.... The rats played ring around the HR 15
	188.	like rats--and too, when rats make rose nozzles of pink HR 27
rattled	99.	Water rattled that stinging coil, your SC 25
rattle	109.	Into the slot. The gongs already rattle Tun 30

rattling	156.	The tarantula rattling at the lily's foot OC 1
raven	73.	And stag teeth foam about the raven throat Dan 70
ravens	93.	Glacial sierras and the flight of ravens CH 158
ravine	21.	My memory I left in a ravine Pass 6
	21.	The evening was a spear in the ravine Pass 23
raw	187.	are naked. Twilights raw Ma 4
ray	193.	The stars are caught and hived in the sun's ray B Tow 8
ray-out	122.	On their own small oasis, ray-cut, an incision Moth 11
razor	91.	With razor sheen they zoom each rapid helix CH 108
reach	10.	Until you reach the muffled floor SM 16
	10.	You cannot ever reach to share SM 24
	69.	Patience! and you shall reach the biding place Riv 131
	108.	Then let you reach your hat Tun 11
reached	181.	Parts of the roof reached Yucatan, I suppose Et 4
reaches	72.	And northward reaches in that violet wedge Dan 35
	90.	The soul, by naphtha fledged into new reaches CH 84
read	88.	Or to read you, Walt,--knowing us in thrall CH 13
	94.	When first I read thy lines, rife as the loam CH 173
	95.	And read thee by the aureole 'round thy head CH 216
	177.	Thou canst read nothing except through ap- petite Rep 1
reads	115.	What cipher-script of time no traveller reads At 30
ready	3.	I am not ready for repentance Leg 3
	7.	And poise them full and ready for explosion SMA 17
	18.	And the key, ready to hand--sifting Pos 3
real	138.	More real than life, the gestures you have spun Port 6
	148.	When one isn't the real Gioconda Loc 10
realitites	3.	Realities plunge in silence by Leg 2
really	88.	Is veined by all that time has really pledged us CH 18
	146.	You ought, really, to try to sleep PA 58
realm	7.	Into a realm of swords, her purple shadow SMA 6
	89.	Dream cancels dream in this new realm of fact CH 39
	116.	Sight, sound and flesh Thou leadest from time's realm At 63
reap	171.	Because these millions reap a dead conclusion KW 9

reaping	127.	And reaping, have mercy and love issued forth Hi 6
rear	40.	I cannot claim: let thy waves rear V-6 14
	167.	And the grey trunk, that's elephantine, rear RP 7
reared	7.	In that ripe nude with head/reared SMA 5
reason	163.	Above all reason lifting, halt serene Id 15
reassuring	31.	This music has a reassuring way F&H II 30
rebound	93.	With vast eternity, dost wield the rebound seed CH 150
rebuffed	27.	Numbers, rebuffed by asphalt, crowd F&H I 9
recall	19.	Anoint with innocence,--recall LC 16
	28.	Without recall,--lost yet poised in traffic F&H I 19
	33.	O brother-thief of time, that we recall F&H III 40
	60.	Rubber bands...Recall--recall/the rapid tongues VW 21
	60.	And once only, as I recall VW 36
	88.	Hearths, there to eat an apple and recall CH 10
	194.	My veins recall and add, revived and sure B Tow 30
recalled	64.	High in a cloud of merriment, recalled Riv 43
recant	109.	Our tongues recant like beaten weather vanes Tun 46
recast	115.	And synergy of waters ever fuse, recast At 46
recedes	23.	And as the alcove of her jealousy recedes WM 20
receive	38.	In this expectant, still exclaim receive V-4 24
	92.	But first, here at this height receive CH 132
receptive	24.	Until my blood dreams a receptive smile WM 33
recesses	11.	Recesses for it from the fury of the street Chap 7
reciting	25.	Reciting pain or glee, how can you bear Rec 4
reckon	92.	To reckon--as thy stilly eyes partake CH 127
reckonings	64.	As final reckonings of fire and snow Riv 36
reclaimed	95.	The Open Road--thy vision is reclaimed CH 210
reconciled	34.	Its lashings charmed and malice reconciled AMT 10
	137.	Forgetfulness is like a bird whose wings are reconciled For 3
reconcilement	170.	Some reconcilement of remotest mind TED 12
recondite	160.	ripe apple-lanterns gush history, recondite lightnings,/irised MT 12
record	17.	May find the record wedged in his soul Par 4
	18.	Record of rage and partial appetites Pos 26
	50.	And record of more, floating in a casque AM 29
recorders	89.	"--Recorders ages hence"--ah, syllables of faith CH 43
	95.	Recorders ages hence, yes, they shall hear CH 214
records	188.	records spurred the Doctor into something nigh those HR 21

recur	111.	Burst suddenly in rain.... The gongs recur Tun 89
red	19.	Twanged red perfidies of spring LC 12
	21.	See where the red and black Pass 17
	40.	Red kelson past the cape's wet stone V-6 8
	48.	Slowly the sun's red caravel drops light AM 13
	70.	The swift red flesh, a winter king Dan 1
	73.	Now snaps the flint in every tooth; red fangs Dan 55
	88.	Whose depth of red, eternal flesh of Pocahontas CH 15
redder	130.	Are warmer with a redder glow Ech 8
redeems	23.	Invariably when wine redeems the sight WM 1
re-descend	66.	And re-descend with corn from querulous crows Riv 84
redskin	66.	Screamed redskin dynasties that fled the brain Riv 77
reel	51.	And biassed by full sails, meridians reel AM 86
references	188.	ans surely slept--whose references to typhus and whose HR 20
refined	90.	Power's script,--wound, bobbin-bound, refined CH 65
reflect	23.	Then glozening decanters that reflect the street WM 5
reflective	28.	Reflective conversion of all things F&H I 32
refractions	108.	Refractions of the thousand theatres, faces Tun 4
refuse	190.	Charms that each by each refuse the clinch Rel 9
regal	167.	Green rustlings, more-than-regal charities RP 1
regard	23.	Regard the forceps of the smile that takes her WM 11
	25.	Regard the capture here, O Janus-faced Rec 1
	92.	Regard the moving turrets! From grey decks CH 118
regarding	104.	While we who press the cider mill, regarding them QH 10
region	38.	And region that is ours to wreathe again V-4 11
regrets	3.	Nor to match regrets. For the moth Leg 4
	133.	The andante of smooth hopes and lost regrets CDB 4
	147.	Of lost hopes and regrets Per 7
regular	10.	The lover's death, how regular SM 1
regularity	188.	of it, its milk-light regularity above my bath partition HR 10
rehearsed	99.	Rehearsed hair--docile, alas, from many arms SC 26
reign	14.	That sometimes take up residence and reign Fern 9
	102.	Crap-shooting gangs in Bleecker reign Va 20

rein	12.	Takes rein Past 10
	78.	She cradled a babe's body, riding without rein Ind 34
reined	48.	The word I bring, O you who reined my suit AM 3
reining	58.	And Cortes rode up, reining tautly in VW 8
rejoin	91.	By convoy planes, moonferrets that rejoin thee CH 114
relapsing	88.	Relapsing into silence, while time clears CH 22
relates	51.	This disposition that thy night relates AM 77
	104.	From four horizons that no one relates QH 28
relatives	30.	All relatives, serene and cool F&H II 22
release	138.	Release,--dismiss the passion from your arms Port 5
	174.	Dear lady--the poet said--release your hair BNOK 2
released	33.	Who dare not share with us the breath released F&H III 42
	56.	The sun, released--aloft with cold gulls hither HD 34
relent	73.	Spark, tooth! Medicine-man, relent, restore Dan 59
relentless	3.	Relentless caper for all those who step Leg 22
religious	32.	religious gunman F&H III 6
relinquishment	184.	Your generosity dispose relinquishment and care Emp 11
reliquary	37.	The sea lifts, also, reliquary hands V-3 8
remember	12.	What woods remember now Past 4
	16.	I could never remember RR 3
	16.	I remember now its singing willow rim RR 16
	60.	The grind-organ says...Remember, remember VW 16
	64.	"Jesus! O I remember watermelon days!" And sped Riv 42
	78.	Yes, Larry, now you're going to sea, remember Ind 46
	78.	First-born, remember Ind 48
	82.	"It's S.S. Ala--Antwerp--now remember kid CS 13
	92.	What alcohol of space...! Remember, Falcon-Ace CH 128
	98.	It is blood to remember; it is fire SC 20
	137.	I can remember much forgetfulness For 11
	145.	I remember one Sunday noon PA 27
	182.	Remember still that strange gratuity of horses Et 38
	185.	Remember the lavender lilies of that dawn Post 7
	188.	me "the True Cross"--let us remember the Doctor and HR 3
remembered	12.	Have you remembered too long Past 15
	39.	Already hang, shred ends from remembered stars V-5 7
	144.	And the Fjords and the Aegean are remembered PA 16

remembering	122.	Blind only in day, but remembering that soon Moth 14
remembers	32.	We know, eternal gunman, our flesh remembers F&H III 19
remembrance	16.	Flags, weeds. And remembrance of steep alcoves RR 6
remembrances	188.	my thoughts, my humble, fond remembrances of the HR 4
remnants	83.	teased remnants of the skeletons of cities CS 30
remorseless	24.	Remorseless line, minting their separate wills WM 25
remote	162.	On skies that gild thy remote dawn OS 7
remotest	170.	Some reconcilement of remotest mind TED 12
rend	180.	Or must we rend our dream Lib 13
render	156.	Let fiery blossoms clot the light, render my ghost OC 24
rendings	64.	Time's rendings, time's blendings they construe Riv 35
rends	36.	The sceptred terror of whose sessions rends V-2 8
	76.	And bison thunder rends my dreams no more Ind 5
repair	33.	The substance drilled and spent beyond repair F&H III 43
repartees	84.	British repartees, skil-/ful savage sea-girls CS 55
repeals	24.	Unwitting the stigma that each turn repeals WM 27
repeated	32.	Repeated play of fire--no hypogeum F&H III 23
repeating	88.	Below grey citadels, repeating to the stars CH 8
repentance	3.	I am not ready for repentance Leg 3
repercussive	92.	Enormous repercussive list-/-ings down CH 137
repetition	109.	And repetition freezes--'What Tun 49
	179.	the vigilance of the ape, the repe-/tition of the parrot. Locks on Len 14-15
replied	22.	"To argue with the laurel," I replied Pass 29
replume	133.	Finale leaves in silence to replume CDB 21
reply	41.	It is the unbetrayable reply V-6 31
	114.	Pouring reply as though all ships at sea At 12
repose	17.	Involves the hands in purposeless repose Par 8
	24.	Before some flame of gaunt repose a shell WM 35
	40.	That smile unsearchable repose V-6 24
reprieve	46.	Vibrant reprieve and pardon thou dost show TBB 28
	92.	The benediction of the shell's deep, sure re-prieve CH 133
reprisals	104.	Shifting reprisals ('til who shall tell us when QH 13
reprobates	66.	Youngsters with eyes like fjords, old reprobates Riv 65
requisitioned	181.	Fernandez' Hotel, was requisitioned into pens Et 11

rescindeth	169.	Rescindeth flesh from bone Hur 7
reservations	104.	Through mapled vistas, cancelled reservations QH 24
residence	14.	That sometimes take up residence and reign Fern 9
resign	38.	The harbor shoulders to resign in mingling V-4 18
resigned	64.	"--But I kept on the tracks." Possessed, re-signed Riv 49
	105.	The resigned factions of the dead preside QH 49
resigns	37.	Resigns a breast that every wave enthrones V-3 4
resolution	12.	For ease or resolution Past 17
	190.	Tenderness and resolution Rel 1
rest	5.	The wanderer later chose this spot of rest EC 12
	12.	A few picked, the rest dead Past 20
	25.	Such eyes at search or rest you cannot see Rec 3
	45.	How many dawns, chill from his rippling rest TBB 1
restlessly	131.	The dawn, a shell's pale lining restlessly Ba 2
restore	73.	Spark, tooth! Medicine-man, relent, restore Dan 59
	148.	Come now, when will they restore me Loc 3
resume	74.	And winds across the llano grass resume Dan 94
	133.	Plaintive yet proud the cello tones resume CDB 3
résumés	108.	Performances, assortments, résumés Tun 1
resurrects	88.	Our lenses, lifts a focus, resurrects CH 23
retarding	104.	Of friendship's acid wine, retarding phlegm QH 12
retching	110.	And when they dragged your retching flesh Tun 79
retiring	70.	Mythical brows we saw retiring--loth Dan 9
retrieve	19.	To music and retrieve what perjuries LC 17
retrieves	37.	Retrieves from sea plains where the sky V-3 3
return	61.	Did not return with the kiss in the hall VW 40
	88.	The ancient names--return home to our own CH 9
	116.	The agile precincts of the lark's return At 58
	160.	Let them return, saying you blush again for the great MT 1
	190.	Return the mirage on a coin that spells Rel 16
returned	159.	Wrap us and lift us; drop us then, returned TCJ 17
returning	48.	One ship of these thou grantest safe returning AM 27
revealed	48.	O where our Indian emperies lie revealed AM 15
reveilles	193.	Pagodas, campaniles with reveilles outleaping B Tow 15
reversed	88.	Where each sees only his dim past reversed CH 27

revived	194.	My veins recall and add, revived and sure B Tow 30
revocation	25.	Defer though, revocation of the tears Rec 11
revolve	111.	Newspapers wing, revolve and wing Tun 98
revolving	116.	Revolving through their harvests in sweet tor- ment At 72
re-wind	110.	Are tunnels that re-wind themselves, and love Tun 59
rhyme	60.	So memory, that strikes a rhyme out of a box VW 30
	190.	Rhyme from the same Tau (closing cinch by cinch Rel 6
rhythm	72.	Within,--I heard it; 'til its rhythm drew Dan 43
rhythmic	30.	Rhythmic ellipses lead into canters F&H II 13
rib	171.	Nor claim me, either, by Adam's spine--nor rib KW 4
ribbon	185.	their ribbon miles, beside the railroad ties Post 8
ribboned	37.	While ribboned water lanes I wind V-3 5
ribs	25.	The highest tower,--let her ribs palisade Rec 21
rich	7.	That are your rich and faithful strength of line SMA 3
	36.	And hasten while her penniless rich palms V-2 17
	104.	Through the rich halo that they do not trouble QH 6
	145.	"One month,--I go back rich PA 31
	149.	What nightmares rich with ingenuity Loc 26
ricochet	30.	Blest excursion! this ricochet F&H II 5
riddle	48.	Of clown nor sage can riddle or gainsay AM 6
riddled	182.	Everything gone--or strewn in riddled grace Et 29
ride	91.	To hedge the seaboard, wrap the headland, ride CH 89
	108.	Or can't you quite make up your mind to ride Tun 18
	110.	And did their eyes like unwashed platters ride Tun 76
	145.	I ride black horse.... Have many sheep PA 32
riders	8.	Delicate riders of the storm PU 8
rides	5.	For joy rides in stupendous coverings EC 5
ridest	169.	Lo, Lord, Thou ridest Hur 1
	169.	Thou ridest to the door, Lord Hur 17
ridiculously	146.	Are ridiculously tapping PA 54
riding	66.	--Memphis to Tallahassee--riding the rods Riv 60
	78.	She cradled a babe's body, riding without rein Ind 34
	110.	--And did their riding eyes right through your side Tun 75

Rip, cont.	60.	And Rip was slowly made aware VW 26
	61.	Keep hold of that nickel for car-change, Rip VW 43
ripe	7.	In that ripe nude with head/reared SMA 5
	20.	(Let sphinxes from the ripe LC 27
	116.	And justified conclamant with ripe fields At 71
	160.	ripe apple-lanterns gush history, recondite lightnings,/irised MT 12
ripened	159.	Past pleasantries...Assert the ripened dawn TCJ 14
ripped	62.	and lands sakes! under the new playbill ripped Riv 4
rippled	16.	Yielded, while sun-silt rippled them RR 10
ripples	131.	Only simple ripples flaunt, and stroke, and float Ba 6
rippling	45.	How many dawns, chill from his rippling rest TBB 1
rip-tooth	45.	A rip-tooth of the sky's acetylene TBB 22
rise	9.	Dumbly articulate in the slant and rise GA 4
	24.	"Rise from the dates and crumbs. And walk away WM 44
	92.	See scouting griffons rise through gaseous crepe CH 119
risen	90.	What ciphers risen from prophetic script CH 82
rises	88.	While rises in the west the coastwise range,/ slowly the hushed land CH 3
	177.	That rises on eternity's long willingness Rep 11
risk	13.	To risk alone the light's decline IS 14
ritual	12.	That ritual of sap and leaves Past 6
rivals	85.	Nimbus? and you rivals two CS 75
riven	20.	From charred and riven stakes, O LC 43
	110.	Puffs from a riven stump far out behind Tun 70
river	46.	O Sleepless as the river under thee TBB 41
	68.	For you, too, feed the River timelessly Riv 107
	69.	The River, spreading, flows--and spends your dream Riv 120
	69.	The River lifts itself from its long bed Riv 139
	111.	Under the river Tun 94
	112.	Lunged past, with one galvanic blare stove up the River Tun 124
	112.	And to be.... Here by the River that is East Tun 131
rivered	109.	subways, rivered under streets Tun 33
river's	64.	The river's minute by the far brook's year Riv 30
	68.	Maybe the breeze will lift the River's musk Riv 97
	79.	Down the dim turnpike to the river's edge Ind 57
rivers	40.	And ocean rivers, churning, shift V-6 3

rivers, cont.	40.	O rivers mingling toward the sky V-6 9
	109.	and rivers.... In the car Tun 34
River-throated	116.	O River-throated--iridescently upborne At 67
riveted	29.	Accept a lone eye riveted to your plane F&H I 49
rivets	115.	Of inchling aeons silence rivets Troy At 36
roach	4.	And a roach spans a crevice in the floor BT 4
road	144.	In the dust of a road PA 23
	161.	At the turning of the road around the roots of the mountain IQ 3
	161.	Where the straight road would seem to ply below the stone, that fierce IQ 4
	161.	Walking the straight road toward thunder IQ 10
	161.	This dry road silvering toward the shadow of the quarry IQ 11
	179.	And the idiot boy by the road, with carbonated eyes, laugh- Len 4
	179.	pebbles among cinders in the road through a twice-opened Len 7
	182.	I beat the dazed mule toward the road. He got that far Et 48
road-gang	64.	Some Sunny Day. I heard a road-gang chanting so Riv 40
roadhouses	105.	In bootleg roadhouses where the gin fizz QH 35
roads	182.	along the roads, begging for buzzards, vultures Et 34
	183.	The roads were being cleared, injured brought in Et 53
roar	62.	and no more sermons windows flashing roar Riv 17
	105.	(Now the New Avalon Hotel) volcanoes roar QH 38
	111.	Blank windows gargle signals through the roar Tun 99
roared	62.	whizzed the Limited--roared by and left Riv 20
	62.	RADIO ROARS IN EVERY HOME WE HAVE THE NORTHPOLE Riv 14
robes	180.	The sea wall. Bring her no robes yet Lib 9
rock	32.	Of wave or rock was good against one hour F&H III 24
	169.	Rock sockets, levin-lathered Hur 11
rocked	30.	Sit rocked in patent armchairs F&H II 23
rocking	37.	Your body rocking V-3 14
rocks	5.	With sulphur and aureate rocks EC 4
	21.	Aprons rocks, congregates pears Pass 8
rod	20.	Once and again; vermin and rod LC 29
rode	58.	And Cortes rode up, reining tautly in VW 8
	76.	How we, too, Prodigal, once rode off, too Ind 13
rods	66.	--Memphis to Tallahassee--riding the rods Riv 60
rolling	144.	Among rolling Ohio hills PA 12
Roman	95.	New integers of Roman, Viking, Celt CH 203

rondure	50.	This turning rondure whole, this crescent ring AM 43
roof	6.	Into a corner of the roof MGLL 9
	6.	And so I stumble. And the rain continues on the roof MGLL 25
	30.	From roof to roof F&H II 6
	181.	Parts of the roof reached Yucatan, I suppose Et 4
room	6.	Yet how much room for memory there is MGLL 3
	6.	There is even room enough MGLL 5
	133.	Sinuously winding through the room CDB 1
	140.	This lamp in our poor room Int 2
	159.	As you have yielded balcony and room TCJ 15
	185.	Dawn's broken arc! the noon's more furbished room Post 12
rooster	30.	Until somewhere a rooster banters F&H II 14
root	72.	--Siphoned the black pool from the heart's hot root Dan 44
roots	69.	And roots surrendered down of moraine clays Riv 126
	129.	of greenery.... Below the roots, a quickening shiver An 3
	161.	At the turning of the road around the roots of the mountain IQ 3
	182.	Long tropic roots high in the air, like lace Et 30
rosary	64.	--Though they'll confess no rosary nor clue Riv 29
rose	40.	To the lounged goddess when she rose V-6 22
	70.	She spouted arms; she rose with maize--to die Dan 4
	78.	It rose up shambling in the nuggets' wake Ind 22
	82.	O Stamboul Rose--dreams weave the rose CS 10
	83.	ATLANTIS ROSE drums wreathe the rose CS 43
	94.	Potomac lilies,--then the Pontiac rose CH 179
	146.	To find the only rose on the bush PA 51
	162.	Thy absence overflows the rose OS 1
	162.	The burden of the rose will fade OS 9
	188.	like rats--and too, when rats make rose nozzles of pink HR 27
Rose of Stamboul	83.	Rose of Stamboul O coral Queen CS 29
roses	17.	Among bruised roses on the papered wall Par 16
	24.	Between black tusks the roses shine WM 28
	130.	Are circles of cool roses,--so Ech 10
	173.	Beyond the roses that no flesh can pass MF 8
	185.	and other gratuities, like porters[,]jokes, roses Post 11
	188.	be doctors, but doctors are rare poets when roses leap HR 26
rosy	188.	rosy (in their basement basinette)--the Doctor sup- HR 16

rose-vines	125.	He has woven rose-vines C 1
rotten	165.	That thin and blistered...just a rotten shell BSEW 4
Roumanian	145.	Roumanian business men PA 37
'round	69.	All fades but one thin skyline 'round...Ahead Riv 137
	95.	And read thee by the aureole 'round thy head CH 216
	159.	What you may cluster 'round the knees of space TCJ 1
round	36.	Close round one instant in one floating flower V-2 20
	51.	Of knowledge,--round thy brows unhooded now AM 84
	84.	Bright skysails ticketing the Line, wink round the Horn CS 61
	88.	But we, who round the capes, the promontories CH 6
	123.	Swinging in spirals round the fresh breasts of day Moth 30
	152.	again round one more fairest day In 21
	163.	In such infernal circles round his door Id 5
rounding	123.	Seething and rounding in long streams of light Moth 37
rounds	110.	That last night on the ballot rounds, did you Tun 81
	111.	Wheels off. The train rounds, bending to a scream Tun 92
rouse	17.	That shall not rouse, how faint the crow's cavil Par 12
	176.	To rouse what sanctions VU 14
rubber	60.	Rubber bands...Recall--recall/the rapid tongues VW 21
	144.	A shift of rubber workers presses down PA 2
rubies	122.	Countless rubies and tapers in the oasis' blue haze Moth 16
ruby	100.	Sprayed first with ruby, then with emerald sheen NWG 14
	123.	The sun saw a ruby brightening ever, that flew Moth 36
rubyless	170.	Leaves Ormus rubyless, and Ophir chill TED 13
ruddy	24.	Ruddy, the tooth implicit of the world WM 40
rue	186.	Are lifted from torn flesh with human rue Shak 7
ruffles	35.	Above the fresh ruffles of the surf V-1 1
rule	89.	Of the ambiguous cloud. We know the strident rule CH 34
rum	82.	and rum was Plato in our heads CS 12
rumbling	144.	Rumbling over the hills PA 9
rum-giver	159.	You, the rum-giver to that slide-by-night TCJ 9
ruminating	64.	Caboose-like they go ruminating through Riv 32

rummaged   181. Where a frantic peacock rummaged amid heaped
                      cans Et 17
rumor   181. From the world outside, but some rumor blew
                      Et 19
rumorous   66. --As I have trod the rumorous midnights, too
                      Riv 70
runaway   64. The ancient men--wifeless or runaway Riv 54
running   62. WIRES OR EVEN RUNning brooks connecting ears
                      Riv 16
                 70. Your hair's keen crescent running, and the
                      blue Dan 19
                 83. or are there frontiers--running sands sometimes
                      CS 38
                 83. running sands--somewhere--sands running CS 39
                187. of wet wind running Ma 2
runs   7. A boy runs with a dog before the sun, straddling
                      SMA 9
rush   50. --Rush down the plenitude, and you shall see
                      AM 49
                100. (Then rush the nearest exit through the smoke
                      NWG 8
                109. --Quite unprepared rush naked back to light
                      Tun 28
                114. The whispered rush, telepathy of wires At 4
                191. And all my countrymen I see rush toward one
                      stall Purg 12
rushed   183. Sliding everywhere. Bodies were rushed into
                      graves Et 51
rushes   148. Your eyes, those pools with soft rushes Loc 1
rushing   17. One rushing from the bed at night Par 3
                 62. a headlight rushing with the sound--can you
                      Riv 11
                115. Silvery the rushing wake, surpassing call At 39
rustlings   167. Green rustlings, more-than-regal charities
                      RP 1

Sabbatical	60.	Or is it the Sabbatical, unconscious smile VW 34
saber	73.	Of lightning deltaed down your saber hair Dan 54
sable	20.	Lean long from sable, slender boughs LC 37
Sachem	72.	--Fall, Sachem, strictly as the tamarack Dan 48
sacked	158.	Though why they bide here, only hell that's sacked Mer 2
sacred	184.	Thy death is sacred to all those who share Emp 12
sacrifice	18.	One moment in sacrifice (the direst Pos 4
sacrosanct	74.	Like one white meteor, sacrosanct and blent Dan 78
sad	192.	Sad heart, the gymnast of inertia, does not count SI 1
saddled	32.	That saddled sky that shook down vertical F&H III 22
safe	48.	One ship of these thou grantest safe returning AM 27
sagas	90.	Stars scribble on our eyes the frosty sagas CH 75
sage	48.	Of clown nor sage can riddle or gainsay AM 6
sagging	181.	The only building not sagging on its knees Et 10
Sagittarius	190.	And the flint tooth of Sagittarius Rel 5
sail	40.	Like a cliff swinging or a sail V-6 19
	51.	Utter to loneliness the sail is true AM 64
sailor	180.	A dead sailor that knew Lib 6
sails	45.	As apparitional as sails that cross TBB 6
	51.	In holy rings all sails charged to the far AM 82
	51.	And biassed by full sails, meridians reel AM 86
	82.	to put me out at three she sails on time CS 14
	178.	So dream thy sails, O phantom bark PB 1
	178.	Of old there was a promise, and thy sails PB 9
saintly	187.	this slate-eyed saintly wraith Ma 17
sakes	62.	and lands sakes! under the new playbill ripped Riv 4
salads	100.	And while legs waken salads in the brain NWG 5
salient	171.	Here has my salient faith annealed me KW 1
saline	168.	This tuft that thrives on saline nothingness AP 1
Sally Simpson	64.	"--And when my Aunt Sally Simpson smiled," he drawled Riv 44
salt	69.	(Anon tall ironsides up from salt lagoons Riv 135
	75.	And when the caribou slant down for salt Dan 97
Saltes	50.	Tomorrow's moon will grant us Saltes Bar AM 53
salty	50.	An herb, a stray branch among salty teeth AM 51

sang, cont.	146.	Your mother sang that in a stuffy parlour PA 46
	164.	I dreamed that all men dropped their names, and sang NA 9
sank	132.	Even, sank in love and choked with flowers MC 10
	158.	But since the Cross sank, much that's warped and cracked Mer 6
San Salvador	36.	And onward, as bells off San Salvador V-2 11
Sanscrit	190.	Who is now left to vary the Sanscrit Rel 12
Sanskrit	92.	Thou hast there in thy wrist a Sanskrit charge CH 129
sap	12.	That ritual of sap and leaves Past 6
sapphire	16.	I heard wind flaking sapphire, like this summer RR 22
	21.	In sapphire arenas of the hills Pass 3
	23.	Octagon, sapphire transepts round the eyes WM 16
	51.	From Moon to Saturn in one sapphire wheel AM 78
sarabande	16.	A sarabande the wind mowed on the mead RR 2
Sarah	182.	When the storm was dying. And Sarah saw them, too Et 41
sat	5.	By a peninsula the wanderer sat and sketched EC 1
	165.	Oozing a-plenty. They sat like baking Buddhas BSEW 7
Satan	157.	You have given me the shell, Satan,--carbonic amulet OC 34
satellited	91.	Of pendulous auroral beaches,--satellited wide CH 113
satin	157.	Congeal by afternoons here, satin and vacant OC 33
saturate	33.	To saturate with blessing and dismay F&H III 30
Saturday	102.	Saturday Mary, mine Va 8
Saturn	51.	From Moon to Saturn in one sapphire wheel AM 78
Saunterer	89.	O Saunterer on free ways still ahead CH 50
saurian	88.	the mammoth saurian/ghoul, the eastern/Cape CH 2
savage	40.	More savage than the death of kings V-6 15
	84.	British repartees, skil-/ful savage sea-girls CS 55
savannahs	51.	Into thy steep savannahs, burning blue AM 63
save	62.	save me the wing for if it isn't Riv 7
	139.	All, save I Lege 9
saves	106.	Breaks us and saves, yes, breaks the heart, yet yields QH 69
saw	34.	The dice of drowned men's bones he saw bequeath AMT 2
	48.	I, wonder-breathing, kept the watch,--saw AM 23
	70.	Mythical brows we saw retiring--loth Dan 9
	70.	But, watching, saw that fleet young crescent die Dan 24

saw, cont.	73.	Wrapped in that fire, I saw more escorts wake Dan 67
	74.	Of his own fate, I saw thy change begun Dan 76
	74.	And saw thee dive to kiss that destiny Dan 77
	78.	Of wagon-tenting looked out once and saw Ind 30
	78.	Until she saw me--when their violet haze Ind 39
	83.	I saw the frontiers gleaming of his mind CS 37
	105.	Who saw the Friends there ever heard before QH 40
	123.	The sun saw a ruby brightening ever, that flew Moth 36
	123.	When below him he saw what his whole race had shunned Moth 42
	161.	Square sheets--they saw the marble only into IQ 1
	179.	the buzz of saw mills, the crunch and blast of quarries Len 2
	181.	But was there a boat? By the wharf's old site you saw Et 14
	182.	When the storm was dying. And Sarah saw them, too Et 41
say	149.	--Which is to be mine, you say? Loc 21
saying	145.	Setting down a glass and saying PA 30
	151.	all america is saying APE 2
scalding	16.	With scalding unguents spread and smoking darts RR 19
scalped	105.	Me farther than scalped Yankees knew to go QH 52
scan	51.	Within whose primal scan consummately AM 67
	163.	That kite aloft--you should have watched him scan Id 11
scanning	179.	a kite high in the afternoon, or in the twilight scanning Len 6
scansions	23.	Narrowing the mustard scansions of the eyes WM 2
scar	164.	And take the wing and scar it in the hand NA 6
scarcely	10.	Scarcely aloud, beyond her door SM 14
	12.	Summer scarcely begun Past 18
	192.	Hours, days--and scarcely sun and moon SI 2
scarcity	171.	O, steel and stone! But gold was, scarcity before KW 13
scarf	102.	O blue-eyed Mary with the claret scarf Va 7
scarfed	84.	--scarfed of foam, their bellies veered green esplanades CS 68
scars	98.	Of lower heavens,--/vaporous scars SC 6
scatter	8.	Scatter these well-meant idioms PU 21
scattered	33.	Delve upward for the new and scattered wine F&H III 39
	34.	A scattered chapter, livid hieroglyph AMT 7
	37.	Are laved and scattered with no stroke V-3 6
scattering	35.	Gaily digging and scattering V-1 5
scene	45.	With multitudes bend toward some flashing scene TBB 10

script	90.	Power's script,--wound, bobbin-bound, refined CH 65
	90.	What ciphers risen from prophetic script CH 82
Scripture	169.	Ay! Scripture flee'th stone Hur 5
scorpion	191.	Where are the bayonets that the scorpion may not grow Purg 10
scrolls	36.	On scrolls of silver snowy sentences V-2 7
scud	30.	Or, plaintively scud past shores F&H II 20
scudding	50.	Was tumbled from us under bare poles scudding AM 30
scurries	73.	And every tendon scurries toward the twangs Dan 53
scuttle	45.	Out of some subway scuttle, cell or loft TBB 17
	108.	As usual you will meet the scuttle yawn Tun 22
scythe	76.	But you who drop the scythe to grasp the oar Ind 11
sea	5.	Where marble clouds support the sea EC 13
	16.	Till age had brought me to the sea RR 5
	21.	I heard the sea Pass 2
	33.	Anchises' navel, dripping of the sea F&H III 36
	34.	This fabulous shadow only the sea keeps AMT 16
	35.	The bottom of the sea is cruel V-1 16
	36.	Take this Sea, whose diapason knells V-2 6
	37.	Retrieves from sea plains where the sky V-3 3
	37.	The sea lifts, also, reliquary hands V-3 8
	38.	I know as spectrum of the sea and pledge V-4 2
	46.	Vaulting the sea, the prairies' dreaming sod TBB 42
	48.	Invisible valves of the sea,--locks, tendons AM 10
	50.	Take of that eastern shore, this western sea AM 47
	68.	You will not hear it as the sea; even stone Riv 116
	69.	No embrace opens but the stinging sea Riv 138
	78.	Yes, Larry, now you're going to sea, remember Ind 46
	89.	Sea eyes and tidal, undenying, bright with myth CH 58
	112.	How far away the star has pooled the sea Tun 134
	114.	Pouring reply as though all ships at sea At 12
	123.	To yellow,--to crystal,--a sea of white spray Moth 32
	131.	Two ivory women by a milky sea Ba 1
	139.	The sand and sea have had their way Lege 7
	157.	Sere of the sun exploded in the sea OC 35
	159.	Of districts where cliff, sea and palm advance TCJ 3
	161.	Palms against the sunset's towering sea, and maybe IQ 6

sea, cont.   172. I had come all the way here from the sea ABP 1
                    172. Sea gardens lifted rainbow-wise through eyes
                          ABP 5
                    180. Hair mocked by the sea, her lover Lib 5
                    180. The sea wall. Bring her no robes yet Lib 9
seaboard   91. To hedge the seaboard, wrap the headland, ride
                          CH 89
sea-girls   84. British repartees, skil-/ful savage sea-girls
                          CS 55
seagull   180. Out of the seagull cries and wind Lib 1
seagull's   45. The seagull's wings shall dip and pivot him
                          TBB 2
seagulls   115. Sheerly the eyes, like seagulls stung with rime
                          At 25
sea-kelp   169. Whip sea-kelp screaming on blond Hur 15
seal   105. Ty-five at Adams' auction,--eats the seal QH 44
sealed   39. Your breath sealed by the ghosts I do not know
                          V-5 24
                    167. And tendril till our deathward breath is sealed
                          RP 11
seal's   36. The seal's wide spindrift gaze toward paradise
                          V-2 25
search   25. Such eyes at search or rest you cannot see
                          Rec 3
                     51. And all the eddying breath between dost search
                          AM 59
                     64. Hobo-trekkers that forever search Riv 55
                    108. Mysterious kitchens.... You shall search them
                          all Tun 5
                    174. Come, search the marshes for a friendly bed
                          BNOK 3
searched   94. O, early following thee, I searched the hill
                          CH 175
searches   115. Searches the timeless laugh of mythic spears
                          At 32
searching   112. Searching, thumbing the midnight on the piers
                          Tun 126
searchlights   92. Cloud-belfries, banging, while searchlights,
                          like fencers CH 121
searing   125. With searing sophistry C 5
sea's   51. The sea's green crying towers a-sway, Beyond
                          AM 88
                    131. Flat lily petals to the sea's white throat
                          Ba 7
seasonable   7. Beloved apples of seasonable madness SMA 14
seasons   36. Bind us in time, O Seasons clear, and awe
                          V-2 21
                     74. Lo, through what infinite seasons dost thou gaze
                          Dan 82
                    104. Even to cast upon the seasons fleeting QH 7
seated   145. Harry and I, "the gentlemen",--seated around
                          PA 28

seaweed	159.	The green preëmption of the deep seaweed TCJ 8
second	25.	Twin shadowed halves: the breaking second holds Rec 5
	89.	Across the hills where second timber strays CH 56
	109.	Where boxed alone a second, eyes take fright Tun 27
	111.	Demented, for a hitching second, humps; then Tun 96
secret	38.	The secret oar and petals of all love V-4 25
secretes	40.	Steadily as a shell secretes V-6 5
secrets	7.	I have seen the spples there that toss you secrets SMA 13
secular	116.	Swift peal of secular light, intrinsic Myth At 65
see	8.	I see now, were inheritances PU 7
	8.	I cannot see that broken brow PU 18
	21.	See where the red and black Pass 17
	25.	Such eyes at search or rest you cannot see Rec 3
	50.	--Rush down the plenitude, and you shall see AM 49
	62.	in the guaranteed corner--see Bert Williams what Riv 5
	64.	Behind/My father's cannery works I used to see Riv 52
	68.	Southward, near Cairo passing, you can see Riv 94
	68.	Yes, turn again and sniff once more--look see Riv 104
	70.	Tugging below the mill-race, I could see Dan 18
	92.	See scouting griffons rise through gaseous crepe CH 119
	92.	Thine eyes bicarbonated white by speed, O Skygak, see CH 124
	95.	And see! the rainbow's arch--how shimmeringly stands CH 212
	104.	These are but cows that see no other thing QH 4
	104.	See them, like eyes that still uphold some dream QH 23
	122.	Some say that for sweetness they cannot see far Moth 5
	122.	That they only can see when their moon limits vision Moth 9
	131.	A dreamer might see these, and wake to hear Ba 4
	133.	And stretches up through mortal eyes to see CDB 16
	142.	I do not know what you'll see,--your vision BE 18
	149.	Don't I see your white swans there Loc 27
	150.	And how much more they cannot see GWP 10

see, cont.	157.	Let not the pilgrim see himself again OC 27
	163.	Sheer over to the other side,--for see Id 1
	191.	And all my countrymen I see rush toward one stall Purg 12
seed	93.	With vast eternity, dost wield the rebound seed CH 150
	99.	Yes, Eve--wraith of my unloved seed SC 27
seeing	89.	Seeing himself an atom in a shroud CH 41
seek	177.	Seek bliss then, brother, in my moment's shame Rep 6
seem	68.	Always they smile out eerily what they seem Riv 109
	126.	On trees that seem dancing O-N 6
	149.	That seem too much impromptu Loc 24
	161.	Where the straight road would seem to ply below the stone, that fierce IQ 4
seemed	66.	Each seemed a child, like me, on a loose perch Riv 57
	78.	And like twin stars. They seemed to shun the gaze Ind 37
	141.	Suddenly he seemed to forget the pain EpH 2
	141.	His own hands seemed to him EpH 13
	141.	Deep hand that lay in his,--seemed beautiful EpH 17
	181.	No one seemed to be able to get a spark Et 18
	183.	And treated, it seemed. In due time Et 54
seen	7.	I have seen the apples there that toss you secrets SMA 13
	11.	The game enforces smirks; but we have seen Chap 19
	31.	Beneath gyrating awnings I have seen F&H II 28
	46.	And we have seen night lifted in thine arms TBB 36
	48.	For I have seen now what no perjured breath AM 5
	48.	Till dawn should clear that dim frontier, first seen AM 20
	60.	nor there. He woke and swore he'd seen Broadway VW 28
	83.	have you seen Popocatepetl--birdless mouth CS 26
	94.	But thou, Panis Angelicus, hast thou not seen CH 198
	104.	But I have seen death's stare in slow survey QH 27
	142.	I had never seen a hand before BE 14
	143.	Seen them again, you won't forget BE 26
	180.	They have not seen her in this harbor Lib 10
	184.	You, who have looked back to Leda, who have seen the Swan Emp 6
	193.	Have you not heard, have you not seen that corps B Tow 5

seer	40.	Some splintered garland for the seer V-6 16
	95.	Above the Cape's ghoul-mound, O joyous seer CH 213
sees	88.	Where each sees only his dim past reversed CH 27
	149.	That my conscience sees double Loc 30
see'st	74.	And see'st thy bride immortal in the maize Dan 84
seething	16.	That seething, steady leveling of the marshes RR 4
	51.	Hushed gleaming fields and pendant seething wheat AM 83
	73.	Flame cataracts of heaven in seething swarms Dan 71
	123.	Seething and rounding in long streams of light Moth 37
seignories	51.	The glistening seignories of Ganges swim AM 68
seizure	116.	Of thy white seizure springs the prophecy At 77
seldom	14.	Seldom, now, meet a mirror in her eyes Fern 2
	185.	Yet seldom was there faith in the heart's right kindness Post 13
selling	83.	then Yucatan selling kitchenware--beads CS 25
	173.	The syphilitic selling violets calmly/and daisies MF 1
semaphores	105.	Here three hours from the semaphores, the Czars QH 30
Seminary Hill	76.	Waved Seminary Hill a gay good-bye Ind 14
sendest	51.	Who sendest greeting by the corposant AM 69
Señor	160.	O mister Señor MT 13
sensed	129.	Aroused by some light that had sensed,--ere the shiver An 4
senses	156.	Is Commissioner of mildew throughout the ambushed senses OC 21
sensibility	148.	Of my lunar sensibility Loc 16
sent	183.	The President sent down a battleship that baked Et 55
sentences	36.	On scrolls of silver snowy sentences V-2 7
sentient	20.	No longer bind. Some sentient cloud LC 30
separate	24.	Remorseless line, minting their separate wills WM 25
Sepulchre	51.	Of Eden and the enchained Sepulchre AM 62
sequel	116.	Of silver sequel, Deity's young name At 79
Sequoia	94.	As vibrantly I following down Sequoia alleys CH 183
Serafin	165.	"Pablo and Pedro, and black Serafin BSEW 1
seraphic	95.	Vast engines outward veering with seraphic grace CH 207
sere	157.	Sere of the sun exploded in the sea OC 35
serenade	110.	The intent escalator lifts a serenade Tun 85

serene	30.	All relatives, serene and cool F&H II 22
	163.	Above all reason lifting, halt serene Id 15
serenely	54.	Serenely now, before day claims our eyes HD 23
	115.	Serenely, sharply up the long anvil cry At 35
serenity	186.	And that serenity that Prospero gains Shak 13
series	50.	Series on series, infinite,--till eyes AM 41
sermons	62.	and no more sermons windows flashing roar Riv 17
serpent	22.	A serpent swam a vertex to the sun Pass 34
	23.	What is it in this heap the serpent pries WM 14
	66.	Time like a serpent down her shoulder, dark Riv 79
	74.	--And laughs, pure serpent, Time itself, and moon Dan 75
	75.	The serpent with the eagle in the boughs Dan 104
	117.	The serpent with the eagle in the leaves At 95
serve	158.	Buddhas and engines serve us undersea Mer 1
serves	151.	memory serves there is still APE 16
service	110.	"But I want service in this office SERVICE Tun 63
sesames	94.	Beyond all sesames of science was thy choice CH 201
sessions	36.	The sceptred terror of whose sessions rends V-2 8
	108.	Channel the congresses, nightly sessions Tun 3
set	94.	Set trumpets breathing in each clump and grass tuft--'til CH 185
	94.	Our Meistersinger, thou set breath in steel CH 193
	122.	Where are set all the myriad jewelleries of night Moth 12
	135.	Set in the tryst-ring has but worn more bright CL 8
setting	145.	Setting down a glass and saying PA 30
settles	32.	And in other ways than as the wind settles F&H III 8
seven	102.	O rain at seven Va 1
	102.	Gone seven--gone eleven Va 5
	114.	So seven oceans answer from their dream At 16
sever	129.	That strives long and quiet to sever the girth An 2
several	82.	or left you several blocks away CS 7
severe	38.	Whose circles bridge, I know, (from palms to the severe V-4 4
severed	24.	Beyond the wall, whose severed head floats by WM 46
sex	149.	With the why-and-wherefore of Your Sex Loc 36
	163.	Fumbling his sex. That's why those children laughed Id 4
sextant	34.	Compass, quadrant and sextant contrive AMT 13
sexton	193.	Of broken intervals...And I, their sexton slave B Tow 12

shad-blow	94.	Cowslip and shad-blow, flaked like tethered foam CH 171
shade	14.	But turning, as you may chance to lift a shade Fern 3
	72.	--And knew myself within some boding shade Dan 38
	78.	The long trail back! I huddled in the shade Ind 29
	122.	So they sleep in the shade of black palm-bark at noon Moth 13
	162.	But here the thorn in sharpened shade OS 11
shadow	4.	Gnats toss in the shadow of a bottle BT 3
	7.	Into a realm of swords, her purple shadow SMA 6
	13.	Like a waiting moon, in shadow swims IS 4
	33.	For golden, or the shadow of gold hair F&H III 44
	34.	This fabulous shadow only the sea keeps AMT 16
	46.	Under thy shadow by the piers I waited TBB 37
	46.	Only in darkness is thy sahdow clear TBB 38
	50.	Laughter, and shadow cuts sleep from the heart AM 35
	161.	This dry road silvering toward the shadow of the quarry IQ 11
	168.	Almost no shadow--but the air's thin talk AP 12
shadowed	25.	Twin shadowed halves: the breaking second holds Rec 5
	92.	Low, shadowed of the Cape CH 117
shadowless	112.	Shadowless in that abyss they unaccounting lie Tun 133
shadows'	23.	--I am conscripted to their shadows' glow WM 8
shadows	9.	Beyond the grass and shadows at her feet GA 12
	13.	Again the shadows at her will IS 8
	13.	Twilight, stiller than shadows, fall IS 12
	21.	The shadows of boulders lengthened my back Pass 13
	30.	White shadows slip across the floor F&H II 11
	33.	The abating shadows of our conscript dust F&H III 35
	156.	In wrinkled shadows--mourns OC 7
	160.	spiders yoked you first,--silking of shadows good under-/drawers for owls MT 5
	192.	--Their shadows even--now can't carry him SI 8
	193.	Of shadows in the tower, whose shoulders sway B Tow 6
shaft	141.	The gash was bleeding, and a shaft of sun EpH 5
shafts	25.	Built floor by floor on shafts of steel that grant Rec 19
shake	50.	Dark waters onward shake the dark prow free AM 56
	174.	It knows its way through India--tropic shake BNOK 14

shaken	123.	Which blue tides of cool moons were slow shaken and sunned Moth 44
shaking	110.	Shaking, did you deny the ticket, Poe Tun 82
shale	69.	Nights turbid, vascular with silted shale Riv 125
shambling	78.	It rose up shambling in the nuggets' wake Ind 22
shame	177.	Seek bliss then, brother, in my moment's shame Rep 6
	177.	And fame is pivotal to shame with every sun Rep 10
	177.	So sleep, dear brother, in my fame, my shame undone Rep 12
shape	163.	Once when he shouted, stretched in ghastly shape Id 6
shapeless	93.	....dispersion...into meshed and shapeless debris CH 143
shaping	109.	girls all shaping up--it used to be Tun 45
share	10.	You cannot ever reach to share SM 24
	33.	Who dare not share with us the breath released F&H III 42
	88.	Our eyes can share or answer--then deflects CH 25
	184.	Thy death is sacred to all those who share Emp 12
shared	16.	Where cypresses shared the noon's RR 7
shark	82.	a nervous shark tooth swung on his chain CS 2
shark-swept	168.	While beachward creeps the shark-swept Spanish Main AP 14
sharp	23.	Sharp to the windowpane guile drags a face WM 19
	78.	But sharp with pain Ind 36
	90.	Stars prick the eyes with sharp ammoniac pro-verbs CH 62
	91.	Wounds that we wrap with theorems sharp as hail CH 98
	104.	The jest is too sharp to be kindly?) boast QH 14
sharpened	162.	But here the thorn in sharpened shade OS 11
sharply	115.	Serenely, sharply up the long anvil cry At 35
shattering	133.	There is a sweep,--a shattering,--a choir CDB 13
she	6.	Through much of what she would not understand MGLL 24
	9.	She is a prisoner of the tree and its green fingers GA 6
	9.	And so she comes to dream herself the tree GA 7
	9.	She has no memory, nor fear, nor hope GA 11
	10.	And she will wake before you pass SM 13
	13.	She hears my step behind the green IS 11
	70.	She spouted arms; she rose with maize--to die Dan 4

she, cont.   110.   the show she cried a little afterwards but
                         Tun 65
                  122.   She will flush their hid wings in the evening to
                         blaze Moth 15
                  139.   She has become a pathos Lege 5
                  145.   As down she knelt for heaven's grace and boon
                         PA 44
                  147.   If she waits late at night Per 1
                  147.   She has drawn her hands away Per 5
                  194.   As flings the question true?)--or is it she
                         B Tow 27

sheaf   106.   Arise--yes, take this sheaf of dust upon your
                         tongue QH 62

shear   91.   They, cavalcade on escapade, shear Cumulus
                         CH 110

sheath   54.   Ask nothing but this sheath of pallid air
                         HD 20

shed   37.   and where death, if shed V-3 15
                  125.   And wavering shoulders with a new light shed
                         C 9
                  174.   Or let us bump heads in some lowly shed BNOK 4

shedding   45.   Shedding white rings of tumult, building high
                         TBB 3

sheds   140.   It sheds a shy solemnity Int 1
                  168.   But this,--defenseless, thornless, sheds no
                         blood AP 11

sheen   13.   Gently yet suddenly, the sheen IS 9
                   91.   With razor sheen they zoom each rapid helix
                         CH 108
                   94.   And filled the forest with what clustrous sheen
                         CH 178
                  100.   Sprayed first with ruby, then with emerald sheen
                         NWG 14

sheened   115.   Sheened harbor lanterns backward fled the keel
                         At 50

sheep   145.   I ride black horse.... Have many sheep PA 32
sheer   163.   Sheer over to the other side,--for see Id 1
sheerly   115.   Sheerly the eyes, like seagulls stung with rime
                         At 25

sheeted   36.   Samite sheeted and processioned where V-2 3
                  182.   Out of the bamboo brake through howling, sheeted
                         light Et 40

sheets   17.   Above the feet the clever sheets Par 5
                  161.   Square sheets--they saw the marble only into
                         IQ 1
                  186.   Sheets that mock lust and thorns that scribble
                         hate Shak 6

shell   24.   Before some flame of gaunt repose a shell WM 35
                   35.   They have contrived a conquest for shell shucks
                         V-1 3
                   40.   Steadily as a shell secretes V-6 5

shining	9.	Shining suspension, mimic of the sun GA 2
shins	24.	Stepping over Holofernes' shins WM 45
ship	48.	One ship of these thou grantest safe returning AM 27
	89.	Wherein your eyes, like the Great Navigator's without ship CH 52
ships	51.	Subscribest holocaust of ships, O Thou AM 66
	114.	Pouring reply as though all ships at sea At 12
shirt	45.	Tilting there momently, shrill shirt ballooning TBB 19
shiver	129.	Of greenery.... Below the roots, a quickening shiver An 3
	129.	Aroused by some light that had sensed,--ere the shiver An 4
	133.	Just as absinthe-sipping women shiver through CDB 6
shivered	25.	The brain's disk shivered against lust. Then watch Rec 14
	93.	That's drained, is shivered back to earth-- thy wand CH 162
shoal	51.	And true appointment from the hidden shoal AM 76
shoe	110.	Of shoes, umbrellas, each eye attending its shoe, then Tun 87
shoes	110.	Of shoes, umbrellas, each eye attending its shoe, then Tun 87
	165.	--Yes, patent-leather shoes hot enough to fry BSEW 11
shone	145.	"Full on this casement shone the wintry moon PA 42
shook	32.	That saddled sky that shook down vertical F&H III 22
shore	34.	Beat on the dusty shore and were obscured AMT 4
	36.	Bequeath us to no earthly shore until V-2 23
	50.	Take of that eastern shore, this western sea AM 47
	50.	The jellied weeds that drag the shore,--perhaps AM 52
	51.	Thy purpose--still one shore beyond desire AM 87
	142.	Clean on the shore some wreck of dreams BE 21
	163.	I hurried by. But back from the hot shore Id 7
	171.	There is no breath of friends and no more shore KW 15
	180.	On this strange shore I build Lib 2
shores	30.	Or, plaintively scud past shores F&H II 20
	123.	Great horizons and systems and shores all along Moth 43
shot	64.	The last bear, shot drinking in the Dakotas Riv 24

shudders	56.	a <u>forest</u> <u>shudders</u> <u>in</u> <u>your</u> <u>hair</u> HD 30
shun	78.	And like twin stars. They seemed to shun the gaze Ind 37
shunned	123.	When below him he saw what his whole race had shunned Moth 42
shunting	88.	Us, shunting to a labyrinth submersed CH 26
shutters	188.	clamour of incessant shutters, trundle doors, and the HR 6
shuttling	114.	Taut miles of shuttling moonlight syncopate At 3
shy	140.	It sheds a shy solemnity Int 1
shyly	185.	at last shyly. My only final friends Post 2
shyness	132.	O blameless shyness;--innocence dissolute MC 4
sibilance	74.	Her hair's warm sibilance. Her breasts are fanned Dan 95
Sibylline	114.	Sibylline voices flicker, waveringly stream At 7
side	37.	Wide from your side, whereto this hour V-3 7
	73.	I could not pick the arrows from my side Dan 66
	91.	Hell's belt springs wider into heaven's plumed side CH 92
	110.	--And did their riding eyes right through your side Tun 75
	163.	Sheer over to the other side,--for see Id 1
	184.	You did not die for conquerors at your side Emp 14
sidelong	115.	Sidelong with flight of blade on tendon blade At 28
sidereal	117.	Sidereal phalanxes, leap and converge At 92
sides	28.	Impinging on the throat and sides F&H I 35
sidestep	11.	We will sidestep, and to the final smirk Chap 9
side-stilting	156.	Side-stilting from the path (that shift, subvert OC 4
siege	73.	Surpassed the circumstance, danced out the siege Dan 64
	91.	Lay siege and hurdle Cirrus down the skies CH 111
sierras	93.	Glacial sierras and the flight of ravens CH 158
sieved	156.	Sieved upward, white and black along the air OC 25
sifting	18.	And the key, ready to hand--sifting Pos 3
	83.	with ashes sifting down CS 27
sigh	46.	Unfractioned idiom, immaculate sigh of stars TBB 34
sighing	167.	Its frondings sighing in aetherial folds RP 8
sight	23.	Invariably when wine redeems the sight WM 1
	51.	A needle in the sight, suspended north AM 74
	62.	ping gimleted and neatly out of sight Riv 23
	95.	On clarion cylinders pass out of sight CH 208
	108.	Someday by heart you'll learn each famous sight Tun 6

sight, cont.	108.	With tabloid crime-sheets perched in easy sight Tun 10
	116.	Sight, sound and flesh Thou leadest from time's realm At 63
	123.	A little time only, for sight burned as deep Moth 45
	131.	But they are wrong.... Ere man was given sight Ba 9
	177.	Where brother passes brother without sight Rep 3
sign	25.	That yield attendance to one crucial sign Rec 12
signs	122.	And had not his pinions with signs mystical Moth 21
signalled	95.	What heritage thou'st signalled to our hands CH 211
signals	54.	Far strum of fog horns...signals dispersed in veils HD 5
signature	38.	In signature of the incarnate word V-4 17
signboard	62.	Stick your patent name on a signboard Riv 1
silence	3.	Realities plunge in silence by Leg 2
	6.	Is the silence strong enough MGLL 19
	88.	Relapsing into silence, while time clears CH 22
	106.	Listen, transmuting silence with that stilly note QH 64
	115.	Of inchling aeons silence rivets Troy At 36
	131.	In silence, beauty blessed and beauty cursed Ba 11
	133.	Finale leaves in silence to replume CDB 21
	140.	Silence and gentle gloom Int 4
	194.	Of pebbles,--visible wings of silence sown B Tow 35
Silencer	170.	O sweet, dead Silencer, most suddenly clear TED 6
silent	3.	As silent as a mirror is believed Leg 1
	34.	And silent answers crept across the stars AMT 12
	78.	Of all our silent men--the long team line Ind 38
	104.	At sunset with a silent, cobwebbed patience QH 22
	138.	Though silent as your sandals, danced undone Port 8
silently	15.	Flings itself silently NL 3
	69.	Meeting the Gulf, hosannas silently below Riv 143
	130.	Silently, now, but that your lips Ech 7
silk	10.	Beneath the green silk counterpane SM 10
	150.	Burrowing in silk is not their way GWP 13
silken	37.	The silken skilled transmemberment of song V-3 18

silking	160.	spiders yoked you first,--silking of shadows good under-/drawers for owls MT 5
sill	19.	And curdled only where a sill LC 6
	56.	The fog leans one last moment on the sill HD 35
silly	100.	Her silly snake rings begin to mount, surmount NWG 19
silted	69.	Nights turbid, vascular with silted shale Riv 125
silver	36.	On scrolls of silver snowy sentences V-2 7
	83.	steel--silver--kick the traces--and know CS 42
	90.	O sinewy silver biplane, nudging the wind's withers CH 77
	114.	With silver terraces the humming spars At 23
	116.	Of silver sequel, Deity's young name At 79
	126.	And gilds the silver on the blotched arbor-seats O-N 4
	159.	Or tempests--in a silver, floating plume TCJ 16
	176.	I watch the silver Zeppelin VU 11
	176.	The silver strophe...the canto VU 15
silvering	161.	This dry road silvering toward the shadow of the quarry IQ 11
silver-paced	45.	And Thee, across the harbor, silver-paced TBB 13
silvery	115.	Silvery the rushing wake, surpassing call At 39
simian	98.	O simian Venus, homeless Eve SC 9
simmering	99.	Insolence. You crept out simmering, accomplished SC 24
simple	131.	Only simple ripples flaunt, and stroke, and float Ba 6
since	79.	And since then--all that's left to me of Jim Ind 49
	83.	interminably/long since somebody's nickel--stopped--/playing CS 46
	135.	My hands have not touched water since your hands CL 1
	135.	No;--nor my lips freed laughter since "farewell CL 2
	158.	But since the Cross sank, much that's warped and cracked Mer 6
	160.	First-plucked before and since the Flood, old hypno- MT 6
	163.	And since, through these hot barricades of green Id 13
	181.	For some hours since--all wireless down Et 22
	192.	His fathers took for granted ages since--and so he looms SI 6
sinewy	90.	O sinewy silver biplane, nudging the wind's withers CH 77
sing	54.	Sing to us, stealthily weave us into day HD 22

sleep	36.	Hasten, while they are true,--sleep, death, desire V-2 19
	39.	The cables of our sleep so swiftly filed V-5 6
	39.	Draw in your head and sleep the long way home V-5 25
	50.	Laughter, and shadow cuts sleep from the heart AM 35
	54.	Insistently through sleep--a tide of voices HD 1
	54.	And if they take your sleep away sometimes HD 10
	56.	Turns in the waking west and goes to sleep HD 38
	83.	and sleep another thousand CS 45
	114.	Two worlds of sleep (O arching strands of song At 20
	122.	So they sleep in the shade of black palm-bark at noon Moth 13
	146.	You ought, really, to try to sleep PA 58
	152.	from sleep forbidden now and wide In 12
	161.	Wide of the mountain--thence to tears and sleep IQ 14
	177.	So sleep, dear brother, in my fame, my shame undone Rep 12
sleepest	51.	O Thou who sleepest on Thyself, apart AM 57
sleepless	46.	O Sleepless as the river under thee TBB 41
Sleepy Hollow	58.	"Is this Sleepy Hollow, friend--?" And he VW 13
sleeves	54.	They give it back again. Soft sleeves of sound HD 11
sleight	159.	The moon's best lover,--guide us by a sleight TCJ 10
sleights	45.	I think of cinemas, panoramic sleights TBB 9
	92.	In guerilla sleights, trapped in combustion gyr- CH 139
slender	20.	Lean long from sable, slender boughs LC 37
	78.	Perhaps a halfbreed. On her slender back Ind 33
	102.	The slender violets stray Va 19
slept	188.	posedly slept, supposedly in #35--thus in my wakeful HR 17
	188.	ans surely slept--whose references to typhus and whose HR 20
slid	98.	Incites a yell. Slid on that backward vision SC 16
slide	100.	A caught slide shows her sandstone grey between NWG 16
slide-by-night	159.	You, the rum-giver to that slide-by-night TCJ 9
sliding	68.	As loth to take more tribute--sliding prone Riv 118
	183.	Sliding everywhere. Bodies were rushed into graves Et 51

slowly, cont.	54.	This wavering slumber.... Slowly HD 18
	56.	The window goes blond slowly. Frostily clears HD 31
	60.	And <u>Rip</u> was <u>slowly</u> <u>made</u> <u>aware</u> VW 26
	88.	While rises in the west the coastwise range,/ slowly the hushed land CH 3
	88.	Or how the priests walked--slowly through Bombay CH 12
	98.	High, cool,/wide from the slowly smoldering fire SC 5
slows	68.	Oh, lean from the window, if the train slows down Riv 100
sluggard	76.	And glistening through the sluggard freshets came Ind 18
sluiced	89.	Is sluiced by motion,--subjugated never CH 30
sluices	19.	Sluices its one unyielding smile LC 7
slumber	54.	This wavering slumber.... Slowly HD 18
	142.	May slumber yet in the moon, awaiting BE 19
slumbering	23.	Asserts a vision in the slumbering gaze WM 4
	74.	Totem and fire-gall, slumbering pyramid Dan 85
slunk	76.	The pebbles sang, the firecat slunk away Ind 17
slung	146.	And a hash of noises is slung up from the street PA 57
sly	76.	But passing sly Ind 16
small	122.	On their own small oasis, ray-cut, an incision Moth 11
	133.	The winers leave too, and the small lamps twinge CDB 24
	180.	Eyes widely planted, clear, yet small Lib 11
smell	60.	Or splits a random smell of flowers through glass VW 31
	128.	The food has a warm and tempting smell Fr 3
smile	19.	Sluices its one unyielding smile LC 7
	20.	Unmangled target smile LC 45
	23.	Regard the forceps of the smile that takes her WM 11
	24.	Until my blood dreams a receptive smile WM 33
	25.	Inquire this much-exacting fragment smile Rec 9
	38.	Whose counted smile of hours and days, suppose V-4 1
	39.	One frozen trackless smile...What words V-5 8
	40.	That smile unsearchable repose V-6 24
	60.	Or is it the Sabbatical, unconscious smile VW 34
	68.	Always they smile out eerily what they seem Riv 109
	72.	Steep, inaccessible smile that eastward bends Dan 34
	78.	She nodded--and that smile across her shoulder Ind 43
	89.	Flickers a moment, consumes us in its smile CH 36

snow, cont.   104.   Than grass and snow, and their own inner being
                            QH 5
                     105.   Dead rangers bled their comfort on the snow
                            QH 50
                     191.   I dream the too-keen cider--the too-soft snow
                            Purg 9
snows   94.   And Klondike edelweiss of occult snows   CH 180
snow-silvered   66.   Snow-silvered, sumac-stained or smoky blue
                            Riv 68
snowy   36.   On scrolls of silver snowy sentences   V-2 7
                      54.   While myriad snowy hands are clustering at the
                            panes   HD 25
scared   167.   As though it soared such wise through heaven
                            too   RP 16
sob   50.   Some inmost sob, half-heard, dissuades the abyss
                            AM 39
sobbed   182.   Sobbed. Yes, now--it's almost over. For they
                            know   Et 42
sober   10.   Not yet is there that heat and sober   SM 5
sobs   127.   Humanity pecks, claws, sobs and climbs   Hi 2
sockets   169.   Rock sockets, levin-lathered   Hur 11
sod   46.   Vaulting the sea, the prairies' dreaming sod
                            TBB 42
                     111.   The sod and billow breaking,--lifting ground
                            Tun 120
soft   6.   In the loose girdle of soft rain   MGLL 4
                       6.   That they are brown and soft   MGLL 10
                      54.   They give it back again. Soft sleeves of sound
                            HD 11
                     148.   Your eyes, those pools with soft rushes   Loc 1
softly   18.   That steals softly direction   Pos 2
soft-pulling   133.   The slit, soft-pulling:-- -- -- and music follows
                            cue   CDB 12
soil   28.   With steel and soil to hold you endlessly
                            F&H I 43
sold   171.   Where gold has not been sold and conscience
                            tinned   KW 16
sole   148.   To the sole end of discovering   Loc 19
solemnity   140.   It sheds a shy solemnity   Int 1
solid   185.   the wren and thrush, made solid print for me
                            Post 3
solstice   40.   The solstice thunders, crept away   V-6 18
solve   158.   Can solve   Mer 4
some   122.   Some say that for sweetness they cannot see far
                            Moth 5
somebody's   82.   "Stamboul Nights"--weaving somebody's nickel--
                            sang   CS 9
                      83.   interminably/long since somebody's nickel--
                            stopped--/playing   CS 46
                     182.   And somebody's mule steamed, swaying right by
                            the pump   Et 31
someday   108.   Someday by heart you'll learn each famous sight
                            Tun 6

somehow	10.	Vestiges of the sun that somehow SM 3
	109.	And somehow anyhow swing Tun 57
	182.	The mule stumbled, staggered. I somehow couldn't budge Et 35
	190.	And pocket us who somehow, do not follow Rel 7
someone	100.	Always you wait for someone else though, always NWG 7
	149.	Doesn't someone come to turn the knob Loc 28
Some Sunny Day	64.	Some Sunny Day. I heard a road-gang chanting so Riv 40
something	66.	Yet they touch something like a key perhaps Riv 62
	94.	But knows it leastwise as death-strife?--O, something green CH 200
	151.	of something--Oh APE 9
	183.	Something like two thousand loaves on the way Et 56
	185.	toward something far, now farther than ever away Post 6
	187.	busy still? For something still Ma 14
	188.	records spurred the Doctor into something nigh those HR 21
	190.	Something of sand and sun the Nile defends Rel 17
	191.	Like something left, forsaken--here am I Purg 4
sometime	7.	The leaves will fall again sometime and fill SMA 1
	17.	When systematic morn shall sometime flood Par 10
	46.	Unto us lowliest sometime sweep, descend TBB 43
sometimes	14.	That sometimes take up residence and reign Fern 9
	54.	And if they take your sleep away sometimes HD 10
	82.	weakeyed watches sometimes snooze--" his bony hands CS 16
	83.	or are there frontiers--running sands sometimes CS 38
	150.	Pathetic yelps have sometimes greeted GWP 16
somewhat	111.	And somewhat emptier than before Tun 95
somewhere	23.	While August meadows somewhere clasp his brow WM 23
	27.	Take them away as suddenly to somewhere F&H I 14
	30.	Until somewhere a rooster banters F&H II 14
	54.	Somewhere out there in blankness steam HD 13
	83.	running sands--somewhere--sands running CS 39
	100.	A tom-tom scrimmage with a somewhere violin NWG 11
	110.	Somewhere above Fourteenth TAKE THE EXPRESS Tun 61
	110.	Bolting outright somewhere above where streets Tun 88

somewhere, cont.	128.	But hold me...somewhere I heard demands FR 7
	188.	the Doctor's rat trap. Where? Somewhere in Vera HR 13
Somme	93.	That then from Appomattox stretched to Somme CH 170
son	79.	You, Larry, traveller--/stranger,/son,/--my friend Ind 64
	141.	And as the fingers of the factory owner's son EpH 8
song	19.	But song, as these LC 24
	31.	The siren of the springs of guilty song F&H II 31
	37.	The silken skilled transmemberment of song V-3 18
	76.	Closes before the dusk, furls in its song Ind 3
	93.	Has beat a song, O Walt,--there and beyond CH 163
	111.	Impassioned with some song we fail to keep Tun 118
	114.	"Make thy love sure--to weave whose song we ply At 14
	114.	Two worlds of sleep (O arching strands of song At 20
	115.	To kneeling wave, one song devoutly binds At 55
	117.	--One Song, one Bridge of Fire! Is it Cathay At 93
	123.	And the torrid hum of great wings was his song Moth 41
	125.	And with it song of minor, broken strain C 11
	137.	Forgetfulness is like a song For 1
	144.	O City, your axles need not the oil of song PA 19
	163.	A Dios gracias, grac--I've heard his song Id 14
	186.	--And fail, both! Yet thine Ariel holds his song Shak 12
songs	88.	The songs that gypsies dealt us at Marseille CH 11
soon	32.	Who faithfully, yourself, will fall too soon F&H III 7
	90.	New latitudes, unknotting, soon give place CH 86
	95.	Not soon, nor suddenly,--no, never to let go CH 219
	122.	Blind only in day, but remembering that soon Moth 14
	179.	soon Len 25
soot	111.	O caught like pennies beneath soot and steam Tun 115
	178.	Imprisoned never, no[,] not soot &[?] steam PB 12
soothings	30.	New soothings, new amazements F&H II 16
sophistry	125.	With searing sophistry C 5
sorted	173.	In bunches sorted freshly--/and bestows MF 4

sought	170.	Being, of all, least sought for: Emily hear TED 5
soul	8.	And such assessments of the soul PU 12
	17.	May find the record wedged in his soul Par 4
	90.	The soul, by naphtha fledged into new reaches CH 84
	142.	A soul, an element in it all BE 8
	148.	My crisp soul will be flooded by a languor Loc 7
sound	6.	With such a sound of gently pitying laughter MGLL 26
	8.	And miss the dry sound of bees PU 19
	11.	And through all sound of gaiety and quest Chap 22
	16.	The willows carried a slow sound RR 1
	16.	And willows could not hold more steady sound RR 23
	34.	And wrecks passed without sound of bells AMT 5
	54.	They give it back again. Soft sleeves of sound HD 11
	62.	a headlight rushing with the sound--can you Riv 11
	109.	of motion is the sound Tun 37
	112.	--A sound of waters bending astride the sky Tun 121
	116.	And like an organ, Thou, with sound of doom At 62
	116.	Sight, sound and flesh Thou leadest from time's realm At 63
	129.	The sound of a dove's flight waved over the lawn An 6
	131.	But there is no sound,--not even a bird-note Ba 5
sounding	51.	Elohim, still I hear thy sounding heel AM 80
	66.	Trains sounding the long blizzards out--I heard Riv 74
soundings	93.	To answer deepest soundings! O, upward from the dead CH 154
	114.	--From black embankments, moveless soundings hailed At 15
sounds	54.	The long, tired sounds, fog-insulated noises HD 3
	141.	And factory sounds and factory thoughts EpH 20
source	6.	To carry back the music to its source MGLL 20
south	66.	Is past the valley-sleepers, south or west Riv 69
	74.	West, west and south! winds over Cumberland Dan 93
	98.	I wanted you, nameless Woman of the South SC 1
	144.	South Main PA 3
Southern Cross	98.	The Southern Cross takes night SC 3

South Street	82.	I met a man in South Street, tall CS 1
southward	68.	Southward, near Cairo passing, you can see Riv 94
souvenir	3.	(Again the smoking souvenir Leg 15
sow	4.	Fox brush and sow ear top his grave BT 7
sowest	92.	Thou sowest doom thou hast nor time nor chance CH 126
sowing	127.	And of all the sowing, and all the tear-tendering Hi 5
sown	194.	Of pebbles,--visible wings of silence sown B Tow 35
space	6.	Over the greatness of such space MGLL 12
	8.	Stretching across a lucid space PU 20
	66.	And space, an eaglet's wing, laid on her hair Riv 80
	88.	The captured fume of space foams in our ears CH 20
	89.	The circle, blind crucible of endless space CH 29
	89.	Of wings imperious...Space, instantaneous CH 35
	90.	The gleaming cantos of unvanquished space CH 76
	91.	This tournament of space, the threshed and chiselled height CH 95
	91.	--Hast splintered space CH 116
	92.	What alcohol of space...! Remember, Falcon-Ace CH 128
	95.	And now, launched in abysmal cupolas of space CH 205
	159.	What you may cluster 'round the knees of space TCJ 1
space-gnawing	91.	Taut motors surge, space-gnawing, into flight CH 100
Spain	166.	The King of Spain IV 13
span	51.	Te Deum laudamus, for thy teeming span AM 72
	64.	Loped under wires that span the mountain stream Riv 25
	94.	Stood up and flung the span on even wing CH 195
	95.	To course that span of consciousness thou'st named CH 209
	123.	But once though, he learned of that span of his wings Moth 25
Spanish Main	166.	The Spanish Main IV 6
	168.	While beachward creeps the shark-swept Spanish Main AP 14
spans	4.	And a roach spans a crevice in the floor BT 4
	33.	The imagination spans beyond despair F&H III 47
spare	115.	Tall Vision-of-the-Voyage, tensely spare At 42
	141.	As his taut, spare fingers wound the gauze EpH 11

spark	73.	Spark, tooth! Medicine-man, relent, restore Dan 59
	124.	I have hunted long years for a spark in the sand Moth 49
	181.	No one seemed to be able to get a spark Et 18
sparkling	24.	Sparkling alone, within another's will WM 32
	91.	Through sparkling visibility, outspread, un-sleeping CH 101
sparrow	27.	The mind is brushed by sparrow wings F&H I 8
spars	114.	With silver terraces the humming spars At 23
spasm	100.	We flee her spasm through a fleshless door NWG 24
spatter	160.	tisms wrench the golden boughs. Leaves spatter dawn MT 7
spawn	99.	Light drowned the lithic trillions of your spawn SC 29
speak	20.	Betrayed stones slowly speak LC 32
	33.	And will persist to speak again before F&H III 26
	156.	To the white sand I may speak a name, fertile OC 12
	178.	That I thy drowned man may speak again PB 2
speakee	166.	No speakee well IV 2
speaking	21.	Died speaking through the ages that you know Pass 19
spear	21.	The evening was a spear in the ravine Pass 23
spears	73.	Spears and assemblies: black drums thrusting on Dan 61
	115.	Searches the timeless laugh of mythic spears At 32
	117.	Like spears ensanguined of one tolling star At 90
spectacles	14.	The lights that travel on her spectacles Fern 1
spectrum	38.	I know as spectrum of the sea and pledge V-4 2
spectrum's	162.	Sped in the spectrum's kiss OS 10
sped	64.	"Jesus! Oh I remember watermelon days!" And sped Riv 42
	70.	Greeting they sped us, on the arrow's oath Dan 11
	72.	Over how many bluffs, tarns, streams I sped Dan 37
	162.	Sped in the spectrum's kiss OS 10
speech	18.	Wounded by apprehensions out of speech Pos 19
speeches	22.	What fountains did I hear? what icy speeches Pass 36
speechful	94.	How speechful on oak-vizored palisades CH 182
speechless	45.	A jest falls from the speechless caravan TBB 20
	74.	Her speechless dream of snow, and stirred again Dan 90
speed	23.	Speed to the arrow into feathered skies WM 18

spine	171.	Nor claim me, either, by Adam's spine--nor rib KW 4
spins	25.	Look steadily--how the wind feasts and spins Rec 13
spinster	105.	The spinster polish of antiquity QH 45
spiracle	83.	"--that spiracle!" he shot a finger out the door CS 34
spiralled	92.	Giddily spiralled/gauntlets, upturned, unlooping CH 138
spires	18.	I, turning, turning on smoked forking spires Pos 21
spiring	116.	Always through spiring cordage, pyramids At 78
spiritual	5.	Luring the living into spiritual gates EC 6
	5.	Dull lips commemorating spiritual gates EC 11
	5.	But only to build memories of spiritual gates EC 17
spittle	98.	The mind is churned to spittle, whispering hell SC 17
spirals	123.	Swinging in spirals round the fresh breasts of day Moth 30
splay	73.	And splay tongues thinly busy the blue air Dan 56
splayed	30.	Splayed like cards from a loose hand F&H II 12
splintered	40.	Some splintered garland for the seer V-6 16
	91.	--Hast splintered space CH 116
	115.	Beams yelling AEolus! splintered in the straits At 40
splinters	14.	--So, while fresh sunlight splinters humid green Fern 7
split	90.	Towards what? The forked crash of split thunder parts CH 68
	176.	the dense mine of the orchid, split in two VU 4
	181.	Two decks unsandwiched, split sixty feet apart Et 15
splits	60.	Or splits a random smell of flowers through glass VW 31
spoke	82.	Murmurs of Leviathan he spoke CS 11
	178.	Perhaps as once Will Collins spoke the lark PB 3
spokes-of-a-wheel	17.	Systole, diastole spokes-of-a-wheel Par 2
spontaneities	7.	Spontaneities that form their independent orbits SMA 10
spools	90.	Is stropped to the slap of belts on booming spools, spurred CH 66
spoon	111.	To spoon us out more liquid than the dim Tun 111
spoor	90.	Where spouting pillars spoor the evening sky CH 60
spot	5.	The wanderer later chose this spot of rest EC 12
spouted	70.	She spouted arms; she rose with maize--to die Dan 4
spouting	32.	Who hurried the hill breezes, spouting malice F&H III 14

spouting, cont.   90.   Where spouting pillars spoor the evening sky
                           CH 60

spray   123.   To yellow,--to crystal,--a sea of white spray
                           Moth 32

sprayed   100.   Sprayed first with ruby, then with emerald sheen
                           NWG 14

spread   16.   With scalding unguents spread and smoking darts
                           RR 19
                     28.   The limbs and belly, when rainbows spread
                           F&H I 34
                     33.   And spread with bells and voices, and atone
                           F&H III 34
                    143.   When your fingers spread among stars   BE 28
                    152.   to spread; the hands to yield their shells   In 4

spreading   23.   Percussive sweat is spreading to his hair.
                           Mallets WM 12
                     64.   Spreading dry shingles of a beard   Riv 51
                     69.   The River, spreading, flows--and spends your
                           dream   Riv 120
                     94.   Evasive--too--as dayspring's spreading arc to
                           trace is   CH 192

spreads   69.   --The Passion spreads in wide tongues, choked
                           and slow   Riv 142

spring   7.   But now there are challenges to spring SMA 4
                      8.   Into the smoky spring that fills   PU 22
                     10.   With lifting spring and starker   SM 2
                     15.   That journey toward no Spring   NL 10
                     19.   Twanged red perfidies of spring   LC 12
                     60.   One day in spring my father took to me   VW 33
                     70.   She ran the neighing canyons all the spring
                           Dan 3
                     72.   O Appalachian Spring! I gained the ledge
                           Dan 33
                     84.   that bloomed in the spring--Heave, weave CS 56
                     94.   Around bared teeth of stallions, bloomed that
                           spring CH 172
                    102.   And Spring in Prince Street   Va 12
                    104.   They keep that docile edict of the Spring QH 2
                    139.   And moons of spring and autumn Lege 8

springs   31.   The siren of the springs of guilty song
                           F&H II 31
                     91.   Hell's belt springs wider into heaven's plumed
                           side CH 92
                    116.   Of thy white seizure springs the prophecy At 77

sprint   73.   Flickering, sprint up the hill groins like a
                           tide Dan 68

sprites   84.   Blithe Yankee vanities, turreted sprites, winged
                           CS 54

sprout   73.   That casts his pelt, and lives beyond! Sprout,
                           horn Dan 58

sprouted   160.   When you sprouted Paradise a discard of chewing-
                           MT 3

spry	35.	Spry cordage of your bodies to caresses V-1 14
spun	90.	Capeward, then blading the wind's flank, banked and spun CH 81
	138.	More real than life, the gestures you have spun Port 6
spurred	90.	Is stropped to the slap of belts on booming spools, spurred CH 66
	188.	records spurred the Doctor into something nigh those HR 21
sputum	191.	Where all your gas lights--faces--sputum gleam Purg 3
square	108.	Out of the Square, the Circle burning bright Tun 25
	161.	Square sheets--they saw the marble only into IQ 1
	188.	crumbled palace in the square--the typhus in a trap HR 12
squared	156.	Squared off so carefully. Then OC 11
squaw	78.	A homeless squaw Ind 32
squeaks	88.	And from above, thin squeaks of radio static CH 19
squint	11.	Facing the dull squint with what innocence Chap 12
	24.	Each chamber, transept, coins some squint WM 24
	163.	With squint lanterns in his head, and it's likely Id 3
squired	70.	Who squired the glacier woman down the sky Dan 2
S.S. Ala	82.	"It's S.S. Ala--Antwerp--now remember kid CS 13
stabbing	18.	And stabbing medley that sways Pos 13
stack	74.	Though other calendars now stack the sky Dan 86
	104.	Portholes the ceilings stack their stoic height QH 19
stacked	27.	Across the stacked partitions of the day F&H I 4
stacks	90.	Under the looming stacks of the gigantic power house CH 61
stag	73.	And stag teeth foam about the raven throat Dan 70
stage	138.	Haunt the blank stage with lingering alarms Port 7
	150.	Alike to stage, equestrian, and pullman GWP 4
staggered	182.	The mule stumbled, staggered. I somehow couldn't budge Et 35
stain	130.	Upward again:--they leave no stain Ech 3
stains	158.	And ponder the bright stains that starred this Throne Mer 14
stair	10.	And every third step down the stair SM 15
stake	73.	And buzzard-circleted, screamed from the stake Dan 65

stars, cont.   30. While nigger cupids scour the stars F&H II 8
                   34. And silent answers crept across the stars
                        AMT 12
                   36. Salute the crocus lustres of the stars V-2 12
                   39. Already hang, shred ends from remembered stars
                        V-5 7
                   46. Unfractioned idiom, immaculate sigh of stars
                        TBB 34
                   78. And like twin stars. They seemed to shun the
                        gaze Ind 37
                   88. Below grey citadels, repeating to the stars
                        CH 8
                   90. Stars prick the eyes with sharp ammoniac
                        proverbs CH 62
                   90. Into the bulging bouillon, harnessed jelly of
                        the stars CH 67
                   90. Stars scribble on our eyes the frosty sagas
                        CH 75
                   90. What marathons new-set between the stars CH 83
                   93. The stars have grooved our eyes with old per-
                        suasions CH 145
                  114. The loft of vision, palladium helm of stars
                        At 24
                  116. Of stars Thou art the stitch and stallion glow
                        At 61
                  143. When your fingers spread among stars BE 28
                  146. The stars are drowned in a slow rain PA 56
                  191. And are these stars--the high plateau--the
                        scents Purg 5
                  193. The stars are caught and hived in the sun's ray
                        B Tow 8
start   83. Or they may start some white machine that sings
                        CS 40
                   93. Is plummet ushered of those tears that start
                        CH 165
                  133. The andante quivers with crescendo's start
                        CDB 9
started   84. I started walking home across the Bridge CS 53
                  146. Where you had started to grow PA 48
star-triggered   75. Alert, star-triggered in the listening vault
                        Dan 99
starved   50. Starved wide on blackened tides, accrete--
                        enclose AM 42
states   66. From pole to pole across the hills, the states
                        Riv 63
                  104. One's glance could cross the borders of three
                        states QH 26
static   88. And from above, thin squeaks of radio static
                        CH 19
Statue of Liberty 84. was putting the Statue of Liberty out--that
                        CS 51

steel, cont.   115.   Eyes stammer through the pangs of dust and
                          steel   At 52
                   171.   O, steel and stone! But gold was, scarcity
                          before   KW 13
steeled   116.   O Thou steeled Cognizance whose leap commits
                          At 57
steel-strung   171.   Of apish nightmares into steel-strung stone
                          KW 12
steely   90.   Of steely gizzards--axle-bound, confined   CH 71
                   122.   Their joy with a barren and steely tide   Moth 8
steep   16.   Flags, weeds. And remembrance of steep alcoves
                          RR 6
                    37.   Upon the steep floor flung from dawn to dawn
                          V-3 17
                    51.   Into thy steep savannahs, burning blue   AM 63
                    72.   Steep, inaccessible smile that eastward bends
                          Dan 34
                   194.   The steep encroachments of my blood left me
                          B Tow 25
steeples   187.   and when the sun taps steeples   Ma 5
steeps   34.   No farther tides...High in the azure steeps
                          AMT 14
                   117.   Now pity steeps the grass and rainbows ring
                          At 94
stem   38.   Shall they not stem and close in our own steps
                          V-4 14
stemming   105.   So, must we from the hawk's far stemming view
                          QH 57
stenographic   27.   The stenographic smiles and stock quotations
                          F&H I 6
step   3.   Relentless caper for all those who step   Leg 22
                    10.   And every third step down the stair   SM 15
                    11.   A famished kitten on the step, and know   Chap 6
                    13.   She hears my step behind the green   IS 11
                    45.   As though the sun took step of thee, yet left
                          TBB 14
stepped   82.   stepped out--forgot to look at you   CS 6
stepping   24.   Stepping over Holofernes' shins   WM 45
steps   6.   Steps must be gentle   MGLL 13
                    38.   Shall they not stem and close in our own steps
                          V-4 14
                   193.   From pit to crucifix, feet chill on steps from
                          hell   B Tow 4
stevedore's   54.   Or a drunken stevedore's howl and thud below
                          HD 8
stick   60.   After day whenever your stick discovered   VW 23
                    62.   Stick your patent name on a signboard   Riv 1
                   182.   To lift a stick for pity of his stupor   Et 36
sticks   35.   Fondle your shells and sticks, bleached   V-1 11
                   105.   Alight with sticks abristle and cigars   QH 32
stiff   149.   A stiff denial to postures   Loc 23

still, cont.   152. still subsist I, wondrous as In 19
                    152. from thine open dugs shall still the sun In 20
                    158. --This Cross, agleam still with a human Face
                          Mer 15
                    164. And still wing on, untarnished of the name NA 2
                    174. From twenty alphabets--we're still unripe
                          BNOK 12
                    181. After it was over, though still gusting bale-
                          fully Et 1
                    182. Remember still that strange gratuity of horses
                          Et 38
                    187. busy still? For something still Ma 14
stiller   13. Twilight, stiller than shadows, fall IS 12
stillness   68. But drift in stillness, as from Jordan's brow
                          Riv 115
                    170. Achieved that stillness ultimately best TED 4
stilly   92. To reckon--as thy stilly eyes partake CH 127
                    106. Listen, transmuting silence with that stilly
                          note QH 64
                    110. Stilly Tun 86
stinging   69. No embrace opens but the stinging sea Riv 138
                     99. Water rattled that stinging coil, your SC 25
stink   151. doesn't stink at all APE 19
stippled   28. Stippled with pink and green advertisements
                          F&H I 26
stir   176. stir your confidence VU 13
stirred   74. Her speechless dream of snow, and stirred again
                          Dan 90
                     76. Back on the gold trail--then his lost bones
                          stirred Ind 10
stirs   194. Whose sweet mortality stirs latent power
                          B Tow 28
stitch   16. Where beavers learn stitch and tooth RR 14
                    116. Of star Thou art the stitch and stallion glow
                          At 61
stock   27. The stenographic smiles and stock quotations
                          F&H I 6
stocks   89. Surviving in a world of stocks,--they also range
                          CH 55
stoic   104. Portholes the ceilings stack their stoic height
                          QH 19
stoke   178. As they were fought--and wooed? They now but
                          stoke PB 7
stolen   21. A thief beneath, my stolen book in hand Pass 27
                    140. Wide from the world, a stolen hour Int 5
stone   10. At doors and stone with broken eyes SM 20
                     18. For this fixed stone of lust Pos 9
                     18. And I, entering, take up the stone Pos 16
                     40. Red kelson past the cape's wet stone V-6 8
                     68. You will not hear it as the sea; even stone
                          Riv 116
                     70. With mineral wariness found out the stone Dan 6

stone, cont.   79. I'm standing still, I'm old, I'm half of stone
                         Ind 53
                    83. <u>snarling stone--green--drums--drown</u> CS 32
                   135. With surging gentleness; and the blue stone
                         CL 7
                   161. Where the straight road would seem to ply below
                         the stone, that fierce IQ 4
                   169. Ay! Scripture flee'th stone Hur 5
                   171. Of apish nightmares into steel-strung stone
                         KW 12
                   171. O, steel and stone! But gold was, scarcity
                         before KW 13
                   194. And builds, within, a tower that is not stone
                         B Tow 33
                   194. (Not stone can jacket heaven)--but slip
                         B Tow 34
stoned   60. Where we stoned the family of young VW 18
stones   18. All but bright stones wherein our smiling plays
                         Pos 29
                    20. Betrayed stones slowly speak LC 32
                    62. WALLSTREET AND VIRGINBIRTH WITHOUT STONES OR
                         Riv 15
                    89. Gleam from the great stones of each prison
                         crypt CH 53
stood   48. That made me exile in her streets, stood me
                         AM 18
                    94. Stood up and flung the span on even wing
                         CH 195
                   182. --I can't account for him! And true, he stood
                         Et 44
                   183. The fever was checked. I stood a long time in
                         Mack's talking Et 58
stop   72. A further valley-shed; I could not stop Dan 30
                   110. The platform hurries along to a dead stop
                         Tun 84
stopped   83. interminably/long since somebody's nickel--
                         stopped--/playing CS 46
store   104. Much of our store of faith in other men QH 15
storied   69. Throb past the City storied of three thrones
                         Riv 133
storm   8. Delicate riders of the storm PU 8
                    31. Dipping here in this cultivated storm F&H II 36
                   130. Of storm or strain an hour ago Ech 4
                   182. When the storm was dying. And Sarah saw them,
                         too Et 41
stove   112. Lunged past, with one galvanic blare stove up
                         the River Tun 124
straddles   68. Straddles the hill, a dance of wheel on wheel
                         Riv 91
straddling   7. A boy runs with a dog before the sun, straddling
                         SMA 9

straggling	163.	The boy straggling under those mimosas, daft Id 2
straight	134.	A gypsy wagon wiggles, striving straight CDB 26
	161.	Where the straight road would seem to ply below the stone, that fierce IQ 4
	161.	Walking the straight road toward thunder IQ 10
straightway	111.	Umbilical to call--and straightway die Tun 114
strain	125.	And with it song of minor, broken strain C 11
	130.	Of storm or strain an hour ago Ech 4
	157.	--Spiked, overturned; such thunder in their strain OC 30
straits	115.	Beams yelling AEolus! splintered in the straits At 40
strands	100.	Pearls whip her hips, a drench of whirling strands NWG 18
	114.	Through the bound cable strands, the arching path At 1
	114.	Two worlds of sleep (O arching strands of song At 20
strange	30.	Where, by strange harmonic laws F&H II 21
	64.	Strange bird-wit, like the elemental gist Riv 37
	78.	Her eyes, strange for an Indian's were not black Ind 35
	88.	Where strange tongues vary messages of surf CH 7
	180.	On this strange shore I build Lib 2
	182.	Remember still that strange gratuity of horses Et 38
stranger	40.	Green borders under stranger skies V-6 4
	79.	You, Larry, traveller--/stranger,/son,/--my friend Ind 64
	156.	Albeit in a stranger tongue. Tree names, flower names OC 13
	182.	--One ours, and one, a stranger, creeping up with dawn Et 39
strangle	39.	Can strangle this deaf moonlight? For we V-5 9
strap	110.	Whose head is swinging from the swollen strap Tun 66
straw	169.	Swept, whistling straw! Battered Hur 9
stray	50.	An herb, a stray branch among salty teeth AM 51
	102.	The slender violets stray Va 19
strays	89.	Across the hills where second timber strays CH 56
streaked	24.	Poor streaked bodies wreathing up and out WM 26
streaks	165.	Luckily the Cayman schooner streaks BSEW 8
stream	25.	The plummet heart, like Absalom, no stream Rec 20
	38.	No stream of greater love advancing now V-4 6
	64.	Loped under wires that span the mountain stream Riv 25

stream, cont.	69.	You are your father's father, and the stream Riv 122
	74.	O stream by slope and vineyard--into bloom Dan 96
	114.	Sibylline voices flicker, waveringly stream At 7
	178.	Have kept no faith but wind, the cold stream PB 10
streamed	70.	Where prayers, forgotten, streamed the mesa sands Dan 7
streams	72.	Over how many bluffs, tarns, streams I sped Dan 37
	123.	Seething and rounding in long streams of light Moth 37
	152.	those streams and slopes untenanted thou In 16
street	10.	Will find the street, only to look SM 19
	11.	Recesses for it from the fury of the street Chap 7
	23.	Then glozening decanters that reflect the street WM 5
	32.	Capped arbiter of beauty in this street F&H III 1
	45.	Down Wall, from girder into street noon leaks TBB 21
	146.	And a hash of noises is slung up from the street PA 57
streets	33.	All stubble streets that have not curved F&H III 27
	48.	That made me exile in her streets, stood me AM 18
	109.	subways, rivered under streets Tun 33
	110.	Bolting outright somewhere above where streets Tun 88
	144.	In the streets and alleys PA 14
	181.	Wires in the streets and Chinamen up and down Et 7
strength	7.	That are your rich and faithful strength of line SMA 3
stretched	93.	That then from Appomattox stretched to Somme CH 170
	163.	Once when he shouted, stretched in ghastly shape Id 6
stretches	133.	And stretches up through mortal eyes to see CDB 16
stretching	8.	Stretching across a lucid space PU 20
strewn	181.	With arms in slings, plaster strewn dense with tiles Et 8
	182.	Everything gone--or strewn in riddled grace Et 29
striated	31.	Striated with nuances, nervosities F&H II 33
stricken	168.	A milk of earth when stricken off the stalk AP 10

strictly   72. --Fall, Sachem, strictly as the tamarack Dan 48
stride   26. All hours clapped dense into a single stride
                      Rec 26
                 45. Some motion ever unspent in thy stride TBB 15
strident   89. Of the ambiguous cloud. We know the strident
                      rule CH 34
strides   68. From tunnel into field--iron strides the dew
                      Riv 90
strike   20. Strike from Thee perfect spheres LC 39
                171. That now has sunk I strike a single march KW 7
strikes   60. So memory, that strikes a rhyme out of a box
                      VW 30
                 74. High unto Labrador the sun strikes free Dan 89
                116. As love strikes clear direction for the helm
                      At 64
                193. Whose thigh embronzes earth, strikes crystal
                      Word B Tow 23
string   3. Shall string some constant harmony Leg 21
                163. One hand dealt out a kite string, a tin can
                      Id 9
strings   46. (How could mere toil align thy choiring strings
                      TBB 30
                114. Upward, veering with light, the flight of strings
                      At 2
                114. As though a god were issue of the strings At 8
                115. The vernal strophe chimes from deathless strings
                      At 56
                117. That bleeds infinity--the orphic strings At 91
strip   188. Let us strip the desk for action--now we have a
                      horse HR 1
striped   35. Bright striped urchins flay each other with sand
                      V-1 2
stripped   60. Is it the whip stripped from the lilac tree
                      VW 32
                182. Blister the mountain, stripped now, bare of palm
                      Et 26
strives   129. That strives long and quiet to sever the girth
                      An 2
striving   134. A gypsy wagon wiggles, striving straight CDB 26
stroke   37. Are laved and scattered with no stroke V-3 6
                131. Only simple ripples flaunt, and stroke, and
                      float Ba 6
                188. and the pharos shine--the mid-wind midnight
                      stroke HR 9
strokes   194. And through whose pulse I hear, counting the
                      strokes B Tow 29
strong   6. Is the silence strong enough MGLL 19
                 75. Now is the strong prayer folded in thine arms
                      Dan 103
strophe   115. The vernal strophe chimes from deathless strings
                      At 56
                176. The silver strophe...the canto VU 15

subways	109.	subways, rivered under streets Tun 33
successive	188.	cherub watchman--tiptoeing the successive patio bal- HR 7
suchwise	167.	As though it soared suchwise through heaven too RP 16
sudden	14.	To darkness through a wreath of sudden pain Fern 6
	89.	And we have laughter, or more sudden tears CH 38
	173.	Fall mute and sudden (dealing change/for lilies MF 7
	190.	What is our life without a sudden pillow Rel 2
suddenly	13.	Gently yet sudenly, the sheen IS 9
	27.	Take them away as suddenly to somewhere F&H I 14
	78.	I held you up--I suddenly the bolder Ind 41
	95.	Not soon, nor suddenly,--no, never to let go CH 219
	111.	Burst suddenly in rain.... The gongs recur Tun 89
	141.	Suddenly he seemed to forget the pain EpH 2
	170.	O sweet, dead Silencer, most suddenly clear TED 6
suet	179.	And there is work, blood, suet and sweat,-- the rigamarole Len 9
suit	48.	The word I bring, O you who reined my suit AM 3
sulking	21.	Sulking, sanctioning the sun Pass 5
sulphur	5.	With sulphur and aureate rocks EC 4
	16.	And mammoth turtles climbing sulphur dreams RR 9
sum	18.	Upon the page whose blind sum finally burns Pos 25
	93.	Hast kept of wounds, O Mourner, all that sum CH 169
sumac-stained	66.	Snow-silvered, sumac-stained or smoky blue Riv 68
summer	5.	By that time summer and smoke were past EC 15
	12.	Summer scarcely begun Past 18
	16.	I heard wind flaking sapphire, like this summer RR 22
	21.	Dangerously the summer burned Pass 11
	68.	And if it's summer and the sun's in dusk Riv 96
	84.	swinging summer entrances to cooler hells CS 48
	141.	Flickering in sunlight over summer fields EpH 15
	146.	One summer day in a little town PA 47
sums	25.	Alike suspend us from atrocious sums Rec 18
summits	169.	Lord God, while summits crashing Hur 14
sun	7.	A boy runs with a dog before the sun, straddling SMA 9
	8.	They are no trophies of the sun PU 24
	9.	Shining suspension, mimic of the sun GA 2

sun, cont.	10.	Vestiges of the sun that somehow SM 3
	12.	The sun drew out Past 7
	15.	No birth, no death, no time nor sun NL 11
	21.	Sulking, sanctioning the sun Pass 5
	22.	A serpent swam a vertex to the sun Pass 34
	35.	The sun beats lightning on the waves V-1 7
	45.	As though the sun took step of thee, yet left TBB 14
	56.	The sun, released--aloft with cold gulls hither HD 34
	74.	That drops his legs and colors in the sun Dan 74
	74.	High unto Labrador the sun strikes free Dan 89
	123.	Til the sun, he still gyrating, shot out all white Moth 33
	123.	The sun saw a ruby brightening ever, that flew Moth 36
	138.	Vault on the opal carpet of the sun Port 1
	141.	The gash was bleeding, and a shaft of sun EpH 5
	141.	That lay in his with the sun upon it EpH 22
	142.	There is a lake, perhaps, with the sun BE 3
	152.	from thine open dugs shall still the sun In 20
	157.	Sere of the sun exploded in the sea OC 35
	158.	Gallows and guillotines to hail the sun Mer 9
	159.	Disclose your lips, O Sun, nor long demure TCJ 6
	177.	And fame is pivotal to shame with every sun Rep 10
	182.	We shoveled and sweated; watched the ogre sun Et 25
	187.	and when the sun taps steeples Ma 5
	190.	Something of sand and sun the Nile defends Rel 17
	192.	Hours, days--and scarcely sun and moon SI 2
sun-cusped	50.	Sun-cusped and zoned with modulated fire AM 44
Sunda	84.	<u>Thermopylae</u>, <u>Black Prince</u>, <u>Flying Cloud</u> through <u>Sunda</u> CS 67
Sunday	145.	I remember one Sunday noon PA 27
	145.	And some Sunday fiddlers PA 36
sundered	105.	Shoulder the curse of sundered parentage QH 53
	136.	An imagined garden grey with sundered boughs Ps 6
sundering	10.	It is the time of sundering SM 9
sun-heap	160.	you Sun-heap, whose MT 11
sunk	171.	That now has sunk I strike a single march KW 7
sunken	66.	Where eyeless fish curvet a sunken fountain Riv 83
sunlight	9.	Drowning the fever of her hands in sunlight GA 10
	13.	The sunlight,--then withdrawing, wear IS 7
	14.	--So, while fresh sunlight splinters humid green Fern 7

sunlight, cont.	69.	O quarrying passion, undertowed sunlight Riv 128
	130.	Jade-green with sunlight, melt and flow Ech 2
	141.	Flickering in sunlight over summer fields EpH 15
	142.	Yet a gash with sunlight jerking through BE 12
sunned	123.	Which blue tides of cool moons were slow shaken and sunned Moth 44
sunning	60.	Some sunning inch of unsuspecting fibre VW 24
sun's	40.	Or as many waters trough the sun's V-6 7
	48.	Slowly the sun's red caravel drops light AM 13
	68.	And if it's summer and the sun's in dusk Riv 96
	167.	I watched the sun's most gracious anchorite RP 4
	193.	The stars are caught and hived in the sun's ray B Tow 8
suns	115.	Into what multitudinous Verb the suns At 45
	116.	Now while thy petals spend the suns about us, hold At 86
sunset	104.	At sunset with a silent, cobwebbed patience QH 22
sunset's	73.	Fed down your anklets to the sunset's moat Dan 72
	161.	Palms against the sunset's towering sea, and maybe IQ 6
sun-shadow	192.	Farther than his sun-shadow--farther than wings SI 7
sun-silt	16.	Yielded, while sun-silt rippled them RR 10
sunward	91.	Surely no eye that Sunward Escadrille can cover CH 106
	172.	Pass sunward. We have walked the kindled skies ABP 8
superscription	36.	Pass superscription of bent foam and wave V-2 18
support	5.	Where marble clouds support the sea EC 13
suppose	28.	And yet, suppose some evening I forgot F&H I 17
	38.	Whose counted smile of hours and days, suppose V-4 1
	156.	And yet suppose OC 8
	181.	Parts of the roof reached Yucatan, I suppose Et 4
supposedly	188.	rosy (in their basement bassinette)--the Doctor sup- HR 16
	188.	posedly slept, supposedly in #35--thus in my wakeful HR 17
surcease	93.	Of love and hatred, birth,--surcease of nations CH 146
	109.	Beyond extinction, surcease of the bone Tun 48
surcharged	88.	Those continental folded aeons, surcharged CH 16

survived	33.	We did not ask for that, but have survived F&H III 25
surviving	89.	Surviving in a world of stocks,--they also range CH 55
suspend	25.	Alike suspend us from atrocious sums Rec 18
suspended	51.	A needle in the sight, suspended north AM 74
suspends	54.	Cool feathery fold, suspends, distills HD 17
suspension	9.	Shining suspension, mimic of the sun GA 2
sustained	116.	Sustained in tears the cities are endowed At 70
swam	22.	A serpent swam a vertex to the sun Pass 34
swan	184.	You, who have looked back to Leda, who have seen the Swan Emp 6
swans	149.	Don't I see your white swans there Loc 27
swarming	115.	Still wrapping harness to the swarming air At 38
swarms	73.	Flame cataracts of heaven in seething swarms Dan 71
	108.	Be minimum, then, to swim the hiving swarms Tun 24
swart	19.	The fox's teeth, and swart LC 9
sway	193.	Of shadows in the tower, whose shoulders sway B Tow 6
swaying	182.	And somebody's mule steamed, swaying right by the pump Et 31
sways	18.	And stabbing medley that sways Pos 13
swears	186.	Swears high in Hamlet's throat, and devils throng Shak 10
sweat	23.	Percussive sweat is spreading to his hair. Mallets WM 12
	167.	Of sweat the jungle presses with hot love RP 10
	179.	And there is work, blood, suet and sweat,-- the rigamarole Len 9
sweated	182.	We shoveled and sweated; watched the ogre sun Et 25
sweating	100.	The world's one flagrant, sweating cinch NWG 4
Swede	144.	The Greek grins and fights with the Swede PA 15
sweep	46.	Unto us lowliest sometime sweep, descend TBB 43
	116.	Within whose lariat sweep encinctured sing At 59
	133.	There is a sweep,--a shattering,--a choir CDB 13
sweeps	58.	Van Winkle sweeps a tenement/way down on Avenue A VW 15
sweet	84.	Sweet opium and tea, Yo-ho CS 58
	85.	(sweet opium and tea CS 71
	116.	Revolving through their harvests in sweet torment At 72
	170.	O sweet, dead Silencer, most suddenly clear TED 6
	174.	From the sweet jeopardy of Anthony's plight BNOK 7

swings	25.	The bridge swings over salvage, beyond wharves Rec 23
swirls	133.	Carmen whirls, and music swirls and dips CDB 19
swirling	72.	Smoke swirling through the yellow chestnut glade Dan 40
swivellings	100.	Her eyes exist in swivellings of her teats NWG 17
swollen	37.	And so, admitted through black swollen gates V-3 9
	110.	Whose head is swinging from the swollen strap Tun 66
swooping	72.	Swooping in eagle feathers down your back Dan 46
sword	39.	Are overtaken. Now no cry, no sword V-5 10
	144.	The plough, the sword PA 17
swords	7.	Into a realm of swords, her purple shadow SMA 6
	177.	Shall come to you through wounds prescribed by swords Rep 8
swore	60.	nor there. He woke and swore he'd seen Broadway VW 28
swung	82.	a nervous shark tooth swung on his chain CS 2
sybil	137.	And it may stun the sybil into prophecy For 9
syllables	76.	In golden syllables loosed from the clay Ind 19
	89.	"--Recorders ages hence"--ah, syllables of faith CH 43
	115.	In myriad syllables,--Psalm of Cathay At 47
	156.	Coils and withdraws. So syllables want breath OC 16
syncopate	114.	Taut miles of shuttling moonlight syncopate At 3
synergy	115.	And synergy of waters ever fuse, recast At 46
synoptic	114.	One arc synoptic of all tides below At 10
syphilitic	173.	The syphilitic selling violets calmly/and daisies MF 1
syrup	151.	that make your colored syrup fairly APE 12
systematic	17.	When systematic morn shall sometime flood Par 10
systems	123.	Great horizons and systems and shores all along Moth 43
systole	17.	Systole, diastole spokes-of-a-wheel Par 2

table   -312-

takes	12.	Takes rein Past 10
	23.	Regard the forceps of the smile that takes her WM 11
	98.	The Southern Cross takes night SC 3
takest	111.	Condensed, thou takest all--shrill ganglia Tun 117
taking	111.	Taking the final level for the dive Tun 93
talk	168.	Almost no shadow--but the air's thin talk AP 12
talking	179.	ing or extending a phallus through the grating, --talking to Len 5
	183.	The fever was checked. I stood a long time in Mack's talking Et 58
	183.	Drinking Bacardi and talking U.S.A. Et 60
tall	39.	Draw in your head, alone and too tall here V-5 22
	69.	(Anon tall ironsides up from salt lagoons Riv 135
	82.	I met a man in South Street, tall CS 1
	115.	Tall Vision-of-the-Voyage, tensely spare At 42
	172.	Yes, tall, inseparably our days ABP 7
	194.	The commodious, tall decorum of that sky B Tow 39
Tallahassee	66.	--Memphis to Tallahassee--riding the rods Riv 60
tally	93.	Thou bringest tally, and a pact, new bound CH 155
talons	24.	New thresholds, new anatomies! Wine talons WM 29
tamarack	72.	--Fall, Sachem, strictly as the tamarack Dan 48
tambourine	4.	Between his tambourine, stuck on the wall BT 11
tape	174.	An old Egyptian jest has cramped the tape BNOK 5
tapers	122.	Countless rubies and tapers in the oasis' blue haze Moth 16
tapestry	133.	The tapestry betrays a finger through CDB 11
	133.	Of whispering tapestry, brown with old fringe CDB 23
tapping	146.	Are ridiculously tapping PA 54
taps	18.	I know the screen, the distant flying taps Pos 12
	187.	and when the sun taps steeples Ma 5
tarantula	156.	The tarantula rattling at the lily's foot OC 1
tardy	4.	Mark tardy judgment on the world's closed door BT 2
	140.	How love blooms like a tardy flower Int 7
target	20.	Unmangled target smile LC 45
tarns	72.	Over how many bluffs, tarns, streams I sped Dan 37
task	170.	Yet fed your hunger like an endless task TED 2
taste	58.	Firmly as coffee grips the taste,--and away VW 9
	104.	We, who with pledges taste the bright annoy QH 11

Tau	190.	Rhyme from the same Tau (closing cinch by cinch Rel 6
taut	91.	Taut motors surge, space-gnawing, into flight CH 100
	114.	Taut miles of shuttling moonlight syncopate At 3
	141.	As his taut, spare fingers wound the gauze EpH 11
tautly	58.	And Cortes rode up, reining tautly in VW 8
tawny	70.	And bridal flanks and eyes hid tawny pride Dan 16
tea	84.	Sweet opium and tea, Yo-ho CS 58
	85.	(sweet opium and tea CS 71
team	78.	Of all our silent men--the long team line Ind 38
tear	24.	This competence--to travel in a tear WM 31
tearful	100.	Least tearful and least glad (who knows her smile NWG 15
tears	20.	Of tears flocks through the tendoned loam LC 31
	25.	Defer though, revocation of the tears Rec 11
	78.	And barren tears Ind 28
	83.	the star floats burning in a gulf of tears CS 44
	89.	And we have laughter, or more sudden tears CH 38
	93.	Is plummet ushered of those tears that start CH 165
	116.	Sustained in tears the cities are endowed At 70
	138.	Despair until the moon by tears be won Port 3
	161.	Wide of the mountain--thence to tears and sleep IQ 14
	162.	Such tears as crowd the dream OS 4
	170.	Else tears heap all within one clay-cold hill TED 14
	184.	You, who contain augmented tears, explosions Emp 1
	186.	Thou wieldest with such tears that every faction Shak 9
tear-tendering	127.	And of all the sowing, and all the tear-tender-ing Hi 5
tear-wet	125.	Can trace paths tear-wet, and forget all blight C 13
teased	83.	teased remnants of the skeletons of cites CS 30
teats	100.	Her eyes exist in swivellings of her teats NWG 17
Te Deum laudamus	51.	Te Deum laudamus, for thy teeming span AM 72
	52.	Te Deum laudamus/O Thou Hand of Fire AM 90
teeming	51.	Te Deum laudamus, for thy teeming span AM 72
teeth	19.	The fox's teeth, and swart LC 9
	32.	Like old women with teeth unjubilant F&H III 17

teeth, cont.	50.	An herb, a stray branch among salty teeth AM 51
	73.	And stag teeth foam about the raven throat Dan 70
	94.	Around bared teeth of stallions, bloomed that spring CH 172
	188.	death around white teeth HR 28
telegraphic	62.	Mazda--and the telegraphic night coming on Thomas Riv 9
telepathy	114.	The whispered rush, telepathy of wires At 4
tell	17.	But from its bracket how can the tongue tell Par 9
	35.	And could they hear me I would tell them V-1 9
	38.	Must first be lost in fatal tides to tell V-4 16
	89.	Walt, tell me, Walt Whitman, if infinity CH 44
	104.	Shifting reprisals ('til who shall tell us when QH 13
	124.	Dim eyes;--a tongue that cannot tell Moth 52
	142.	How can you tell where beauty's to be found BE 9
	166.	And they shall tell IV 5
tellurian	91.	Tellurian wind-sleuths on dawn patrol CH 103
tempest	114.	White tempest nets file upward, upward ring At 22
	186.	Of all our days, being pilot,--tempest, too Shak 5
tempest-lash	50.	Yet under tempest-lash and surfeitings AM 38
tempests	159.	Or tempests--in a silver, floating plume TCJ 16
temples	159.	As you raise temples fresh from basking foam TCJ 12
tempting	128.	The food has a warm and tempting smell Fr 3
ten	108.	Ten blocks or so before? But you find yourself Tun 20
tended	125.	And he tended with far truths he would form C 6
tendered	37.	This tendered theme of you that light V-3 2
tenderness	190.	Tenderness and resolution Rel 1
tendon	73.	And every tendon scurries toward the twangs Dan 53
	115.	Sidelong with flight of blade on tendon blade At 28
tendoned	20.	Of tears flocks through the tendoned loam LC 31
tendons	48.	Invisible valves of the sea,--locks, tondons AM 10
tendril	167.	And tendril till our deathward breath is sealed RP 11
tenement	58.	Van Winkle sweeps a tenement/way down on Avenue A VW 15
Teneriffe's	51.	And Teneriffe's garnet--flamed it in a cloud AM 70

Tennessee	68.	The Ohio merging,--borne down Tennessee Riv 95
tennis	141.	That knew a grip for books and tennis EpH 9
tensely	115.	Tall Vision-of-the-Voyage, tensely spare At 42
tensile	32.	The tensile boughs, the nimble blue plateaus F&H III 20
tent	74.	There, where the first and last gods keep thy tent Dan 80
tentacles	168.	Its tentacles, horrific in their lurch AP 6
tepees	72.	Grey tepees tufting the blue knolls ahead Dan 39
terminals	95.	Toward endless terminals, Easters of speeding light CH 206
termless	66.	Holding to childhood like some termless play Riv 58
terraced	193.	O terraced echoes prostrate on the plain B Tow 16
terraces	114.	With silver terraces the humming spars At 23
terrapin	157.	For slow evisceration bound like those huge terrapin OC 28
terrible	115.	From gulfs unfolding, terrible of drums At 41
	176.	the terrible puppet of my dreams, shall VU 2
terrific	46.	Terrific threshold of the prophet's pledge TBB 31
terror	36.	The sceptred terror of whose sessions rends V-2 8
tests	50.	This third, of water, tests the word; lo, here AM 33
tethered	94.	Cowslip and shad-blow, flaked like tethered foam CH 171
text	174.	An able text, more motion than machines BNOK 10
theatres	108.	Refractions of the thousand theatres, faces Tun 4
thee	20.	Strike from Thee perfect spheres LC 39
	45.	And Thee, across the harbor, silver-paced TBB 13
	45.	As though the sun took step of thee, yet left TBB 14
	45.	Implicitly thy freedom staying thee TBB 16
	46.	O Sleepless as the river under thee TBB 41
	74.	And saw thee dive to kiss that destiny Dan 77
	91.	By convoy planes, moonferrets that rejoin thee CH 114
	92.	Toward thee, O Corsair of the typhoon,--pilot, hear CH 123
	93.	O Walt!--Ascensions of thee hover in me now CH 148
	94.	O, early following thee, I searched the hill CH 175
	95.	And read thee by the aureole 'round thy head CH 216
	116.	Unspeakable Thou Bridge to Thee, O Love At 83
	152.	Thy time is thee to wend In 1

thee, cont.	152.	thyself, bestow to thee In 6
	152.	unfurling thee untried,--until In 11
	152.	partitions in thee--goes In 13
	162.	So eyes that mind thee fair and gone OS 5
	166.	But peace to thee IV 9
their	7.	Their own perennials of light SMA 11
	23.	--I am conscripted to their shadows' glow WM 8
	64.	But some men take their liquor slow--and count Riv 28
	104.	Perspective never withers from their eyes QH 1
	110.	And did their eyes like unwashed platters ride Tun 76
	122.	That their land is too gorgeous to free their eyes wide Moth 6
	122.	Their joy with a barren and steely tide Moth 8
	122.	That they only can see when their moon limits vision Moth 9
	122.	Their mother, the moon, marks a halo of light Moth 10
	122.	On their own small oasis, ray-cut, an incision Moth 11
	122.	She will flush their hid wings in the evening to blaze Moth 15
	133.	Their brown eyes blacken, and the blue drop hue CDB 8
	139.	The sand and sea have had their way Lege 7
	157.	Each daybreak on the wharf, their brine-caked eyes OC 29
	157.	--Spiked, overturned; such thunder in their strain OC 30
	164.	I dreamed that all men dropped their names, and sang NA 9
	164.	As only they can praise, who build their days NA 10
	176.	with all their zest for doom VU 8
	192.	--Their shadows even--now can't carry him SI 8
	193.	Of broken intervals...And I, their sexton slave B Tow 12
them	7.	Put them again beside a pitcher with a knife SMA 16
	16.	Yielded, while sun-silt rippled them RR 10
	35.	And could they hear me I would tell them V-1 9
	66.	Propitiate them for their timber torn Riv 86
	100.	Some cheapest echo of them all--begins NWG 12
	104.	See them, like eyes that still uphold some dream QH 23
	171.	As draws them toward a doubly mocked confusion KW 11
theme	37.	This tendered theme of you that light V-3 2
	69.	A liquid theme that floating niggers swell Riv 123
	89.	Of you--the theme that's statured in the cliff CH 49

thin, cont.	151.	the nation's lips are thin and fast APE 14
	165.	That thin and blistered...just a rotten shell BSEW 4
	168.	Almost no shadow--but the air's thin talk AP 12
thine	20.	Names peeling from Thine eyes LC 33
	46.	And we have seen night lifted in thine arms TBB 36
	74.	Across what bivouacs of thine angered slain Dan 83
	75.	Of dusk?--And are her perfect brows to thine Dan 100
	75.	Now is the strong prayer folded in thine arms Dan 103
	92.	Thine eyes bicarbonated white by speed, O Skygak, see CH 124
	93.	And this, thine other hand, upon my heart CH 164
	117.	So to thine Everpresence, beyond time At 89
	152.	from thine open dugs shall still the sun In 20
	186.	--And fail, both! Yet thine Ariel holds his song Shak 12
thing	104.	These are but cows that see no other thing QH 4
things	16.	And finally, in that memory all things nurse RR 17
	26.	Forgive me for an echo of these things Rec 27
	28.	There is the world dimensional for/those un-twisted by the love of things/irreconcilable F&H I 16
	28.	Reflective conversion of all things F&H I 32
	123.	When the others were blinded by all waking things Moth 27
	124.	These things I have:--a withered hand Moth 51
	129.	Hush! these things were all heard before dawn An 9
	143.	Of things irreconcilable BE 23
think	28.	There is some way, I think, to touch F&H I 24
	45.	I think of cinemas, panoramic sleights TBB 9
	142.	Do not think too deeply, and you'll find BE 7
	142.	A mesh of belts down into it, made me think BE 13
thinking	151.	or, even thinking APE 8
thinly	73.	And splay tongues thinly busy the blue air Dan 56
	123.	But they burned thinly blind like an orange peeled white Moth 40
third	10.	And every third step down the stair SM 15
	50.	This third, of water, tests the word; lo, here AM 33
	108.	You'll find the garden in the third act dead Tun 8
thirst	75.	Do arrows thirst and leap? Do antlers shine Dan 98

thou, cont.	95.	Thou, Vedic Caesar, to the greensward knelt CH 204
	111.	Kiss of our agony thou gatherest Tun 116
	111.	Condensed, thou takest all--shrill ganglia Tun 117
	112.	Kiss of our agony Thou gatherest Tun 136
	116.	O Thou steeled Cognizance whose leap commits At 57
	116.	Of stars Thou art the stitch and stallion glow At 61
	116.	And like an organ, Thou, with sound of doom At 62
	116.	Sight, sound and flesh Thou leadest from time's realm At 63
	116.	Forever Deity's glittering Pledge, O Thou At 73
	116.	Unspeakable Thou Bridge to Thee, O Love At 83
	116.	(O Thou whose radiance doth inherit me At 87
	152.	those streams and slopes untenanted thou In 16
	169.	Lo, Lord, Thou ridest Hur 1
	169.	Thou ridest to the door, Lord Hur 17
	169.	Thou bidest wall nor floor, Lord Hur 18
	177.	Thou canst read nothing except through appetite Rep 1
	186.	Thou wieldest with such tears that every faction Shak 9
though	25.	Defer though, revocation of the tears Rec 11
	58.	--It is the same hour though a later day VW 6
	64.	--Though they'll confess no rosary nor clue Riv 29
	64.	"There's no place like Booneville though, Buddy Riv 46
	74.	Though other calendars now stack the sky Dan 86
	123.	But once though, he learned of that span of his wings Moth 25
	136.	Though now but marble are the marble urns Ps 1
	136.	Though fountains droop in waning light and pain Ps 2
	146.	Even though, in this town, poetry's a PA 59
	158.	Though why they bide here, only hell that's sacked Mer 2
	163.	Its course, though he'd clamped midnight to noon sky Id 12
thought	5.	The apostle conveys thought through discipline EC 9
	48.	I thought of Genoa; and this truth, now proved AM 17
thoughts	8.	His thoughts, delivered to me PU 5
	141.	And factory sounds and factory thoughts EpH 20
	188.	my thoughts, my humble, fond remembrances of the HR 4
thousand	18.	Through a thousand nights the flesh Pos 5

throat, cont.	56.	<u>my</u> <u>tongue</u> <u>upon</u> <u>your</u> <u>throat</u>--<u>singing</u> HD 27
	73.	And stag teeth foam about the raven throat Dan 70
	106.	In one last angelus lift throbbing throat QH 63
	131.	Flat lily petals to the sea's white throat Ba 7
	152.	the cup again wide from thy throat to spend In 15
	168.	The lizard's throat, held bloated for a fly AP 7
	186.	Swears high in Hamlet's throat, and devils throng Shak 10
throats	32.	Let us unbind our throats of fear and pity F&H III 10
throb	69.	Throb past the City storied of three thrones Riv 133
throbbing	54.	As winch engines begin throbbing on some deck HD 7
	95.	Wherewith to bind us throbbing with one voice CH 202
	106.	In one last angelus lift throbbing throat QH 63
	168.	Balloons but warily from this throbbing perch AP 8
throbs	176.	The window weight throbs in its blind VU 19
throne	70.	He holds the twilight's dim, perpetual throne Dan 8
	158.	And ponder the bright stains that starred this Throne Mer 14
thrones	69.	Throb past the City storied of three thrones Riv 133
throng	186.	Swears high in Hamlet's throat, and devils throng Shak 10
through	48.	Assure us through thy mantle's ageless blue AM 28
	51.	Urging through night our passage to the Chan AM 71
	54.	Insistently through sleep--a tide of voices HD 1
	60.	Or splits a random smell of flowers through glass VW 31
	111.	Blank windows gargle signals through the roar Tun 99
	122.	Never came light through that honey-thick glaze Moth 20
	133.	The tapestry betrays a finger through CDB 11
	134.	Morning: and through the foggy city gate CDB 25
	179.	ing or extending a phallus through the grating, --talking to Len 5

through, cont.	179.	pebbles among cinders in the road through a twice-opened Len 7
	194.	And through whose pulse I hear, counting the strokes B Tow 29
throughout	156.	Is Commissioner of mildew throughout the ambushed senses OC 21
throve	21.	That throve through very oak. And had I walked Pass 24
throw	142.	Far consummations of the tides to throw BE 20
thrush	185.	the wren and thrush, made solid print for me Post 3
thrust	60.	It flashed back at your thrust, as clean as fire VW 25
	168.	Thrust parching from a palm-bole hard by the cove AP 3
thrusting	73.	Spears and assemblies: black drums thrusting on Dan 61
thud	54.	Or a drunken stevedore's howl and thud below HD 8
thumb	11.	Dally the doom of that inevitable thumb Chap 10
thumbing	112.	Searching, thumbing the midnight on the piers Tun 126
thunder	35.	The waves fold thunder on the sand V-1 8
	76.	And bison thunder rends my dreams no more Ind 5
	90.	Toward what? The forked crash of split thunder parts CH 68
	92.	Hung low...until a conch of thunder answers CH 120
	111.	Thunder is galvothermic here below.... The car Tun 91
	157.	--Spiked, overturned; such thunder in their strain OC 30
	159.	With snore of thunder, crowding us to bleed TCJ 7
	161.	Walking the straight road toward thunder IQ 10
thunder-bud	72.	A distant cloud, a thunder-bud--it grew Dan 41
thunder's	94.	Heard thunder's eloquence through green arcades CH 184
thunders	40.	The solstice thunders, crept away V-6 18
thunder-shod	74.	Thewed of the levin, thunder-shod and lean Dan 81
thy	19.	Thy Nazarene and tinder eyes LC 26
	20.	Thy face LC 42
	20.	Dionysus, Thy LC 44
	40.	--Thy derelict and blinded guest V-6 12
	40.	I cannot claim: let thy waves rear V-6 14
	45.	Some motion ever unspent in thy stride TBB 15
	45.	Implicitly thy freedom staying thee TBB 16

thy, cont.

45.	A bedlamite speeds to thy parapets	TBB 18
45.	Thy cables breathe the North Atlantic still TBB 24	
46.	Thy guerdon...Accolade thou dost bestow	TBB 26
46.	(How could mere toil align thy choiring strings TBB 30	
46.	Again the traffic lights that skim thy swift TBB 33	
46.	Beading thy path--condense eternity	TBB 35
46.	Under thy shadow by the piers I waited	TBB 37
46.	Only in darkness is thy shadow clear	TBB 38
48.	Assure us through thy mantle's ageless blue AM 28	
50.	Yet yield thy God's, thy Virgin's charity	AM 48
51.	Cruelly with love thy parable of man	AM 60
51.	Into thy steep savannahs, burning blue	AM 63
51.	Te Deum laudamus, for thy teeming span	AM 72
51.	This disposition that thy night relates	AM 77
51.	The orbic wake of thy once whirling feet	AM 79
51.	Elohim, still I hear thy sounding heel	AM 80
51.	Of knowledge,--round thy brows unhooded now AM 84	
51.	Thy purpose--still one shore beyond desire AM 87	
74.	Of his own fate, I saw thy change begun	Dan 76
74.	There, where the first and last gods keep thy tent Dan 80	
74.	And see'st thy bride immortal in the maize Dan 84	
74.	Thy freedom is her largesse, Prince, and hid Dan 87	
92.	How from thy path above the levin's lance CH 125	
92.	To reckon--as thy stilly eyes partake	CH 127
92.	Thou hast there in thy wrist a Sanskrit charge CH 129	
93.	That's drained, is shivered back to earth--thy wand CH 162	
94.	When first I read thy lines, rife as the loam CH 173	
94.	Beyond all sesames of science was thy choice CH 201	
95.	The Open Road--thy vision is reclaimed	CH 210
95.	In their own veins uncancelled thy sure tread CH 215	
95.	And read thee by the aureole 'round thy head CH 216	
112.	And this thy harbor, O my City, I have driven under Tun 129	
114.	"Make thy love sure--to weave whose song we ply At 14	
115.	O Love, thy white, pervasive Paradigm At 48	

tides, cont.   38. Must first be lost in fatal tides to tell
                            V-4 16

                      48. Witness before the tides can wrest away AM 2

                      50. Starved wide on blackened tides, accrete--
                            enclose AM 42

                      93. Of tides awash the pedestal of Everest, fail
                            CH 152

                   114. One arc synoptic of all tides below At 10

                   123. Which blue tides of cool moons were slow shaken
                            and sunned Moth 44

                   139. Waif of the tides Lege 6

                   142. Far consummations of the tides to throw BE 20

tied   122. They had scorned him, so humbly low, bound there
                            and tied Moth 23

                   142. Tied bundle-wise with cords of smoke BE 6

tidy   14. In crowns less grey--O merciless tidy hair
                            Fern 10

tiers   104. Long tiers of windows staring out toward former
                            QH 20

ties   185. their ribbon miles, beside the railroad ties
                          Post 8

tiger-lilies   132. She hazards jet; wears tiger-lilies MC 5

tightened   141. And as the bandage knot was tightened EpH 23

'til   94. Blue-writ and odor-firm with violets, 'til
                          CH 176

                    94. Set trumpets breathing in each clump and grass
                            tuft--'til CH 185

                 104. Shifting reprisals ('til who shall tell us when
                          QH 13

tiles   181. With arms in slings, plaster strewn dense with
                          tiles Et 8

tilted   163. The other tilted, peeled end clapped to eye
                          Id 10

tilting   45. Tilting there momently, shrill shirt ballooning
                          TBB 19

                    92. Lift agonized quittance, tilting from the in-
                          visible brink CH 135

timber   66. Propitiate them for their timber torn Riv 86

                    89. Across the hills where second timber strays
                          CH 56

time   5. By that time summer and smoke were past EC 15

                     8. Of glories proper to the time PU 16

                  10. It is the time of sundering SM 9

                  15. No birth, no death, no time nor sun NL 11

                  21. The dozen particular decimals of time Pass 25

                  23. Whose skin, facsimile of time, unskeins WM 15

                  26. And let us walk through time with equal pride
                          Rec 28

                  33. O brother-thief of time, that we recall
                          F&H III 40

                  35. By time and the elements; but there is a line
                          V-1 12

                  36. Bind us in time, O Seasons clear, and awe
                          V-2 21

timeless, cont.	115.	Searches the timeless laugh of mythic spears At 32
timelessly	68.	For you, too, feed the River timelessly Riv 107
time's	64.	Time's rending, time's blendings they construe Riv 35
	68.	Down, down--born pioneers in time's despite Riv 112
	115.	Pacific here at time's end, bearing corn At 51
	116.	Sight, sound and flesh Thou leadest from time's realm At 63
times	27.	The mind has shown itself at times F&H I 1
	58.	Times earlier, when you hurried off to school VW 5
	132.	Charred at a stake in younger times than ours MC 12
	161.	Against mankind. It is at times IQ 7
	161.	--It is at times as though the eyes burned hard and glad IQ 12
<u>Times</u>	61.	Have you got your "<u>Times</u>" VW 44
Times Square	108.	Up Times Square to Columbus Circle lights Tun 2
tin	163.	One hand dealt out a kite string, a tin can Id 9
tinder	19.	Thy Nazarene and tinder eyes LC 26
tinned	171.	Where gold has not been sold and conscience tinned KW 16
tinselled	100.	Each other--turquoise fakes on tinselled hands NWG 20
tintex	62.	Tintex--Japalac--Certain-teed Overalls ads Riv 3
tiny	145.	With four tiny black-eyed girls around her PA 34
tiptoeing	188.	cherub watchman--tiptoeing the successive patio bal- HR 7
tired	54.	The long, tired sounds, fog-insulated noises HD 3
	83.	in Panama--got tired of that CS 24
tireless	150.	Are tireless GWP 2
tissues	21.	Casual louse that tissues the buckwheat Pass 7
	122.	But over one moth's eyes were tissues at birth Moth 17
Titicaca	174.	It's Titicaca till we've trod it through BNOK 15
titters	30.	While titters hailed the groans of death F&H II 27
tobacco	33.	A goose, tobacco and cologne F&H III 31
tobacconist	27.	To druggist, barber and tobacconist F&H I 12
to-day	38.	Bright staves of flowers and quills to-day as I V-4 15

tongues, cont.	133.	On smokey tongues of sweetened cigarettes CDB 2
	193.	And swing I know not where. Their tongues en-grave B Tow 10
to-night	6.	There are no stars to-night MGLL 1
tonight	174.	You've overruled my typewriter tonight BNOK 8
tonnage	69.	Damp tonnage and alluvial march of days Riv 124
took	45.	As though the sun took step of thee, yet left TBB 14
	60.	One day in spring my father took to me VW 33
	72.	I took the portage climb, then chose Dan 29
	123.	And he ventured the desert,--his wings took the climb Moth 28
	160.	gum took place. Up jug to musical, hanging jug just gay MT 4
	179.	chorea took him away--there is the Nine of Len 12
	192.	His fathers took for granted ages since--and so he looms SI 6
too-keen	191.	I dream the too-keen cider--the too-soft snow Purg 9
too-soft	191.	I dream the too-keen cider--the too-soft snow Purg 9
tooth	16.	Where beavers learn stitch and tooth RR 14
	24.	Ruddy, the tooth implicit of the world WM 40
	73.	Now snaps the flint in every tooth; red fangs Dan 55
	73.	Spark, tooth! Medicine-man, relent, restore Dan 59
	82.	a nervous shark tooth swung on his chain CS 2
	190.	And the flint tooth of Sagittarius Rel 5
toothpaste	110.	Below the toothpaste and the dandruff ads Tun 74
top	4.	Fox brush and sow ear top his grave BT 7
	72.	One white veil gusted from the very top Dan 32
torch	84.	torch of hers you know CS 52
	180.	Light the last torch in the wall Lib 8
torment	116.	Revolving through their harvests in sweet torment At 72
torn	11.	Or warm torn elbow coverts Chap 8
	32.	On rifts of torn and empty houses F&H III 16
	66.	Propitiate them for their timber torn Riv 86
	76.	As once my womb was torn, my boy, when you Ind 6
	186.	Are lifted from torn flesh with human rue Shak 7
torrent	74.	She is the torrent and the singing tree Dan 91
torrid	123.	And the torrid hum of great wings was his song Moth 41
	186.	Through torrid entrances, past icy poles Shak 1
tortoise	4.	Heaven with the tortoise and the hare BT 6
tortured	69.	Tortured with history, its one will--flow Riv 141
toss	4.	Gnats toss in the shadow of a bottle BT 3

toss, cont.   7.   I have seen the apples there that toss you
                           secrets SMA 13
tossed   18.   Tossed on these horns, who bleeding dies Pos 23
                   112.   Tossed from the coil of ticking towers....
                           Tomorrow Tun 130
tossing   139.   The tossing loneliness of many nights Lege 1
total   18.   Account the total of this trembling tabulation
                           Poss 11
totem   74.   Totem and fire-gall, slumbering pyramid Dan 85
touch   28.   There is some way, I think, to touch F&H I 24
                    39.   --As if too brittle or too clear to touch
                           V-5 5
                    39.   Knowing I cannot touch your hand and look
                           V-5 15
                    66.   Yet they touch something like a key perhaps
                           Riv 62
                   105.   Our love of all we touch, and take it to the
                           Gate QH 59
touched   68.   As though you touched hands with some ancient
                           clown Riv 101
                   132.   Though I have touched her flesh of moons MC 1
                   135.   My hands have not touched water since your
                           hands CL 1
touching   8.   Touching as well upon our praise PU 15
                    21.   Touching an opening laurel, I found Pass 26
tournament   91.   This tournament of space, the threshed and
                           chiselled height CH 95
toward   8.   Once moved us toward presentiments PU 10
                    11.   That slowly chafes its puckered index toward us
                           Chap 11
                    15.   That journey toward no Spring NL 10
                    36.   The seal's wide spindrift gaze toward paradise
                           V-2 25
                    45.   With multitudes bent toward some flashing scene
                           TBB 10
                    73.   And every tendon scurries toward the twangs
                           Dan 53
                    92.   Toward thee, O Corsair of the typhoon,--pilot,
                           hear CH 123
                    94.   Years of the Modern! Propulsions toward what
                           capes CH 197
                    95.   Toward endless terminals, Easters of speeding
                           light CH 206
                   104.   Long tiers of windows staring out toward former
                           QH 20
                   110.   Probing through you--toward me, O evermore
                           Tun 78
                   111.   Lets go.... Toward corners of the floor Tun 97
                   111.   With antennae toward worlds that glow and sink
                           Tun 110
                   150.   Toward lawyers and Nevada GWP 9

toward, cont.   161. Walking the straight road toward thunder IQ 10

                161. This dry road silvering toward the shadow of
                      the quarry IQ 11

                182. I beat the dazed mule toward the road. He got
                      that far Et 48

                185. toward something far, now farther than ever away
                      Post 6

                191. And all my countrymen I see rush toward one
                      stall Purg 12

towards   90. Towards what? The forked crash of split thunder
                      parts CH 68

                171. As draws them towards a doubly mocked confusion
                      KW 11

tower   25. The highest tower,--let her ribs palisade
                      Rec 21

                 25. Wrenched gold of Nineveh;--yet leave the tower
                      Rec 22

                102. O Mary, leaning from the high wheat tower Va 15

                102. Out of the way-up nickel-dime tower shine Va 23

                167. Drift coolly from that tower of whispered light
                      RP 2

                193. Of shadows in the tower, whose shoulders sway
                      B Tow 6

                193. The bells, I say, the bells break down their
                      tower B Tow 9

                194. No answer (could blood hold such a lofty tower
                      B Tow 26

                194. And builds, within, a tower that is not stone
                      B Tow 33

                194. That shrines the quiet lake and swells a tower
                      B Tow 38

towering   115. Pick biting way up towering looms that press
                      At 27

                161. Palms against the sunset's towering sea, and
                      maybe IQ 6

towers   51. The sea's green crying towers a-sway, Beyond
                      AM 88

                 56. From Cyclopean towers across Manhattan waters
                      HD 32

                 89. For you, the panoramas and this breed of towers
                      CH 48

                112. Tossed from the coil of ticking towers....
                      Tomorrow Tun 130

town   64. Bind town to town and dream to ticking dream
                      Riv 27

                 78. A dream called Eldorado was his town Ind 21

                109. to dig in the field--travlin the town--too
                      Tun 43

                146. One summer day in a little town PA 47

                146. Even though, in this town, poetry's a PA 59

                181. At the base of the mountain. But the town, the
                      town Et 6

town, cont.	183.	Without ceremony, while hammers pattered in town Et 52
	191.	That I prefer to country or to town Purg 16
trace	94.	Evasive--too--as dayspring's spreading arc to trace is CH 192
	125.	Can trace paths tear-wet, and forget all blight C 13
	159.	We hold in vision only, asking trace TCJ 2
	193.	To trace the visionary company of love, its voice B Tow 18
traces	83.	steel--silver--kick the traces--and know CS 42
trackless	39.	One frozen trackless smile...What words V-5 8
tracks	62.	a Ediford--and whistling down the tracks Riv 10
	62.	three men, still hungry on the tracks, ploddingly Riv 21
	64.	"--But I kept on the tracks." Possessed, re-signed Riv 49
trade	84.	those bright designs the trade winds drive CS 57
traffic	28.	Without recall,--lost yet poised in traffic F&H I 19
	46.	Again the traffic lights that skim thy swift TBB 33
	89.	Of canyoned traffic...Confronting the Exchange CH 54
tragedy	85.	(last trip a tragedy)--where can you be CS 74
trail	76.	Back on the gold trail--then his lost bones stirred Ind 10
	78.	The long trail back! I huddled in the shade Ind 29
trailed	98.	Furrow of all our travel--trailed derision SC 14
train	68.	Or stay the night and take the next train through Riv 93
	68.	Oh, lean from the window, if the train slows down Riv 100
	111.	Wheels off. The train rounds, bending to a scream Tun 92
	185.	as one nears New Orleans, sweet trenches by the train Post 9
trains	66.	Trains sounding the long blizzards out--I heard Riv 74
trance	159.	The falling wonder of a rainbow's trance TCJ 4
tranquil	94.	Panis Angelicus! Eyes tranquil with the blaze CH 187
transept	24.	Each chamber, transept, coins some squint WM 24
transepts	23.	Octagon, sapphire transepts round the eyes WM 16
transfer	28.	The fare and transfer, yet got by that way F&H I 18
transience	22.	"Am justified in transience, fleeing Pass 30
transient	125.	The transient bosoms from the thorny tree C 7
translating	115.	Of deepest day--O Choir, translating time At 44

transmemberment	37.	The silken skilled transmemberment of song V-3 18
transmuting	106.	Listen, transmuting silence with that stilly note QH 64
transparent	114.	Transparent meshes--fleckless the gleaming staves At 6
transpiring	38.	Mutual blood, transpiring as foreknown V-4 19
trap	188.	crumbled palace in the square--the typhus in a trap HR 12
	188.	the Doctor's rat trap. Where? Somewhere in Vera HR 13
trapeze	101.	Yet, to the empty trapeze of your flesh NWG 25
trapped	92.	In guerilla sleights, trapped in combusion gyr- CH 139
travail	93.	The competent loam, the probable grass,--travail CH 151
	129.	The moans of travail of one dearest beside me An 7
travel	14.	The lights that travel on her spectacles Fern 1
	24.	This competence--to travel in a tear WM 31
	98.	Furrow of all our travel--trailed derision SC 14
traveller	79.	You, Larry, traveller--/stranger,/son,/--my friend Ind 64
	115.	What cipher-script of time no traveller reads At 30
travlin	109.	to dig in the field--travlin the town--too Tun 43
tread	95.	In their own veins uncancelled thy sure tread CH 215
treason	24.	How much yet meets the treason of the snow WM 43
treated	183.	And treated, it seemed. In due time Et 54
treble	35.	And in answer to their treble interjections V-1 6
tree	9.	She is prisoner of the tree and its green fingers GA 6
	9.	And so she comes to dream herself the tree GA 7
	50.	Some Angelus environs the cordage tree AM 55
	60.	Is it the whip stripped from the lilac tree VW 32
	74.	She is the torrent and the singing tree Dan 91
	125.	The transient bosoms from the thorny tree C 7
	137.	Forgetfulness is white,--white as a blasted tree For 8
	156.	Albeit in a stranger tongue. Tree names, flower names OC 13
	191.	Of Eden--and the dangerous tree--are these Purg 6
trees	126.	On trees that seem dancing O-N 6
	145.	Twinkling like little Christmas trees PA 35

trellises	126.	Dives through the filter of trellises O-N 3
trembles	6.	It trembles as birch limbs webbing the air MGLL 15
trembling	18.	Account the total of this trembling tabulation Pos 11
	52.	And kingdoms/naked in the/trembling heart AM 89
	94.	Gold autumn, captured, crowned the trembling hill CH 186
	110.	Your trembling hands that night through Baltimore Tun 80
tremolo	30.	Magnetic to their tremolo F&H II 3
tremorous	3.	Imploring flame. And tremorous Leg 6
tremors	187.	twigs in tremors. Walls Ma 3
trenchant	18.	In Bleecker Street, still trenchant in a void Pos 18
trenches	185.	as one nears New Orleans, sweet trenches by the train Post 9
trespass	163.	My trespass vision shrinks to face his wrong Id 16
trestle	114.	New octaves trestle the twin monoliths At 18
tribal	73.	Lie to us,--dance us back the tribal morn Dan 60
tribunal	193.	Of that tribunal monarch of the air B Tow 22
tributaries	68.	Grimed tributaries to an ancient flow Riv 113
tribute	68.	As loth to take more tribute--sliding prone Riv 118
trick	178.	And who trick back the leisured winds again PB 6
trillion	19.	Are trillion on the hill LC 13
	115.	Some trillion whispering hammers glimmer Tyre At 34
trillions	99.	Light drowned the lithic trillions of your spawn SC 29
trip	85.	(last trip a tragedy)--where can you be CS 74
triple-noted	106.	That triple-noted clause of moonlight QH 67
trod	64.	He trod the fire down pensively and grinned Riv 50
	66.	--As I have trod the rumorous midnights, too Riv 70
	174.	It's Titicaca till we've trod it through BNOK 15
troopers	181.	And Cuban doctors, troopers, trucks, loose hens Et 9
trophies	8.	They are no trophies of the sun PU 24
tropic	156.	I count these nacreous frames of tropic death OC 9
	174.	It knows its way through India--tropic shake BNOK 14
	182.	Long tropic roots high in the air, like lace Et 30
trouble	104.	Through the rich halo that they do not trouble QH 6

troubled	28.	The press of troubled hands, too alternate F&H I 42
	149.	And my heart fishes in troubled water Loc 31
trough	40.	Or as many waters trough the sun's V-6 7
troughed	22.	Sand troughed us in a glittering abyss Pass 33
troughing	48.	Crested and creeping, troughing corridors AM 11
trounce	100.	And the lewd trounce of a final muted beat NWG 23
trouting	64.	"--For early trouting." Then peering in the can Riv 48
trout's	70.	I learned to catch the trout's moon whisper; I Dan 22
trowel	144.	The trowel,--and the monkey wrench PA 18
Troy	115.	Of inchling aeons silence rivets Troy At 36
truck	54.	And then a truck will lumber past the wharves HD 6
	84.	Outside a wharf truck nearly ran him down CS 49
trucks	181.	And Cuban doctors, troopers, trucks, loose hens Et 9
true	36.	Hasten, while they are true,--sleep, death, desire V-2 19
	51.	Utter to loneliness the sail is true AM 64
	51.	And true appointment from the hidden shoal AM 76
	79.	Where gold is true Ind 56
	148.	True, I nibble at despondencies Loc 17
	182.	--I can't account for him! And true, he stood Et 44
	188.	me "the True Cross"--let us remember the Doctor and HR 3
	194.	As flings the question true?)--or is it she B Tow 27
truly	148.	Ah, madame! truly it's not right Loc 9
	170.	--Truly no flower yet withers in your hand TED 9
trumpets	94.	Set trumpets breathing in each clump and grass tuft--'til CH 185
trundle	188.	clamour of incessant shutters, trundle doors, and the HR 6
trunk	167.	And the grey trunk, that's elephantine, rear RP 7
trust	18.	Witness now this trust! the rain Pos 1
	35.	You must not cross nor ever trust beyond it V 1 13
	135.	Yet,--much follows, much endures...Trust birds alone CL 5
truth	48.	I thought of Genoa; and this truth, now proved AM 17
truths	125.	And he tended with far truths he would form C 6
try	146.	You ought, really, to try to sleep PA 58

turning, cont.	36.	Mark how her turning shoulders wind the hours V-2 16
	50.	This turning rondure whole, this crescent ring AM 43
	161.	At the turning of the road around the roots of the mountain IQ 3
	177.	Go then, unto thy turning and thy blame Rep 5
turnpike	79.	Down the dim turnpike to the river's edge Ind 57
turns	39.	Where nothing turns but dead sands flashing V-5 17
	56.	Turns in the waking west and goes to sleep HD 38
	69.	Down two more turns the Mississippi pours Riv 134
turnstile	109.	And down beside the turnstile press the coin Tun 29
	156.	Without a turnstile? Who but catchword crabs OC 18
turquoise	100.	Each other--turquoise fakes on tinselled hands NWG 20
turreted	84.	Blithe Yankee vanities, turreted sprites, winged CS 54
turrets	92.	Regard the moving turrets! From grey decks CH 118
turtles	16.	And mammoth turtles climbing sulphur dreams RR 9
tusks	24.	Between black tusks the roses shine WM 28
tusseling	85.	Buntlines tusseling (91 days, 20 hours and anchored!)/Rainbow, Leander CS 73
twain	116.	In single chrysalis the many twain At 60
twanged	19.	Twanged red perfidies of spring LC 12
twangs	73.	And every tendon scurries toward the twangs Dan 53
twelve	108.	to twelve upward leaving Tun 15
twentieth	62.	So the 20th Century--so Riv 19
twenty	85.	Buntlines tusseling (91 days, 20 hours and anchored!)/Rainbow, Leander CS 73
	174.	From twenty alphabets--we're still unripe BNOK 12
twice	3.	Twice and twice Leg 14
twice-opened	179.	pebbles among cinders in the road through a twice-opened Len 7
twigs	187.	twigs in tremors. Walls Ma 3
twilight	13.	Twilight, stiller than shadows, fall IS 12
	179.	a kite high in the afternoon, or in the twilight scanning Len 6
twilight's	70.	He holds the twilight's dim, perpetual throne Dan 8
twilights	187.	are naked. Twilights raw Ma 4
twin	25.	Twin shadowed halves: the breaking second holds Rec 5

twin, cont.   78.   And like twin stars. They seemed to shun the
                           gaze   Ind 37
                    114.   New octaves trestle the twin monoliths At 18
twine   41.   Which rainbows twine continual hair V-6 27
twinge   133.   The winers leave too, and the small lamps twinge
                           CDB 24
twinkling   145.   Twinkling like little Christmas trees PA 35
twinship   90.   Two brothers in their twinship left the dune
                           CH 79
twist   25.   As double as the hands that twist this glass
                           Rec 2
twisted   60.   We launched--with paper wings and twisted VW 20
                    143.   But some are twisted with the love BE 22
twisting   92.   Now eagle-bright, now/quarry-hid, twist-/-ing,
                           sink with CH 136
two   50.   For here between two worlds, another, harsh
                           AM 32
                     56.   --Two--three bright window-eyes aglitter, disk
                           HD 33
                     69.   Down two more turns the Mississippi pours
                           Riv 134
                     85.   Nimbus? and you rivals two CS 75
                     90.   Two brothers in their twinship left the dune
                           CH 79
                    114.   Two worlds of sleep (O arching strands of song
                           At 20
                    131.   Two ivory women by a milky sea Ba 1
                    141.   The two men smiled into each other's eyes
                           EpH 24
                    176.   the dense mine of the orchid, split in two
                           VU 4
                    181.   Two decks unsandwiched, split sixty feet apart
                           Et 15
                    183.   Something like two thousand loaves on the way
                           Et 56
twos   105.   Of golf, by twos and threes in plaid plusfours
                           QH 31
tympanum   112.   Lights, coasting, left the oily tympanum of
                           waters Tun 127
type   174.   Have levers for,--stampede it with fresh type
                           BNOK 11
typewriter   174.   You've overruled my typewriter tonight BNOK 8
typhoid   188.   metaphysics that are typhoid plus and had
                           engaged HR 22
typhoon   92.   Toward thee, O Corsair of the typhoon,--pilot,
                           hear CH 123
typhus   188.   crumbled palace in the square--the typhus in a
                           trap HR 12
                    188.   ans surely slept--whose references to typhus and
                           whose HR 20
typical   188.   conies with a typical pistol--trying to muffle
                           doors HR 8

ubiquitous	91.	Behold the dragon's covey--amphibian, ubiquitous CH 88
ubiquity	105.	What eats the pattern with ubiquity QH 47
ultimately	170.	Achieved that stillness ultimately best TED 4
umbilical	111.	Umbilical to call--and straightway die Tun 114
	191.	I am unraveled, umbilical anew Purg 17
umbrellas	110.	Of shoes, umbrellas, each eye attending its shoe, then Tun 87
unaccounting	112.	Shadowless in that abyss they unaccounting lie Tun 133
unbelievably	151.	unbelievably--Oh APE 10
unbetrayable	41.	It is the unbetrayable reply V-6 31
unbind	32.	Let us unbind our throats of fear and pity F&H III 10
unburned	159.	Like water, undestroyed,--like mist, unburned TCJ 18
uncancelled	95.	In their own veins uncancelled thy sure tread CH 215
unceasing	112.	Unceasing with some Word that will not die Tun 122
uncoiled	135.	Between us, voiceless as an uncoiled shell CL 4
unconscious	60.	Or is it the Sabbatical, unconscious smile VW 34
uncontested	28.	Prodigal, yet uncontested now F&H I 22
uncoy	104.	And they are awkward, ponderous and uncoy QH 9
uncurls	17.	For what skims in between uncurls the toe Par 7
undelivered	10.	Her mound of undelivered life SM 11
undenying	89.	Sea eyes and tidal, undenying, bright with myth CH 58
under	142.	Lapped under it,--or the dun BE 4
underbrush	156.	Patrols the dry groins of the underbrush OC 19
underdrawers	160.	spiders yoked you first,--silking of shadows good under-/drawers for owls MT 5
underground	109.	underground, the monotone Tun 36
	109.	of other faces, also underground Tun 38
underneath	108.	A walk is better underneath the L a brisk Tun 19
undersea	158.	Buddhas and engines serve us undersea Mer 1
understand	6.	Through much of what she would not understand MGLL 24
	39.	"--And never to quite understand!" No V-5 18
	164.	But we must die, as you, to understand NA 8
	170.	The harvest you descried and understand TED 10
undertowed	69.	O quarrying passion, undertowed sunlight Riv 128
undeserved	189.	not heed the negative--so might go on to unde-served HR 31
undestroyed	159.	Like water, undestroyed,--like mist, unburned TCJ 18
undimming	20.	And their undimming lattices of flame LC 34
undinal	36.	Her undinal vast belly moonward bends V-2 4
undirected	18.	Hidden,--O undirected as the sky Pos 7
undone	46.	The City's fiery parcels all undone TBB 39

undone, cont.	138.	Though silent as your sandals, danced undone Port 8
	177.	So sleep, dear brother, in my fame, my shame undone Rep 12
uneaten	167.	Uneaten of the earth or aught earth holds RP 6
uneven	5.	The uneven valley graves. While the apostle gave EC 2
unexpected	141.	The unexpected interest made him flush EpH 1
unfended	19.	First blood. From flanks unfended LC 11
unfettered	36.	Of rimless floods, unfettered leewardings V-2 2
unfolded	41.	--Unfolded floating dais before V-6 26
unfolding	115.	From gulfs unfolding, terrible of drums At 41
unfolds	105.	That unfolds a new destiny to fill QH 56
unfractioned	46.	Unfractioned idiom immaculate sigh of stars TBB 34
unfurling	152.	unfurling thee untried,--until In 11
unguents	16.	With scalding unguents spread and smoking darts RR 19
unhooded	51.	Of knowledge,--round thy brows unhooded now AM 84
unhusks	106.	Yes, whip-poor-will, unhusks the heart of fright QH 68
unique	148.	What is her unique propensity Loc 20
universe	5.	Orators follow the universe EC 7
	90.	The nasal whine of power whips a new universe CH 59
unjubilant	32.	Like old women with teeth unjubilant F&H III 17
unkind	176.	And it is always the day, the farewell day unkind VU 23
unknotting	90.	New latitudes, unknotting, soon give place CH 86
unlooping	92.	Giddily spiralled/gauntlets, upturned, unlooping CH 138
unloved	99.	Yes, Eve--wraith of my unloved seed SC 27
unmake	23.	Her eyes, unmake an instant of the world WM 13
unmangled	20.	Unmangled target smile LC 45
unmended	136.	And broken branches, wistful and unmended Ps 7
unpaced	22.	--On unpaced beaches leaned its tongue and drummed Pass 35
unprepared	109.	--Quite unprepared rush naked back to light Tun 28
unraveled	191.	I am unraveled, umbilical anew Purg 17
unresigned	152.	illimitable and unresigned In 7
unripe	174.	From twenty alphabets--we're still unripe BNOK 12
unrocking	17.	Your head, unrocking to a pulse, already Par 14
unsandwiched	181.	Two decks unsandwiched, split sixty feet apart Et 15
unseals	194.	Unseals her earth, and lifts love in its shower B Tow 40
unsearchable	40.	That smile unsearchable repose V-6 24

utmost	94.	And onward yielding past my utmost year CH 190
utter	51.	Utter to loneliness the sail is true AM 64
	116.	Whose fell unshadow is death's utter wound At 66
utterly	98.	No wraith, but utterly--as still more alone SC 2

vacant	157.	Congeal by afternoons here, satin and vacant OC 33
vagrant	187.	The vagrant ghost of winter Ma 12
vain	32.	That waited faintly, briefly and in vain F&H III 18
	162.	Such words as it were vain to close OS 3
	170.	You who desired so much--in vain to ask TED 1
	178.	Their vanity, and dream no land in vain PB 8
	186.	Conflicting, purposeful yet outcry vain Shak 4
vainly	98.	Whatever call--falls vainly on the wave SC 8
	152.	(no instinct flattering vainly now In 8
valentine	24.	Petrushka's valentine pivots on its pin WM 49
validities	159.	Expose vaunted validites that yawn TCJ 13
valley	5.	The uneven valley graves. While the apostle gave EC 2
	7.	In the valley where you live/(called Brandywine SMA 12
	171.	Out of the valley, past the ample crib KW 2
valleys	21.	Vine-stanchioned valleys--": but the wind Pass 18
	94.	White banks of moonlight came descending valleys CH 181
valley-shed	72.	A further valley-shed; I could not stop Dan 30
valley-sleepers	66.	Is past the valley-sleepers, south or west Riv 69
valves	48.	Invisible valves of the sea,--locks, tendons AM 10
vanes	109.	Our tongues recant like beaten weather vanes Tun 46
vanities	84.	Blithe Yankee vanities, turreted sprites, winged CS 54
vanity	178.	Their vanity, and dream no land in vain PB 8
vantage	192.	How more?--but the lash, lost vantage--and the prison SI 5
Van Winkle	58.	And Rip Van Winkle bowing by the way VW 12
	58.	Van Winkle sweeps a tenement/way down on Avenue A VW 15
	60.	that he, Van Winkle, was not here VW 27
	61.	And hurry along, Van Winkle--it's getting late VW 45
vaporous	98.	Of lower heavens,--/vaporous scars SC 6
variants	190.	As though we knew (those who are variants Rel 8
vary	88.	Where strange tongues vary messages of surf CH 7
	190.	Who is now left to vary the Sanscrit Rel 12
vascular	69.	Nights turbid, vascular with silted shale Riv 125
vast	34.	Then in the circuit calm of one vast coil AMT 9
	36.	Her undinal vast belly moonward bends V-2 4
	64.	Keen instruments, strung to a vast precision Riv 26

Venus	98.	O simian Venus, homeless Eve SC 9
	131.	They say that Venus shot through foam to light Ba 8
Vera Cruz	188.	in Mexico.... That night in Vera Cruz--verily for HR 2
	188.	The Doctor's rat trap. Where? Somewhere in Vera/Cruz--to bring--to take--to mix--to ransom-- to de- HR 13-14
verb	115.	Into what multitudinous Verb the suns At 45
verdigris	109.	This answer lives like verdigris, like hair Tun 47
verily	172.	Where cliff and citadel--all verily ABP 3
	188.	in Mexico.... That night in Vera Cruz--verily for HR 2
verities	90.	New verities, new inklings in the velvet hummed CH 63
vermeil	122.	That emerge black and vermeil from yellow cocoons Moth 4
vermin	20.	Once and again; vermin and rod LC 29
vernal	115.	The vernal strophe chimes from deathless strings At 56
vertex	22.	A serpent swam a vertex to the sun Pass 34
vertical	32.	That saddled sky that shook down vertical F&H III 22
vest	64.	One said, excising a last burr from his vest Riv 47
vestibule	190.	My wrist in the vestibule of time--who Rel 14
vestiges	10.	Vestiges of the sun that somehow SM 3
vibrant	25.	I crust a plate of vibrant mercury Rec 7
	46.	Vibrant reprieve and pardon thou dost show TBB 28
	114.	Complighted in one vibrant breath made cry At 13
vibrantly	94.	As vibrantly I following down Sequoia alleys CH 183
view	105.	So, must we from the hawk's far stemming view QH 57
	167.	A fountain at salute, a crown in view RP 14
vigilance	179.	the vigilance of the ape, the repe- Len 14
vigils	93.	What memories of vigils, bloody, by that Cape CH 166
Viking	95.	New integers of Roman, Viking, Celt CH 203
village	70.	I left the village for dogwood. By the canoe Dan 17
vine	33.	Gathered the voltage of blown blood and vine F&H III 38
	76.	Over the lintel on its wiry vine Ind 2
vines	19.	Perpetual fountains, vines LC 25
vine-stanchioned	21.	Vine-stanchioned valleys--": but the wind Pass 18
vineyard	74.	O stream by slope and vineyard--into bloom Dan 96

violet		
violet	72.	And northward reaches in that violet wedge Dan 35
	78.	Until she saw me--when their violet haze Ind 39
violets	12.	No more violets Past 1
	12.	And violets Past 19
	94.	Blue-writ and odor-firm with violets, 'til CH 176
	102.	The slender violets stray Va 19
	173.	The syphilitic selling violets calmly/and daisies MF 1
violin	100.	A tom-tom scrimmage with a somewhere violin NWG 11
virgin	70.	O Princess whose brown lap was virgin May Dan 15
	74.	And she is virgin to the last of men Dan 92
	159.	Your light lifts whiteness into virgin azure TCJ 5
	180.	The virgin. They laugh to hear Lib 3
virginal	27.	Virginal perhaps, less fragmentary, cool F&H I 15
virginbirth	62.	WALLSTREET AND VIRGINBIRTH WITHOUT STONES OR Riv 15
virgin's	50.	Yet yield thy God's, thy Virgin's charity AM 48
visage	110.	And why do I often meet your visage here Tun 72
visible	194.	Of pebbles,--visible wings of silence sown B Tow 35
visibility	91.	Through sparkling visibility, outspread, un-sleeping CH 101
vision	23.	Asserts a vision in the slumbering gaze WM 4
	95.	The Open Road--thy vision is reclaimed CH 210
	98.	Incites a yell. Slid on that backward vision SC 16
	114.	The loft of vision, palladium helm of stars At 24
	122.	That they only can see when their moon limits vision Moth 9
	139.	And even my vision will be erased Lege 10
	142.	I do not know what you'll see,--your vision BE 18
	150.	The little voices of prairie dogs GWP 1
	159.	We hold in vision only, asking trace TCJ 2
	163.	My trespass vision shrinks to face his wrong Id 16
	192.	The warp is in the woof--and his keen vision SI 3
visionary	193.	To trace the visionary company of love, its voice B Tow 18
Vision-of-the-Voyage	115.	Tall Vision-of-the-Voyage, tensely spare At 42

wafer   28. The white wafer cheek of love, or offers
                        words F&H I 30
wage   184. To wage you surely back to memory Emp 10
wagon   134. A gypsy wagon wiggles, striving straight CDB 26
wagon-tenting   78. Of wagon-tenting looked out once and saw Ind 30
waif   139. Waif of the tides Lege 6
wail   66. Wail into distances I knew were hers Riv 75
wails   54. Gongs in white surplices, beshrouded wails HD 4
wainscoting   23. Against the imitation onyx wainscoting WM 9
wait   13. Nor has the evening long to wait IS 15
                   68. You have a half-hour's wait at Siskiyou Riv 92
                   79. Good-bye...Good-bye...oh, I shall always wait
                        Ind 63
                  100. Always you wait for someone else though, always
                        NWG 7
                  100. We wait that writhing pool, her pearls collapsed
                        NWG 21
                  105. Wait for the postman driving from Birch Hill
                        QH 54
                  188. And during the wait over dinner at La Diana,
                        the HR 29
waited   32. That waited faintly, briefly and in vain
                        F&H III 18
                   46. Under thy shadow by the piers I waited TBB 37
waiting   13. Like a waiting moon, in shadow swims IS 4
                   40. Waiting, afire, what name, unspoke V-6 13
                  102. And I'm still waiting you Va 6
                  147. Waiting for morning Per 10
waits   147. If she waits late at night Per 1
wake   10. And she will wake before you pass SM 13
                   34. Monody shall not wake the mariner AMT 15
                   51. The orbic wake of thy once whirling feet AM 79
                   73. Wrapped in that fire, I saw more escorts wake
                        Dan 67
                   78. It rose up shambling in the nuggets' wake
                        Ind 22
                   89. From which we wake into the dream of act CH 40
                   98. And this long wake of phosphor,/iridescent
                        SC 13
                  115. Silvery the rushing wake, surpassing call At 39
                  131. A dreamer might see these, and wake to hear
                        Ba 4
                  191. So absolution? Wake pines--but pines wake here
                        Purg 8
wakeful   188. posedly slept, supposedly in #35--thus in my
                        wakeful HR 17
waken   10. Filter in to us before we waken SM 4
                  100. And while legs waken salads in the brain NWG 5
wakens   21. And wakens alleys with a hidden cough Pass 10
waking   56. Turns in the waking west and goes to sleep
                        HD 38

wanderer, cont.	5.	The wanderer later chose this spot of rest EC 12
wanders	4.	Wanders in some mid-kingdom, dark, that lies BT 10
	54.	Spills into steam, and wanders, washed away HD 14
	137.	That, freed from beat and measure, wanders For 2
wands	72.	Of Adirondacks!--wisped of azure wands Dan 36
wanes	187.	of winter wanes Ma 18
waning	136.	Though fountains droop in waning light and pain Ps 2
	187.	and knows its waning Ma 19
want	82.	I don't want to know what time it is--that CS 20
	109.	"what do you want? getting weak on the links Tun 50
	110.	"But I want service in this office SERVICE Tun 63
	156.	Coils and withdraws. So syllables want breath OC 16
wanted	98.	I wanted you, nameless Woman of the South SC 1
	98.	I wanted you...The embers of the Cross SC 18
war	50.	Palos again,--a land cleared of long war AM 54
warehouses	142.	Bellies and estuaries of warehouses BE 5
warily	168.	Balloons but warily from this throbbing perch AP 8
wariness	70.	With mineral wariness found out the stone Dan 6
warm	11.	Or warm torn elbow coverts Chap 8
	74.	Her hair's warm sibilance. Her breasts are fanned Dan 95
	78.	As long as Jim, your father's memory, is warm Ind 45
	128.	The food has a warm and tempting smell Fr 3
	130.	Are warmer with a redder glow Ech 8
	145.	And threw warm gules on Madeline's fair breast PA 43
warmly	141.	Fell lightly, warmly, down into the wound EpH 7
warp	192.	The warp is in the woof--and his keen vision SI 3
warped	158.	But since the Cross sank, much that's warped and cracked Mer 6
warping	90.	Warping the gale, the Wright windwrestlers veered CH 80
war's	91.	War's fiery kennel masked in downy offings CH 94
wars	194.	The angelus of wars my chest evokes B Tow 31
warted	142.	And the hand was thick and heavily warted BE 15
wash	98.	God--your namelessness. And the wash SC 22
washed	54.	Spills into steam, and wanders, washed away HD 14
washerwoman	111.	Wop washerwoman, with the bandaged hair Tun 101

watch	25.	The brain's disk shivered against lust. Then watch Rec 14
	48.	I, wonder-breathing, kept the watch,--saw AM 23
	108.	And watch the curtain lift in hell's despite Tun 7
	127.	And I watch, and say, "These the anguish are worth Hi 8
	176.	I watch the silver Zeppelin VU 11
watched	34.	An embassy. Their numbers as he watched AMT 3
	163.	That kite aloft--you should have watched him scan Id 11
	167.	I watched the sun's most gracious anchorite RP 4
	182.	We shoveled and sweated; watched the ogre sun Et 25
watches	82.	weakeyed watches sometimes snooze--" his bony hands CS 16
	88.	What whisperings of far watches on the main CH 21
	188.	watches at least--the lighthouse flashed... whirled HR 18
watching	62.	watching the tail lights wizen and converge, slip- Riv 22
	70.	But, watching, saw that fleet young crescent die Dan 24
watchman	188.	cherub watchman--tiptoeing the successive patio bal- HR 7
water	37.	While ribboned water lanes I wind V-3 5
	50.	This third, of water, tests the word; lo, here AM 33
	70.	What laughing chains the water wove and threw Dan 21
	99.	All night the water combed you with black SC 23
	99.	Water rattled that stinging coil, your SC 25
	131.	She came in such still water, and so nursed Ba 10
	135.	My hands have not touched water since your hands CL 1
	144.	With the stubbornness of muddy water PA 4
	149.	And my heart fishes in troubled water Loc 31
	159.	Like water, undestroyed,--like mist, unburned TCJ 18
	171.	And here is water, and a little wind KW 14
	181.	Was halfway under water with fires Et 21
	182.	Yet water, water Et 47
watergutted	83.	and galleries, galleries of watergutted lava CS 31
watermelon	64.	"Jesus! Oh I remember watermelon days!" And sped Riv 42
waters	40.	Or as many waters trough the sun's V-6 7
	45.	Over the chained bay waters Liberty TBB 4
	50.	Dark waters onward shake the dark prow free AM 56

way, cont.

28. There is some way, I think, to touch   F&H I 24
31. This music has a reassuring way   F&H II 30
39. Draw in your head and sleep the long way home
    V-5 25
58. And Rip Van Winkle bowing by the way   VW 12
58. <u>Van Winkle sweeps a tenement/way down on Avenue
    A</u>   VW 15
84. --he lunged up Bowery way while the dawn   CS 50
115. Pick biting way up towering looms that press
    At 27
139. The sand and sea have had their way   Lege 7
149. And it's your fault that I'm this way   Loc 29
150. Burrowing in silk is not their way   GWP 13
151. feeling them in every way and   APE 4
172. I had come all the way here from the sea   ABP 1
174. It knows its way through India--tropic shake
    BNOK 14
183. Something like two thousand loaves on the way
    Et 56

ways

29. Bent axle of devotion along companion ways
    F&H I 50
32. And in other ways than as the wind settles
    F&H III 8
89. O Saunterer on free ways still ahead   CH 50

way-up

102. Out of the way-up nickel-dime tower shine
    Va 23

wayward

68. They win no frontier by their wayward plight
    Riv 114

we

11. We make our meek adjustments   Chap 1
11. For we can still love the world, who find
    Chap 5
11. We will sidestep, and to the final smirk
    Chap 9
11. We can evade you, and all else but the heart
    Chap 17
11. The game enforces smirks; but we have seen
    Chap 19
30. Know, Olympians, we are breathless   F&H II 7
31. That we are heir to: she is still so young
    F&H II 34
31. We cannot frown upon her as she smiles
    F&H II 35
32. We even   F&H III 11
32. We know, eternal gunman, our flesh remembers
    F&H III 19
33. We did not ask for that, but have survived
    F&H III 25
33. O brother-thief of time, that we recall
    F&H III 40
39. Can strangle this deaf moonlight? For we
    V-5 9
46. And we have seen night lifted in thine arms
    TBB 36

we, cont.	60.	Where we stoned the family of young VW 18
	75.	We danced, O Brave, we danced beyond their farms Dan 101
	88.	But we, who round the capes, the promontories CH 6
	104.	While we who press the cider mill, regarding them QH 10
	115.	We left the haven hanging in the night At 49
	130.	I dream we quarreled long, long ago Ech 12
	140.	We claim, and none may know Int 6
	145.	And we overpayed them because we felt like it PA 39
	158.	Here where we finger moidores of spent grace Mer 13
	159.	We hold in vision only, asking trace TCJ 2
	164.	We pinion to your bodies to assuage NA 3
	164.	Our envy of your freedom--we must maim NA 4
	164.	Because we are usurpers, and chagrined NA 5
	164.	Names we have, even, to clap on the wind NA 7
	164.	But we must die, as you, to understand NA 8
	172.	Pass sunward. We have walked the kindled skies ABP 8
	177.	And here we join eyes in that sanctity Rep 2
	180.	Or must we rend our dream Lib 13
	182.	We shoveled and sweated; watched the ogre sun Et 25
	188.	Let us strip the desk for action--now we have a horse HR 1
	190.	As though we knew (those who are variants Rel 8
weak	109.	"what do you want? getting weak on the links Tun 50
weakeyed	82.	weakeyed watches sometimes snooze--" his bony hands CS 16
wear	13.	The sunlight,--then withdrawing, wear IS 7
	23.	Wear me in crescents on their bellies. Slow WM 6
	190.	Will hold it--wear the keepsake, dear, of time Rel 15
weariness	144.	Absorbing and conveying weariness PA 8
wearing	176.	I'm wearing badges VU 9
wears	132.	She hazards jet; wears tiger-lilies MC 5
weather	109.	Our tongues recant like beaten weather vanes Tun 46
weather's	182.	The weather's in their noses. There's Don--but that one, white Et 43
weathers	162.	Weathers all loneliness OS 12
weave	54.	Sing to us, stealthily weave us into day HD 22
	82.	O Stamboul Rose--dreams weave the rose CS 10
	83.	O Stamboul Rose--drums weave CS 22
	84.	that bloomed in the spring--Heave, weave CS 56

weave, cont.	114.	"Make thy love sure--to weave whose song we ply At 14
weaving	9.	The wind possessing her, weaving her young veins GA 8
	82.	"Stamboul Nights"--weaving somebody's nickel-- sang CS 9
	156.	His Carib mathematics web the eyes' baked lenses OC 22
webbing	6.	It trembles as birch limbs webbing the air MGLL 15
webs	72.	Feet nozzled wat'ry webs of upper flows Dan 31
wedge	39.	Can fasten or deflect this tidal wedge V-5 11
	72.	And northward reaches in that violet wedge Dan 35
wedged	17.	May find the record wedged in his soul Par 4
weed	35.	And their fingers crumble fragments of baked weed V-1 4
weeds	16.	Flags, weeds. And remembrance of steep alcoves RR 6
	50.	The jellied weeds that drag the shore,--perhaps AM 52
week	165.	Bought a launch last week. It might as well BSEW 2
weekenders	105.	Weekenders avid of their turf-won scores QH 29
weep	161.	But went on into marble that does not weep IQ 15
weeps	28.	Weeps in inventive dust for the hiatus F&H I 37
weight	144.	Until you feel the weight of many cars PA 6
	176.	The window weight throbs in its blind VU 19
welcome	105.	A welcome to highsteppers that no mouse QH 39
well	8.	Touching as well upon our praise PU 15
	36.	As her demeanors motion well or ill V-2 9
	128.	The host, he says that all is well Fr 1
	166.	No speakee well IV 2
	165.	Bought a launch last week. It might as well BSEW 2
	165.	Have been made of--well, say paraffin BSEW 3
well-known	21.	Compiles a too well-known biography Pass 22
well-meant	8.	Scatter these well-meant idioms PU 21
wend	152.	Thy time is thee to wend In 1
went	161.	But went on into marble that does not weep IQ 15
west	56.	Turns in the waking west and goes to sleep HD 38
	62.	brother--all over--going west--young man Riv 2
	66.	Is past the valley-sleepers, south or west Riv 69
	74.	West, west and south! winds over Cumberland Dan 93
	88.	While rises in the west the coastwise range,/ slowly the hushed land CH 3
	144.	North-bound, and East and West PA 7

western	50.	Take of that eastern shore, this western sea AM 47
	185.	after the western desert and the later cattle country Post 10
westward	78.	Bent westward, passing on a stumbling jade Ind 31
wet	40.	Red kelson past the cape's wet stone V-6 8
	136.	Glitters on the edges of wet ferns Ps 3
	187.	of wet wind running Ma 2
whaler	82.	got to beating time..."A whaler once CS 17
wharf	84.	Outside a wharf truck nearly ran him down CS 49
	157.	Each daybreak on the wharf, their brine-caked eyes OC 29
wharf's	181.	But was there a boat? By the wharf's old site you saw Et 14
wharves	25.	The bridge swings over salvage, beyond wharves Rec 23
	54.	And then a truck will lumber past the wharves HD 6
whatever	98.	Whatever call--falls vainly on the wave SC 8
wheat	51.	Hushed gleaming fields and pendant seething wheat AM 83
	102.	O Mary, leaning from the high wheat tower Va 15
wheel	51.	From Moon to Saturn in one sapphire wheel AM 78
	68.	Straddles the hill, a dance of wheel on wheel Riv 91
wheeled	91.	Wheeled swiftly, wings emerge from larval-silver hangars CH 99
wheels	111.	Wheels off. The train rounds, bending to a scream Tun 92
	141.	That glittered in and out among the wheels EpH 6
wheezing	112.	A tugboat, wheezing wreaths of steam Tun 123
whelming	50.	Bewilderment and mutiny heap whelming AM 34
whenever	60.	After day whenever your stick discovered VW 23
wherein	18.	All but bright stones wherein our smiling plays Pos 29
	24.	Wherein new purities are snared; where chimes WM 34
	89.	Wherein your eyes, like the Great Navigator's without ship CH 52
whereof	94.	Of that great Bridge, our Myth, whereof I sing CH 196
whereto	37.	Wide from your side, whereto this hour V-3 7
wherewith	95.	Wherewith to bind us throbbing with one voice CH 202
whine	90.	The nasal whine of power whips a new universe CH 59
whip	60.	Is it the whip stripped from the lilac tree VW 32

whip, cont.	84.	Fins whip the breeze around Japan CS 60
	100.	Pearls whip her hips, a drench of whirling strands NWG 18
	169.	Whip sea-kelp screaming on blond Hur 15
whip-poor-will	106.	Yes, whip-poor-will, unhusks the heart of fright QH 68
whips	90.	The nasal whine of power whips a new universe CH 59
	126.	With crimson feathers whips away the mists O-N 2
whirl	150.	Whirl by them centred in the lap GWP 7
whirled	188.	watches at least--the lighthouse flashed... whirled HR 18
whirling	37.	Past whirling pillars and lithe pediments V-3 11
	51.	The orbic wake of thy once whirling feet AM 79
	90.	Our hearing momentwise; but fast in whirling armatures CH 69
	100.	Pearls whip her hips, a drench of whirling strands NWG 18
whirls	133.	Carmen whirls, and music swirls and dips CDB 19
whisper	50.	Like pearls that whisper through the Doge's hands AM 45
	70.	I learned to catch the trout's moon whisper; I Dan 22
	125.	But you who hear the lamp whisper thru night C 12
	144.	I will whisper words to myself PA 20
whispered	23.	--From whom some whispered carillon assures WM 17
	114.	The whispered rush, telepathy of wires At 4
	167.	Drift coolly from that tower of whispered light RP 2
whispering	24.	With Baptist John's. Their whispering begins WM 47
	98.	The mind is churned to spittle, whispering hell SC 17
	115.	Some trillion whispering hammers glimmer Tyre At 34
	133.	Of whispering tapestry, brown with old fringe CDB 23
whisperings	88.	What whisperings of far watches on the main CH 21
whispers	32.	In whispers, naked of stool F&H III 5
	117.	Whispers antiphonal in azure swing At 96
whistle	19.	Inaudible whistle, tunneling LC 22
whistles	64.	Under a world of whistles, wires and steam Riv 31
whistling	62.	a Ediford--and whistling down the tracks Riv 10
	73.	A birch kneels. All her whistling fingers fly Dan 49
	169.	Swept, whistling straw! Battered Hur 9

white

white, cont.	127.	Mercy, white milk, and honey, gold love Hi 7
	131.	Flat lily petals to the sea's white throat Ba 7
	137.	Forgetfulness is white,--white as a blasted tree For 8
	149.	Ah! without the moon, what white nights Loc 25
	149.	Don't I see your white swans there Loc 27
	156.	Across the feet of the dead, laid in white sand OC 2
	156.	To the white sand I may speak a name, fertile OC 12
	156.	Sieved upward, white and black along the air OC 25
	171.	The oar plash, and the meteorite's white arch KW 5
	182.	Leather, which the rimed white wind has glazed Et 28
	182.	The weather's in their noses. There's Don--but that one, white Et 43
	188.	death around white teeth HR 28
whitely	19.	Whitely, while benzine LC 1
whiteness	7.	From whiteness that cries defiance to the snow SMA 8
	159.	Your light lifts whiteness into virgin azure TCJ 5
whiter	100.	And shall we call her whiter than the snow NWG 13
whitest	116.	Thy pardon for this history, whitest Flower At 84
whither	193.	An instant in the wind (I know not whither hurled B Tow 19
Whitman	89.	Walt, tell me, Walt Whitman, if infinity CH 44
	95.	My hand/in yours,/Walt Whitman--/so CH 220
whittlings	169.	To quivering whittlings thinned Hur 8
whizzed	62.	whizzed the Limited--roared by and left Riv 20
whizzing	92.	Ing, dance the curdled depth/down whizzing CH 140
whole	50.	This turning rondure whole, this crescent ring AM 43
	123.	When below him he saw what his whole race had shunned Moth 42
wholly	69.	Poised wholly on its dream a mustard glow Riv 140
	148.	O prodigal and wholly dilatory lady Loc 2
why-and-wherefore	149.	With the why-and wherefore of Your Sex Loc 36
wicker-neat	84.	A wind worried those wicker-neat lapels, the CS 47
wide	34.	Often beneath the wave, wide from this ledge AMT 1
	35.	Too lichen-faithful from too wide a breast V-1 15
	36.	The seal's wide spindrift gaze toward paradise V-2 25

wide, cont.	37.	Wide from your side, whereto this hour V-3 7
	50.	Starved wide on blackened tides, accrete--enclose AM 42
	56.	arms close; eyes wide, undoubtful HD 28
	66.	--They know a body under the wide rain Riv 64
	69.	--The Passion spreads in wide tongues, choked and slow Riv 142
	91.	Of pendulous auroral beaches,--satellited wide CH 113
	98.	High, cool,/wide from the slowly smouldering fire SC 5
	122.	That their land is too gorgeous to free their eyes wide Moth 6
	123.	And without one cloud-car in that wide meshless blue Moth 35
	140.	Wide from the world, a stolen hour Int 5
	141.	The knots and notches,--many in the wide EpH 16
	148.	Bland as the wide gaze of a Newfoundland Loc 8
	152.	from sleep forbidden now and wide In 12
	152.	the cup again wide from thy throat to spend In 15
	161.	Wide of the mountain--thence to tears and sleep IQ 14
widely	180.	Eyes widely planted, clear, yet small Lib 11
widening	38.	And widening noon within your breast for gathering V-4 20
	194.	In azure circles, widening as they dip B Tow 36
wider	91.	Hell's belt springs wider into heaven's plumed side CH 92
	190.	In wider letters than the alphabet Rel 11
widowed	184.	Nor that fruit of mating which is widowed pride Emp 15
wield	93.	With vast eternity, dost wield the rebound seed CH 150
wieldest	186.	Thou wieldest with such tears that every faction Shak 9
wife	145.	And his wife, like a mountain, coming in PA 33
wifeless	64.	The ancient men--wifeless or runaway Riv 54
wiggles	134.	A gypsy wagon wiggles, striving straight CDB 26
wild	141.	They were like the marks of wild ponies' play EpH 18
wilderness	11.	Have heard a kitten in the wilderness Chap 23
	64.	An empire wilderness of freight and rails Riv 56
will	13.	Again the shadows at her will IS 8
	24.	Sparkling alone, within another's will WM 32
	25.	A wind abides the ensign of your will Rec 24
	69.	Tortured with history, its one will--flow Riv 141
Will Collins	178.	Perhaps as once Will Collins spoke the lark PB 3
willingness	177.	That rises on eternity's long willingness Rep 11

willow	16.	I remember now its singing willow rim RR 16
willows	16.	The willows carried a slow sound RR 1
	16.	And willows could not hold more steady sound RR 23
	41.	Hushed willows anchored in its glow V-6 30
	187.	willows, a little hungry Ma 11
wills	24.	Remorseless line, minting their separate wills WM 25
	188.	antagonistic wills--into immunity. Tact, horsemanship HR 24
win	15.	"Has no one come here to win you NL 5
	68.	They win no frontier by their wayward plight Riv 114
	140.	The world, at last, must bow and win Int 11
	189.	yield to--by which also you win and gain mastery and HR 34
winch	54.	As winch engines begin throbbing on some deck HD 7
wind	9.	The wind possessing her, weaving her young veins GA 8
	11.	As the wind deposits Chap 3
	12.	Bronze and brass. The wind Past 9
	16.	A sarabande the wind mowed on the mead RR 2
	16.	I heard wind flaking sapphire, like this summer RR 22
	18.	Whose heart is fire shall come,--the white wind rase Pos 28
	21.	(I had joined the entrainments of the wind) Pass 12
	21.	Vine-stanchioned valleys--": but the wind Pass 18
	25.	Look steadily--how the wind feasts and spins Rec 13
	25.	A wind abides the ensign of your will Rec 24
	32.	And in other ways than as the wind settles F&H III 8
	36.	Mark how her turning shoulders wind the hours V-2 16
	37.	While ribboned water lanes I wind V-3 5
	50.	Merges the wind in measure to the waves AM 40
	58.	There was Priscilla's cheek close in the wind VW 10
	84.	A wind worried those wicker-neat lapels, the CS 47
	111.	The conscience navelled in the plunging wind Tun 113
	137.	A bird that coasts the wind unwearyingly For 5
	147.	Hearing the wind Per 2
	147.	The wind plays andantes Per 6
	147.	Below the wind Per 9
	156.	The wind that knots itself in one great death OC 15

wiry	76.	Over the lintel on its wiry vine Ind 2
wish	108.	Finger your knees--and wish yourself in bed Tun 9
	174.	And then it pleads again, "I wish I knew BNOK 16
wisped	72.	Of Adirondacks!--wisped of azure wands Dan 36
wistful	136.	And broken branches, wistful and unmended Ps 7
wit	24.	--Anguished, the wit that cries out of me WM 37
	170.	Needs more than wit to gather, love to bind TED 11
withdrawing	13.	The sunlight,--then withdrawing, wear IS 7
withdraws	156.	Coils and withdraws. So syllables want breath OC 16
withered	124.	These things I have:--a withered hand Moth 51
withers	90.	O sinewy silver biplane, nudging the wind's withers CH 77
	104.	Perspective never withers from their eyes QH 1
	170.	--Truly no flower yet withers in your hand TED 9
without	149.	Ah! without the moon, what white nights Loc 25
witless	48.	Nigh surged me witless.... Hearing the surf near AM 22
witness	18.	Witness now this trust! the rain Pos 1
	48.	Witness before the tides can wrest away AM 2
wizen	62.	watching the tail lights wizen and converge, slip- Riv 22
woke	60.	nor there. He woke and swore he'd seen Broadway VW 28
woman	70.	Who squired the glacier woman down the sky Dan 2
	98.	I wanted you, nameless Woman of the South SC 1
	181.	The old woman and I foraged some drier clothes Et 2
	185.	and a paralytic woman on an island of the Indies Post 15
womb	76.	As once my womb was torn, my boy, when you Ind 6
women	32.	Like old women with teeth unjubilant F&H III 17
	131.	Two ivory women by a milky sea Ba 1
	133.	Just as absinthe-sipping women shiver through CDB 6
won	3.	Until the bright logic is won Leg 17
	78.	Won nothing out of fifty-nine--those years Ind 26
	122.	And rings macrocosmic won envy as thrall Moth 22
	138.	Despair until the moon by tears be won Port 3
wonder	22.	Under the constant wonder of your eyes Pass 31
	159.	The falling wonder of a rainbow's trance TCJ 4
wonder-breathing	48.	I, wonder-breathing, kept the watch,--saw AM 23

world, cont.	89.	Surviving in a world of stocks,--they also range CH 55
	127.	Of the hive of the world that is my heart Hi 4
	136.	Mine is a world foregone though not yet ended Ps 5
	140.	Wide from the world, a stolen hour Int 5
	140.	The world, at last, must bow and win Int 11
	140.	And even should the world break in Int 9
	147.	No world can offer Per 4
	148.	For snaring the poor world in a blue funk Loc 12
	150.	The world moves by so fast these days GWP 12
	181.	From the world outside, but some rumor blew Et 19
	193.	And so it was I entered the broken world B Tow 17
world's	4.	Mark tardy judgment on the world's closed door BT 2
	100.	The world's one flagrant, sweating cinch NWG 4
worlds	50.	For here between two worlds, another, harsh AM 32
	111.	With antennae toward worlds that glow and sink Tun 110
	114.	Two worlds of sleep (O arching strands of song At 20
worm	169.	Nor, Lord, may worm outdeep Hur 12
worm's	105.	Must we descend as worm's eye to construe QH 58
worms'	19.	Distilling clemencies,--worms' LC 21
worn	135.	Set in the tryst-ring has but worn more bright CL 8
worried	84.	A wind worried those wicker-neat lapels, the CS 47
worth	3.	The only worth all granting Leg 9
	127.	And I watch, and say, "These the anguish are worth Hi 8
wound	34.	The portent wound in corridors of shells AMT 8
	90.	Power's script,--wound, bobbin-bound, refined CH 65
	116.	Whose fell unshadow is death's utter wound At 66
	141.	Fell lightly, warmly, down into the wound EpH 7
	141.	As his taut, spare fingers wound the gauze EpH 11
	141.	Around the thick bed of the wound EpH 12
wounded	18.	Wounded by apprehensions out of speech Pos 19
wounds	91.	Wounds that we wrap with theorems sharp as hail CH 98
	93.	Hast kept of wounds, O Mourner, all that sum CH 169
	177.	Shall come to you through wounds prescribed by swords Rep 8

wounds, cont.	193.	In wounds pledged once to hope--cleft to despair B Tow 24
wove	70.	What laughing chains the water wove and threw Dan 21
woven	125.	He has woven rose-vines C 1
wraith	89.	Near Paumanok--your lone patrol--and heard the wraith CH 46
	98.	No wraith, but utterly--as still more alone SC 2
	99.	Yes, Eve--wraith of my unloved seed SC 27
	187.	this slate-eyed saintly wraith Ma 17
wrap	91.	To hedge the seaboard, wrap the headland, ride CH 89
	91.	Wounds that we wrap with theorems sharp as hail CH 98
	159.	Wrap us and left us; drop us then, returned TCJ 17
wrapped	66.	The old gods of the rain lie wrapped in pools Riv 82
	73.	Wrapped in that fire, I saw more escorts wake Dan 67
wrapping	115.	Still wrapping harness to the swarming air At 38
wrapt	36.	Laughing the wrapt inflections of our love V-2 5
	116.	To wrapt inception and beatitude At 75
wrath	179.	wrath Len 28
wreath	14.	To darkness through a wreath of sudden pain Fern 6
wreathe	38.	And region that is ours to wreathe again V-4 11
	83.	ATLANTIS ROSE drums wreathe the rose CS 43
wreathing	24.	Poor streaked bodies wreathing up and out WM 26
wreaths	112.	A tugboat, wheezing wreaths of steam Tun 123
wreck	142.	Clean on the shore some wreck of dreams BE 21
wrecks	34.	And wrecks passed without sound of bells AMT 5
wren	185.	the wren and thrush, made solid print for me Post 3
wrench	144.	The trowel,--and the monkey wrench PA 18
	160.	tisms wrench the golden boughs. Leaves spatter dawn MT 7
wrenched	25.	Wrenched gold of Nineveh;--yet leave the tower Rec 22
wrest	48.	Witness before the tides can wrest away AM 2
wrestling	37.	Light wrestling there incessantly with light V-3 12
	73.	I heard the hush of lava wrestling your arms Dan 69
Wright	90.	Warping the gale, the Wright windwrestlers veered CH 80
wrinkled	156.	In wrinkled shadows--mourns OC 7
wrist	92.	Thou hast there in thy wrist a Sanskrit charge CH 129

Yankee	84.	Blithe Yankee vanities, turreted sprites, winged CS 54
Yankees	105.	Me farther than scalped Yankees knew to go QH 52
yard	146.	In the front yard PA 52
yarn	23.	(Painted emulsion of snow, eggs, yarn, coal, manure WM 10
yawn	108.	As usual you will meet the scuttle yawn Tun 22
	111.	Daemon, demurring and eventful yawn Tun 106
	159.	Expose vaunted validities that yawn TCJ 13
yawning	48.	That fall back yawning to another plunge AM 12
yawns	108.	The subway yawns the quickest promise home Tun 23
ye	151.	to india, o ye faithful APE 24
year	12.	And the year Past 2
	20.	Compulsion of the year, O Nazarene LC 36
	46.	Already snow submerges an iron year TBB 40
	64.	The river's minute by the far brook's year Riv 30
	94.	And onward yielding past my utmost year CH 190
	167.	Climb up as by communings, year on year RP 5
year's	19.	Thorns freshen on the year's LC 10
	104.	Though they should thin and die on last year's stubble QH 8
years	33.	Distinctly praise the years, whose volatile F&H III 45
	38.	All bright insinuations that my years have caught V-4 21
	70.	Now lie incorrigibly what years between Dan 12
	78.	Won nothing out of fifty-nine--those years Ind 26
	79.	There's where the stubborn years gleam and atone Ind 55
	94.	Years of the Modern! Propulsions toward what capes CH 197
	124.	I have hunted long years for a spark in the sand Moth 49
yell	98.	Incites a yell. Slid on that backward vision SC 16
yelling	73.	O yelling battlements,--I, too, was liege Dan 62
	115.	Beams yelling AEolus! splintered in the straits At 40
yellow	72.	Smoke swirling through the yellow chestnut glade Dan 40
	122.	That emerge black and vermeil from yellow cocoons Moth 4
	123.	To yellow,--to crystal,--a sea of white spray Moth 32
	134.	Yellow, pallid, like ancient lace CDB 28
yelps	150.	Pathetic yelps have sometimes greeted GWP 16

yes	95.	Recorders ages hence, yes, they shall hear CH 214
	95.	yes, Walt,/Afoot again, and onward without halt CH 218
	99.	Yes, Eve--wraith of my unloved seed SC 27
	106.	His news already told? Yes, while the heart is wrung QH 61
	106.	Arise--yes, take this sheaf of dust upon your tongue QH 62
	106.	Yes, whip-poor-will, unhusks the heart of fright QH 68
	106.	Breaks us and saves, yes, breaks the heart, yet yields QH 69
	151.	PULSE!--yes, PULSE APE 13
	165.	--Yes, patent-leather shoes hot enough to fry BSEW 11
	172.	Yes, tall, inseparably our days ABP 7
	176.	Yes, I being VU 1
	176.	Yes, light. And it is always VU 21
	185.	across dawn's broken arc. No; yes...or were they Post 4
yesteryear	115.	--Tomorrows into yesteryear--and link At 29
yield	25.	That yield attendance to one crucial sign Rec 12
	48.	Yet lost, all, let this keel one instant yield AM 16
	50.	Yet yield thy God's, thy Virgin's charity AM 48
	152.	to spread; the hands to yield their shells In 4
	167.	Forever fruitless, and beyond that yield RP 9
	189.	yield to--by which also you win and gain mastery and HR 34
yielded	16.	Yielded, while sun-silt rippled them RR 10
	76.	Yielded your first cry at the prairie's door Ind 7
	78.	But gilded promise, yielded to us never Ind 27
	159.	As you have yielded balcony and room TCJ 15
yielding	32.	The mounted, yielding cities of the air F&H III 21
	51.	Yielding by inference and discard, faith AM 75
	94.	And onward yielding past my utmost year CH 190
	152.	Madonna, natal to thy yielding In 18
yields	106.	Breaks us and saves, yes, breaks the heart, yet yields QH 69
Yo-ho	04.	Sweet opium and tea, Yo-ho CS 58
yoked	160.	spiders yoked you first,--silking of shadows good under-/drawers for owls MT 5
yoking	115.	Of heaven's meditation, yoking wave At 54
yonder	66.	They lurk across her, knowing her yonder breast Riv 67
	161.	Profile of marble spiked with yonder IQ 5
you	11.	We can evade you, and all else but the heart Chap 17

you, cont.

14. But turning, as you may chance to lift a shade
    Fern 3
18. As quiet as you can make a man Pos 17
24. Has followed you. Though in the end you know
    WM 41
25. Such eyes at search or rest you cannot see
    Rec 3
25. Borne cleft to you, and brother in the half
    Rec 8
26. In alternating bells have you not heard Rec 25
30. And you may fall downstairs with me F&H II 18
39. Nothing like this in the world," you say V-5 14
48. To you, too, Juan Perez, whose counsel fear
    AM 7
58. You walked with Pizarro in a copybook VW 7
89. For you, the panoramas and this breed of towers
    CH 48
100. Always you wait for someone else though, always
    NWG 7
115. And you, aloft there--Jason! hesting Shout
    At 37
125. But you who hear the lamp whisper thru night
    C 12
142. How can you tell where beauty's to be found
    BE 9
143. O Beauty's fool, though you have never BE 25
143. Seen them again, you won't forget BE 26
143. Nor the Gods that danced before you BE 27
143. And you others--follow your arches BE 29
143. To what corners of the sky they pull you to
    BE 30
146. Where you had started to grow PA 48
146. And you were outside as soon as you PA 49
146. You ought, really, to try to sleep PA 58
149. --Which is to be mine, you say Loc 21
156. You have given me the shell, Satan,--carbonic
    amulet OC 34
158. Leave us, you idols of Futurity--alone Mer 12
159. What you may cluster 'round the knees of space
    TCJ 1
159. You, the rum-giver to that slide-by-night TCJ 9
159. As you have yielded balcony and room TCJ 15
159. Whose arrow must have pierced you beyond pain
    TCJ 20
160. you Sun-heap, whose MT 11
163. That kite aloft--you should have watched him
    scan Id 11
164. But we must die, as you, to understand NA 8
176. lavish this on you VU 3
184. You, who contain augmented tears, explosions
    Emp 1
184. You, who have looked back to Leda, who have seen
    the Swan Emp 6

zenith	93.	Hermetically past condor zones, through zenith havens CH 159
Zeppelin	176.	I watch the silver Zeppelin VU 11
zest	176.	with all their zest for doom VU 8
zigzag	156.	Near the coral beach--nor zigzag fiddle crabs OC 3
zigzags	14.	The zigzags fast around dry lips composed Fern 5
Zodiacs	92.	Zodiacs, dashed/(now nearing fast the Cape CH 141
zoned	50.	Sun-cusped and zoned with modulated fire AM 44
zones	93.	Hermetically past condor zones, through zenith havens CH 159
zoom	91.	With razor sheen they zoom each rapid helix CH 108